CRIMINAL TRAJECTORIES

PSYCHOLOGY AND CRIME

General Editors: Brian Bornstein, University of Nebraska, and
Monica Miller, University of Nevada, Reno

Criminal Trajectories

A Developmental Perspective

David M. Day and Margit Wiesner

NEW YORK UNIVERSITY PRESS

New York

NEW YORK UNIVERSITY PRESS
New York
www.nyupress.org

References to Internet websites (URLs) were accurate at the time of writing. Neither the author nor New York University Press is responsible for URLs that may have expired or changed since the manuscript was prepared.

A portion of Chapter 5 appeared in a previous form in a 2015 research report by Day, D. M., Koegl, C. J., Rossman, L., & Oziel, S entitled *The monetary cost of criminal trajectories for an Ontario sample of offenders,* submitted to Public Safety Canada's (PSC) National Crime Prevention Centre (NCPC).

Library of Congress Cataloging-in-Publication Data
Names: Day, David M., 1957– author. | Wiesner, Margit, author.
Title: Criminal trajectories : a developmental perspective /
David M. Day and Margit Wiesner.
Description: New York : New York University Press, [2019] | Series: Psychology and crime |
Includes bibliographical references and index.
Identifiers: LCCN 2018041756 | ISBN 9781479880058 (cl : alk. paper) |
ISBN 9781479864607 (pb : alk. paper)
Subjects: LCSH: Criminal behavior. | Criminal behavior, Prediction of. |
Crime—Sociological aspects. | Criminal psychology.
Classification: LCC HV6080 .D3686 2019 | DDC 364.3—dc23
LC record available at https://lccn.loc.gov/2018041756

CONTENTS

Introduction

Criminal Trajectories and Life-Course Development

"Welcome to my Nightmare": The words on the chalkboard greeted people as they entered the room. This was a prisoner's first "treatment review" meeting, a part of the comprehensive rehabilitation program offered at a treatment-oriented prison for adult male offenders. An offender's treatment review is held about every 5 months at this particular facility, and an offender is allowed to invite five or six of his peers to attend. The unit social worker, who also is present, invites another five or six inmates, and a correctional officer and unit correctional manager round out the list of those in attendance.

The purpose of the meeting is to give the offender an opportunity to openly discuss his offenses and any other relevant information he may wish to share. Those in attendance are permitted to ask questions and comment on what they have heard. Treatment reviews are often intense sessions because sensitive and personal information is shared in a supportive environment led by the social worker. For this particular individual, the message on the board was meant to convey how challenging, difficult, and even horrific his life had been. The social worker started off by asking, "What makes you think your life has been any more of a nightmare than anyone else here?" The room fell silent. Indeed, prisons are filled with individuals whose early lives had been far from a dream.

Crime is a major concern in our society. Prison populations are growing. The cost to maintain the justice system is escalating. Some of the putative factors that give rise to crime, such as economic instability, downward social mobility, and substance abuse, particularly of opioids, have become more prevalent. Especially concerning is when antisocial behavior begins at an early age, such as before adolescence. Child onset crime has a particularly pernicious, disruptive effect on development. Not only that, but the effects are also cumulative such that a consequence at one age (e.g., poor academic performance) continues to roll out its effects at other ages and in other life domains (e.g., peer relations), taking the person off a normative developmental trajectory. In other words, development generally unfolds in a manner that is coherent, predictable, organized, and hierarchical. Any perturbations to the normative developmental path arising from early risk factors for antisocial behavior are likely to substantially alter the course of development for the individual, resulting in a trajectory that is far from normative. When criminal behavior begins early, there is a high likelihood that the course of the behavior will be long, the crimes will be varied and serious, and the social, personal, and financial burden on society will be substantial (M. Cohen, Piquero, & Jennings, 2010; A. Piquero, Farrington, & Blumstein, 2003). Therefore, it is important to study the course of development of criminal behavior, whenever it begins.

This book explores the topic of criminal trajectories from a developmental perspective. For more than 25 years, the notions of *developmental trajectories*, in general, and *criminal trajectories*, in particular, have taken hold as important areas of investigation for researchers interested in the longitudinal study of behavioral phenomena, like crime. A search of *PsycInfo* indicates a dramatic increase in the number of published articles that refer to developmental trajectories in the 1990–2018 period compared to the 1880–1989 period, an increase from 49 articles to 6,320 articles! Driven by a wave of seminal longitudinal studies and inspired by major technical advances in the statistical analysis of longitudinal data at the level of the individual, the study of criminal trajectories has led to new ways of investigating the past, present, and future of criminal offenders. Informed by rich developmental theories (Farrington, 2005a), the accumulated body of literature has generated a wealth of information about criminal behavior, brought about new insights on crime, challenged old ideas, and fostered new research questions for future investigation.

Although this work has been of tremendous importance, to date, the study of criminal trajectories has been more descriptive to identify the patterns of growth trajectories across latent classes, with less emphasis on explanation, to account for differences in the shapes and patterns of the trajectories. We argue that, by placing criminal trajectory research within the context of a broad developmental perspective, key concepts and meta-theoretical propositions from developmental science, such as process models linking past events to future outcomes, relationships between normative and nonnormative development, adaptive functioning and developmental needs across the life span, and the interdependence between the individual and the environment, could be brought forward into the research to a greater extent than they currently are. Incorporating these concepts into investigations of criminal trajectories could aid in advancing knowledge about the dynamic and developmental processes underlying the onset, course, and desistance of criminal activity.

This book examines criminal trajectories as both a concept and a statistical method and makes the case for a developmental perspective to frame the topic. The overarching argument of the book is that crime is a product of developmental processes and that different types of offenders, characterized by distinctive developmental trajectories of criminal behavior, are the result of unique etiological pathways and processes. These pathways and processes are set out in developmentally informed theories of crime that are tested through research. A developmental perspective is important from a practical standpoint because it can inform the design of theoretically and empirically sound prevention and early intervention programs and policies to prevent or forestall the onset of antisocial and criminal activity, particularly when it begins in childhood. It is known that an early onset of antisocial activity portends a lengthy and protracted criminal career. Moreover, the results of trajectory research and the identification of unique predictors of distinct trajectory groups (e.g., late starters, early onset, high-rate persisters, low-rate persisters) may contribute to the development of effective targeted interventions aimed at reducing malleable risk factors and strengthening protective factors for different types of offenders.

The Notion of a Developmental Trajectory: A Brief Introduction

The thrill of a roller coaster comes from the undulating track, abrupt changes in direction and speed, and banking through sharp curves and corners. Although life rarely takes us on a virtual roller coaster ride, the *trajectory* of the roller coaster, that is, the path it follows through space, provides a useful metaphor with which to describe the course of development of psychological phenomena as they unfold over age or time. Across the life span, aspects of our lives wax and wane, pitch upward, crest and fall, and reach a plateau. A trajectory represents the course, evolution, or progression on some dimension of those aspects of our lives over age or time. Once launched, individuals follow different trajectories over the course of their lives, some with steep curves, some with shallow curves, some of long duration, and some of short duration. That is, within a population, individual variation (i.e., heterogeneity) in the trajectories that we follow for a given phenomenon is to be expected. Trajectory research aims to capture the heterogeneity of those "time paths" (Blokland & Nieuwbeerta, 2010, p. 66). Moreover, the unfolding of a trajectory is a dynamic process that is subject to environmental and individual influences and their interaction. This dynamic process is in keeping with a key tenet of developmental psychology, that the individual and environment are interdependent (Lerner, Hershberg, Hilliard, & Johnson, 2015; Mash & Wolfe, 2019; Overton, 2015).

Continuity and change are defining features of development (Sroufe, 1979), and developmental researchers interested in capturing the unfolding undulations in the manifestation of psychological traits, behaviors, characteristics, and experiences have embraced trajectories as both a concept and a statistical technique. The notion of a developmental trajectory maps well onto the conceptualization of growth and maturation put forth by researchers about a broad array of behavioral phenomena (Curran & Willoughby, 2003; Nagin & Odgers, 2010a). The study of trajectories also cuts across many disciplines, including psychology, sociology, and criminology, and subdisciplines and subspecialties, such as developmental psychology, developmental psychopathology, developmental criminology, life-course criminology, the risk and resilience literature, developmental pathways, and developmental systems theory. Over the course of one's life, we may speak of trajectories of brain volume growth (P. Shaw et al., 2008), handedness in infancy (Michel, Babik, Sheu, & Campbell, 2014), language skill development (Farkas & Beron, 2004), bullying experiences (Reijntjes et al., 2013), physical aggression (B. Brame, Nagin, & Tremblay, 2001), substance use (Zucker, Fitzgerald, & Moses, 1995), social and emotional development (Miers, Blöte, deRooij, Bokhorst, & Westenberg, 2013), self-esteem (Hirsch & DuBois, 1991), social competence (Monahan & Steinberg, 2011), and symptoms of mental illness such as depression (Costello, Swendsen, Rose, & Dierker, 2008) and anxiety (Feng, Shaw, & Silk, 2008), among others.

A study by Costello et al. (2008) provides a good illustration of trajectory research. Costello and his colleagues examined the longitudinal course of depressed mood from age 12 to 25 years in a nationally representative sample of nearly 12,000 male and female youth. Using a cohort-sequential design—a design that involved three waves of data with multiple overlapping age groups (e.g., 12–16 years, 14–17 years)—they found from their trajectory analysis that the sample clustered into four distinct trajectory groups, each following a different progression of symptoms over the course of the follow-up period. The four groups, with the percentage of youth in each group in parentheses (see Figure I.1), were descriptively labeled: no depressed mood (28.7%), which showed a minimal level of depressed mood over time with a slight rise in mid-adolescence; stable low depressed mood (59.4%), which showed a slightly higher level of depressed mood that remained constant over time; early-high declining depressed mood (9.5%), which showed a relatively high level of depressed mood from early to mid-adolescence, followed by a sharp decline into adulthood; and late-escalating depressed mood (2.4%), which showed a sharp increase from about age 14.5 years to a high level of depressed mood that continued into adulthood. The important point drawn from these results is that the youth composed a heterogeneous population with respect to their experience of depressed mood over time and that trajectory analysis was able to capture this underlying heterogeneity. A next question to examine is whether the groups differed on any pertinent characteristics that might suggest distinct developmental pathways.

Costello et al. (2008) compared the groups and found that, relative to youth in the no-depressed-mood group, youth in the late-escalating group were more likely to be female and to have higher levels of self-reported delinquent behavior. Also, youth from two-parent households who also reported a greater connection to their parents, peers, or school and who had higher self-esteem were less likely to be classified in the stable-low-depressed-mood group, compared to the no-depressed-mood group. Taken together, the study is illustrative in showing the

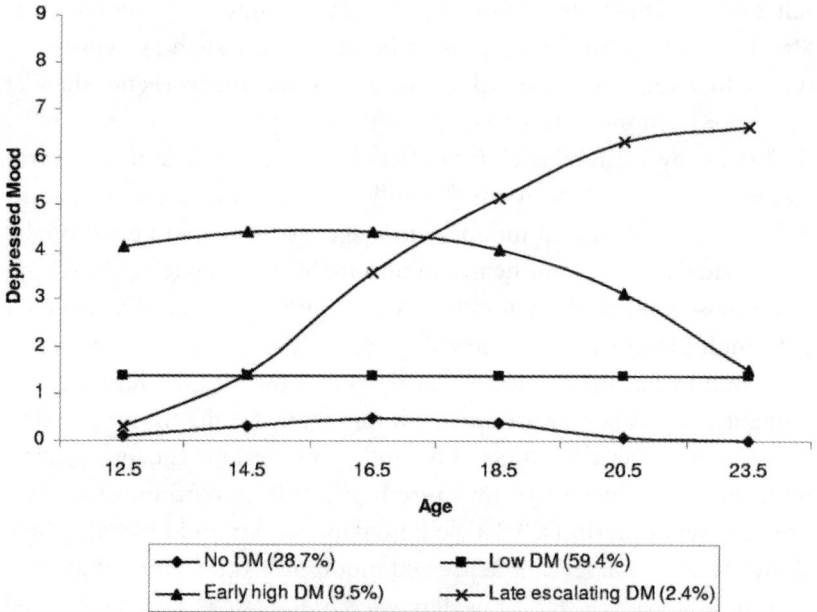

Figure I.1. Predicted depressed mood score for each trajectory group in a sample of American adolescents and young adults (N = 11,559)
Source: Costello, D. M., Swendsen, J., Rose, J. S., & Dierker, I. C. (2008). Risk and protective factors associated with trajectories of depressed mood from adolescence to early adulthood. Journal of Consulting and Clinical Psychology, 76, pp. 173–183. American Psychological Association. Reprinted with permission.
Note: DM = depressed mood.

kinds of heuristic clusters that might be generated through the statistical method of trajectory analysis and the variability that exists in the course of development of psychological phenomena, such as depressed mood, that may be observed in a study sample. This study also illustrates that the resulting trajectory groups may be distinguished based on individual and family characteristics. Finally, if the data were available, the study might also have assessed whether early childhood factors could distinguish the trajectory groups. The identification of such developmental variables might suggest differences in the etiologies of the trajectory groups that might inform the development of unique preventative strategies to forestall a more serious course of depressive symptomatology in young people.

The Nature and Time Course of Crime

Moving to the realm of criminality, researchers have examined trajectories on a wide range of variables, including police contacts (Bushway, Paternoster, & Brame, 2003), arrests (Marshall, 2006; Natsuaki, Ge, & Wenk, 2008; Wiesner, Capaldi, & Kim, 2007), court appearances (Livingston, Stewart, Allard, & Griffith, 2008; A. Ward et al., 2010), self-reported offenses (Fergusson, Horwood, & Nagin, 2000; MacDonald, Haviland, & Morral, 2009; Monahan, Steinberg, Cauffman, & Mulvey, 2009; Tzoumakis, Lussier, Le Blanc, & Davies, 2013; Wiesner & Capaldi, 2003), convictions generally (Blokland, Nagin, & Nieuwbeerta, 2005; McCuish, Corrado, Lussier, & Hart, 2014; A. Piquero, Farrington, et al., 2007; Piquero, Farrington, Nagin, & Moffitt, 2010; Yessine & Bonta, 2009), and convictions for specific offense types, including violent (Bersani, Nieuwbeerta, & Laub, 2009), nonviolent (i.e., property and drug; Sampson & Laub, 2003; van der Geest, Blokland, & Bijleveld, 2009), and sex (Freiburger, Marcum, Iannacchione, & Higgins, 2012) offenses.

Over the course of their criminal "careers" offenders may display changes and continuities in criminal activity on various dimensions, including the rate, type, timing, frequency, versatility, and severity of offending (Blumstein, Cohen, Roth, & Visher, 1986). Moreover, offenders differ in their patterns of offending on these various dimensions (Moffitt, 1993; A. Piquero, Sullivan, & Farrington, 2010). For example, some offenders commit only a few offenses of mild severity and over a short period, perhaps limited to the adolescent period. Other offenders commit a larger number of offenses and of greater variety and increasing severity over a long period, perhaps starting in childhood and continuing well into adulthood. Other variations in offending patterns include everything between. As noted earlier, a primary aim of trajectory research is to capture this underlying heterogeneity in the population of criminal offenders and to tease apart patterns among those following different offense trajectories.

In broad terms, a criminal trajectory represents the course, progression, or evolution of criminal activity at the level of the individual over age or time. Offenders compose a diverse and varied population (Wolfgang, Figlio, & Sellin, 1972), but the statistical analysis of trajectories allows for variation in the topography of crime and, as a statistical tool, seeks to aggregate individuals into homogeneous latent (i.e., unobserved or unmeasured) classes who follow similar trajectories that are heterogeneous across trajectory groups (B. Muthén & Muthén, 2000). With its focus on within-individual or person-centered analyses of behavior and an emphasis on continuity and change over time, the study of criminal trajectories is well suited to advance the goal of developmental science to uncover factors associated with the onset and course of a given outcome. It has thus become an important tool for "charting and understanding" (Nagin, 2011, p. 53) the progression of criminal activity over the life course.

A Developmental Perspective

This book makes the case for a developmental perspective as essential to advancing knowledge about criminal trajectories and gaining a deeper, more nuanced understanding of criminal behavior across the life span. A developmental perspective begins with the assumption that criminal behavior is developmentally embedded throughout the life course (Brown et al., 2008). The goal of a developmental approach to the study of crime, then, is to fully explore the meaning and implications of this position. How and why is criminal behavior embedded in the development of the individual? What does this mean in terms of acting to prevent or forestall the onset of delinquency? Can a developmental perspective provide insights into salient questions about criminal behavior, for example, about the intergenerational transmission of crime?

To aid in this endeavor, this book highlights five points to capture what is meant by a developmental perspective, each of which links back to the study of criminal trajectories: (a) There is a focus on *developmental processes* and an understanding of the causal mechanisms or causal chains that link past events to future outcomes; (b) there is a focus on change and continuity at the level of the *individual* rather than of groups, with an emphasis on person-centered or within-individual data analysis; (c) there is a focus on *developmental tasks* and their role in typical and atypical development over the life course; (d) there is a focus on *dynamic transactions* between salient age-graded individual and contextual developmental systems over the life course; and (e) there is a focus on *longitudinal research* to allow for assessments of change at the level of the individual, whereby repeated measures are gathered on the same individuals over time.

First, a developmental perspective places an emphasis on the study of *developmental processes* that shape the nature and pattern of change. The focus is on uncovering the likely pathways that lead to a given outcome, such as criminal behavior, and the causal mechanisms through which the risk of crime is transmitted, that is, the determinants of developmental change and continuity. A developmental perspective is thus *process-oriented*. A developmental perspective aims to move beyond a simple descriptive analysis of development toward an understanding of the reasons underlying the observed changes in behavioral phenomena; its goal is to *explain*, not just to describe. Research questions may be framed in terms of identifying the developmental pathways and causal mechanisms that link past events to future outcomes. For example, how might a childhood history of physical maltreatment lead to the onset of violent crime in adolescence, and what are the mediating variables that compose a purported causal chain linking these variables? Theory plays an important role in the formulation and specification of a purported causal chain, providing a theoretical road map of those developmental pathways. In other words, theory provides an outline of and a rationale for the relevant variables composing the pathway and the expected direction of effects among the variables, in a sense, ordering the expected trail of events from risk factors to outcomes (Cullen, Benson, & Makarios, 2012).

Second, a developmental perspective emphasizes an examination of the patterns of change and continuity at the *level of the individual*; that is, the unit of analysis is the person. Research questions may be framed in terms of understanding how behavior in one stage of development carries forward (or not) for individuals into a subsequent stage of development. For example, do those individuals who engage in aggressive behavior in middle childhood become violent offenders in late adolescence? To properly answer this question, a statistical approach referred to as within-individual or person-centered (Bergman, 1998; Magnusson, 1998), as opposed to variable-centered methods, such as analysis of variance or linear regression analysis, is required. Person-centered approaches advocate for the person, viewed holistically, as the unit of analysis and use cluster analysis, latent class analysis, latent transition analysis, (growth) mixture modeling, and similar statistical techniques to identify configurations, patterns, or clusters of variables (Bauer & Shanahan, 2007). This person-centered approach is the essential basis for the empirical derivation of criminal trajectories. Moreover, understanding the causal mechanisms by which this (dis)continuity would occur also is important. With a focus on the individual as the unit of analysis, a developmental perspective is sensitive to individual differences and variations in developmental pathways, processes, and outcomes. In other words, across individuals, variability is to be expected because not all individuals develop at the same speed, rate, or time. As we will see, this notion lends itself well to the concept and methodology of developmental trajectories, which also hold that individuals follow distinct courses of development toward a common outcome. Indeed, an essential objective of the criminal trajectory methodology is to capture the heterogeneity among a set of individuals in their patterning of criminal behavior over time, to identify *a set* of trajectories within a population.

Third, understanding the individual from a developmental perspective takes into consideration age-salient *developmental tasks* and how the achievement of these tasks (or lack thereof) enables (or undermines) the individual to move competently into the next stage of development (Masten, Burt, & Coatsworth, 2006; Sroufe & Rutter, 1984). Examples of developmental tasks from birth to adolescence include attachment and language development (from infancy to preschool), academic achievement and rule-based conduct (in middle childhood), and the formation of close peer relations within and across gender and development of a cohesive sense of self (in adolescence; Masten & Coatsworth, 1998). Moving beyond adolescence, developmental tasks involve those that prepare the individual to successfully negotiate the transition to adult relationships and occupational roles (Roisman, Aguilar, & Egeland, 2004) and, thereafter, to adjust to age-related changes, such as in physical health (Baltes, Reese, & Lipsitt, 1980; Brown et al., 2008; McCormick, Kuo, & Masten, 2011; Sroufe, 2013).

Achieving these psychological milestones is associated with developmental competence across the life span, which is associated with attainment of positive developmental outcomes (e.g., social competence, good coping skills) within and across major developmental periods (e.g., childhood, adolescence, adulthood; Cicchetti & Rogosch,

2002). Failing to navigate these developmental tasks, referred to as *adaptational failure*, undermines healthy psychological and psychosocial growth and takes an individual off a normative developmental track relative to his or her peers, creating challenges for the person as he or she struggles to continue to attain normative societal expectations. The consequences of adaptational failure are cumulative and can be particularly devastating when they begin early in life, such as in infancy (Sroufe, 2013). Adaptation is thus conceptualized as hierarchical in nature in that successful adaptation at one developmental stage increases the likelihood (but not the certainty) of successful resolution of subsequent stage-salient tasks (Cicchetti & Rogosch, 2002).

When considering the developmental course of a given individual, salient issues for the person may be contextualized in terms of her or his successful management of salient age-appropriate developmental tasks. For example, a 6-year-old child struggling with schoolyard bullying may experience challenges in forming positive peer relations, a psychosocial task of this developmental period. Such challenges may further impede normative developmental processes in this particular domain; create or exacerbate the conditions that give rise to experiences of acute stress, school refusal, and the onset of social anxiety; and result in a cascade of secondary problems that lead to negative consequences across other domains, such as family relations and academic performance, that carry forward over time.

To remedy the situation, the child might engage in therapy with a mental health practitioner to achieve the dual goals of alleviating the symptoms of social anxiety and providing opportunities that enable the young person to build age-appropriate adaptation skills to regain a normative course of development, leading to more successful adaption moving forward. These opportunities might include strengthening the child's social skills through modeling and role-playing and arranging playdates with a positive peer group. A developmental perspective thus integrates an understanding of typical developmental processes, that is, universal and adaptive principles of growth and maturation, with an understanding of processes associated with atypical development. Research questions may be framed, for example, in terms of asking how continued failure of developing skills necessary for normative academic achievement and positive peer relations in middle childhood might contribute to circumstances that lead to increased social isolation, feelings of low self-esteem and hopelessness, and perhaps later involvement in street-gang activity in adolescence.

In the context of criminal offending, questions might be posed about how early involvement in the criminal justice system (e.g., before age 15), an example of a nonnormative transition, could potentially undermine achieving normative developmental tasks and result in a cumulative risk for maladaptive functioning later in life. Questions about treatment and rehabilitation for individuals involved in the criminal justice system might be formulated in terms of normative and nonnormative developmental paths and how best to provide opportunities that enable the individual to reenter a normative developmental track. Psychologists Elizabeth Cauffman (Cauffman, 2012; Cauffman & Steinberg, 2012; Dmitrieva, Monahan, Cauffman, & Steinberg, 2012) and David Farrington (Farrington, Loeber, & Howell, 2012) have argued that, in its current form, the criminal justice system serves to undermine the positive growth and development of system-involved individuals, leading to an increased risk of poor psychosocial outcomes and criminal recidivism, particularly for juvenile offenders. Unfortunately, all too often, the justice system fails to provide opportunities and experiences that enable youth to normalize their lives and catch up with their nondelinquent peers (National Research Council, 2013). From a *stage-environment fit* perspective (Eccles et al., 1993), there is a mismatch between the developmental needs of the individual and the opportunities available in the criminal justice system (Cauffman, Cavanagh, Donley, & Thomas, 2016).

Fourth, a developmental perspective emphasizes the *dynamic transactions* between an individual's prior developmental history and current social environments (or contexts) over the life course within a framework that is sensitive to the individual's developmental stage or salient age-graded developmental systems (e.g., Cairns & Cairns, 1995; Capaldi & Wiesner, 2009; Caspi & Elder, 1988). Developmental systems theory may be viewed as a metamodel that subsumes leading frameworks of human development (Lerner et al., 2015; Overton, 2015). A central tenet of this metamodel is that a developmental system comprises multilayered, age-graded individual and contextual systems (e.g., biological, psychological, social, cultural-historical) that interact with each other across the life span and are integrated into a synthetic coactional system. Put differently, the process of development, including the development of criminal behavior, is "conceptualized as the functioning of, and transactions across and within, biological, psychological, and social systems, with constant feedback and interaction over time" (Capaldi & Wiesner, 2009, p. 376).

The incorporation of such thinking into criminology requires more integrated and focused theories about how individual factors and context interact at different developmental periods (Mulvey, 2014). More refined, developmentally informed theory also holds promise to enrich practice regarding system-involved offenders. In fact, contemporary developmental systems theory is heavily invested in not only describing and explaining but also optimizing within-person development across the life span (e.g., Lerner, Lerner, von Eye, Bowers, & Lewin-Bizan, 2011; Lerner et al., 2015).

Along these lines, as noted earlier, what is needed is a criminal justice system that is sensitive to age-graded developmental processes across the life span, particularly processes pertaining to criminal behavior and its desistance (Cesaroni, 2015). In other words, to assist a person to change or modify his or her behavior, it is important to understand the function served by certain behaviors (e.g., crime) for a given person at that particular point in his or her development. This functional analysis of the behavior may translate into asking, from the person's perspective, what it means to commit a crime (e.g., Brown et al., 2008; Cicchetti & Rogosch, 2002; Selman & Adalbjarnardottir, 2000). It also means being sensitive to age-graded levels of functioning and psychosocial maturity as individuals mature to adulthood, based on social, emotional, behavioral, and biological (e.g., neurological) growth and development, including reasoning, judgment, decision-making capacity, brain development of the prefrontal cortex, and the role that antisocial behavior plays in different developmental periods (Capaldi & Wiesner, 2009; Cauffman et al., 2016; Cauffman & Steinberg, 2012; Farrington et al., 2012; Steinberg, Chung, & Little, 2004). From a developmental perspective, the goal of the criminal justice system is to alter the criminal trajectory of individuals by providing developmentally appropriate programming and treatment or alternative sentencing options to enable offenders to achieve the developmental tasks of acquiring social skills, basic educational and vocational skills, and temperance skills to behave in a socially mature and responsible manner and to facilitate their positive growth and development, putting them back on a normative developmental track (Cauffman, 2012; National Research Council, 2013). This rehabilitative goal of fostering positive growth and adaptation extends across the life course.

Fifth and finally, as might be expected from the preceding discussion, a developmental perspective places a premium on longitudinal data. In a longitudinal study, the same sample of individuals is followed over time with repeated assessments or observations taken at different periods. Such data allow for within-individual analyses such that patterns of change and continuity on variables of interest may be examined. Longitudinal data also allow for an unambiguous temporal sequence of life events to be established, enabling the researcher to draw conclusions about time-ordered relations between developmental precursors and outcomes (Farrington, 2013; Wohlwill, 1973). These developmental chains or pathways are essential for drawing conclusions about putative causality, testing for both direct and indirect effects. For example, a researcher interested in the study of risk factors of school dropout, when viewed as "the outcome of a long process of disengagement from school" (Christenson & Thurlow, 2010, p. 149), might conduct a prospective longitudinal study whereby data are gathered on family experiences in early childhood (e.g., home environment, parental monitoring and involvement in school), academic and behavioral problems and attitudes toward school in middle childhood, and poor attendance and school truancy in late childhood and early adolescence (e.g., Jimerson, Egeland, Sroufe, & Carlson, 2000; Lowe & Dotterer, 2013). The statistical association among each of these developmentally sequenced experiences would be tested in support of the putative causal pathway. Relations could be examined between each variable and the next for direct effects, and the relation between earlier experiences and later outcomes could be examined via the mediating variables for indirect effects.

In essence, a developmental perspective is quite important to the study of criminal trajectories. The notion of criminal trajectories maps well onto the conceptualization of growth and maturation held by researchers about a wide range of behavioral phenomena (Nagin & Odgers, 2010a). Applying a developmental perspective to the study of criminal trajectories provides a framework for posing meaningful research questions about change and continuity in criminal behavior from a life-course perspective, developing and testing theories about the developmental course of antisocial and criminal behavior across the life span, and investigating different etiologies of criminality for individuals who follow distinct criminal trajectories.

In addition, applying a developmental perspective has implications for the development of strategic early intervention and prevention programs and policies to prevent or forestall the development of antisocial and delinquent behavior in children and youth (B. Welsh & Farrington, 2012). There is now a growing appreciation for the theoretical and practical utility of developmentally based perspectives of crime to understand the mechanisms underlying the onset and maintenance of criminal behavior (Farrington et al., 2012; Grisso & Schwartz, 2000; Skeem, Scott, & Mulvey, 2014). Developmental and life-course models of crime (Cullen et al., 2012; Farrington, 2005a) have led the way in embracing the principles and knowledge drawn from the developmental sciences. The research questions that emanate from a developmental perspective include those concerned with charting and describing the nature and course of criminal behavior across the life span and uncovering the factors associated with the onset of crime and with the multiple trajectories of offending, as well as patterns of desistance from crime. These considerations have been the primary interests of criminal trajectory research for the past few decades, but there is still a great deal more to learn.

Three Premises of This Book

This book is based on three premises: (a) Crime is a product of developmental processes, (b) criminals compose a heterogeneous population, and (c) process models are essential for understanding criminal behavior in a developmental context, that is, advancing the notion that "crime happens over time, not at a time," given its distal and proximal (in time) influences. Each of these premises is described in the following.

CRIME IS A PRODUCT OF DEVELOPMENTAL PROCESSES. The first premise states that crime is embedded in developmental processes and pathways (DeLisi, 2005). Like the onset of psychopathology or mental illness (Sroufe, 1997, 2009), the processes and pathways associated with the onset and maintenance of criminal behavior are seen as deviations from what may be considered typical or normative development. Therefore, research and theory on both normative and non-normative development and adaptive and maladaptive functioning are mutually informative (Farrington & Loeber, 2013). In this context, the term *pathway* is used to refer to an orderly and interconnected set of behaviors, events, and experiences that are probabilistically associated with a given outcome. Pathways are distinguished from trajectories in that, whereas a pathway comprises a set of linked antecedents that are associated with a given consequence or outcome, such as mental illness or criminal behavior, a trajectory represents the unfolding course or progression of the outcome once initiated. An example of a trajectory would be the course or progression of symptoms of a mental disorder that wax and wane over time with changing personal circumstances, life transitions, exposure to stress, and so forth. In the context of criminal behavior, a trajectory refers to the course or progression of some dimension of criminal offending, such as the number of convictions a person has at different ages, sampled over time.

Although written in the context of developmental psychopathology, Sroufe's (2009) remarks about understanding a given outcome within a developmental context are equally applicable to the field of developmental criminology and the developmental study of crime:

> To fully understand the origins and course of psychopathology, we need to understand the developmental history of the person. This is not always obvious because development linkages are often complex. Not only is there heterotypic continuity, in which the same characteristic or tendency may be manifest in different ways over time, there is also developmental coherence of patterns of adaption. Thus, for example, conduct problems in childhood may predict adult depression better than does childhood depression (Robins & Price, 1991). Such complexities are what made the discipline of developmental psychopathology necessary. (p. 180)

According to developmental theories of crime, criminal behavior is thought not to arise within the person de novo, without prior indications (Farrington, 1986). Stated more bluntly by Loeber (1990, p. 31), "delinquents do not 'spring out of the cabbage patch' when they commit their first delinquent act; instead chronic problematic behavior often precedes the delinquent act by many years." Indeed, based on analyses of the Pittsburgh Youth Study, a longitudinal study of 1,500 inner-city boys, a first contact with the criminal justice system was preceded by serious conduct problem behaviors seven years earlier (Loeber, Farrington, Stouthamer-Loeber, Moffitt, & Caspi, 1998). Therefore, a first contact with the criminal justice system by a 15-year-old youth may have been predicted 7 years prior, at age 8, by the onset of early conduct problem behavior. This finding has implications for the development of early intervention and prevention programs to prevent or forestall early involvement in the criminal justice system that targets "the pathogenic processes that contribute to onset or to maintenance" (Shirk, Talemi, & Olds, 2000, p. 846) of the criminal behavior.

Also, key to a developmental perspective is the notion that early experiences shape and influence later outcomes (Sroufe & Rutter, 1984). The onset and maintenance of antisocial and delinquent behaviors are seen as the result of a complex interplay of multiple developmental processes across various life domains (i.e., individual, family, peer, school, community) that unfold over time. These developmental processes may either be proximal (i.e., in the recent past) or distal (i.e., in the distant past) to the event and can have either direct or indirect (or both) effects on the outcome. For example, a history of early childhood maltreatment (a distal risk factor) may place a young person on a developmental pathway toward externalizing problems later in life. Early trauma exposure disrupts normative developmental processes and neurochemical functioning that sets into motion a cascade of negative events leading to mental health problems, involvement in antisocial behavior, and possibly incarceration (Coleman & Stewart, 2010). In adolescence, association with a deviant peer group (a proximal risk factor), whose activities and values are reinforced through the process of *deviancy training* (Dishion, 2000; Dishion & Piehler, 2007), may lead to involvement in property offenses, such as shoplifting or break and enters; in drug offenses, such as possession or trafficking; or in weapons use, violence, gang activity, and other delinquent acts. Proximal risk factors also may involve developmental transitions and turning points, such as the transition from grade school to middle school. Transitions create opportunities or vulnerabilities for individuals. Either way, transitions may upend an individual's sense of self, self-esteem, and self-confidence and lead to heightened feelings of incompetence and vulnerability (Stewart, 1982). Such negative feelings could persist until the person is able to consolidate the new roles and expectations and demonstrate a renewed sense of resilience. Moreover, until the person is able to regain a stable sense of self, he or she may exhibit poor coping behaviors and be particularly susceptible to negative social influences. At the same time, the discussion of antecedents and outcomes must be tempered by the probabilistic nature of the empirical findings. Risk factors are meant to be understood as probabilistic rather than deterministic (Dumas & Nilsen, 2003). For example, Robins (1966) demonstrated that not all children identified as antisocial develop into antisocial adults. This observation leads to the search for moderator variables that influence the direction (positive or negative) of the relation between the risk factor and the outcome and for protective factors, defined as "an antecedent condition that is associated with a decrease in the likelihood of a maladaptive outcome" (Day, Wanklyn, & Yessine, 2014, p. 100).

CRIMINALS COMPOSE A HETEROGENEOUS POPULATION. The second premise highlights the notion that offenders do not comprise one singular, monolithic, homogeneous class of individuals. Offenders, after all, are a collective of individuals classified together by a single common characteristic—that they have, on one or more occasion, engaged in an act that is in violation of a law for which they may (in the case of official criminal records) or may not (in the case of self-report data) have been criminally prosecuted. Indeed, the offender population is quite heterogeneous. In this context, the issue is not how offenders differ from non-offenders (Rutter, Giller, & Hagell, 1998) but how offenders differ among themselves (A. Piquero et al., 2010). Variability among offender populations should not be a surprise given that the range of offenses that constitute criminal acts is, in itself, heterogeneous. Indeed, an impressive amount of research has accumulated to show the myriad ways in which offenders differ from one another, both in terms of their patterns of offending (e.g., frequency, severity, type, and duration) and in the developmental pathways (i.e., the successive ordering of risk factors) leading to offending. Therefore, gaining a better understanding of and appreciation for this variability can potentially lead to a more focused understanding of how early interventions may be tailored to benefit the lives of children and youth and their families who come from diverse backgrounds and with a diverse range of experiences and characteristics.

So, the question becomes, How best to "slice up the pie"? Offenders may be partitioned into various subgroups, for example, by age of onset (i.e., in childhood, adolescence, or adulthood; Moffitt, 1993; Patterson & Yoerger, 1993; Zara & Farrington, 2009), by offender type (i.e., sex, property, violent, or drug; Chaiken & Chaiken, 1984), or by the range of offense types they commit (i.e., specialists versus versatiles; Loeber, 1990). Three lines of research provide supporting evidence for the heterogeneity of offenders: (a) studies on chronic offenders, (b) efforts at classifying offenders, and (c) research on developmental pathways to offending.

Our discussion of the first line of research begins with the Philadelphia Birth Cohort Study. In an important contribution to the field of criminology, Wolfgang et al. (1972) followed 9,945 youth born in Philadelphia in 1945 from ages 10 to 18. In their detailed account of the results, they reported that 6.3% of their sample (18% of the cohort offenders) were responsible for 52% of the delinquent acts committed by the cohort. These "chronic" offenders, as they were labeled, were identified as such because they had five or more arrests. Indeed, this remarkable finding was replicated in a subsequent study of a second Philadelphia cohort (Tracy, Wolfgang, & Figlio, 1990). In this investigation, Tracy and colleagues (1990) followed 27,160 male and female participants born in Philadelphia in 1958. Once again, the results indicated that 7.5% of the cohort (23% of the cohort offenders) accounted for 61% of all police contacts. That a small percentage of offenders, commonly referred to as habitual, persistent, or chronic offenders, accounts for a large proportion of crimes is a robust finding (see Martinez, Lee, Eck, & O, 2017) that has been replicated with samples in the United States (A. Piquero & Buka, 2002; Shannon, 1982), Canada (Day, Bevc, Theodor, Rosenthal, & Duchesne, 2008), Sweden (Stattin & Magnusson, 1991), New Zealand (Moffitt, Caspi, Rutter, & Silva, 2001), Germany (Block, Brettfeld, & Wetzels, 2009), and the United Kingdom (Farrington, 2002). Studies also have found that high-rate offenders tend to have an early onset for misbehavior; commit serious offenses, including violence; and have a lengthy criminal career (A. Piquero et al., 2003).

A number of problems exist with this research, however, including the arbitrary distinction between chronic and nonchronic offenders (i.e., the 5+ cutoff for police contacts to define chronicity). As a result of the use of such subjective and ad hoc categorizations to slice up the pie, different cutoffs have been applied in different studies (P. Jones, Harris, Fader, & Grubstein, 2001), particularly those involving samples of female offenders where cutoff levels need to be set lower than the cutoff used by Wolfgang et al. (1972; e.g., A. Piquero, 2000; A. Piquero & Buka, 2002) because of the smaller number of crimes committed by women, in general. Moreover, these cutoffs fail to consider either the seriousness of the offenses or the time frame over which the offending took place (Hoge, 2001). Nonetheless, identification of persistent offenders has highlighted the individual differences in offending and has shined a light on the importance of making distinctions between high-rate and non-high-rate (e.g., low- and moderate-rate) offenders. This work also led to efforts toward the strategic allocation of resources in the criminal justice system and of matching the intensity of programs to offenders based on criminogenic risk needs (Bonta & Andrews, 2017; P. Jones et al., 2001) as well as the early identification of chronic offenders and the development of intervention and prevention programs targeted at children who may be on a track toward a chronic offense trajectory (MacLeod, Grove, & Farrington, 2012).

A second line of research that supports the heterogeneity of offenders comes from efforts to classify criminals into homogeneous subgroups and the search for offender typologies and taxonomies (Gibbons, 1975). According to Ferdinand (1966), "a typology consists essentially of a collection of types that are clearly distinguishable from one another but that are sufficiently similar to form a set" and are "generally concerned with patterns that are revealed in the empirical world" (p. 43). According to Moffitt (1993, p. 674),

> a classification becomes a taxonomy if it engenders assertions about origins and outcomes by weaving a nomological net of relationships between the taxa and their correlates (Meehl & Golden, 1982). A taxon carries a network of meaning over and above a behavioral description; it includes implications for etiology, course, prognosis, treatment, and relations with other taxa.

Both Ferdinand and Moffitt maintain that classification systems are not theories per se but can be developed into theories and tested against reality through empirical investigation. Ferdinand (1966, p. 45) noted that

> typologies . . . are based on types that describe complex, empirical associations. The orientation of typologies is to the complexity of the empirical world, whereas the orientation of theory is to the analytical simplicity of the conceptual world. A major difference between theories and typologies, therefore, is the object of their concern; for typologies it is the uniformities in nature, but for theories it is the logical relationships that exist between concepts. Typologies strive to clear up and explain the patterns that exist in nature, whereas theories attempt to clarify the implications that inhere in certain basic concepts.

The development of classification systems to sort offenders into categories has a long and rich tradition in criminology, beginning with the work of the 19th-century Italian psychiatrist and criminologist, Cesare Lombroso (1876; Gibson, 2002). With an aim toward understanding the causes of crime, and drawing on the theories of the time, including Charles Darwin's biological theory and Franz Joseph Gall's phrenology theory (based on the shape of the skull), Lombroso distinguished five types of offenders: the born criminal, the epileptic criminal, the criminal by passion, the insane and feebleminded criminal, and the occasional criminal (Roebuck, 1967). However, a lack of solid evidence to support these "types" has led Lombroso's work to be largely discredited today, although he is credited for ushering in a modern era of scientifically based criminal typologies. Since then, offender typologies have been based on physical-constitutional factors, such as the body shape (i.e., William Sheldon's ectomorph, endomorph, mesomorph types); psychological-psychiatric characteristics, including the work of Sigmund Freud and his constructs of the id, ego, and superego; personality characteristics, such as neuroticism, impulsivity, and psychopathic traits; and sociological approaches, based on, for example, socioeconomic status and socialization patterns (for early reviews of criminal typologies see Ferdinand, 1966, and Roebuck, 1967). Since these early works, over the years, numerous classification systems have been proffered, particularly since the 1950s

(Gibbons, 1975), although none has gained much traction (Moffitt, 1993). This is, in part, due to the often speculative nature of the typologies, the fuzzy boundaries between types, the complexity of the phenomenon under investigation, and the lack of empirical evidence to substantiate the taxonomic conjecture (Lenzenweger, 2004).

Contemporary efforts toward the development of typologies and taxonomic systems have improved upon the limitations of the earlier work (T. Brennan & Beitenbach, 2008; T. Brennan, Beitenbach, & Dieterich, 2008). The most frequently cited is Terrie Moffitt's (1993) dual taxonomy model. Moffitt proposed two groups, a dual taxonomy, that could be distinguished by etiological factors, types of offenses in which each engages, and the length of the criminal career. Moffitt proposed that young people follow one of two trajectories of antisocial behavior, life-course persistent (LCP) or adolescence limited (AL). On one hand, the small number of youth (about 5%–10%) who follow the LCP trajectory usually initiate their conduct problem behavior in childhood. The theory proposes that their high offending rates are a result of a confluence of biopsychosocial factors, including neurological problems, experiences of abuse and neglect, poor parental monitoring and supervision, community disadvantage, and, in later childhood and adolescence, school truancy, school failure, and delinquent peer association. Moreover, with the passage of time, these risk factors carry their own momentum through a cascade of cumulative risk, affecting multiple domains of the person's life (e.g., family, social, academic, employment), leading the individual to become ensnared in a criminal lifestyle and a lifelong, persistent pattern of criminality.

On the other hand, the larger number of youth who follow the AL trajectory experience relatively normal development until about age 15, at which time a striving for personal independence and association with like-minded individuals lead them to mimic the antisocial lifestyle of their delinquent peers. As a group, they experience few developmental risk factors and live a normal childhood. As adolescents, no longer children but not yet entitled to the rights and freedoms of adulthood, they experience a *maturity gap* that fuels some, usually minor, forms of antisocial behavior. The criminal acts of the AL group are often mild in nature, and their "criminal careers" are of short duration, usually terminating within several years of onset when opportunities for postsecondary education and job prospects become available. These taxonomic distinctions are useful because they suggest different etiological factors and different outcomes for those following each of the two distinct trajectories.

Support for Moffitt's (1993) theory has been provided by a number of trajectory studies (Moffitt, 2006a, 2018; Nagin, Farrington, & Moffitt, 1995; A. Piquero & Brezina, 2001; van Domburgh, Vermeiren, Blokland, & Doreleijers, 2009), including research with female-specific samples (Odgers et al., 2008). Chung, Hill, Hawkins, Gilchrist, and Nagin (2002), for example, found that their chronic trajectory group (of five trajectory groups generated by their analyses), composing 7% of their community sample, was characterized by a childhood onset of aggressive behavior and a persistence of offending into adulthood, similar to Moffitt's LCP group. Their late-onset group, composing about 14% of their community sample, showed an adolescence onset of antisocial behavior. Contrary to Moffitt's model, however, this group persisted in their offending into adulthood (see also Moffitt, Caspi, Harrington, & Milne, 2002). Similarly, Fergusson et al. (2000) identified a chronic group, composing 6.3% of their community sample. As predicted by Moffitt, this group was characterized by a high degree of childhood personal and environmental adversity and risk factors. An adolescent-onset group of offenders also was extracted from their sample. The support for Moffitt's theory notwithstanding, both studies generated more than the two trajectory groups predicted by the model. These findings highlight the "work-in-progress" nature of the dual taxonomy model, which, although elegant and parsimonious, is incomplete. Further work is needed to extend taxonomic models to match the accumulating empirical evidence (DeLisi & Piquero, 2011). Put another way, Moffitt's early work was theoretical. Once researchers began working out the mathematical means of generating trajectory groups, more than two groups were generated from samples, including the low-level-chronic (Nagin et al., 1995), and adult-onset (Zara & Farrington, 2009) groups. But these were *empirical* results and new theories followed after more trajectories than predicted by the original version of Moffitt's dual taxonomy were identified.

A third line of research that supports the heterogeneity of offenders comes from work on understanding the *causes* of crime from a developmental perspective. Bear in mind, however, that crime is a complex human behavior and so accounting for its causes must take into consideration this complexity. The complexity lies in the multiplicity of factors that may influence the onset, course, maintenance, and desistance of the behavior at the level of the individual. This position is consistent with the developmental principle of *equifinality* (Cicchetti & Rogosch, 1996), whereby different risk factors (e.g., child maltreatment, exposure to punitive parenting, low impulse control) may lead to the same outcome (e.g., criminal activity). However, as Albert Einstein famously stated, "everything should be made as simple as possible, but not simpler."

In recent years, a number of developmentally minded researchers have advanced the notion of multiple pathways leading to antisocial behavior (Frick, 2004; Loeber & Hay, 1997; Pickles & Hill, 2006). As noted earlier, a pathway represents a successive ordering or developmental sequence of events that lead to a given outcome (Farrington & Loeber, 2013; Loeber & Hay, 1997). According to Kazdin (Kazdin, Kraemer, Kessler, Kupfer, & Offord, 1997, p. 398, emphasis in original), "the term *path* refers to a sequence of characteristics, events, experiences and behaviors, that define successive steps or stages by which the outcome becomes manifest. The research task is to identify how one moves through those steps resulting in some outcome, such as delinquency in adolescence." Given the developmental nature of multiple pathways models, this work is most relevant for accounting for the onset of early conduct problem behaviors, which is seen as one step in the larger sequence of events that leads to more serious forms of antisocial behavior (Loeber & Hay, 1997). As a result, developmental pathways also have implications for criminal offending later in life. Note that the notion of multiple pathways to delinquency stands in contrast to single pathway models, such as Gottfredson and Hirschi's (1990) general theory of crime. Gottfredson and Hirschi stated that offenders only differ in degree and not kind (A. Piquero et al., 2003). The propensity to commit crimes, then, is rooted in early childhood experiences and in the trait of self-control, which varies across individuals but remains invariant over time (see Loeber & Stouthamer-Loeber, 1996).

An example of a multiple pathways model was proffered by developmental psychologist Rolf Loeber. Loeber and his colleagues used data from the Pittsburgh Youth Study (Loeber et al., 1993) to postulate that children with antisocial tendencies follow one of three pathways of behavioral development toward different forms of delinquency (see Figure I.2).

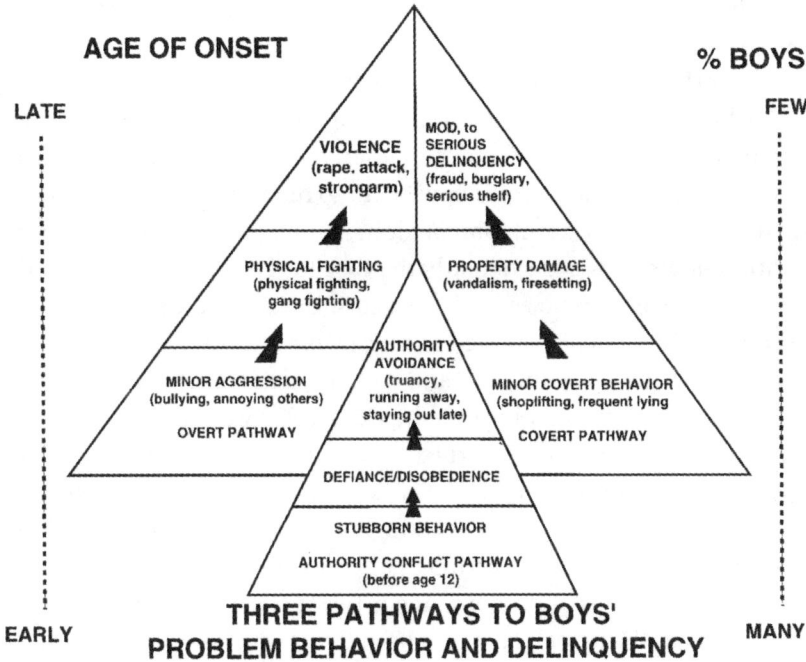

Figure I.2. Three developmental pathways
Source: Loeber, R., & Hay, D. (1997). Key issues in the development of aggression and violence from childhood to early adulthood. *Annual Review of Psychology, 48,* pp. 371–410. Reprinted with permission.

The pathways represent ordered sequences in which increasingly serious levels of behavior become manifest over time. The first pathway, called the *Overt Pathway*, describes a developmental sequence that begins with minor aggression as a first step, physical fighting as a second step, and serious violent behavior, such as rape, as a third step. The second pathway, called the *Covert Pathway*, describes the developmental sequence from minor antisocial acts, such as lying and stealing, to property damage and vandalism and finally to more serious delinquent acts, such as car theft, burglary, and fraud. The third pathway, called the *Authority Conflict Pathway*, describes the developmental sequence that begins with obstinate behavior and moves to defiant and oppositional behavior and finally to authority avoidance, including truancy and running away, as a third step. As a further refinement to the model, Loeber distinguished between youngsters whose antisocial behavior was temporary, labeled *experimenters*, and youngsters who continued in their antisocial behavior, labeled *persisters* (Loeber & Stouthamer-Loeber, 1996).

Loeber also reported that development along one pathway may be a precursor to development along another pathway (Loeber et al., 1993). In other words, young people may begin to develop along one path and then continue their development along a dual path. In the Pittsburgh Youth Study, this was particularly the case for boys on the Overt Pathway, who seemed to be as likely to also slide into the Covert Pathway, becoming what Loeber referred to as *versatile* offenders, that is, offenders who engaged in both overt and covert types of behaviors. This was not the case, however, for boys on the Covert Pathway, who did not seem likely to also slide into the Overt Pathway. Finally, it was determined that boys on the Authority Conflict Pathway were also likely to develop along either of the other two paths. Although these developmental pathways have been replicated with various samples (Loeber, Wei, Stouthamer-Loeber, Huizanga, & Thornberry, 1999; Tolan, Gorman-Smith, & Loeber 2000), to date, the models have only been tested with boys. It remains to be seen whether the same pathways are exhibited in girls, although some evidence suggests that this might be the case (Gorman-Smith & Loeber, 2005).

Another developmental pathways model was advanced by Canadian researchers Ray Corrado and Lauren Freedman (2011). These researchers posited that early exposure to developmental risk factors, including prenatal risk factors, affects the likelihood of exposure to subsequent risk factors. Similar to Loeber's model, Corrado and Freedman contend that "changes in antisocial behaviour are predictable, hierarchical, and orderly" (2011, p. 199). In the Corrado and Freedman model, which was developed in keeping with the large body of research on risk factors, youth who end up engaging in antisocial and delinquent behavior may be seen as having followed one of five developmental pathways leading to the onset of their delinquency. Each of the five pathways is initiated by exposure to a distinct set of risk factors. Exposure to or experience with the following risk factors may set an individual onto one of the five pathways: (a) prenatal risk; (b) extreme child maltreatment; (c) childhood personality disorder, including oppositional defiant disorder, conduct disorder, and early psychopathic traits; (d) extreme temperament, including high emotional reactivity; and (e) adolescent-onset antisocial behavior. Moreover, Corrado and Freeman argue that, in keeping with the multiple pathways, different intervention strategies are needed to address the distinct needs of youth following each of the pathways. To illustrate their model, we describe one of the pathways in the following.

According to the *extreme temperament pathway*, Corrado and Freedman (2011) propose that some youth are born with a difficult temperament. This risk factor predisposes the individual toward experiencing extreme (heightened or dampened) behavioral and emotional responses to internal and external stimuli, such as fussiness or fearfulness, compared to a moderate response of an optimal temperament. This trait is referred to as high/low emotional reactivity and is associated with an increased risk for antisocial behavior. Temperament is considered a stable characteristic that manifests early in a person's life, by 4 months of age (Kagan & Snidman, 2004). It is also considered a developmental precursor to an individual's personality that is shaped over time by reciprocal interactions with the environment (Stright, Gallagher, & Kelley, 2008).

Children with a difficult temperament can pose challenges for parents in managing their child's emotional and behavior states. This situation may hinder the emotional bonding between parent and child and result in the use of harsh and punitive responses by parents. High/low emotional reactivity also may impede normative socialization processes by interfering with parents' ability to inculcate prosocial behaviors in their child. Chronic irritability in the child, for example, may be (mis) perceived by parents as willful defiance and oppositionality that create an acute and heightened sense of frustration and anger. This negative perception and the ensuing negative feelings are perpetuated through the continual repetition of such damaging parent–child interactions. This transactional, dynamic process leads parents to use punitive and physical discipline, such as yelling and hitting, resulting in mutually coercive and negative experiences that maintain both the child's aggressive behavior, through positive reinforcements, and the parents' ineffective behavior management techniques, through negative reinforcements (Patterson, 1986). All this serves to undermine children's ability to achieve emotional and behavioral self-regulation, a critical psychosocial task of childhood.

In the presence of additional risk factors, such as single parenthood, low socioeconomic status, or limited social support and social isolation,

Corrado and Freedman (2011) contend that these processes are further compounded, creating an environment that substantially disrupts effective parenting behavior as well as the child's achievement of normative developmental tasks that begins in infancy and carries forward into childhood and adolescence. Children following this developmental pathway are at heightened risk of poor peer relations and peer rejection, marginalizing them from prosocial peer groups and opportunities to develop prosocial skills. Relations with teachers and other authority figures also are compromised, as the child may react to routine school activities with aggressive outbursts that parallel the hostile interactions with parents. This dynamic leads to heightened risk for school truancy, suspension, and expulsion and further marginalization from normative social institutions. In late childhood and early adolescence, boredom and low self-control may lead the young person to substance abuse problems and other forms of risky, reckless, or self-destructive behavior, including severe violence, out of a lack of fear or a drive toward novelty and sensation-seeking. Proposed interventions for youth on this developmental pathway include efforts aimed at teaching the child to develop effective emotional and behavioral self-regulation and coping skills. Parents and teachers may be taught nonpunitive responses to difficult behavior and creating positive, as opposed to overly critical, learning environments that are based on success.

At present, Corrado and Freedman's (2011) model remains at the theoretical stage and, although based on the extant literature, is yet to be tested against reality. Further work is needed to determine whether the proposed model is consistent with the "lived experiences" of youth, whether five pathways are sufficient for accounting for the onset of antisocial behavior in young people and whether the proposed interventions associated with each pathway are able to divert youth on a given pathway onto a more normative pathways of development.

In summary, multiple pathways models share conceptual similarities with the typology models described earlier but focus more directly on articulating the etiological factors and developmental sequences that give rise to the different forms of antisocial and delinquent behavior. However, further work is needed on multiple pathways models. For example, pathways models fall short in a number of areas, including articulating the timing of the progression through the pathways, whether a step on the pathway could be skipped but still result in the same out-come, and what form the process takes as an individual moves from one pathway to another. The advantage of multiple pathways models is that each pathway has its own unique set of causal mechanisms. As delinquency is multiply determined, the same intervention may not be effective for all children with conduct problem behavior (Frick, 2004). As a result, to move beyond the multiple pathways models, there is a need for an understanding of the causal processes and mechanisms that connect past events to future outcomes that can be targeted by an inter-vention rather than targeting the risk factor, which might be immutable. This aspect of developmental pathways leads to the next section, which emphasizes the need to identify and articulate the specific processes that link past events with future outcomes (Pickles & Hill, 2006).

PROCESS MODELS ARE ESSENTIAL FOR UNDERSTANDING CRIMINAL BEHAVIOR IN A DEVELOPMENTAL CONTEXT. As the developmental psychologist Dante Cicchetti stated, "all pathology is, strictly speaking, a process" (1984, p. 2). Consistent with this position, the third premise of this book states that process models are needed to explain the mechanisms of effects of risk and protective factors on the onset, maintenance, and desistance of antisocial, delinquent, and crimi-nal behavior. As discussed earlier, there is a growing body of research that suggests that the onset of criminal behavior follows age-related pat-terns of behavior, suggesting that its etiology is developmentally deter-mined (Loeber & Hay, 1997; Moffitt, 2006a); that is, prior experiences (e.g., in infancy or childhood) influence later outcomes (e.g., in adoles-cence or adulthood). Again, we remind the reader that these associa-tions are to be understood as probabilistic, not deterministic (Dumas & Nilsen, 2003). The question that arises, then, is, By what mechanisms or processes does this occur? The identification of developmental risk factors is critical to understanding the causes and course of crime, and an abundance of research exists, yielding veritable laundry lists of risk variables (Allard, Chrzanowski, & Stewart, 2012) that aid in this en-deavor. However, studies are needed to uncover the underlying causal mechanisms that link these risk factors to outcomes, to identify not just the *what* but also the *why* (Farrington, 2003; Farrington & Loeber, 2013; Frick, 2004; Kazdin et al., 1997). Although knowing that punitive dis-cipline is statistically associated with antisocial behavior is one thing, understanding the causal mechanisms that link them, what the mediating variables are between harsh parenting and delinquency, is another. Once again, this work has implications for the development of effective early interventions. For example, a program may target not the specific risk factor, which may be unchangeable, but the particular mechanisms and mediators that are disrupted when developmental processes go awry (Kazdin & Nock, 2003; Rutter et al., 1998; Shirk et al., 2000).

Within psychology, an understanding of process models has been greatly advanced by the field of developmental psychopathology. Developmental psychopathology is largely concerned with the factors that give rise to the onset, course, and termination of psychiatric disorders in children and youth (Rutter & Sroufe, 2000; Sroufe & Rutter, 1984). In this regard, obvious parallels exist between developmental psychopathology and the field of developmental criminology, which is concerned with the onset and course of crime and desistance from crime (Le Blanc & Loeber, 1998; Loeber & Le Blanc, 1990; Nagin & Tremblay, 2005a). As McMillan Hastings, Salter, and Skuse (2008, p. 883) noted, "risk factors early in life can be linked to a temporally distant outcome through a developmental chain that results from maladaptation at an early stage." According to Kazdin et al. (1997, p. 378, emphasis in original),

> a risk factor is a *process concept* insofar as it refers to a characteristic, event, or experience that in some way influences, initiates, or alters critical processes within a person's life or the systems within which he or she functions. These processes or intervening steps explain why or how the risk factors presage the outcome.

As stated previously, theory plays an important role in the development and evaluation of process models. Theory provides a road map for the steps that compose the process model. Theory also provides an outline of the relevant variables of the model and the purported direction of effects, in a sense, ordering the expected trail from risk factors to outcomes. Last, theory provides an explanation for the underlying causal mechanisms of the risk factors. In other words, theory *explains* the relationship between risk factors and outcomes.

The developmental theory of antisocial behavior by Gerald Patterson (Patterson, DeBaryshe, & Ramsey, 1989) provides a good illustration

Early Childhood   Middle Childhood   Late Childhood and Adolescence

```
                              ┌──────────────┐
                              │  Rejection by│
                              │ normal peers │        ┌────────────┐
┌──────────┐    ┌─────────┐   └──────────────┘        │ Commitment │   ┌────────────┐
│Poor parental│ │  Child  │                           │ to deviant │   │ Delinquency│
│ discipline  │→│ conduct │→                        → │ peer group │ → │            │
│and monitoring│ │problems │   ┌──────────────┐        └────────────┘   └────────────┘
└──────────┘    └─────────┘   │   Academic   │      →
                              │   failure    │
                              └──────────────┘
```

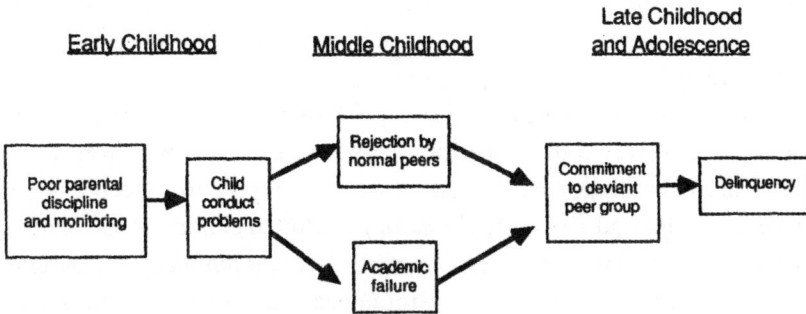

Figure I.3. Developmental model of antisocial behavior
Source: Patterson, G. R., DeBaryshe, B. D., & Ramsey, E. (1989). A developmental perspective on antisocial behavior. *American Psychologist, 44*, pp. 329–335. American Psychological Association. Reprinted with permission.

(see Figure I.3). Patterson et al. (1989) posited that, from early childhood to adolescence, antisocial behavior unfolds in an orderly and predictable sequence of experiences. The process begins with exposure to harsh and punitive discipline, which undermines the child's opportunities to achieve positive outcomes in school and peer relations in middle childhood. These experiences of failure lead the young person to associate with deviant peer groups in adolescence. The model draws on behavioral principles of conditioned learning, modeling, and contingent reinforcements to explain the mechanisms linking past events to future outcomes. The aim is to understand the origins and the course of criminal behavior and to trace the developmental processes and pathways that link past events with future outcomes.

Complex causal models, such as Patterson and colleagues', that involve multiple intervening variables may be empirically tested through the use of a serial (versus parallel) multiple mediation statistical technique, proposed by Andrew Hayes (2013). In this analytical approach, a series of mediating variables is strung together in a theoretical causal chain. Each mediator is posited as having an influence on the next mediator, which influences the next, and so on. Such models are useful as they are likely to be consistent with real-world complexities in that many causal effects likely involve multiple mechanisms operating through serial causal chains. Also, competing (or compatible) theories postulating different mechanisms of influence may be tested simultaneously as a formal statistical comparison of the different theoretical paths of influence (Hayes, 2013). Two examples are helpful for illustrating the value of this approach.

In a prospective longitudinal study, Chassin, Curran, Hussong, and Colder (1996) tested three distinct pathways leading from parental alcohol use to self-reported alcohol and illicit drug use in a sample of 316 male and female adolescents. The sample included children of alcoholics (COAs) and matched controls, that is, children of nonalcoholic parents of similar ethnicity, family composition, age, and socioeconomic status. Each of the three pathways involved a series of mediators that represented specific causal chains. The first pathway, labeled the *socialization pathway*, tested the effects of maternal and paternal alcohol use on parental monitoring of the youth's behavior, the association with substance using peers, and the youth's own substance use. The second pathway, labeled the *stress and negative affect regulation pathway*, tested the effects of maternal and paternal alcohol use on adolescents' stress experiences, negative affect, the association with substance using peers, and the youth's own substance use. The third pathway, labeled the *temperament pathway*, tested the effects of maternal and paternal alcohol use on youth's emotionality (i.e., inadequate emotional coping, emotionally labile), negative affect (i.e., anxious, sadness, feelings of derogation), sociability, the association with substance using peers, and the youth's own substance use. These three pathways were tested as mediated effects in purported causal chains in relation to the adolescents' substance use assessed over a 3-year period. The longitudinal pattern of substance use was represented as a single, average change trajectory called a growth curve. The growth curve yielded an upward slope, indicating a linear increase in substance use over time.

Results of the study indicated that, first, paternal (but not maternal) alcohol use had a different effect on the youth's substance use between the two subsamples; not only were COA youth with alcoholic fathers more likely to use substances; paternal alcohol use also *increased* the use of substances more quickly in the COA youth than in the non-COA peers. Second, analyses of the three pathways yielded mixed support. Although both the socialization and the stress and negative affect regulation pathways were supported by the data, the pathways did not fully account for the youth's substance use growth. Paternal alcohol use still exerted an influence on the outcome variable after controlling for the mediators. Last, no support was found for the relation between paternal alcohol use and sociability and emotionality. This study nicely illustrates the empirical investigation of multiple mediators that are tested in serial (vs. parallel) fashion and the ways in which different theoretical models that reflect distinct processes accounting for relations between explanatory variables and outcomes may be examined simultaneously.

A second illustration of a process model comes from the work of criminologist Marvin Krohn (Krohn, Ward, Thornberry, Lizotte, & Chu, 2011). In this study, the authors tested a model of the relation between youth gang involvement at age 14 and involvement in street crime and experiences of arrests at age 31 via a serial mediator model that included precocious transitions into early adulthood, economic hardship, and poor family relations. Using data from the Rochester Youth Development Study (Thornberry, Lizotte, Krohn, Smith, & Porter, 2003), Krohn et al. (2011) found support for the model. Greater youth gang involvement undermined the successful transition from adolescence to adulthood, which resulted in greater economic hardship and family problems in adulthood, which had the subsequent effect of increasing the likelihood the individual will continue to be involved in criminal activity and experience arrests as an adult. Like Chassin et al. (1996), in investigating a theoretically derived causal chain, this study illustrates the use of mediational analyses to test complex process models that describe purported causal mechanisms underlying the linkages between past events and future outcomes. Such models help shed light on the critical steps involved in the unfolding nature of developmental processes (Bushway, 2013a; Farrington, 2003; Rutter & Sroufe 2000).

Overview of This Book

Over the last few years, a number of excellent reviews of criminal trajectory research have appeared either as journal articles (Jennings & Reingle, 2012; Nagin & Odgers, 2010a, 2010b; Nagin & Piquero, 2010) or book chapters (Nagin, 2011; A. Piquero, 2008). To date, however, there has not been a fuller discussion of criminal trajectories. With the broad and rich body of research that has now accumulated over the last 25 years and the wide range of well-refined and well-articulated developmentally informed theoretical models (Farrington, 2005a), the time is right to review the state-of-the-art trajectory research in its own volume. In addition, our aim with this book is to place the notion of a criminal trajectory within the broader context of a developmental framework.

This book offers an overview of what we know about criminal trajectories. It draws on theory and research from a number of fields, including developmental psychology, developmental criminology, and crime prevention, to explore the intersection between developmental psychology and criminal trajectories. The book also illustrates and explicates the theoretical, empirical, and practical utility of considering the heterogeneity underlying offender populations (in the form of multiple criminal trajectories) over the life course in the conceptualization, response to, and prevention of crime. The volume draws on the first author's (D. M. D.) 30 years of experience as a researcher in developmental criminology and criminal trajectories and his personal experience as a staff psychologist at a medium-security prison for adult male offenders in Ontario, Canada, and on the second author's (M. W.) research experience in life-span developmental psychology, dynamic developmental systems theory, developmental criminology, longitudinal data analysis, and trajectory work using crime (and substance use) data from the United States and Germany. It also draws on the accumulated literature that has grown broad and deep over the past two-and-a-half decades in its coverage of the theoretical, empirical, methodological, and practical considerations of understanding the longitudinal nature and pattern of crime from a trajectory approach. This book argues that a developmental perspective, informed by the accumulated body of criminal trajectory research and process-oriented theoretical models, can advance knowledge of the mechanisms underlying the onset, course, and desistance of crime. This understanding may lead to better, more effective crime prevention policies and practices and an overall reduction in the incidence and prevalence of crime in our society.

The goals of this book are as follows:

• Introduce the reader to the concept of criminal trajectories and to the trajectory statistical methodology
• Review current debates and controversies about criminal trajectory research

- Describe the main findings from the accumulated criminal trajectory research
- Illustrate ways in which criminal trajectory research informs knowledge of developmental pathways of crime
- Critically examine the policy and programming implications of the criminal trajectory literature
- Suggest new areas for further investigation to advance criminal trajectory research and its broader applications and implications

Although perhaps not as thrilling as a roller coaster, we hope you enjoy the ride!

1

Theoretical Backdrop

The contemporary study of criminal trajectories emerged in 1993 with the publication of the article "Age, Criminal Careers, and Population Heterogeneity—Specification and Estimation of a Nonparametric, Mixed Poisson Model" by Daniel Nagin and Kenneth Land. This seminal work came in the wake of key theoretical and methodological developments in the 7-year period preceding it. Each development represents a milestone in a series of intellectual advances that opened new ways of thinking about, conceptualizing, and generating and testing hypotheses about crime from a developmental perspective. These milestones include the publication in 1986 by Alfred Blumstein, Cohen, Roth, and Visher of the report on criminal careers; the launch in 1986 of the *Causes and Correlates of Delinquency Studies*; the publication in 1990 of the chapter by Rolf Loeber and Marc Le Blanc on developmental criminology; the publication in 1993 by Terrie Moffitt of the dual taxonomy model of offending; and the publication in the same year by Nagin and Land of the methodology for analyzing developmental trajectories. This scientific lineage represents what we call the *short* historical view of the theoretical backdrop of criminal trajectories.

The theoretical backdrop also has a *long (or broad)* historical view that places the concept of criminal trajectories, and developmental trajectories, more generally, and the developmental context in which they are embedded within several other theoretical frameworks that came before 1986. These frameworks include those of Glen H. Elder (Elder, 1985a; Elder & Rockwell, 1979) and Paul B. Baltes (Baltes, Reese, & Lipsitt, 1980) and their life-course sociology and life-span psychology perspectives, respectively, and the field of developmental psychopathology (Achenbach, 1974; Cicchetti, 1984). This chapter reviews both the short and long views of the theoretical backdrop of criminal trajectories. Although not a focus of this chapter, we note that the foundation that underpins the statistical methodology for group-based trajectory analysis (i.e., as a special application of finite mixture models) has its own intellectual lineage dating back to the 1890s (Bauer & Curran, 2003a; Curran & Hussong, 2003).

The Short Historical View

In 1986, Alfred Blumstein, Jacqueline Cohen, Jeffrey Roth, and Christy Visher published their seminal two-volume edited report *Criminal Careers and Career Criminals*. We see this work as marking the first milestone of the short historical view of the theoretical backdrop of criminal trajectories because it set forth a comprehensive plan for the study of crime with the individual as the unit of analysis. The report was the product of the Panel on Research on Criminal Career, convened in 1983 by the National Academy of Science under the sponsorship of the National Institute of Justice (NIJ). In these two volumes, the contributing authors defined the parameters of a criminal career, reviewed the empirical literature on criminal career dimensions, outlined the relevance of the criminal career perspective to crime control and criminal justice policy and practice, and set out a blueprint for the future investigation of the criminal career paradigm.

Blumstein et al. (1986) defined a criminal career as "the longitudinal sequence of crimes committed by an individual offender" (p. 12) that is characterized during a lifetime by three components: an initiation or onset; a termination or end; and a duration or career length (Blumstein, Cohen, & Farrington, 1988). Criminal career research is concerned with how "careers are initiated, how they progress, and why they are discontinued" (Petersilia, 1980, p. 322). Consistent with the developmental approach to the study of crime discussed in the introduction, the focus was on patterns of offending behavior at the level of the individual. During their careers, offenders may display changes and continuities in criminal activity on various dimensions, including rate, type, timing, versatility, and severity. Drawing a parallel with developmental psychopathology, this is akin to following individuals with a mental disorder in terms of the intensity (or severity), duration, and frequency of the symptoms— important dimensions for monitoring the effectiveness of a clinical treatment plan. It is the patterns of transition (change) and stability (continuity) on these sorts of variables (i.e., rate, type, timing, versatility, severity) across major developmental periods, as well as the underlying reasons for the observed patterns, that are of interest to criminal justice researchers, theoreticians, practitioners, and policy makers (Barnett, Blumstein, & Farrington, 1987; A. Piquero & Mazerolle, 2001).

Also, consistent with the developmental approach, the criminal career paradigm is concerned with risk factors and the effects of early experiences (e.g., adverse family background, early onset overt and covert conduct problems) on the onset and course of delinquency and criminal activity. As such, the criminal career paradigm advocates for the use of prospective longitudinal (vs. cross-sectional) research methods to test hypotheses about putative causal associations between antecedents and consequences, whereby the temporal ordering of events can be clearly established and extraneous variables can be controlled (Blumstein, Cohen, & Farrington, 1988). The criminal career paradigm favors dynamic models of crime rather than static models, such as the general theory of crime proffered by Gottfredson and Hirschi (1986, 1988, 1990), a theory that David Farrington described as "explicitly anti-developmental" (Farrington, 2003, p. 228). As an organizing framework, the criminal career paradigm has had a major influence on all subsequent developmental theories concerned with factors associated with the onset, course, and termination of crime.

Another key proposition of the criminal career paradigm, which is particularly relevant to the study of criminal trajectories, is that researchers should investigate age–crime curves at the level of the individual (denoted by the Greek letter *lambda*, λ) rather than groups, as the aggregate age–crime curve, with its familiar sharp rise in early adolescence and gradual decline into adulthood after about age 17, may mask distinct subgroups of offenders whose own growth curves depart from this pattern (A. Piquero, Farrington, et al., 2003). It may be that, although a large group of offenders fit the age–crime curve, a smaller group of offenders remain active criminals into adulthood. Furthermore, these groups may differ on some dimensions of the criminal career, such as career length, offense frequency, type, or severity (Blumstein et al., 1988). In a prescient statement foreshadowing the emergence of the trajectory analysis methodology that would appear 7 years later, Blumstein et al. (1986, p. 10) suggested that future research "should focus especially on the path of λ over time as offenders age, variation in λ with age for active offenders, the factors associated with intermittent spurts of high-rate and low-rate offending, and differences in λ by crime type." Indeed, trajectory research provides a means of mathematically modeling the heterogeneity in the rate of offending in a sample at the level of the individual over the duration of the criminal career.

A second important initiative in 1986 was the launch by the Office of Juvenile Justice and Delinquency Prevention of three large-scale prospective longitudinal studies in the United States, collectively referred to as the *Causes and Correlates of Delinquency Studies*. These studies were the Pittsburgh Youth Study (Loeber, Farrington, Stouthamer-Loeber, & van Kammen, 1998), the Denver Youth Study (Huizinga, Wylie Weiher, Espiritu, & Esbensen, 2003) and the Rochester Youth Development Study (Thornberry, Lizotte, Krohn, Smith, & Porter, 2003). Together, over the years, these investigations have generated important contributions to the understanding of the causes of crime that would not have been detected through cross-sectional studies (Thornberry & Krohn, 2003a).

As exemplified by the *Causes and Correlates Studies*, the 1980s saw a tremendous growth in interest in longitudinal and developmentally informed research and in the burgeoning study of developmental risk factors. The decade saw a flurry of studies in a number of countries, including the United States, Australia, and New Zealand, that examined risk and protective factors for a range of maladaptive outcomes in children and youth, including mental health problems and antisocial behavior. Sometimes these outcomes were studied simultaneously in the same investigation, for example, when conduct disorder was the dependent variable, given the significant overlap between conduct disorder diagnosis and delinquent behavior. These studies took up the earlier work on risk and protective factors by such eminent developmental researchers as Emmy Werner, Lee Robins, and Sheldon and Eleanor Glueck. The new line of research was advanced by Norman Garmezy, Rolf Loeber, and Sir Michael Rutter, among others.

One such longitudinal study of developmental risk factors was the launch in Ontario, Canada of the Ontario Child Health Study (Ontario Child Health Centre, 2018). With funding from the (Ontario) provincial government, the Ontario Child Health Study was a large-scale, epidemiological study that investigated the prevalence and continuity of, and risk factors for, four mental disorders (neurosis, somatization, hyperactivity, and conduct disorder) in a stratified cluster sample of 3,294 children and youth, ages 4 to 16 in Ontario. The children were assessed at two time points, in 1983 and again in 1987. Variables included in the 1983 assessment were used to predict outcomes 4 years later (a third follow-up, not reported on here, was conducted in 2000 to examine predictors of various psychosocial outcomes when the sample reached adulthood).

Among the many findings that came out of this research, Offord et al. (1992) reported that conduct disorder had the highest rate of stability of all the disorders, with 45% of the children who met criteria for the disorder in 1983 continuing to manifest the disorder in 1987. This figure is compared with 34% and 26% of the youth with hyperactivity and emotional disorder, respectively. This finding is consistent with Robins (1966), who also found a high rate of stability for conduct disorder. Also, family dysfunction and getting along with others predicted the persistence of psychiatric disorder over the duration of the study. Moreover, economic disadvantage in 1983 was associated with the onset of a disorder in 1987 among children who had no prior disorder. In a subsequent study, Lipman, Offord, and Boyle (1994) found that economic disadvantage in 1983 predicted poor school performance and social impairment 4 years later. Last, Szatmari, Boyle, and Offord (1993) reported that psychiatric disorders aggregated within families in the Ontario Child Health Study sample, particularly for conduct and emotional disorders. This study added to the previous literature with clinic-based samples that showed a tendency for disorders to aggregate within families. The authors, however, were unable to discern the extent to which genetic or environmental influences (or their interaction) accounted for the effect. As with the *Causes and Correlates Studies*, the Ontario Child Health Study had an important impact on research on risk factors for conduct problems and antisocial behavior (MacMillan et al., 1997; Offord et al., 1987).

We now turn to the third milestone contributing to the criminal trajectory research. In an essay published in 1990 titled "Toward a Developmental Criminology," Loeber and Le Blanc picked up on some of the themes of the criminal career paradigm initiated by Blumstein et al. (1986) and developed them further to define a new line of inquiry within criminology. Loeber and Le Blanc felt that a coherent, clearly articulated, and formalized description of a dynamic, developmental criminology was needed to move the field forward in terms of understanding crime at the level of the individual from an explicitly developmental framework. Provocatively, what this meant was that the more familiar tradition in criminology and sociology of analyzing cross-sectional data was thought to be inadequate for exploring within-individual developmental progressions and that longitudinal data were needed, in which study participants served as their own controls. Like the criminal career paradigm, developmental criminology places emphasis on studying within-person changes through longitudinal research designs that can disentangle causes from correlates.

According to Loeber and Le Blanc (1990), developmental criminology refers simply to "temporal within-individual changes in offending" (pp. 376–377). The focus of developmental criminology is twofold: (a) to understand the progression of conduct problem behavior and criminal offending with age and (b) to identify the risk factors that are causally related or correlated with criminal offending and that affect its course of development. Developmental criminology brings in concepts of development to better understand the factors and processes that give rise to the various dimensions of criminal behavior, such as offending severity, crime mix, and desistance. For example, the notion that development occurs in a predictable, organized, and hierarchical manner underlies the study of crime from a developmental criminology perspective. The simple question posed by Loeber and Le Blanc was whether criminal offending unfolds in the same way as other developmental phenomena (i.e., in a predictable, organized, and hierarchical manner).

Both the criminal career paradigm and developmental criminology are interested in the factors associated with the causes and correlates of the onset (referred to within developmental criminology as *activation*) and desistance of crime (conceptualized by the developmental criminology framework as a process, not an event), as well as with change and continuity of various dimensions of offending during the course of offending, including severity (referred to as *aggravation*), frequency (referred to as *acceleration*), and versatility (referred to as *diversification*). At the same time, whereas Blumstein et al. (1986) were concerned with offending across the life span, Loeber and Le Blanc (1990) were interested in the adolescent period, given the major changes in the biological, psychological, and social domains that occur during the teen years.

Of relevance to the study of criminal trajectories, Loeber and Le Blanc (1990) also were interested in developmental trajectories, which they defined quite broadly as "the systematic developmental changes in offending involving one or more of the processes of activation, aggravation, and desistance" (p. 382). Moreover, anticipating the method for extracting multiple criminal trajectories from a data set that would emerge a few years later, they noted that "researchers may need to distinguish between multiple, rather than single, trajectories that reflect different dynamic career types" (Loeber & Le Blanc, 1990, p. 382). At the same time, however, in a follow-up essay in which they updated the developmental criminology literature, Le Blanc and Loeber (1998) used the term "developmental trajectory" to refer to something more akin to a developmental pathway, as defined earlier, that is, an ordered sequence of developmental processes and behavior that leads to a particular outcome, such as involvement in substance use, violent offending, or property crime (e.g., Loeber, 1985; Loeber & Hay, 1997). Indeed, they do state that the terms *trajectories* and *pathways* may be used interchangeably (Le Blanc & Loeber, 1998, p. 152). Le Blanc and Loeber provide the example of normative developmental trajectories for men described by Hogan (1978), in which the behavioral sequence is ordered from the completion of school to obtaining employment to starting a family. They also use the term *metatrajectories* (Le Blanc & Loeber, 1998, p. 153) to refer to robust life-course offending patterns, such as patterns of the chronic offenders found in the Wolfgang, Figlio, and Sellin (1972) study and the adolescence-limited and life-course-persistent offending trajectories proposed by Moffitt (1993). Within these contexts, their use of the terms *trajectories* and *pathways* interchangeably serves only to obfuscate the distinctions between these two concepts that are made in this book.

In the early 1990s, what was still needed to move the developmental study of crime forward was an explicitly developmentally framed *theory* of crime from which hypotheses could be generated and tested. If criminal offenders are a heterogeneous population with different age–crime curves, what would these groups look like? How would groups be constituted? Would they have unique origins, and what would those look like? The two most prominent developmental theories of criminality were proposed by Terrie Moffitt (1993) and Gerald Patterson (Patterson, Capaldi, & Bank, 1991; Patterson & Yoerger, 1993). Taken together, their work marks the fourth milestone of the short historical view of the theoretical backdrop of criminal trajectories. According to these theorists, offenders begin their criminal careers in either childhood (early starters) or adolescence (late starters). Patterson and Yoerger (1993) state that the early starters experience high rates of aggressive and "coercive" family experiences during childhood, which place them on a developmental pathway toward a protracted criminal career in adolescence and adulthood. By contrast, the late starters experience fewer developmental risk factors and begin to engage in delinquent behavior in adolescence because of an association with a deviant peer group. Taking a more biopsychosocial approach, Moffitt (1993) postulates that the early starters (i.e., life-course-persistent group) have neurological problems that interact with aversive environmental conditions to yield a lifelong, highly stable pattern of antisocial behavior. The late starters (i.e., adolescent-limited group), on the other hand, experience relatively normal development until about age 15, at which time a striving for personal independence leads them to mimic the antisocial lifestyle of their delinquent counterparts. The criminal acts in which the late-starter group engages are often relatively mild in nature and tend to desist within a few years of onset. These theories, particularly Moffitt's (1993) dual taxonomy model, have generated numerous studies using data sets from several countries, including the United States, the United Kingdom, and New Zealand, to test their validity.

Finally, in the same year that Moffitt's paper was published, Nagin and Land (1993) published their approach to the longitudinal analysis of criminal career data to examine within-individual patterns of offending across latent groups into which individuals are sorted, referred to as a *nonparametric mixed Poisson model* (later called semiparametric mixed model). This seminal work was followed over the next decade by a steady stream of articles by statistically minded criminologists and criminology-minded statisticians that further developed, refined, advanced, and extended the use of semiparametric group-based trajectory models for the analysis of developmental trajectories of crime. Also, several years later, Muthén contributed further developments to the statistical methodology for performing trajectory analysis, based on the more generalized growth mixture modeling (GMM) approach (B. Muthén & Shedden, 1999).

The Long Historical View

The roots of criminal trajectory research can be traced further back to earlier theoretical frameworks. Just as juvenile offenders do not "spring from the cabbage" when they commit their first offense (Loeber, 1990, p. 31), so, too, do theoretical concepts not emerge out of thin air (Benson, 2013); they are rooted in broad theoretical and conceptual ideas that preceded them. The notion of a criminal trajectory may be grounded in a number of broad theoretical frameworks, including the life-course and life-span traditions of Elder and Baltes, respectively. In addition, concepts from the field of developmental psychopathology, which concerns the nature and pattern of onset, course, and recovery from mental illness, have become immensely important for describing developmental processes of crime (DeLisi & Piquero, 2011). Taken together, these three rich theoretical traditions have contributed to shaping the criminal trajectories construct and the developmental context they inhabit.

GLEN ELDER AND THE LIFE COURSE. According to sociologist Glen Elder (1985b), "life course analysis is oriented to the process of change and ultimately to the task of explaining such change" (p. 17). Moreover, Elder (1985c) provided a useful heuristic for conceptualizing life-course dynamics in terms of (a) trajectories, which are lifelines, careers, or pathways of behavior or some aspect of a person's life (e.g., education, work, marriage) and which represent the *long view* of the life course, and (b) transitions, which are events or turning points that are embedded in trajectories "that give them distinctive form and meaning" (p. 31) and that represent the *short view* of the life course. For example, age-graded transitions within an education trajectory include the passage from grade school to middle school, from high school to college, and eventually from college to work life. Across individuals, multiple trajectories across various domains, each uniquely shaped by normative and nonnormative transitions, intersect to coalesce into "the uniqueness of individual life courses" (Blokland & Nieuwbeerta, 2010, p. 58). Elder's sociological life-course perspective, therefore, aims to examine and explain stability and change of social trajectories across the life span in terms of life events, including historical events (what others would refer to as stochastic or random events) such as war, economic depression, and social revolutions.

Armed with rich longitudinal data from the Berkeley Guidance Study and the Oakland Growth Study, Elder (1986, 1987) studied how military service shaped the life course in two samples of men, of which 70% and 90%, respectively, served in the armed forces during or after World War II (Elder, 1998a). For these men, entry into the army may have represented an escape from economic disadvantage and a route toward a more successful life path, it may have represented an opportunity to accelerate the transition from boyhood to manhood, or it may have represented a chance to build a positive sense of self, an identity as a strong, self-reliant, efficacious young man contributing to the war effort. Moreover, the life circumstances of the men may have influenced the timing at which they entered the army in that early joiners (before age 21) were more likely than late joiners to have experienced family hardship and low academic achievement and self-competence prior to entering the armed forces.

Timing also was also found to be particularly influential in shaping their life-course trajectory, interestingly, in favor of the early joiners, a group whose members were more disadvantaged. Compared to the late joiners, early joiners were more likely to have experienced a delayed transition to full-time employment, marriage, and parenthood, which worked toward their advantage on return to civilian life into midlife; they were able to come back with discipline, positive experiences, and self-confidence. Late joiners were more likely to have experienced a disruption to their life course in terms of strained family relations and marriage and a delayed career, which adversely affected their adjustment on return to postmilitary life. Taken together, these results support an "early timing hypothesis" (Elder, 1998a, p. 8); positive benefits were conferred for an early entry into the army, on one hand, and disruptions to the life course resulted for late joiners, on the other hand.

What these findings further highlight is the role of timing of entry into the military as an important turning point in the life trajectory of these men. In the same way, Elder (1998a) described the impact of timing on the life course of the birth of a child. The early arrival (i.e., off time) of parenthood, for example, as a teenager, disrupts the normative developmental life course, with a cumulative impact over time relative to becoming a parent later in life.

Likewise, in the context of crime, although arrest is a nonnormative life event, for the individual, early involvement in the criminal justice system renders the transition from childhood to adolescence perilous. We know from life-span psychology that transitions across major developmental periods afford both opportunities and challenges. Most individuals navigate them well; but for some they are highly stressful and overwhelming (Petersen & Leffert, 1995). Developmental transitions tend to result in a decrement in adaptation and psychosocial functioning, a lowered self-evaluation, and heightened feelings of incompetence (Stewart, 1982). These negative feelings persist until the person is able to consolidate the new roles and expectations and demonstrates a renewed sense of resilience. As we saw from Elder's work, two factors that may conspire against such a normative developmental process are the *timing* and *number* of simultaneous transitions (Graber & Brooks-Gunn, 1996). Premature timing and an increased number of transitions can pose difficulties for the individual, compromising his or her ability to cope with the vicissitudes of the emerging and subsequent developmental periods. Thornberry, Ireland, and Smith (2001) examined whether age at the time of maltreatment affects its impact on psychosocial development. They found that the timing of the maltreatment did affect the relationship between the maltreatment and its outcome such that the proximal impact on adolescent outcomes was greater than the distal impact. Physical and sexual abuse and neglect that occurred only in adolescence or persisted from childhood to adolescence had a greater negative impact on development in the teen years than did maltreatment that only occurred in childhood. Effects were seen in a number of areas, including greater rates of delinquency, alcohol and drug use, and teen pregnancy. The authors speculated that coping mechanisms accessed by youth in response to such stressors may lead them to either rebel through antisocial behavior or escape through alcohol or drug use. It was also thought that the effects of maltreatment limited to childhood either may fade over time because of the resilience of children or be mitigated by successful intervention.

Involvement in serious antisocial behavior during adolescence, especially if it (a) begins at an early age, (b) is protracted, and (c) involves contact with the justice system, may lead to a disruption in the normative developmental processes bringing about a premature transition from adolescence into adulthood and a concomitant redefinition of roles and contexts (e.g., being processed as a "criminal," making court appearances, and spending a great deal of time with police and correctional, probation, and parole officers; L. Johnson, Simons, & Conger, 2004). It also leads to an increase in the number of transitions and non-normative stressors with which the person must contend (Petersen & Leffert, 1995) and impedes the young person's ability to accomplish the developmental tasks of adolescence, such as completing school, developing positive peer relations, and forming a healthy and integrated sense of self (Masten & Coatsworth, 1998). The cumulative impact is a continued disruption in normative functioning that can interfere with the person's ability to develop the requisite skills and capabilities to assume the socially accepted roles and expectations of adulthood. This process can result in an increased likelihood of maintaining criminal activity into adulthood, as opportunities for completing high school and entering the labor force diminish. However, caution must be exercised in describing these outcomes, as developmental pathways are meant to be understood as probabilistic not deterministic (Dumas & Nilsen, 2003). Considerable plasticity in adaptation and adjustment allows for both continuity and discontinuity in developmental outcomes. This, of course, opens the possibility for rehabilitative efforts to provide missed opportunities for individuals involved in the justice system to facilitate their positive growth and development. Ideally, such intervention strategies are informed by a thorough understanding of developmental trajectories of offending behavior and the developmental processes that link to the patterns of escalation and de-escalation.

PAUL BALTES AND LIFE-SPAN PSYCHOLOGY. Paul Baltes's life-span psychology is concerned with change and continuity across the full age spectrum and the processes and mechanisms that influence the development of the individual (i.e., ontogenesis). Development, to German psychologist Baltes, is a lifelong process (Baltes et al., 1980). The theoretical framework has much in common with Elder's work. Indeed, Baltes (1987) uses the terms *life span* and *life course* interchangeably, although he acknowledged that the latter term tended to be favored by sociologists. Both are broad orientations rather than theories. Life-span psychology is not one single theory but "a *family of perspectives* that together specify a coherent metatheoretical view of the nature of development" (Baltes, 1987, p. 612, emphasis in original). Second, both are concerned with development from birth to death. According to Baltes et al. (1980, p. 66), "life-span developmental psychology is concerned with the description, explanation, and modification (optimization) of developmental processes in the human life course from conception to death." Life-span development is about long-term, rather than short-term, patterns of change over the course of human development, although studies of either contribute to the life-span psychology field. This theoretic approach stands in contrast to some theories (e.g., Piagetian, Freudian) that propose that psychosocial development is essentially complete by adolescence. Third, both are interested in the integration of historical context and processes of human development. In particular, Baltes was interested in normative history-graded events that "define the developmental context of a given birth cohort" (Lerner, Theokas, & Bobek, 2005, p. 16), including wars, epidemics, and downturns in the economy, as well sociocultural shifts, such as in sex-role expectations. Life-span psychology differs from life-course sociology in that, although not exclusively, as a subdiscipline of psychology, life-span psychology is concerned with the ontogenesis of *psychological* phenomena, notably cognition (e.g., memory, intelligence) and personality and the nature and pattern of their trajectories over the life course, particularly across adulthood and into old age.

Baltes, Linderberger, and Staudinger (2006, p. 570) identify four broad objectives of life-span psychology: "1) To offer an organized account of the overall structure and sequence of development across the life span; 2) to identify the interconnections between earlier and later developmental events and processes; 3) to delineate the biological, psychological, social, and environmental factors and mechanisms which are the foundation of life span development; and 4) to specify the biological and environmental opportunities and constraints that shape life span development of individuals, including their range of plasticity (modifiability)." Of relevance to the notion of criminal trajectories, although Baltes does not explicitly define a "trajectory," the use of the term in life-span psychology (e.g., Baltes et al., 1980) suggests a course or progression of development of some psychological phenomenon, such as attachment (Lerner & Ryff, 1978) and achievement behavior (Brim, 1976) over age or time. In this regard, Baltes's use of the term is consistent with the way in which it is defined for this book.

In the next section, we discuss Baltes's contribution to the notion of adaptation and adaptive functioning, from a life-span psychology perspective. Specifically, we describe the *Selection, Optimization,* and *Compensation* (SOC) theory, which has become a dominant model of successful aging (Ouwehand, de Ridder, & Bensing, 2007). We present this material as an upward extension (i.e., for adults) of the notions of adaptation and adaptive functioning that we discussed in the introduction, primarily in relation to children and youth. The SOC model illustrates how successful adaptation and adaptive functioning can be achieved in adulthood. The section ends with a discussion of the relevance of the theory to a developmental approach to the study of offenders on a criminal trajectory.

SELECTION, OPTIMIZATION, AND COMPENSATION THEORY. Recall from the introduction that adaptive functioning is a central concept in developmental psychology. By effectively adapting to changing internal and external stimuli, the individual is able to maintain an optimal growth and development. We also noted that effective adaptation is tied to achievement of life-span tasks (Baltes et al., 1980). You may recall that *adaptational failure* refers to the circumstance whereby a person fails to achieve normative tasks of development in the formative years, which can undermine positive psychological and psychosocial growth. The effects of adaptational failure are cumulative, resulting in a cascade of negative consequences that continue to undermine development (Sroufe, 2013).

Baltes put forth one of the leading theories of successful aging (Freund & Baltes, 2002; Ouwehand et al., 2007), a life-span theory of adaptive development and adaptive functioning, referred to as the SOC theory. To Baltes, effective adaptation refers to the process of enacting positive life-management strategies across the life course that lead to subjective well-being and successful aging (Freund & Baltes, 2002). Life-management strategies refer to self-regulatory and goal-directed behaviors that are used to cope with changing life circumstances. Effective life management reflects an ability to monitor, respond to, and cope with experiences that either brings one closer to or further away from the achievement of personal goals. In this regard, successful life management is achieved through the three processes of self-regulation: selection, optimization, and compensation.

Selection refers to the identification and selection of and commitment to personal goals or domains of functioning from the broad array of possible goals available to an individual because of biological, social, and psychological opportunities and constraints of one's life circumstances. The process of setting personal goals enables one to have a feeling that one's life has meaning. Freund and Baltes (2002) suggest that there are two types of selection, elective selection and loss-based selection. Elective selection is focused on achieving a desired and self-directed outcome, such as settling down to start a family rather than volunteering one's time to help in a third-world country. Loss-based selection is focused on revising one's goals when faced with an impediment to achieving the original goal or threatened by an inability to maintain functioning in a given goal domain. For example, loss-based selection may involve committing to quit smoking when smoking-related health problems, like emphysema, begin to impair one's quality of life. Loss-based selection can involve shifting goals or modifying goals in keeping with the available resources, reprioritizing goals, or developing new goals. Loss-based selection represents an important feature of adaptive functioning because it requires one to shift from an originally planned course of action and to effectively cope with changes in the means to achieve a personal goal.

Optimization refers to the acquisition, recruitment, and coordination of internal and external resources to achieve a system of goals, that is, "the acquisition and investment in goal-relevant means" (Freund & Baltes, 2002, p. 643, emphasis in original). Optimization is about the pursuit of one's personal goals and can take many forms, including persistence in a behavior or task, practicing new skills to provide the means to achieve the goal, or modeling the behavior of successful others to achieve a desired end.

Compensation refers to the modification of behaviors when goals are blocked or the means to achieve a goal are no longer available. Compensation is based on the premise that a person experiences both growth (gains) and deficits (losses) in resources throughout the life course that require one to make optimal use of the resources he or she has at his or her disposal (i.e., maximize gains and minimize losses). For example, struggling in a high school science course may necessitate enlisting the aid of an academic tutor to help pass the course. Note that compensation is different than loss-based selection in that compensation refers to the use of alternative means to maintain functioning in a goal domain, that is, to compensate for a change in resources, whereas loss-based selection involves a change in goals themselves. Moreover, the notion of gains and losses is central to life-span psychology. Paul and Margret Baltes (1990) proposed that successful aging involves a continual process of effectively balancing the gains and losses in skills, abilities, competencies, and resources experienced throughout the life course. To summarize, according to SOC theory, "people select life domains that are important to them, optimize the resources and aids that facilitate success in these domains, and compensate for losses in these domains in order to adapt to biological, psychological, and socio-economic changes throughout their lives and create an environment for lifelong successful development" (Ouwehand et al., 2007, p. 875).

It has been emphasized throughout this discussion that the optimal use of the three SOC processes is correlated with successful aging. Baltes was primarily concerned with healthy, successful aging and adaptive functioning throughout the life span rather than with maladaptive functioning, with typical and normal development rather than with atypical or abnormal development. In this regard, Baltes and his colleagues found that older individuals who are able to effectively adapt to life's exigencies through the processes of selection, optimization, and compensation and to achieve a positive balance between the gains and losses that one experiences during aging show greater resilience in life and report a greater subjective state of well-being (Ouwehand et al., 2007). For example, Freund and Baltes (2002) found that, in two samples of 218 and 181 men and women, ages 18 to 89 years, those who scored higher on a 48-item self-report measure of SOC processes (i.e., develop a few, clear goals that are prioritized; identify behaviors to access resources to achieve the goals; suggest alternative means to achieve the goals in the face of loss of means) also reported higher levels on seven indicators of adaptive mastery (Ryff, 1989): (1) positive emotions, (2) autonomy, (3) environmental mastery, (4) personal growth, (5) positive relations, (6) purpose in life, and (7) self-acceptance. Correlations were generally in the moderate range, varying between .29 and .44. Freund and Baltes (2002) also found that, except for the Elective Selection scale, all the SOC indicators increased from young adulthood (18–43 years) to a peak in middle adulthood (43–67 years), followed by a decline into older adulthood (67–89 years). Only elective selection continued to ascend into older adulthood. Young adults are still exploring multiple pathways and have not settled on their life goals, unlike adults in the middle age group. The linear trend of elective selection was interpreted as suggesting that middle and older adults become more aware of their life ambitions and pathways and focus on selected goals. The cross-sectional nature of the samples, however, limits the conclusions that can be drawn either about causality or intra-individual growth trajectories.

SOC processes have also been identified as important in adolescent development, specifically in relation to intentional self-regulation. Developmental psychologist Richard Lerner (2005) proposed that the SOC theory fits well as a process model of goal-directed behavior and intentional self-regulation; the latter may be particularly salient to teenagers. Intentional self-regulation refers to "the conscious control of goal-directed thought and action" (Bowers, Gestsdóttir et al., 2011, p. 1193) and, because of the biological, psychological, social, and contextual changes experienced during adolescence, is particularly important for healthy psychosocial functioning in this period of development. It is expected that the ability to self-regulate effectively would be related to indicators of successful, healthy development, including social competence, empathy, and moral development (S. Zimmerman, Phelps, & Lerner, 2007). In one study, Lerner (2005; see also Gestsdóttir & Lerner, 2007) found that high scores on an 18-item self-report measure of SOC representing successful adaptation were related to positive psychosocial development in a sample of 1,700 Grade 5 youth in 13 states of the United States from the 4-H Positive Youth Development Study. Across two waves of data, in Grades 5 and 6, correlations were in the order of .13 to .38 (all rs significant at $p <$ .001). Likewise, as expected, low scores on the SOC measure were associated with high levels of self-reported delinquent and risky behavior and depression. Correlations with these three outcome variables ranged from −.12 to −.31 (all rs significant at $p < $ .001). These results were subsequently replicated in several studies (S. Zimmerman et al., 2007; S. Zimmerman, Phelps, & Lerner, 2008). For example, S. Zimmerman et al. (2007) used three waves of Positive Youth Development data (Grades 5–7) and found that low SOC scores in Grade 5 predicted high scores on measures of depression, delinquency, and risky behavior in Grade 7.

More recently, in an investigation that followed 1,574 young people from the Positive Youth Development study across seven waves of data, from Grades 5 to 11, Bowers, Gestsdóttir et al. (2011) examined the relationship between longitudinal trajectories of self-regulation, using a self-report measure of SOC processes, and measures of depression and externalizing behaviors. Using GMM, Bowers, Gestsdóttir et al. identified four trajectories of self-regulation, labeled elevated, steady decline, late onset, and pronounced decline. Interestingly, Bowers, Gestsdóttir et al. found that the majority of the youth (79%) were on the steady decline trajectory from ages 10 to 16, showing a marked decrease in self-reported SOC functioning over time. They speculated that this pattern was considered normative and consistent with decrements seen in other areas of functioning over the course of early to mid-adolescence, including academic grades, intrinsic motivation, self-perceptions, self-concepts, and confidence in academic abilities. In other words, across early to mid-adolescence, young people show a decrement in intentional self-regulation as they begin to engage in the process of active self-exploration that leads to the formation of a stable self-identity (Gestsdóttir & Lerner, 2008). These results also dovetail with Freund and Baltes (2002), who found that SOC scores were lowest in adolescence and early adulthood and gradually climbed as life pathways became crystallized. Moreover, although not specifically referred to in the literature, the results of the Bowers, Gestsdóttir et al. (2011) study also may be seen as consistent with the adolescence-limited group of Moffitt's (1993) dual taxonomy model in which normative adolescent development is characterized by some involvement in minor and time-limited antisocial behavior. The same social, emotional, and cognitive mechanisms underlying the decrement in planning and self-regulatory behavior of lower SOC functioning could be associated, perhaps even in a causal manner, with an increased involvement in risky behaviors in this stage of development. The point at which the person reaches the nadir of his or her SOC trajectory (see Bowers, Gestsdóttir et al., 2011) represents a critical juncture in his or her development, a transition (Elder, 1985c), which is likely characterized by an increase in psychosocial maturity (Steinberg & Cauffman, 1996), enhanced executive functioning skills (Gestsdóttir & Lerner, 2008), and, from the SOC perspective, the acquisition of "more developed planning skills, increased understanding of resources, and a more realistic view of one's own abilities" (Gestsdóttir, Lewin-Bizan, von Eye, Lerner, & Lerner, 2009, p. 586). These developments would be expected to be associated with an increase in SOC functioning and a concomitant decrease in risky behavior as one moves in a positive direction toward the attainment of goals related to academic, social, and occupational pursuits.

Last, results from the Positive Youth Development studies fit with the conclusions by Mulvey, Schubert, and Piquero (2014) in a recent report on desistance from delinquency. Mulvey et al. suggested that finding ways to accelerate mature thinking in youthful offenders about what they want in life and how to achieve it might promote greater desistance from criminal activity. Although no study has applied the SOC theory to an offender population, it would be expected that, based on the extant literature, an increase in the three SOC processes would be associated with a greater likelihood of criminal desistance. Although concerned primarily with positive, adaptive, successful aging, Baltes was mindful of the potential applications of life-span psychology to helping individuals live a fulfilling life and avoid dysfunctional and undesirable outcomes. From a developmental perspective, rehabilitation within the criminal justice system might work toward assisting youthful and adult offenders to develop the skills for adaptive functioning consistent with the three processes of selection, optimization, and compensation.

Of course, although purely speculative, it may be the case that, at least for a portion of offenders (e.g., those on a high-rate chronic trajectory), involvement in criminal activity may have been the result of a purposeful, deliberate thoughtful, and conscious life choice (i.e., selection), albeit not in line with the positive, healthy goals Baltes envisioned when he conceptualized the SOC theory. Indeed, Bowers, Gestsdóttir et al. (2011) conceded that "ISR [intentional self-regulation] behaviors can equally be successfully (or unsuccessfully) used in regard to problematic behaviors" (p. 1204). For some offenders, the choice of a criminal lifestyle may have looked promising in terms of opportunities for affiliation and earning a decent (although dangerous) living; that is, it was seen as a desirable life goal (Sampson & Laub, 2005a). Enlisting the adaptive skills to recruit the skills and resources necessary for achieving the goals characterizes the second SOC process (i.e., optimization). When opportunities to achieve prosocial goals, such as academic advancement, formation of healthy, intimate relationships, and gainful employment, are no longer available and resources to succeed through socially acceptable and legitimate avenues become limited, the adaptive and pragmatic response would be to optimize one's available skills and resources, even through illegitimate means. The third process of the SOC model (i.e., compensation), however, may be seen as lacking among some criminal offenders when the inherent dangers of the criminal lifestyle and the greater risks of arrests, convictions, and jail time become salient and suspend or threaten to cut short one's "criminal career." These consequences might suggest that a change in life goals may be in store. Failure to compensate for lost or blocked opportunities reflects poor adaptive functioning from the perspective of the SOC model. Likewise, the process of desistance from crime may be a function of recognizing the need to engage in compensation actions to minimize one's losses and change one's direction in life, which Carlsson (2012), in his research on change processes in offending, refers to as a "turning point" (see also Laub & Sampson, 1993).

DEVELOPMENTAL PSYCHOPATHOLOGY. The final broad theoretical contribution to the concept and study of criminal trajectories we consider is developmental psychopathology. Developmental psychopathology was born of the union between developmental psychology and abnormal psychology (Achenbach, 1974). Developmental psychopathology takes a developmental perspective to account for the onset and course of and recovery from mental health disorders in children and youth. Developmental psychopathology is a broad and interdisciplinary field that integrates contributions from psychiatry, psychology, biology, neuroscience, genetics, and related fields (Cicchetti & Sroufe, 2000). As a result, a complete description of the field is beyond the scope of this chapter. Our focus is on the parallels between the study of mental illness and the study of crime from a developmental perspective (Morizot & Kazemian, 2015). For example, both fields are concerned with the developmental trajectories of a behavioral phenomenon (i.e., mental illness or crime) that may cause distress in the person or others and that (a) is considered abnormal or deviant by the standards of society and (b) has an onset, a course, and a desistance or termination. Both developmental psychopathology and developmental criminology are concerned with understanding the underlying causal mechanisms of a given phenomenon, and both have taken up the task of reducing its prevalence and incidence in the population. Both fields are invested in advancing knowledge through theory and empirical research focused on explicating the developmental processes and pathways leading to criminal activity or mental illness. For both fields, an early onset portends a more serious, intractable, and lengthy course.

Some central concepts of the field of developmental psychopathology are equifinality, multifinality, plasticity, risk and protective factors, and the practical mission of applying the basic science of developmental psychopathology to the development of effective early intervention and prevention programs. The principles of equifinality and multifinality state that mental illness is multiply determined; that, across individuals, different risk factors may contribute to the development of a mental disorder (equifinality); and that a single risk factor can lead to different mental disorders (multifinality). For example, exposure to domestic violence, child maltreatment, poverty, low verbal intelligence, harsh discipline, and poor parental supervision all may be risk factors for a conduct disorder diagnosis (equifinality); likewise, child maltreatment may lead to different disorders, including conduct disorder, depression, or borderline personality disorder (multifinality). The tasks for developmental psychopathology researchers are to (a) disentangle the role of various risk factors for the onset of a disorder and (b) identify the moderators that differentiate the developmental pathways leading from a given risk factor to a particular outcome. Developmental plasticity states that outcomes are not predetermined destinies to be realized. Rather, pathways (and hence individuals) are open to modification and transformation either by accident (e.g., epigenetics through the process of methylation) or design (e.g., early interventions). The identification of risk and protective factors has come to define the field of developmental psychopathology (Rutter & Sroufe, 2000). The search for causal mechanisms for mental disorders has been advanced by key developments within the risk factor research paradigm (Farrington, 2003; Kazdin, Kraemer, Kessler, Kupfer, & Offord, 1997). Beginning in the 1980s, risk factor research, including, more recently, the search for protective and promotive factors (Day, Wanklyn, & Yessine, 2014), has led to the emergence of veritable laundry lists of factors implicated in the development of mental disorders. Bringing some semblance of order and organization to these lists has been accomplished through the development of theoretical models that describe the putative and purported processes by which risk factors influence each other leading to the emergence of mental health problems in young people. These models have been subjected to considerable empirical research to test the models against reality. Last, consistent with the recent field of prevention science (Catalano et al., 2012), the practical mission of this work in developmental psychopathology has been the application of the findings from basic science to the development of programs and policies to reduce the prevalence of mental disorders in the population. This line of investigation has seen moderate success (B. Welsh & Farrington, 2012), with significant gains made in the reduction in the severity, if not the prevalence, of a disorder, the length or duration of a course of a disorder, and a delay in the onset of a disorder.

Conclusion

This chapter has examined the long and short (intellectual) historical contexts for the concept of a criminal trajectory. As with any idea of importance, the roots of the criminal trajectory notion run deep in several disciplines, including the life-course and life-span theoretical frameworks of Elder and Baltes, respectively, and the field of developmental psychopathology. Also, the more recent contributions to the criminal trajectory notion were traced through the criminal career paradigm, developmental criminology field, and important developmentally informed longitudinal studies on antisocial behavior. The next chapter reviews the concept of criminal trajectories from a statistical perspective. In nontechnical terms, we consider the mathematical underpinnings of the trajectory methodology and illustrate it with examples from the "Toronto" data set, a longitudinal database of 764 male offenders whose offense trajectories were followed for about 17.5 years, the Oregon Youth Study, and other literature.

Suggested Supplemental Readings

A number of excellent sources provide up-to-date overviews of the key theories and fields described in this chapter. These sources include *The Oxford Handbook of Developmental and Life-Course Criminology* (Farrington, Kazemian, & Piquero, 2018) and the special issue of the *Journal of Research in Crime and Delinquency* on the criminal career paradigm (Sullivan & Piquero, 2016a). Loeber, Byrd, and Farrington (2015) provide an update on the developmental criminology framework in light of current developments on the biology of offending behavior. Criminologists Christoffer Carlsson and Jerzy Sarnecki (2016) provide a comprehensive introduction to the field of life-course criminology. Overton (2015) and Lerner, Hershberg, Hilliard, and Johnson (2015) explicate how the life-course and life-span approaches from Elder and Baltes, along with other leading frameworks of human development, may be subsumed under a developmental systems theory metamodel that has become the dominant paradigm in contemporary developmental psychology. The third edition of the four-volume collection of *Developmental Psychopathology* (Cicchetti, 2016) provides an up-to-date and state-of-the-art review of the field. Finally, several books describe the design of and key findings from major longitudinal studies of criminal behavior, including those by Thornberry and Krohn (2003a) and Farrington and Welsh (2007).

2

Methodological Approaches to
Modeling Criminal Trajectories

To say that even the most prolific criminal was at one time a child may be axiomatic, even trite. Yet underlying this simple statement are some complex questions about the cause, course, and optimal response to crime. What can be learned by looking backward into a life lived in crime? Looking back into the life of a criminal we may pinpoint the age at which the conduct problems first began and observe the life circumstances that gave rise to the nascent misbehavior and the factors that, once initiated, maintained it across major developmental periods of childhood, adolescence, and adulthood. We could track the progression of the criminal activity over time from onset to desistance across the life span and chart the course of the offending in terms of the rate at which crimes were committed, their severity, and the range of offense types, including property, violent, drug, and sex offenses. We may also proffer a guess as to how the criminal behavior may have been prevented or forestalled in the first place to identify and target the causal variables that, if altered, would have resulted in a different outcome. Last, it would be informative to examine the extent to which, and at what ages, the person's psychosocial, emotional, and behavioral development departed from what might be considered a typical or normative developmental progression (Masten & Coatsworth, 1998). Such are some of the advantages of studying crime and the individuals who commit them from a developmental perspective.

A single case, of course, reveals little about the population of criminal offenders, in general; across individuals, there can be as many progressions in the developmental patterning to antisocial and criminal behavior as there are individuals. Indeed, that offenders compose a heterogeneous population is widely presumed. Within a scientific framework, the goal of discovery is to make sense of this heterogeneity and uncover general patterns that best represent the "reality" of offenders to generate empirically supported theoretical models that succinctly and precisely describe and account for developmental processes derived from observed data.

For example, criminal behavior is multiply determined and the number of risk factors that can influence its onset and course is large (Farrington, 1997). Generally, risk factors fall into five domains: individual, family, peer, school, and neighborhood (Farrington, 2003). Reppucci, Fried, and Schmidt (2002) provided a useful organizational framework for risk factors for antisocial (and, by extension, criminal) behavior that draws on the ecological systems theory of developmental psychologist Urie Bronfenbrenner (1979). According to Reppucci and colleagues, risk factors may be categorized using three levels of analysis. At the level of the individual are biological, cognitive, and emotional factors; at the level of the immediate systems are variables close or proximal to the individual, including family, peers, school, and neighborhood; and at the cultural and societal levels are variables that are distal to the individual and include media portrayals of crime, poverty, racism, and social and political influences such as firearms accessibility, employment opportunities, and drug and alcohol consumption patterns.

Importantly, these three systems do not exert their influence on individual antisocial and criminal behavior in isolation; rather, they are posited to interact in multifaceted ways over the life course. Furthermore, the influence of these variables on the onset and course of antisocial and criminal behavior will differ across individuals such that explaining crime at the individual level is akin to explaining the cause of a car accident. Although we may know all the variables that can lead to a collision, this does not necessarily tell us which specific factors were causally related in any given incident. Therefore, theories of the development of crime need to be sensitive to the complex interplay among the multiplicity of risk factors contributing to the onset and course of antisocial behavior and to the multiple pathways leading to criminal involvement. Earlier, we presented two examples of multiple pathways models (Corrado & Freedman, 2011; Loeber & Hay, 1997) that account for the array of risk factors leading to the onset of antisocial and delinquent behavior (i.e., equifinality) and for the complexity of the relations among them. Several branches of criminology have taken up the task of explaining the causal influences of crime across the life span from a developmental perspective. These branches include developmental criminology (Loeber & Le Blanc, 1990) and the developmental and life-course framework (Farrington, 2003, 2005b). Indeed, the study of criminal trajectories is firmly located under the big tent of these broad developmental frameworks. In the next section, we describe the concept of a criminal trajectory.

The Concept of a Trajectory

With a primary focus on developmental questions of crime and taking the individual as the unit of analysis to account for intraindividual or within-individual patterns of change over time or age, we may begin to describe the notion of a criminal trajectory. As both a concept and a statistical method, the aim of trajectory research is twofold: (a) to capture the development or growth of criminal activity on some dimension (e.g., frequency or severity) over age or time from a within-individual perspective and (b) to reduce the number of individual trajectories in a given sample to a meaningful and manageable number of groups that are homogeneous within trajectory classes and heterogeneous across classes (B. Muthén & Muthén, 2000). In other words, the aim of trajectory analysis is to identify the multiple dynamic growth patterns of individuals in a given sample.

The term *trajectory* is used as a metaphor in the social sciences borrowed from the natural sciences. It is a word that is widely used, commonly understood, but rarely defined (George, 2009). The notion of a trajectory of an object moving through space is a concept borrowed by the social sciences from the natural sciences to characterize the pattern of change and continuity of some behavioral phenomena over time. In physics, a trajectory refers to a course taken by an object launched onto a path (the trajectory). For example, according to one physics textbook, "the path along which an object moves, which might be a straight line or might be curved, is called the object's trajectory" (Knight, 2008, p. 3). In the social sciences, we may speak of being on a metaphorical trajectory on some social or psychological phenomena, for example, the trajectory of a relationship, career, or involvement in criminal activity.

A criminal trajectory represents the course, progression, or evolution of criminal behavior over age or time at the level of the individual. The objective of studying criminal trajectories is to understand the developmental course of offending at the level of the individual and the factors that influence its progression. In other words, trajectory researchers are interested in how the topography of crime unfolds across a developmental landscape, using such dimensions as rate, type, or severity, to measure the peaks and valleys. According to Sampson and Laub (1997), "a *trajectory* is a pathway or line of development over the life span, such as work life, marriage, parenthood, self-esteem, or criminal behavior. Trajectories refer to long-term patterns of behavior and are marked by a sequence of transitions" (p. 142, emphasis in original). Blokland and Nieuwbeerta (2010, p. 66) refer to a trajectory as a "time path." Finally, Curran and Willoughby (2003) provide a more technical definition of a trajectory:

> Although there are many possible ways to define a trajectory, we begin with the basic premise that a trajectory is a continuous and individual-specific underlying process that gave rise to an observed set of repeated measures over time for a particular individual. For example, although we may have observed four repeated measures of antisocial behavior for a particular child, we may theoretically believe that these observations were generated by some unobserved underlying trajectory of antisociality that is unique to this child. It is this unobserved (or "latent") trajectory that is of key theoretical interest. However, because the trajectory was not directly observed (and, implicitly, is *unobservable*), we must empirically infer its existence as a function of the set of repeated measures that we did observe. These trajectories may take the form of individual intercepts, linear slopes, curvatures, asymptotes, or many other types of values. However, the core belief is that these individual parameters help us to accurately and parsimoniously summarize a larger set of observed data in a way that is maximally consistent with developmental theory. (pp. 582–583, emphasis in original)

Individual Trajectory Profiles: Illustrative Examples

To further develop the notion of a criminal trajectory, we present graphical representations of the raw offense profiles for five individuals taken from the "Toronto" sample, a longitudinal data set of 764 offenders from Toronto, Canada. The sample represents the entire population of juvenile offenders who had been sentenced between 1986 and 1996 to one of two open-custody facilities for youth. The youth were, on average, 17.6 years at the time of admission into the facility (range 16–24 years), and the average sentence length was 123 days (range 1–1,087 days). Youth could have been older than 17 years at the time of admission if they were under 18 at the time of committing their index offense but 18 years or older at the time of sentencing. The criminal activity of the Toronto sample was followed with archival criminal records for about 17.5 years (range 9.8–29.3 years), from late childhood/early adolescence until the end of the follow-up on September 27, 2007. They were on average 33 years at the end of the follow-up. Their average age at the time of their first court contact was 15.5 years and their average trajectory length (difference in years between their first and last court contact) was 10 years. Further details about the sample, including trajectory analyses, can be found in Ward et al. (2010) and Day et al. (2010).

Figure 2.1 presents the "unsmoothed" profiles of the raw data for five individuals from the Toronto sample (using pseudonyms). The profiles are meant to be descriptive depictions of their offense "trajectories." Such individual profiles are useful to convey key points about longitudinal offending patterns (A. Piquero, Sullivan, et al., 2010). For each graph in Figure 2.1, the y-axis is fixed to a specified range (0–7 convictions) to aid comparison across cases. In addition to examining the raw data, it is helpful to summarize individual trajectory profiles using "smoothed" methods. Singer and Willett (2003) recommend applying both "non-parametric" (i.e., smoothing across temporal idiosyncrasies without imposing a specific polynomial growth function) and "parametric" approaches (i.e., fitting a regression line to each individual after selecting a specific polynomial growth function) for providing smoothed individual trajectory profiles. "Smoothed" nonparametric profiles are presented in Figure 2.2 for the same five individuals, from ages 10 to 30. To provide a sense of the general direction of change (i.e., upward, level, or downward) of the five profiles, linear trajectories fitted with Ordinary Least Squares regression are presented in Figure 2.3. Last, Figure 2.4 presents the fitted trajectories with a cubic function to show the estimated individual growth curves for the five offenders.

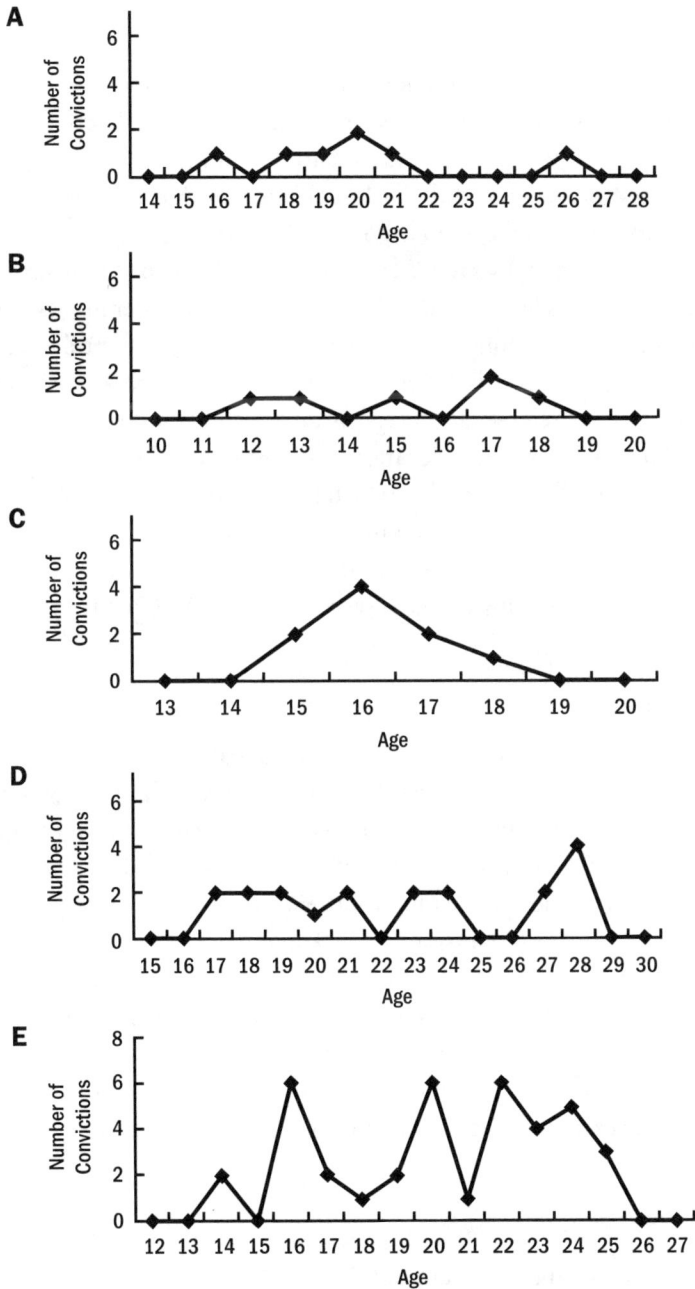

Figure 2.1. Graph of participant's offending by age; Panel A: "Martin";
Panel B: "Sam"; Panel C: "John"; Panel D: "Danny"; Panel E: "Joe"

"Martin"

Martin may be described as a low-rate offender who committed a range of offense types; that is, he was versatile in his criminal activity, which included property, violent, and administration of justice (e.g., escape from custody and being unlawfully at large) offenses. His offense trajectory spanned 10 years, from ages 16 to 26. Five days after turning 16, Martin was convicted of arson and sentenced to 10 months in a prison for juveniles followed by 6 months on probation. Twenty-one months after his first charge, he was convicted a second time, for failure to comply with probation, and was given a 4-month prison sentence. He was convicted a third time, 18 months after his release, at the age of 19, for break and enter. Within 12 months, he was convicted twice more, for possession of stolen credit cards and escaping lawful custody, for which he received sentences of 4 months and 1 month, respectively. Seven months later he was charged with uttering a death threat and, 5 years after that, with simple assault. A profile of Martin's rate of offending by age is shown in Panel A of Figure 2.1.

"Sam"

Across his trajectory, Sam committed offenses at a low rate and was limited in the range of offense types he committed, which included sex and property crimes. His trajectory spanned only 6 years, from ages 12 to 18. At the age of 12, Sam was convicted of a sexual offense. He was convicted a second time at the age of 13 for another sexual offense. Two years later, he was convicted of possession of break and enter instruments, his only property crime. He had three more convictions between the ages of 17 and 18, two for sexual assault and one for sexual interference. He was incarcerated at the age of 18 and served a 2-month sentence, followed by 1 year of probation. Based on available data, he committed no subsequent offenses after his release from prison (see Panel B of Figure 2.1).

"John"

Over the course of his trajectory, John committed offenses at a low rate; he was also a versatile offender who committed a range of offense types, including property, violent, and sex crimes. His trajectory was brief, as he desisted at age 18, 4 years after his first conviction at age 15. However, during this period, he incurred a total of nine convictions. John's first conviction was for robbery. Less than a month later he was convicted of a second robbery. One year later, he was convicted of a weapons offense. Over the next 10 months, he would be convicted six more times for failure to comply with recognizance, weapons, possession of stolen property under $1,000, break and enter, and sexual assault. As a juvenile, he received mostly probation for his offenses as well as several short custodial sentences of between 3 and 6 months (see Panel C of Figure 2.1).

"Danny"

Danny committed offenses at a moderate rate and was versatile in the range of offense types he committed, which included property, violent, drug, and administration of justice crimes. He was convicted 19 times over a period of 8 years, starting at age 17. Over his trajectory, he typically incurred one or two convictions each year for minor offenses, including theft under $1,000 and failure to comply with probation, a breach offense. At age 21, he was convicted of his first violent offense, a robbery, for which he was sentenced to 9 months in prison. He was convicted a second time of robbery, at the age of 23 and, a year later, of trafficking narcotics, adding to his repertoire of offenses. At age 28 he was convicted on four separate occasions, three for assault and one for a property offense (see Panel D of Figure 2.1). For his convictions, he served multiple prison sentences, although typically for short periods, between 1 and 10 months.

"Joe"

Joe committed offenses at a high rate and was versatile in the types of offenses he committed, which included property, violent, and drug crimes. He also had a lengthy criminal record that spanned a period of 11 years. He was first convicted at the age of 14 and tended to have many convictions in rapid succession, for example, every 3 or 4 months. His

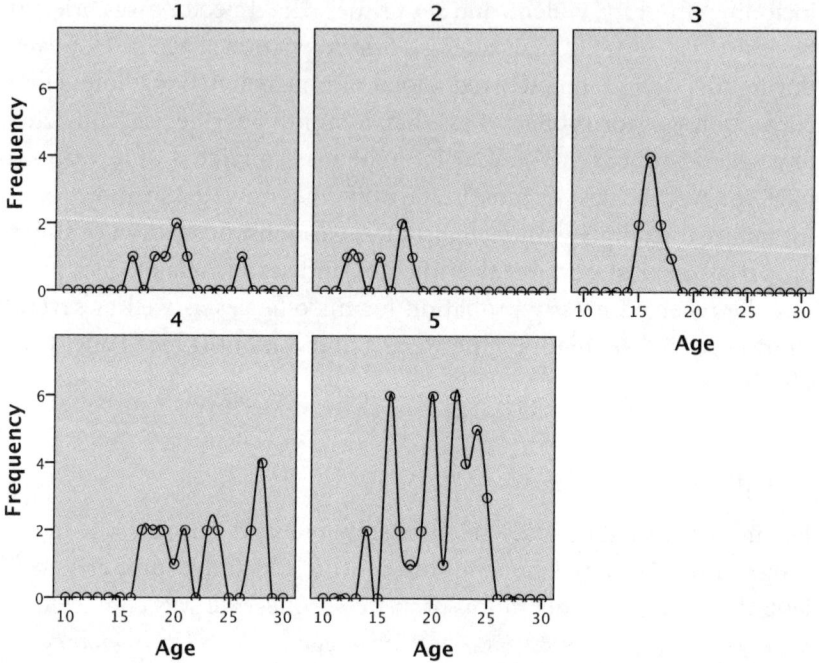

Figure 2.2. Smooth nonparametric trajectories for five offense profiles from the Toronto sample

first conviction was for a break and enter. Two days later, he was convicted of assault. After a 2-year break from offending, he was convicted of assault, followed in rapid succession by five more convictions at the age of 16 for failure to comply with recognizance, break and enter, trafficking, and possession over $1,000. Over the next 9 years, he would be convicted 30 more times for a range of offenses, mostly property, including break and enter and related (e.g., possession of break-and-enter instruments), mischief property, and theft. He was also convicted of various violent crimes including robbery, weapons, uttering a death threat, assaulting a peace officer, and resisting arrest, as well as once for trafficking. For his crimes, he received mostly short prison sentences of 4 months or less; however, for his last two convictions (both for property offenses), he received longer sentences, including 2 years in prison (see Panel E of Figure 2.1).

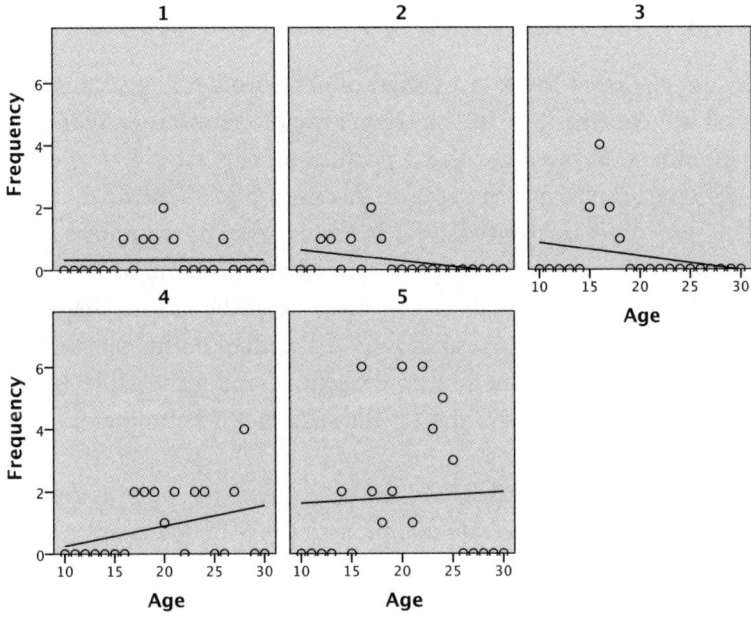

Figure 2.3. Linear Ordinary Least Squares trajectory fit for five offense profiles from the Toronto sample

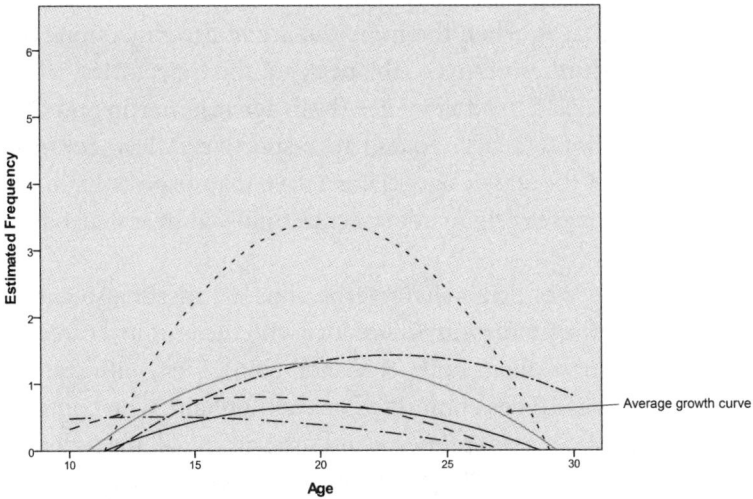

Figure 2.4. Fitted Ordinary Least Squares regression lines for five offense trajectories from the Toronto sample using a cubic polynomial function, showing the average growth curve

Describing Individual Trajectory Profiles

A casual glance at these individual offense profiles suggests the considerable heterogeneity in the frequency of criminal activity across the offenders. How might these profiles be characterized to capture the differences among the profiles? According to Wohlwill (1973), the parameters or characteristics of a trajectory (or "developmental function" as he called them) may be described in terms of five sets of features: (a) the presence, direction, and rate of change; (b) shape of the trajectory; (c) the age corresponding to specified points on the trajectory; (d) the values of the minima, maxima, and terminal level of the response on the trajectory; and (e) the sequence and timing of changes in the trajectory.

Turning to our five cases, two of the profiles (i.e., Martin and Sam) may be described as low-rate offenders because their maximum number of convictions never went above one. John and Danny may be characterized as moderate-rate offenders as their maximum values reached a value of 4, and Joe may be described as a high-rate offender whose maximum value reached six convictions three times, in fact, at ages 16, 20, and 22. Second, with the exception of John, all the profiles showed considerable changes in direction with some periods of intermittency, that is, when the individuals had no convictions (Martin and Sam). Third, in terms of the peaks of the trajectories, whereas Sam and John peaked in adolescence (both age 16), Martin and Danny peaked in adulthood (at ages 20 and 28, respectively). Last, John's profile appears to fit the classic age–crime curve (Sampson & Laub, 1993) with a rapid increase early in adolescence followed by a sharp decline thereafter.

In addition to Wohlwill's characterizations, we might also consider other aspects of the profiles, in accordance with the criminal career paradigm (Blumstein, Cohen, Roth, & Visher, 1986). First, with respect to the range of offense types committed, except for Sam, who committed only two types of offenses (property and sex crimes), all the individuals committed at least three different types of offenses, typically property, violent, and drug or sex crimes. This pattern of offending might suggest that, for these men, versatility is less the exception than the rule, a conclusion for which there is considerable empirical support, particularly for violent offenders (A. Piquero, Farrington, et al., 2003; A. Piquero, Jennings, & Barnes, 2012).

Considerable research has been dedicated to examining the issue of offense specialization and versatility (A. Piquero et al., 2003). The issue goes to the heart of the generality of offense propensities (Gottfredson & Hirschi, 1990) debate. On one hand, versatility is to be expected due to the singular propensity of poor self-control that underlies all criminal offending. On the other hand, differential reinforcement contingencies, for example, might lead some offenders to specialize in their offense pattern, particularly as they get older. Developmental approaches, including pathway models (e.g., Loeber & Hay, 1997) and taxonomic theories of crime (e.g., Moffitt, 1993), also support a potential for specialization. In general, studies have found some specialization amid considerable versatility (Farrington, Snyder, & Finnegan, 1988; A. Piquero et al., 2003). Studies also find that sex offenders tend to be the most specialized (Stander, Farrington, Hill, & Altham, 1989). Moreover, recent studies using statistical techniques that control for static, that is, nonmodifiable, covariates (e.g., age of onset, sex, and race) and time-varying covariates (e.g., the number and type of prior offenses) reveal a greater degree of specialization than previously reported (Baker, Metcalfe, & Jennings, 2013).

Last, in keeping with behavioral theories of crime, evidence indicates there is a positive linear relationship between age and offense specialization (Farrington, 1997; Le Blanc & Loeber, 1998; A. Piquero, Paternoster, Mazerolle, Brame, & Dean, 1999). This association suggests that, over time, behavior may be shaped by experiences and reinforcers. However, further work is needed to better understand the causal mechanisms underlying the observed pattern of offense specialization. Also, a corollary issue to the specialization question that may be examined is the age-graded distribution of certain offense types, that is, whether some offense types are more likely to occur earlier than other offense types. In an analysis of the Toronto sample data, Day, Bevc, Theodor, Rosenthal, and Duchesne (2008, see Figure 7) found that property offenses were the primary offense type committed by the sample in the early part of their offense trajectory in early adolescence; involvement in violent offenses increased between the ages of 16 and 20; and this pattern was followed by an increase in drug offenses between the ages of 20 and 25 (see also Farrington, 1997; Sampson & Laub, 2003). Some have suggested that less severe offense types serve as stepping-stones to more serious offense types (Farrington, 2003).

Second, with respect to the number of offenses committed relative to the length of the trajectory (Farrington, 1997), on one hand, with nine convictions in only 4 years, John might be described as a short-term high-rate offender. On the other hand, with seven convictions over 10 years, Joe might be considered a long-term low-rate offender. This particular distinction, between short-term high-rate offenders and long-term low-rate offenders, was explored in an interesting paper by A. Piquero, Sullivan, et al. (2010), who suggested that such a characterization may have considerable policy and practice implications for the justice system. A. Piquero et al. compared the offense patterns of individuals identified from Cambridge Study of Delinquent Development data (A. Piquero, Farrington, et al., 2007) as on either a short-term high-rate trajectory or a long-term low-rate trajectory. The former group composed 5.4% of the sample, and the latter group composed 11.3% of the sample. They found that the short-term high-rate offenders had an earlier age of onset for a first conviction (M age was 13.5 years) than did the long-term low-rate offenders (M age was 17.8 years); committed a larger average number of offenses per year (referred to as lambda or λ; $M = 1.25$) than did the long-term low-rate offenders ($M = .42$); and committed more property offenses than did the long-term low-rate group whereas the long-term low-rate offenders committed more violent offenses. Last, more of the short-term high-rate offenders had spent time in prison (61.9%) than did the long-term low-rate offenders (9.1%).

Each group, A. Piquero, Sullivan, et al. (2010) suggest, poses unique challenges to the justice system. The short-term high-rate offenders committed a large volume of crime, in spite of a relatively short criminal career length, and had an earlier age of onset. Therefore, it would seem to make sense to pay attention to young people who come in contact with the justice system at an early age and respond at the appropriate level to not overrespond and ensnare them within the system. A thorough assessment of the individual's risk factors and treatment needs to guide appropriate intervention would be warranted (Hoge &

Andrews, 1996). The long-term low-rate offenders committed a lower volume of offenses but remained involved in criminal activity over a longer period. A. Piquero, Sullivan, et al. (2010) speculated that the long-term low-rate offenders might experience problems with alcohol and substance use that may account for the lengthy criminal careers. More generally, it may be that persistent offenders who do not commit offenses at a high rate (i.e., moderate- and low-rate offenders) may be holding firm to an active involvement in a criminal lifestyle because of being "stuck" in a situation from which they cannot easily extricate themselves. This pattern of behavior may be due to experiences with psychosocial problems, such as substance use and abuse, low levels of social support, and poor coping, rather than a hardened commitment to a criminal lifestyle (Brook, Lee, Finch, Brown, & Brook, 2013; Hussong, Curran, Moffitt, Caspi, & Carrig, 2004; Monahan & Piquero, 2009; A. Ward et al., 2010). As a result, long-term, low-rate offenders represent an interesting and perhaps challenging subgroup for the justice system in their own right largely because of their persistence in offending. They also may be prime targets for treatment interventions and rehabilitation programming to address their issues. However, this hypothesis needs further investigation. Moreover, this conclusion is based on studies conducted only with male offenders. Whether the same effects for substance abuse are observed in long-term low-rate female offenders remains to be seen.

Beyond this brief analysis of criminal profiles, the next task is to move beyond the description of change to inferring the causes of change (Campbell, 1963). What accounts for the shape of these profiles, that is, the continuities and changes in direction? In keeping with the developmental perspective, we could ask about the developmental pathways that led these individuals to their respective trajectories, about the early risk factors that set them onto a pathway, and about the risk factors that supported a course toward the outcome. What factors might account for individuals ending up with different trajectory profiles? In other words, what might account for the heterogeneity of offense trajectories? What can examining a criminal trajectory tell us about the past (prior to the start of the trajectory), present (during the trajectory), and future (after the trajectory has ceased to be tracked) of offenders? We also need to move beyond individuals' trajectory profiles to trajectories of samples of offenders. Can these trajectories be clustered into groups that show common or similar growth patterns that also differ across groups? Do they fall into various classes? Do they represent subtypes or subpopulations (taxonomies or typologies)? These questions are central to the study of criminal trajectories and are explored throughout this book.

Trajectory Analysis

Rather than depicting one line for each individual in a study sample, resulting in a tangled mess of lines across a graph (see Figure 2.5), statistical techniques referred to as semiparametric group-based trajectory modeling (SGBTM), also known as latent class growth analysis (LCGA; Nagin, 1999, 2005; Roeder, Lynch, & Nagin, 1999), and latent growth mixture modeling (GMM; B. Muthén, 2004; B. Muthén & Muthén, 2000; B. Muthén & Shedden, 1999) may be used to cluster individuals into homogeneous groups with statistically similar trajectories based on longitudinal data. In the remainder of this chapter, we present a nontechnical overview of the methodological foundations of these modeling approaches and describe the core practical considerations that must be negotiated during any SGBTM or GMM analysis. The purpose of this section is twofold. First, it provides a solid foundation for being an informed consumer of the results of SGBTM and GMM studies. Second, it introduces background that aids in the understanding of the major debates and controversies surrounding this methodology, which we discuss later. In consideration of the main thrust of our book, mathematical formulae are only presented in this chapter and kept at an absolute minimum to

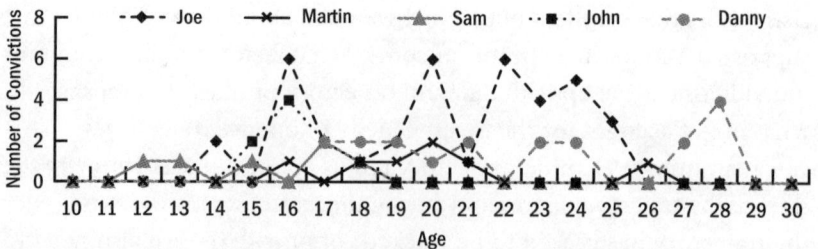

Figure 2.5. Putting it all together for five cases from the Toronto sample

make the text as accessible as possible while still addressing the key statistical underpinnings of the group-based trajectory methodology.

Using SGBTM or GMM helps to reduce the individual offense profiles in a sample to a manageable and meaningful number of prototypical clusters or groupings of trajectories. Both approaches have much in common from a conceptual perspective, but they also differ in some important ways. Before we present the statistical underpinnings and methodology for performing SGBTM or GMM analysis, conventional growth curve modeling is briefly reviewed. Several practical considerations pertaining to the analysis and interpretation of conventional growth curve models also apply to group-based analysis but are easier to understand without the added complexity of dealing with multiple unobserved trajectory groupings. Examples of such practical issues include how the data set should be structured (wide vs. long format), how time should be coded, how the estimated intercept should be interpreted, which growth function should be chosen, how the effects of time-varying covariates should be interpreted, and how the residual covariance structure should be specified.

Moreover, conventional growth curve modeling may be viewed as a special case of the more general GMM framework. Therefore, the following brief overview of conventional growth curve modeling serves as a useful backdrop to better understand how SGBTM and GMM relate to some other well-established techniques for analyzing longitudinal data. However, it is beyond the scope of this book to describe the differences of SGBTM and GMM to other major approaches to modeling longitudinal data, such as intensive longitudinal methods for experience sampling and diary data, generalized estimating equations, latent transition analysis, or event-history analysis. A useful overview of statistical techniques for the analysis of longitudinal data through the lens of a developmental perspective is given in Laursen, Little, and Card (2012). McArdle and Nesselroade (2014) summarize decades of groundbreaking work on longitudinal analysis using structural equation models.

Conventional Growth Curve Modeling

From a trajectory analysis perspective, a trajectory is a latent construct that cannot be observed directly from the data but is estimated by the statistical analysis of the set of repeated measures for the sample (Curran & Willoughby, 2003; B. Muthén & Muthén, 2000; Nagin, 2005). The objective of conventional growth curve modeling techniques is to capture the mean trend of the trajectory in the sample as well as individual deviations from the average trajectory trend. In doing so, it is assumed that individuals are drawn from the same population and that the trajectory can be described by a parsimonious set of parameters, such as the estimated average rate of growth in offending and variability in the rate of change over time. Two popular approaches to conventional growth curve modeling are available.

First, analyses can be performed within a multilevel or hierarchical linear modeling framework (e.g., Goldstein, 1995; Hedecker, 2004; Raudenbush & Bryk, 2002; Singer & Willett, 2003). Repeated measures for a sample of individuals generate two-level data structures where measurement occasions or time are nested within persons. Within this framework, "within-person" change is described as a function of time in the Level 1 model, whereas "between-person" differences in these changes are described in the Level 2 model using a random-effects specification. Second, the structural equation modeling framework in the form of latent growth curve or latent growth modeling can be used (e.g., Bollen & Curran, 2006; T. Duncan, Duncan, & Strycker, 2006; McArdle & Epstein, 1987; Meredith & Tisak, 1990; Preacher, Wichman, MacCallum, & Briggs, 2008; Willett & Sayer, 1994). This statistical technique applies a multivariate latent variable approach in which the parameters of the individual growth curves are specified as continuous latent variables (i.e., latent intercept and latent slope growth factors). Latent growth curve models are actually applications of multilevel (two-level) models because the repeated observations are nested within individuals; for a large subset of models, it is possible to fit analytically equivalent growth curve models across the multilevel and structural equation modeling frameworks (Curran, 2003; Preacher et al., 2008; Willett & Sayer, 1994).

Despite their similarities, these frameworks differ in certain ways (Hox & Stoel, 2005; Little, 2013; B. Muthén, 2004), including the format of the data structure (i.e., multilevel modeling requires data in a "long" format; structural equation modeling requires data in a "wide" format) and the incorporation of time in the statistical model. In particular, multilevel frameworks allow time to be a variable, for example, age, age^2, *age³*, that reflects individually varying times of observation and has a random slope. In contrast, structural equation modeling frameworks allow time to be a parameter in the model (by specifying time scores, that is, factor loadings, in such a way that they represent a specific form or pattern of change over time) so that the underlying trajectory, or latent growth factors, can be estimated. Structural equation modeling frameworks also need time-structured data, which means that all cases are observed at the same—equal or unequal—time intervals. In contrast, multilevel modeling frameworks do not require time-structured data. In recent years, some structural equation modeling software programs have become able to relax this requirement. Finally, these frameworks differ in the flexibility with which complex extensions to the fitted growth curve model can be added. For example, higher-order growth models with multiple indicators of the outcome at each time point are more readily implemented in structural equation modeling, relative to multilevel modeling, frameworks, whereas the latter more easily allow for adding more levels to the analysis.

For the purposes of this chapter, we present conventional growth curve modeling mostly from the perspective of the structural equation modeling framework. As mentioned earlier, latent growth curve modeling may be viewed as applying multilevel modeling within the framework of structural equation modeling. From a conceptual point of view, this characteristic allows us to describe latent growth curve modeling as involving two levels of analysis. At the first analysis level, the repeated measures of each individual across time are analyzed as a function of an underlying linear or nonlinear growth trajectory. The second analysis level involves using the individual parameters (slope and intercept values) to determine the differences in growth from a baseline measure. Consistent with this view, many texts introduce latent growth curve modeling by distinguishing Level 1 from Level 2 model equations. We adhere to this common practice in our overview but could not agree more with Curran and Willoughby (2003), who emphasized that this distinction between Level 1 ("within-person") and Level 2 ("between-person") models is heuristic because both models are, in fact, estimated simultaneously during any latent growth curve modeling analysis.

Growth curve models are often analyzed in two steps. A common starting point is to fit an "unconditional growth curve model" without predictors to infer the shape of the trajectory from the observed repeated measures. Given an acceptable unconditional growth curve model, this is followed by estimation of a "conditional growth curve model" in which predictors are added to explain "between-person" differences in the trajectory parameters. Researchers can choose from a broad array of possible growth functions, but many applications use polynomial functions of time (or age). A simple unconditional linear latent growth curve model of offending for $T = 5$ time points and i individuals is depicted in Figure 2.6. In the diagram, rectangles represent manifest variables and ovals indicate latent variables. Within the structural equation modeling framework, the Level 1 ("within-person") model corresponding to Figure 2.6 can be expressed as

$$Y_{ti} = \eta_{0i} + \eta_{1i}\,\lambda_t + \varepsilon_{ti},$$

where parameter Y_{ti} is person i's $(i = 1, \ldots, n)$ rate of offending at time t $(t = 1, \ldots, T)$; $\lambda_t = 0, 1, \ldots, (T - 1)$ represents equally spaced linear change (where T equals the total number of observed time points and time-structured data are assumed); η_{0i} is the intercept of the underlying trajectory for person i; η_{1i} is the linear slope of the underlying trajectory for person i; and ε_{ti} is the residual for person i at time t. As can be seen, both the intercept and linear slope terms are indexed with a subscript i to indicate that these estimates are unique to each person in the given sample. Put differently, this specification implies that the observed rate of offending for person i at time t is a function of the underlying trajectory parameters for the person (i.e., the intercept and linear slope estimates for the given person) plus an individual- and time-specific residual (Curran & Willoughby, 2003). Some other characteristics of the model depicted in Figure 2.6 are noteworthy. First, the coding of time starts with the value of zero, which means that the intercept represents the model implied rate of offending at the initial time point. Biesanz, Deeb-Sossa, Papadakis, Bollen, and Curran (2004) present an excellent discussion of other options for coding time and their effects on the interpretation of findings. Second, the linear (straight-line) growth function implies that a one-unit change in time is related to a η_1-unit change in the rate of offending and the magnitude of this association is constant across all observed time points. Third, the time scores (i.e., factor loadings) that define the scaling

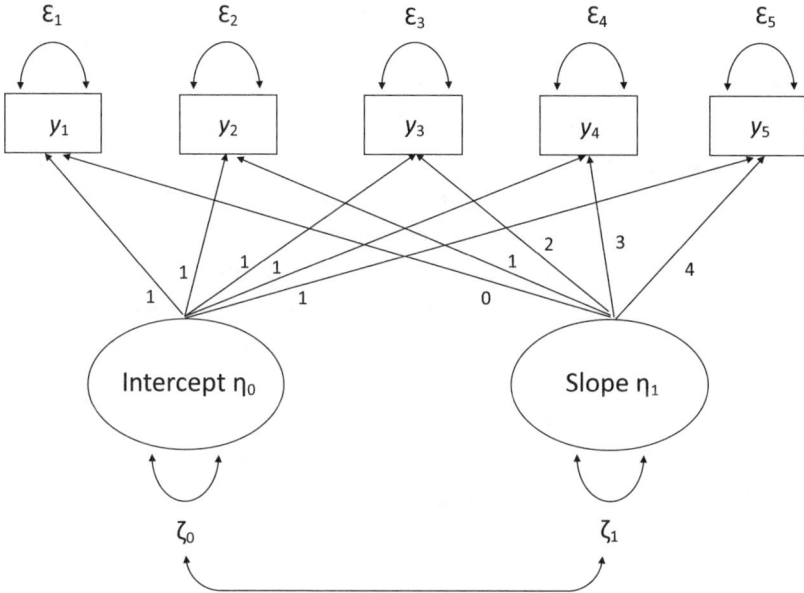

Figure 2.6. Path diagram for an unconditional linear latent growth curve model of offending

of the growth factors (Stoolmiller, 1995) reflect equal spacing of the intervals between the observed time points. Alternative specifications of time scores can be used with unequally spaced measurement occasions. Some, but not all, structural equation modeling software packages offer ways to accommodate individually varying times of observations (e.g., Sterba, 2014). Fourth, the residuals (ε_{ti}) are specified as being uncorrelated, but this restriction can be relaxed.

Within the structural equation modeling framework, the Level 2 ("between-person") model corresponding to Figure 2.6 can be expressed as

$$\eta_{0i} = \mu_0 + \zeta_{0i}, \text{ and}$$

$$\eta_{1i} = \mu_1 + \zeta_{1i},$$

where the two random coefficients (η_{0i} and η_{1i}) from the Level 1 model serve as dependent variables, μ_0 is the model estimated average level of offending at the initial time point pooling over all persons in the sample, μ_1 represents the estimated average rate of linear change in offending over time pooling over all persons in the sample, and ζ_{0i} and ζ_{1i} are error terms representing the deviations of each person i from the average linear trajectory parameters. Individual variation of the growth parameters is assumed to take on a normal distribution (see Kreuter & Muthén, 2008b). Put differently, these two equations reflect that an intercept (or slope) for a particular person is estimated as a combination of the average of *all* the intercepts (or slopes) in the sample plus the deviation of the person's intercept (or slope) from this sample average (Curran & Willoughby, 2003). Practically speaking, we can view these estimates as the four most critical pieces of information resulting from the unconditional linear growth model depicted in Figure 2.6. The variance of the deviations of each person from the estimated sample mean (denoted as ψ_0 for the intercepts, ψ_1 for the linear slopes, and ψ_{01} for the covariance between the intercepts and slopes) indicates the extent to which the study participants differ from one another in their individual trajectory parameters (a variance of zero reflects that all study participants follow the same trajectory over time). For this reason, these variance estimates are referred to as the *random-effects* part of the growth curve model, whereas the mean estimates are referred to as the *fixed-effects* part of the growth curve model. Details about various assumptions underlying growth curve models within the structural equation modeling framework are provided in Bollen and Curran (2006) and Preacher et al. (2008).

One or more correlated exogenous predictors can be readily included in a conventional growth curve model to explain the variability between study participants in the estimated trajectory parameters. This procedure allows the researcher to ask questions about which between-person characteristics are associated with trajectories that start lower versus higher or increase (or decrease) more steeply versus less steeply. We briefly illustrate this method by adding two correlated time-invariant predictors, such as male gender and a continuous measure of mental health problems, to the linear growth model (predictors not shown in Figure 2.6). Time-invariant predictors are measured only once, whereas time-varying covariates are repeatedly assessed, typically at the same intervals as the indicators of the growth factors. Within the structural equation modeling framework, the Level 1 model equation is the same as presented earlier (albeit it would have changed if a time-varying covariate had been added); the Level 2 model, however, can now be expressed as

$$\eta_{0i} = \mu_0 + \sum_k \gamma_{0k} X_{ki} + \zeta_{0i}, \text{ and}$$

$$\eta_{1i} = \mu_1 + \sum_k \gamma_{1k} X_{ki} + \zeta_{1i},$$

where the two random coefficients (η_{0i} and η_{1i}) again serve as the dependent variables, the gamma parameters (γ_{0k} and γ_{1k}) reflect the predictive effects of the K exogenous variables x (here, $k = 2$ time-invariant predictors that are correlated with each other) on the person i's intercept and linear slope estimates that define the trajectories of offending; the means (μ_0 and μ_1) now represent regression intercepts given the presence of predictor variables, and the error terms (ζ_{0i} and ζ_{1i}) are correlated but now represent *residual* individual variation after accounting for the set of predictors. Conditional growth curve models allow for tests of theoretical questions pertaining to between-person differences in the prediction of the individual trajectory parameters (Curran & Willoughby, 2003).

Multiple extensions of the growth curve model depicted in Figure 2.6 are possible. As discussed earlier, the multilevel and structural equation modeling frameworks differ somewhat in the ease, technical details, and flexibility with which these extensions can be implemented. To name but a few, estimating nonlinear trajectories, contingent on the availability of an adequate number of repeated measures for the individuals in a given sample, is possible. A common approach is using higher-order polynomials where additional model parameters represent quadratic, cubic, or even higher-order polynomial growth functions. Alternatively, nonlinear growth functions can be modeled using techniques such as piecewise, spline, or exponential growth functions. Second, time-varying covariates can be added to the growth curve model. Third, analyses are not restricted to using continuous repeated measures data; for example, categorical outcomes, ordinal measures, or count data with floor effects can be analyzed. Fourth, it is possible to accommodate missing values in the repeated measures data as well as higher-order growth models that include multiple measures of the outcome at each time point. Fifth, antecedents, time-varying covariates, and outcomes may be simultaneously included in a growth curve analysis. Sixth, several options are available to test for differences in growth over time among known groups, such as treatment groups or ethnic/racial groups. Seventh, additional levels of clustering can be incorporated using three-plus-level modeling approaches, such as clustering by classrooms, schools, or neighborhoods. Last, multiple complex growth curve modeling variants exist that allow for trajectory analyses of more than one outcome at the same time. Numerous excellent statistical and nontechnical texts describe the statistical underpinnings of these extensions and provide instructive examples for both modeling frameworks (e.g., Biesanz et al., 2004; Bollen & Curran, 2006; Curran & Willoughby, 2003; T. Duncan et al., 2006; Hedecker, 2004; Little, 2013; Masyn, Petras, & Liu, 2014; Preacher et al., 2008; Singer & Willett, 2003; Stoolmiller, 1995). Many of these extensions can also be incorporated into the GMM framework.

To summarize, conventional growth curve modeling may be sufficient for capturing random individual deviations from the average trajectory trend if theory and observed data are consistent with the assumption that all individuals in the sample are from a single homogeneous population and follow a similar average functional form of growth over time. However, this assumption of homogeneity in the overall mean growth trajectory is often unrealistic. As we discussed previously, multiple pathways models and developmental taxonomies of criminal behavior (e.g., Moffitt, 1993) explicitly posit homogeneous subgroups that follow distinctive trajectories of offending over time. In this case, group-based modeling approaches are better aligned with the underlying theoretical model from a conceptual point of view. Nagin and Odgers (2010b) point out that they may have the secondary benefit of better approximating the observed data. In the next section, group-based modeling approaches are described, which encompass conventional growth curve modeling as a special and restricted case.

Semiparametric Group-Based Trajectory Modeling and Latent Growth Mixture Modeling

When researchers are interested in subtypes or subpopulations but information about the distinct developmental trajectories of the subpopulations is not known or the subpopulations are unobserved, latent GMM (B. Muthén, 2004; B. Muthén & Muthén, 2000; B. Muthén & Shedden, 1999) and SGBTM, also referred to as latent class growth analysis (Nagin, 1999; 2005; Roeder, Lynch, & Nagin, 1999), are useful. Both approaches are embedded in the finite mixture modeling (McLachlan & Peel, 2000; Titterington, Smith, & Makov, 1985) framework, which is predicated on the assumption that the population of interest consists of a finite number of heterogeneous subpopulations with varying parameters (a finite mixture of distributions). Unlike multigroup models, which use observable characteristics, such as gender or ethnic/racial group membership, to distinguish known groups of individuals with differing trajectories, growth mixture analyses divide the population of interest into an unknown number of mutually exclusive and exhaustive K subpopulations (or latent classes) that are defined by their own distinct trajectory parameters.

More practically, GMM and SGBTM extend conventional growth curve modeling by classifying individuals into different latent classes (groups) to accommodate unobserved population heterogeneity in trajectories. For example, the trajectory could be linear in one class and nonlinear in another class. Conventional growth curve modeling uses continuous latent variables (when conducted within the structural equation modeling framework); in contrast, group-based trajectory modeling approaches additionally use a categorical latent variable, also known as a latent class variable, to represent a mixture of subpopulations where latent class membership of the individual is not known ex ante (i.e., unobserved) but is inferred from the data.

SGBTM is typically viewed as a special case of the more generalized GMM approach because it only assumes a homogeneous trajectory *within* each group (e.g., B. Muthén, 2004; Kreuter & Muthén, 2008b). That is, SGBTM models are characterized by zero variances and covariances for the Level 2 error terms, resulting in the elimination of the latent variance-covariance matrix from the model (Morin et al., 2011). Individuals within each given latent class are thus implicitly assumed to follow the same developmental trajectory in SGBTM applications and to differ only due to random perturbations. GMM relaxes this restriction by allowing for variability in trajectories within classes; that is, individuals from a given latent class are allowed to vary around their class-specific mean growth curve. The SGBTM approach, in contrast, "requires trajectory variability to lie at the between-class level" (Preacher et al., 2008, p. 58). For this reason, SGBTM has a slight tendency to lead to the identification of more trajectory groups than does GMM (Bauer & Curran, 2004; B. Muthén & Muthén, 2000), although this issue has not been widely studied.

Both approaches differ somewhat in their purpose and distributional assumptions. SGBTM was developed to statistically approximate a complex but *unspecified continuous* distribution with a linear combination of discrete distributions; the derived trajectory groups are not literal entities but, rather, are semiparametric approximations of local areas of support of the distribution of individual differences in growth (Nagin & Odgers, 2010b). In contrast, standard GMM relies on a *parametric* specification by invoking the multivariate normality assumption for *within-class* random effects or growth parameters (Kreuter & Muthén, 2008a, 2008b). The mixture components in this case correspond to true unobserved subpopulations that are characterized by different patterns of developmental trajectories. A limitation of the GMM approach is that nonnormal distributions of the growth parameters (i.e., violations of the within-class normality assumption) can lead to incorrect conclusions about the number and even the existence of latent trajectory classes (Bauer & Curran, 2003a). Although not discussed in the following, a nonparametric extension of the GMM model has been proposed that does not rely on any distributional assumption for the random effects (Kreuter & Muthén, 2008b).

Next, the statistical underpinnings of group-based trajectory analysis are presented in reference to the more general GMM framework. Similar to our presentation of conventional growth curve modeling, we describe the standard GMM approach using multilevel modeling notation so that the differences between both analytical techniques are more easily seen. Figure 2.7 depicts an unconditional linear GMM model of offending, where i is the index for the individual and t is the index for time. In this case, we assume that continuous outcome measures are used, but other types of outcome measures can be readily analyzed, such as categorical, censored, and/or count variables. In the path diagram, c represents a categorical latent variable, that is, a latent class variable, with k levels that are estimated from the data, where each individual i has a probability of membership p in each of the k latent classes. The categorical latent variable c is included in the path diagram to represent latent trajectory classes underlying the latent growth variables. The Level 1 and Level 2 models corresponding to Figure 2.7 can be expressed as

$$Y_{ti}^k = \sum_{k=1}^{K} p\,(c = k)\,[\eta_{0i}^k + \eta_{1i}^k\,\lambda_t^k + \varepsilon_{ti}^k],$$

$$\eta_{0i}^k = \mu_0^k + \zeta_{0i}^k, \text{ and}$$

$$\eta_{1i}^k = \mu_1^k + \zeta_{1i}^k,$$

where Y_{ti}^k in the Level 1 model is person i's ($i = 1, \ldots, n$) rate of offending at time t ($t = 1, \ldots, T$) for latent class k ($k = 1, 2, \ldots, K$). The superscript k indicates that all parameters in the Level 1 and Level 2 model equations are class-specific. However, it is possible to incorporate invariance constraints across latent classes for specific model parameters and fully class-varying GMM are rarely tested, in part because of frequent convergence problems. Nevertheless, we can think of GMM as an analytical technique that considers a separate latent growth curve model for each latent class. The two latent growth parameters (η_{0i}^k and η_{1i}^k) are continuous latent variables with a normal distribution that represent the underlying trajectory of offending for individual i in latent class k. As before, λ_t^k represents time scores, which may be specified as class-varying (linear or nonlinear trajectories could be specified in each class; trajectories could be specified as noninvariant or invariant across classes). Time intervals may be equally or unequally spaced, just as in conventional growth curve modeling, and the researcher must specify the desired coding of time. Here, the intercept coefficient represents the model-implied rate of offending at the initial time point. The parameter ε_{ti}^k represents the residual for person i at time t in latent class k. In our case, the residuals are specified as uncorrelated, but this restriction can be relaxed in GMM (see Bauer & Curran, 2004). The fixed-effects parameters in the Level 2 model (i.e., the intercept coefficients μ_0^k and μ_1^k) represent model-estimated overall mean levels of

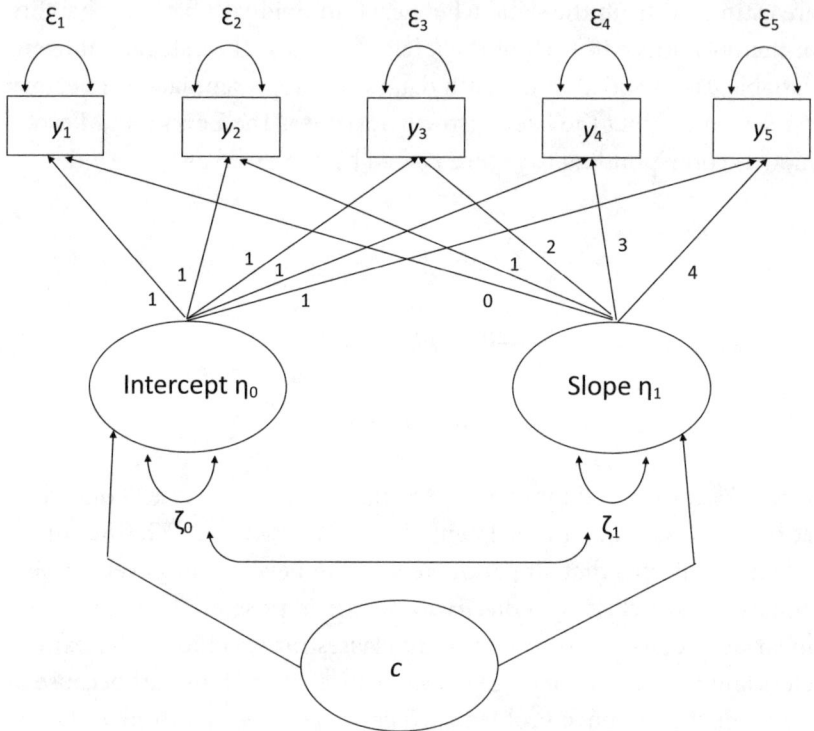

Figure 2.7. Path diagram for an unconditional linear latent growth mixture model of offending

offending at the initial time point and the average rate of change in offending over time in latent class k. The random-effects parameters in the Level 2 model (i.e., the error terms ζ_{0i}^k and ζ_{1i}^k) represent the variability of the estimated intercepts and slopes across cases within the given latent class k.

As mentioned earlier, situations in which group membership is unknown (unobserved) for individuals in a sample may be addressed via GMM analysis. GMM includes a categorical latent variable (or latent class variable), that is accommodated by incorporating probabilistic classification. Specifically, GMM estimates the predicted probability of membership in each latent class for all individuals, which is reflected in the first part of the Level 1 model equation $\sum_{k=1}^{K} p(c = k)$. For example, a given person i may have a probability of 0.11 to belong to Class 1, a probability of 0.29 to belong to Class 2, and a probability of 0.60 to belong to Class 3 for a GMM with three latent classes. These estimated posterior probabilities sum up to one for each person across all classes and unconditionally over all classes. Most applications of GMM use the default maximum posterior probability rule, which assigns individuals to a latent class based on the highest predicted probability of class membership (i.e., individuals are assigned to the most probable, that is, modal, class). This approach is sometimes referred to in the literature as *modal assignment*. In our hypothetical example, the person would be assigned to Latent Class 3. Some authors have proposed alternative assignment procedures that are not used as often in the applied literature. These methods include the *randomized class assignment* procedure from Bandeen-Roche (Wang, Brown, & Bandeen-Roche, 2005). This approach uses random "pseudo-class draws" to account for imperfect classification accuracy when individuals are assigned to latent classes. It is useful for the construct validation of latent trajectory classes (for an application, see Morin et al., 2011) and may, therefore, gain more popularity in future research. Matrix equation notations and other statistical details for GMM and SGBTM are presented in several texts (e.g., B. Muthén, 2004; B. Muthén & Shedden, 1999; Nagin, 1999, 2005; Petras & Masyn, 2010).

Analyses typically do not stop after selecting a best-fitting, interpretable GMM model with a specific number of latent trajectory classes but extend the model to include exogenous time-invariant predictors, time-varying covariates, and/or later life outcomes (consequences). It is at this stage of the analysis that substantive researchers draw on developmental taxonomies to generate testable hypotheses about the antecedents, correlates, and outcomes of the uncovered trajectory groups. In the methodological literature, these modeling extensions are increasingly framed within a construct validation argument. Scholars have posited that construct validation is critical to support the substantive interpretation of latent trajectory classes as representing meaningful subpopulations (Morin et al., 2011; Petras & Masyn, 2010). Within the context of group-based trajectory modeling, the validation of a model requires evidence of relations of latent trajectory classes to theoretically significant antecedents/outcomes that were not included in the classification algorithm. The ease, technical details, and flexibility with which these extensions can be incorporated in group-based trajectory modeling differ

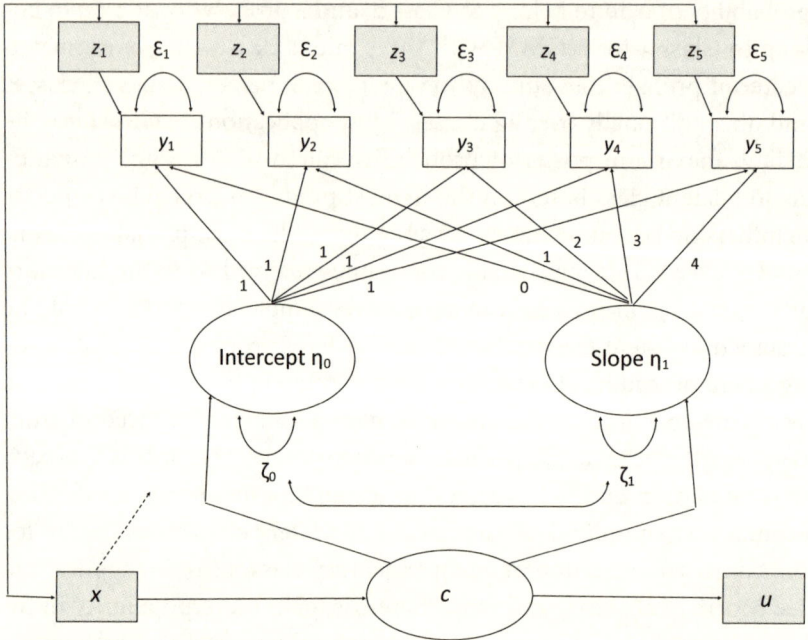

Figure 2.8. Path diagram for a conditional linear latent growth mixture model of offending with a time-invariant predictor, a time-varying covariate, and a distal outcome

slightly between SGBTM and GMM. For example, only GMM allows the researcher to specify direct predictive effects of time-invariant predictors on latent growth factors *within* trajectory classes. Here, we focus on summarizing the main issues for these model extensions within the GMM approach.

Figure 2.8 depicts a conditional linear GMM model of offending with a time-invariant predictor x, a time-varying covariate z, and a distal outcome u. For visual clarity, the rectangles representing these additional variables are shaded in the path diagram. Including auxiliary information in the form of theoretically significant antecedents and consequences may help distinguish between true mixture distributions and homogeneous nonnormal distributions and is necessary from a construct validation perspective (Morin et al., 2011; Petras & Masyn, 2010).

In GMM, exogenous time-invariant predictors are linked to latent class membership via multinomial logistic regression. Specifically, the impact of a time-invariant predictor x on the probability of latent class membership is expressed as $p(C_i = k \mid x_i)$ and estimated with a multinomial logistic regression model. Note that one of the latent trajectory classes must be designated as the reference class. As discussed later, it is important to verify that the inclusion of time-invariant predictors of class membership does not substantially alter the enumeration (size and meaning) of classes when compared to the solution from the final unconditional GMM model. It was already mentioned that time-invariant predictors may also be allowed to predict *within-class* interindividual variability in the underlying trajectory of offending when analyses are performed within the GMM framework (this is indicated by the dashed line in Figure 2.8). In this case, the Level 2 model equations for our GMM example would change to $\eta_{0i}^k = \mu_{00}^k + \beta_{01}^k x + \zeta_{0i}^k$ and $\eta_{1i}^k = \mu_{10}^k + \beta_{11}^k x + \zeta_{1i}^k$ (for a single covariate x). This optional modeling specification is not possible in SGBTM for reasons described earlier. Second, similar to conventional growth curve modeling, time-varying covariates z may be included in the Level 1 model (equation not shown). Alternative approaches are possible, such as dual trajectory modeling, which estimates unobserved population heterogeneity in parallel growth processes. Third, distal outcomes u may be incorporated in the GMM model. This can be done using two approaches (equations not shown). The distal outcome(s) may either be treated as an additional indicator of the latent class variable or as a true causal outcome of latent class membership (for details, see Petras & Masyn, 2010).

This section provided an overview of the underlying concepts, statistical underpinnings, and methodology of group-based trajectory modeling and clarified how SGBTM and GMM relate to each other and to more traditional techniques for longitudinal data analysis, such as conventional growth curve modeling. In the next section, we summarize important practical considerations and steps for conducting GMM and SGBTM analyses.

Model-Building Considerations in SGBTM and GMM

Group-based trajectory models can be estimated with varying degrees of flexibility in several software packages. Examples include SAS PROC TRAJ (B. Jones & Nagin, 2007; B. Jones, Nagin, & Roeder, 2001), STATA

Traj (B. Jones & Nagin, 2013), Mplus (L. Muthén & Muthén, 1998–2012), Mx (Neale, Boker, Xie, & Maes, 2003), Latent Gold (Vermunt & Magidson, 2005), and programs for use within the R statistical programming environment (R Development Core Team, 2009), such as *crimCV* (Nielsen et al., 2014) and OpenMx (Boker et al., 2011). By far the most widely used software programs in the criminological and developmental psychology literature are PROC TRAJ for the SAS platform and Mplus. Both can accommodate missing data and multiple types of measured outcomes (e.g., continuous, censored, categorical, count variables) but differ in the models that can be tested. SAS PROC TRAJ is restricted to tests of SGBTM models. Mplus uses the more general GMM framework, which allows for estimation of latent class growth analysis models as a special case by imposing certain model constraints (Kreuter & Muthén, 2008b). We have no vested interest in any particular software package and do not promote any one above the others. As software packages continue to evolve and further extension opportunities are added, all have their strengths. Often, specific details (e.g., the need to account for exposure time and intermittency periods) will tip the balance toward a particular software program for the analysis at hand. In our own work with data from multiple samples, we have used more than one software program over the years.

GMM and SGBTM analyses are not easy to implement; model evaluation and selection are not straightforward, require subjective decisions at various modeling steps, usually occur within an iterative model fitting process, and are vulnerable to convergence problems, local maxima, improper solutions, and violations of distributional assumptions (Preacher et al., 2008). Frequently untested class-invariance assumptions may affect substantive interpretations of analysis results (Morin et al., 2011). A thorough evaluation of multiple alternative model specifications is essential for these reasons. Some model-building guidelines are offered next.

The first model-building step involves specifying the functional form of growth in the outcome over time. How does one decide which linear or nonlinear growth function(s) should be examined for the data at hand? In most cases, a mix of theoretical considerations and descriptive data exploration will inform decisions of the researcher at this step. Developmental taxonomies of antisocial and criminal behavior (e.g.,

Moffitt, 1993) offer predictions about the number of expected latent trajectory classes and their hypothesized shape of growth over time. For example, if empirical investigations encompass the adolescent and young adult years of study participants, a preponderance of increasing (linear or nonlinear) trajectories of offending might be expected, whereas distinct declining trajectories might be posited to be more prevalent during the individuals' middle-aged adult years. Other theoretical considerations relate to the possible need to statistically account for (a) exposure time (the fraction of time the individual was not institutionalized and "free" to commit crimes), (b) mortality information (to safeguard against treating individuals who died as desisters from crime), and (c) intermittency periods (periods of dormancy during which the probability of criminal activity is strictly zero) during group-based trajectory modeling of criminal behavior (e.g., Eggleston, Laub, & Sampson, 2004).

In addition to theoretical considerations, exploratory data screening of the observed outcome variables is critical for guiding the specification of growth functions for latent trajectory classes. Exploratory data screening may reveal "commonalities across individuals and idiosyncrasies between individuals" (Petras & Masyn, 2010, p. 77). Regarding their individual offense trajectories over time, smooth nonparametric, as well as Ordinary Least Squares, trajectories should be examined for at least a randomly selected subset of study participants. This approach to data screening was illustrated earlier for five individuals from the Toronto sample (see Figures 2.2–2.4). Depending on the type of the outcome variables, researchers can choose among several modeling options. For example, zero-inflated Poisson models (Nagin & Land, 1993) are available in most software programs for GMM and SGBTM analyses of count variables with a large number of zeros; such variables are quite common in the criminological literature, especially when using official records measures of criminal behavior. Finally, model parsimony may be another guiding principle when deciding on the specification of growth functions in GMM and SGBTM analyses.

A second model-building step consists of identifying the number of latent trajectory classes. Taking into consideration the possibility that the derived trajectory classes might be a methodological artifact of skewed or nonnormally distributed data (Bauer & Curran, 2003a), how does one determine how many latent trajectory classes there are? This topic is often referred to as *class enumeration*. Several issues are relevant for determining the optimal number of latent trajectory classes. Considerable debate has centered on the question of whether predictors or covariates should be included in this model-building step and positions have shifted a number of times. Much early work relied on unconditional (i.e., without predictors or covariates) GMM and SGBTM models as the unquestioned approach for determining the number of latent trajectory classes. It was subsequently argued that the inclusion of predictors and covariates might be advantageous in some cases to avoid model misspecification and distorted modeling results (B. Muthén, 2004). Yet, Tofighi and Enders (2008) found that the inclusion of covariates was detrimental to class enumeration, especially for sample sizes with fewer than 1,000 individuals. At a minimum, this effect suggests that it is difficult to come up with one-size-fits-all rules for determining the optimal number of latent trajectory classes in GMM analyses.

Other practical considerations are also relevant for the second model-building step. Detailed but accessible explanations of these issues, which apply to mixture modeling in general, are presented in Pastor and Gagné (2013). For example, inadequate start values might result in GMM and SGBTM models that converge on local maxima (i.e., false maximum likelihood solutions) rather than on a global maximum (i.e., the model with the "real" largest log likelihood). Therefore, it is generally recommended to use a large number of random sets of start values to avoid modeling solutions that converge on local maxima (Hipp & Bauer, 2006). If random start values are not available for use in the software program at hand, then GMM and SGBTM models should be repeatedly estimated with different sets of user-supplied start values to verify that the largest log likelihood is replicated and to ensure the stability of trajectory-class solutions (B. Jones et al., 2001). Improper or unacceptable solutions are signaled in manifold ways, such as negative variance estimates, a nonpositive definite Fisher information matrix, and empty or very small latent trajectory classes (e.g., less than 1% of the sample). These indicators often suggest that more parsimonious models might be more appropriate (e.g., Nylund, Asparouhov, & Muthén, 2007). Models that specify different numbers of latent trajectory classes are not nested;

therefore, the classical likelihood ratio tests cannot be used to compare the fit of models with different numbers of latent trajectory classes (McLachlan & Peel, 2000; see also Petras & Masyn, 2010). Instead, information criteria such as the Bayesian Information Criterion and other statistical tests and indices may be used to compare SGBTM and GMM models with varying numbers of latent trajectory classes (Kass & Raftery, 1995; Raftery, 1995). These objective criteria should be complemented by evaluations of the statistical adequacy of the solutions and their substantive interpretability or conformity with theoretical expectations (Bauer & Curran, 2003a). However, the field has not reached full agreement about the most effective criteria for making these decisions. Reflecting this continued controversy, the software programs differ in the criteria and statistical tests and indexes that they offer for evaluations of GMM and SGBTM models with varying numbers of latent trajectory classes. Our comments on this issue focus on the most popular software programs in the criminological and developmental psychology literature on group-based trajectory modeling.

Simulation studies using Mplus (Nylund, Asparouhov, & Muthén, 2007; Peugh & Fan, 2012; Tofighi & Enders, 2008; Tolvanen, 2007) suggest four statistical tests and indices that are especially helpful for determining the best-fitting model: the Bayesian Information Criterion (Schwarz, 1978), the Consistent Akaike Information Criterion (Bozdogan, 1987), the sample-size adjusted Bayesian Information Criterion (Sclove, 1987), and the Bootstrap Likelihood Ratio Test (McLachlan & Peel, 2000). Lower values on the Bayesian Information Criterion, Consistent Akaike Information Criterion, and the sample-size adjusted Bayesian Information Criterion suggest a better fitting model. Regarding the Bootstrap Likelihood Ratio Test, which is not available in SAS PROC TRAJ, a significant p value indicates that the $k - 1$ class model should be rejected in favor of a k-class model. Some have argued that the Bayesian Information Criterion is a flawed criterion because it tends to suggest finite mixture models with too many classes and instead proposed a cross-validation approach to class enumeration, which is implemented in the software package *crimCV* (Nielsen et al., 2014). It may be useful to graphically depict several information criteria via "elbow plots" (Petras & Masyn, 2010). In these plots, the point of formation of the first angle reveals the optimal number of latent trajectory classes for the given study sample. Additional diagnostic checks have been proposed to evaluate the parameter estimates for statistical conformity (Bauer & Curran, 2003a), including goodness-of-fit tests based on model-implied multivariate skewness and kurtosis values (B. Muthén, 2004) and residual graphical diagnostics (Wang et al., 2005), but their performance in class enumeration has not been studied very much. Finally, the classification accuracy of the chosen models should be considered. Mplus provides the Entropy (Ramaswamy, Desarbo, Reibstein, & Robinson, 1993) value as a summary of the overall accuracy of classification or class separation of the model. Entropy varies from 0 to 1, with values closer to 1 indicating fewer classification errors of the model at hand. Kreuter and Muthén (2008b), among others, caution against overemphasizing the importance of the entropy value during decisions about class enumeration because it is, by definition, a function of the number of specified latent trajectory classes. Average posterior probabilities for each latent trajectory class should also be inspected; values close to 1 on the main diagonal of the classification table reflect reasonable classification accuracy. Nagin (2005) suggests for these average posterior probabilities to exceed a minimum threshold of .70; he also advises to establish that the odds of correct classification based on the posterior probabilities of group membership exceed a minimum threshold of 5. We reiterate that debates about the best criteria for class enumeration in SGBTM and GMM are continuing and that this summary simply reflects the current state of thinking on this issue.

The final GMM and SGBTM models are often graphically displayed with fitted and observed mean trajectory curves for each latent class. Sometimes just the fitted mean trajectory curves are depicted, such as depicted in Figure 2.9 for a subsample of 378 offenders from the Toronto data set. In this case, a four-group solution best represented the trajectories of the number of court contacts, consisting of a moderate-rate, a low-rate, a high-rate adult-peaked, and a high-rate adolescent-peaked pathway (further details on the Toronto data are available from Day et al., 2010; A. Ward et al., 2010). This common practice in criminological and developmental psychology research has been met with criticism and more contemporary texts emphasize that the additional plotting of within-class trajectories is essential for interpretation of the derived latent trajectory classes (Erosheva, Matsueda, & Telesca, 2014). Relatedly,

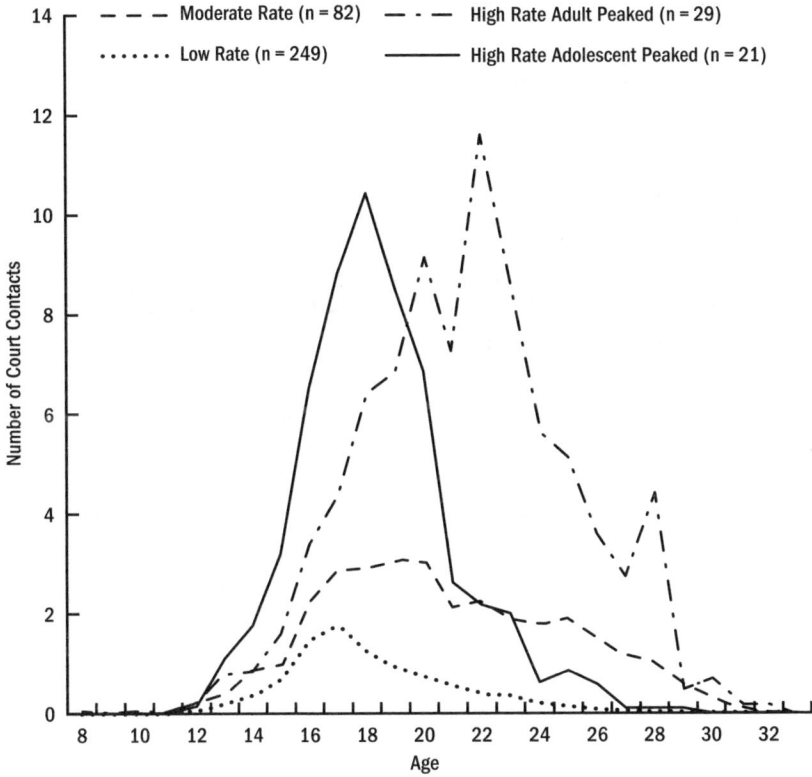

Figure 2.9. Criminal trajectories of four-group model for the Toronto subsample (n = 378)
Source: Reprinted with permission from *Criminal Justice and Behavior*, vol. 37, pp. 1278–1300. Copyright @2010 American Association of Correctional Psychologists. All rights reserved.

plotting confidence intervals for predicted individual trajectories around the group means has also been suggested.

A more detailed example with data from the Oregon Youth Study may be helpful at this point. The Oregon Youth Study is an ongoing multiagent and multimethod longitudinal study in a medium-sized metropolitan region in the Pacific Northwest of the United States. Initiated in 1983–1984, the Oregon Youth Study has tracked a sample of at-risk men from ages 9 or 10 to their 30s (Capaldi & Patterson, 1987). As part of the Oregon Youth Study, juvenile or adult court record searches were conducted locally for the study participants each year, which yielded data

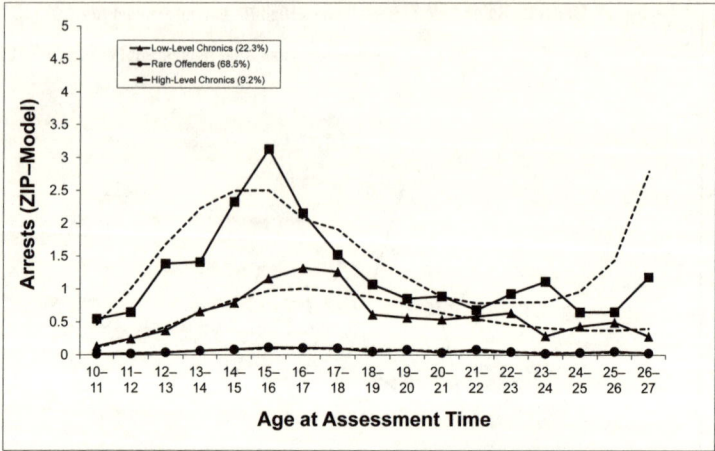

Figure 2.10a. Fitted (dashed lines) versus empirical (solid lines) trajectories of officially recorded offending for 203 young men from the Oregon Youth Study
Source: Reprinted with permission from *Criminology*, 2007, vol. 45, pp. 835–863.
Copyright @2007 American Society of Criminology. All rights reserved.
Note: Empirical trajectories represent the observed arrest rates; fitted trajectories are statistically adjusted for exposure time.

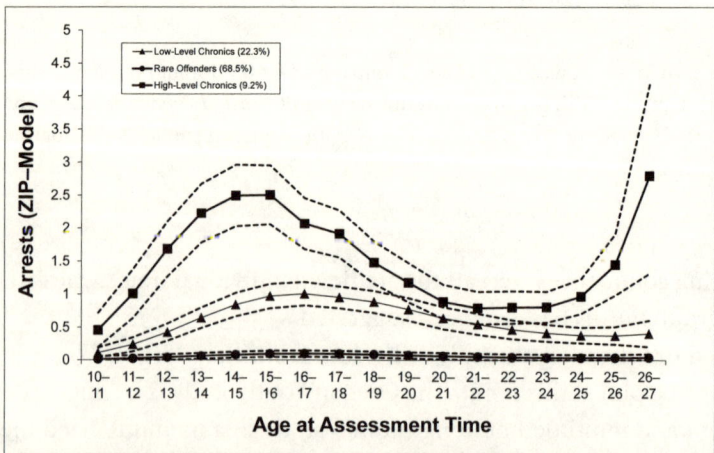

Figure 2.10b. Fitted mean (solid lines) trajectories of officially recorded offending with 95% confidence intervals (dashed lines) for 203 young men from the Oregon Youth Study
Source: Abridged with permission from *Criminology*, 2007, vol. 45, pp. 835–863.
Copyright @2007 American Society of Criminology. All rights reserved.

on the number of official arrests in the past year for the Oregon Youth Study men. These data were used by Wiesner, Capaldi, and Kim (2007) to model unobserved heterogeneity in trajectories of officially recorded offending behavior from age 10 and 11 to 26 and 27. SGBTM analyses were performed using the zero-inflated Poisson model with statistical controls for exposure time. Figure 2.10a depicts the fitted and observed mean trajectory curves for each of the three resulting latent classes; 95% confidence intervals around the three fitted mean trajectory curves are shown in Figure 2.10b and indicative of good class separation. The average posterior probabilities exceeded .91 for each trajectory class, and the odds of correct classification ranged from 21.44 to 123.50 for the three trajectory classes. Overall, the findings revealed high classification accuracy for the chosen three-class SGBTM model.

The final step, construct validation of latent trajectory classes, requires the inclusion of theoretically significant antecedents, time-varying covariates, and/or consequences. This step poses many challenges in applied research. Researchers must judge whether a modal assignment of individuals to latent trajectory classes, which ignores the model's classification accuracy, is justifiable for the data at hand. Alternative approaches that account for classification accuracy of the model might be preferred, such as randomized assignment via "pseudo-class draws" and the single-step approach. The importance of examining how class enumeration might be impacted by the inclusion of antecedents (i.e., time-invariant predictors of latent trajectory class membership) cannot be overstated (L. Li & Hser, 2011). Petras and Masyn (2010), among others, have proposed model-building strategies for construct validation analyses within the GMM framework; Morin et al. (2011) provide a concrete example. Yet, "what particular steps should be taken to obtain validity evidence for a mixture modeling solution is an active area of research . . . and guidance on the issue is likely forthcoming" (Pastor & Gagné, 2013, pp. 377–378).

Extensions and Trends of SGBTM and GMM

Group-based trajectory modeling is an area of active study that continues to rapidly advance our understanding of the underlying methodology, its implementation in various software programs, and the development of innovative extensions to existing modeling approaches. In this final section, we briefly outline three active areas of research for this methodology.

First, considerable methodological work focuses on extending the standard GMM methodology in manifold ways, such as the specification of nonlinear structured growth mixture models (e.g., Grimm, Ram, & Estabrook, 2010) and piecewise growth mixture models with unknown random knots (e.g., Zopluoglu, Harring, & Kohli, 2014). These extensions offer appealing alternatives for modeling distinct nonlinear growth patterns over time and the presumed underlying causal mechanisms. For example, turning points hypothesized to alter the direction of criminal trajectories, such as getting married, play a major role in some leading criminological theories (e.g., Sampson & Laub, 2016). Yet, the turning points (also known as knots) may not always be observable and the knots or change points may differ among individuals. In this case, the model may be accommodated with the inclusion of *unknown* random knots in GMM.

Second, other methodological work examines how various features of the observed data, including outliers and nonnormality (S. Lee & McLachlan, 2014; Muthén & Asparouhov, 2015), missing data, nonrandom participant attrition, mortality of study participants (e.g., Bauer, 2007; Eggleston et al., 2004; Haviland, Jones, & Nagin, 2011), length of follow-up or number of time points (e.g., Eggleston et al., 2004; Farrington, Piquero, & Jennings, 2013), impact class enumeration, and substantive findings and how these might be addressed during statistical analysis. Many of these observed data features are encountered in criminological research. For example, death may be a nontrivial source of attrition in samples with high risk for antisocial or criminal behavior (Haviland et al., 2011). Innovative ways to accommodate such data features in SGBTM and GMM analyses continue to be proposed. Over time, these new methodologies may succeed in more effectively addressing pitfalls of the group-based trajectory modeling method.

Third, interest in advanced causal inference analysis has been rejuvenated by the introduction of new statistical tools (e.g., propensity score matching) into criminology and other disciplines. Parallel to these methodological advances, longitudinal-experimental research has drawn much more attention in the last two decades (Farrington,

Loeber, & Welsh, 2010), the need for cost-effective evidence-based prevention/intervention programs has become ever more apparent (Elliott, 2013), and there has been increased focus on studying presumed causal impacts in quasi-experimental research (Apel & Sweeten, 2010). It is perhaps not surprising that these challenges have been recognized among the SGBTM and GMM proponents. Multigroup GMM modeling strategies have been proposed and used for the analysis of unobserved distinct trajectory patterns in randomized intervention trials and quasi-experimental prevention studies (e.g., B. Muthén et al., 2002; Spaeth, Weichold, Silbereisen, & Wiesner, 2010). Other efforts have concentrated on combining SGBTM with propensity score matching techniques (e.g., Haviland, Nagin, Rosenbaum, & Tremblay, 2008; Nieuwbeerta, Nagin, & Blokland, 2009).

This concludes our admittedly subjective list of trends for group-based trajectory modeling. On one hand, these developments offer exciting possibilities for future substantive and methodological research with group-based trajectory modeling. On the other hand, best practices in SGBTM and GMM evolve at such a rapid pace that responsible researchers must make a concerted effort to keep up with the ever-changing (growth) mixture modeling literature.

Conclusion

This chapter has introduced the concept of a trajectory, illustrated ways to graphically depict individual trajectory profiles and describe their key features, and presented the statistical underpinnings and methodology for performing group-based trajectory analyses. The relation of these techniques to more traditional methods of analyzing longitudinal data was also examined. Key model-building steps and considerations in the application of SGBTM and GMM methods were described. The next chapter reviews the main controversies and criticisms of the group-based trajectory methodology.

Suggested Supplemental Readings

Numerous excellent texts provide technical and conceptual overviews of SGBTM (e.g., Nagin, 1999, 2005; Nagin & Odgers, 2010b). B. Muthén

(2004) presents an overview of the general mixture modeling integrative framework for combining categorical and continuous latent variables that focuses on GMM and related techniques for longitudinal analysis (see also Kreuter & Muthén, 2008a). An excellent description of GMM that includes detailed recommendations for the incorporation of antecedents and consequences can be found in Petras and Masyn (2010). An illustration of how tests of nonlinear GMM may be implemented in two software programs can be found in Grimm et al. (2010). Authoritative papers from Bauer and colleagues (e.g., Bauer, 2007; Bauer & Curran, 2003a, 2004) discuss potential pitfalls of GMM. Finally, a critical review of the practices of group-based trajectory modeling applications in criminology and developmental science is offered by Erosheva et al. (2014).

3

Debates and Controversies

Despite the rapid growth in the number of researchers who employ the semiparametric group-based trajectory modeling (SGBTM) and latent growth mixture modeling (GMM) methodology, the study of trajectories is not without controversy (Erosheva, Matsueda, & Telesca, 2014). As Petras and Masyn (2010) astutely observe in the introduction to their book chapter on GMM,

> in concert with the growing popularity of these data-driven, group-based methods for studying developmental and life-course behavior trajectories, have come active and spirited ontological discussions about the nature of the emergent trajectory groups resulting from the analyses . . . , i.e., whether the resultant trajectory typology defined by the subgroups derived from the data represent a "true" developmental taxonomy. Further debate involves whether it is reasonable to even apply these methods if there is not a true taxonomy underlying the data, under what conditions these methods should be applied, and how the results should be interpreted if we consider the fact that, for any given dataset, we cannot know the "truth" of the population distribution from which the observations were drawn. (p. 70)

Although we do not share the deep-seated skepticism that some scholars have expressed about the suitability of group-based trajectory modeling methodology for advancing scientific knowledge in a meaningful manner (e.g., Bauer, 2007; Sampson & Laub, 2005b; Skardhamar, 2010), we firmly believe that researchers and public policy makers need to be cognizant of its limitations. To this end, the observations from Petras and Masyn (2010) set the perfect preface for this chapter.

This chapter explores the major controversies and debates about criminal trajectory modeling. Debates in the literature include issues at the conceptual, theoretical, and methodological level, some of which were briefly touched on earlier. This chapter builds on and extends many prior works by others (e.g., Bauer, 2007; Bauer & Curran, 2003a; Brame, Paternoster, & Piquero, 2012; Erosheva et al., 2014; Greenberg, 2016; Nagin & Tremblay, 2005b; Sampson & Laub, 2003; Skardhamar, 2010; Sterba, Baldasaro, & Bauer, 2012). A key objective of this chapter was to cover new methodological developments (e.g., bootstrapping, new software package *crimCV*, inclusion of covariates, results of new Monte Carlo simulations, and new approaches to the assessment of model adequacy) that have not been synthesized in prior reviews while at the same time providing a representative sampling of longer-standing debates. The chapter begins with a discussion of the danger of interpreting uncovered trajectory groups too literally as real-existing entities ("reification" of groups). Next, the pros and cons of direct versus indirect applications of the SGBTM and GMM methodology are examined. The chapter concludes with an extensive review of the current knowledge on multiple practical challenges in SGBTM and GMM analysis: (a) statistical criteria for class enumeration; (b) distributional issues, model misspecification, and overextraction of trajectory classes; (c) dependency on antecedents and covariates; and (d) robustness or sensitivity of trajectory solutions in relation to various methodological factors.

Reification of Trajectory Groups

Questions about the nature of the criminal trajectory groups that are uncovered during statistical analysis have been a recurring theme across the extant literature. In general, trajectory groups that emerge from SGBTM or GMM analysis can be conceptualized in one of two ways: as a device for approximating a complex continuum of unknown form or as concrete entities that are distinctive and theoretically meaningful (Nagin & Land, 1993). Theory-based construct validation of trajectory groups that are uncovered during statistical analysis is of paramount importance for the second conceptualization. Even if supplemental data support the construct validity of statistically constructed offender trajectory groups, they should not be interpreted as literally existing entities to which individuals in that trajectory group follow in lockstep fashion, an overinterpretation of SGBTM and GMM findings that is referred to as "reification" of groups in the literature (e.g., Brame et al., 2012; Erosheva et al., 2014; Laub & Sampson, 2003; McAra & McVie, 2012; Nagin & Tremblay, 2005b).

The distinction between both conceptualizations is not just an issue of labels that are assigned to trajectory groups but can have far-reaching public-policy implications. Specifically, the identification of a set of trajectory groups lends legitimacy to them, which raises the danger that they will be viewed by consumers of trajectory studies, including policy makers, as more than heuristic devices (Sampson & Laub, 2003). Nagin and Tremblay (2005b) eloquently warn of this danger with the following example: "If a group is small and its behavior is socially undesirable, such as committing crimes, reifying the group as a distinct entity–rather than as an extreme on a continuum, may provoke draconian responses to the behavior by creating the impression of a bright line of separation between 'them' and 'us.' Human history is replete with tragic instances in which a fictional group-based separation is the first step to dehumanizing them" (p. 883). Such concerns are even more pertinent given results of simulation studies that have raised questions about the circumstances under which latent trajectory groups can be reliably identified. Specifically, simulation studies found that SGBTM and GMM will uncover trajectory groups when the true data-generating process is continuous and those groups do not necessarily resemble the process that was employed for generating the data (Bauer & Curran, 2003a; Skardhamar, 2010; Weakliem & Wright, 2009; see also Greenberg, 2016). In light of these findings, Skardhamar (2010) cautions that the mere uncovering of trajectory groups in an SGBTM and GMM analysis does not permit decisions about the veracity of taxonomic theories because the resultant groups might equally well be explained by nontaxonomic theories, rendering these statistical techniques little more than a descriptive or exploratory data reduction tool. Brame et al. (2012) assert that this judgment is too harsh and argue that

> the GBT [group-based trajectory] method will always identify groups of cases in accordance with the number of groups specified. . . . This is so because GBT models are explicitly designed to identify distinct groups of offenders in the data–the models exploit the clustering of individuals by locating distinct points of support in the data. . . . One can hardly be too critical of a modelling technique that only does what it is supposed to do. The controversial issue is not that GBT methods identify distinct clusters of offenders, since that is what the model does, but characterizing

the *meaning* the groups have. The latter is not a modelling question, it is a *theoretical* question. . . . Estimating a GBT model (a model explicitly designed to identify distinct groups of offenders) that produces some number of groups *does not, by itself, provide evidence that the groups identified have any significance or importance, theoretical or otherwise.* . . . If one estimates a GBT model with theory in hand, then the results of this analysis can be compared to the theory just like the results of any other analysis (assumptions and all) are compared with a theory. (pp. 478–480, emphasis in original)

To be sure, the points of both sides of this controversy are well taken. The uncovering of statistically constructed trajectory groups through GMM and SGBTM analysis is not sufficient by itself for demonstrating the existence of these groups, in part because researchers cannot know, for any given data set, the true underlying population distribution (discrete or continuous) from which the observations were gathered. Just as with any other statistical technique, it is problematic if the SGBTM and GMM methodology is used in an atheoretical manner; the theory-based construct validation of statistically constructed trajectory groups is critical to support their significance. For these reasons, the SGBTM and GMM literature cautions that there is a danger of reifying a set of criminal trajectories that emerges from the statistical analysis. This situation means that researchers must be careful not to speak of a trajectory as if it were a real entity, existing in reality, to which individuals in that trajectory group follow in lockstep fashion. Rather, a trajectory is a heuristic device generated by the statistical analysis of data, and the researcher plays a role in the ensuing results, for example, in the specification, selection, and interpretation of a resultant statistical model. To emphasize this aspect of the model fitting process, Ram and Grimm (2009) refer to the SGBTM and GMM methodology as "a constrained exploratory technique" (p. 572).

Approximation to an Unknown Continuous Distribution of Population Trajectories

Erosheva et al. (2014) surmised in a recent review that most applications of the SGBTM and GMM methodology tend to interpret trajectory groups as representative of distinct population subgroups, that is, as latent strata or subpopulations that are reflective of a true developmental taxonomy underlying the data. Such applications are generally referred to as *direct* applications in finite mixture modeling (McLachlan & Peel, 2000; Titterington, Smith, & Makov, 1985). It is typical for researchers in these situations to relate the results from their analysis to a specific taxonomic theory. In the field of criminology, the developmental taxonomy of antisocial behavior from Moffitt (1993) serves as a prime example of such a taxonomic theory. However, it has not gone unchallenged (e.g., Sampson & Laub, 2003) and other scholars have taken the position that the criminological literature is not clear on whether the uncovered latent trajectory groups indeed represent substantively meaningful classes (e.g., Kreuter & Muthén, 2008a).

Methodologists tend to conceptualize latent trajectory groups as discrete approximations to a complex, unspecified continuum of growth trajectories, in part because the existence of truly distinct groups is deemed to be rare and not the norm in the social sciences (Erosheva et al., 2014; Nagin, 2005; Nagin & Tremblay, 2005b). Moreover, social sciences theory is seldom specific about the exact form of continuously distributed growth trajectories (Sterba et al., 2012). Applications that use latent trajectory groups as a device to approximate complex continuous distributions that are difficult to capture by conventional parametric statistical models are referred to as *indirect* applications in finite mixture modeling (McLachlan & Peel, 2000; Titterington et al., 1985). In fact, this idea was a major motivating factor for developing the SGBTM approach. Specifically, the trajectory groups are intended as an *indirect* (discrete) approximation of a more complex continuous population distribution of growth trajectories for which the exact form is unknown (e.g., Nagin, 1999, 2005; Nagin & Tremblay, 2005b). We draw on the excellent graphical illustration of this idea in Sterba et al. (2012), reprinted in Figure 3.1:

> The smooth curve depicts a one-dimensional distribution of individual differences in growth (say, differences in initial level, or intercept) in the population. An SPGM [semiparametric group-based model] would extract $k = 1 \ldots K$ classes, which would serve as points of support for this continuous individual difference distribution, much like histobars in a

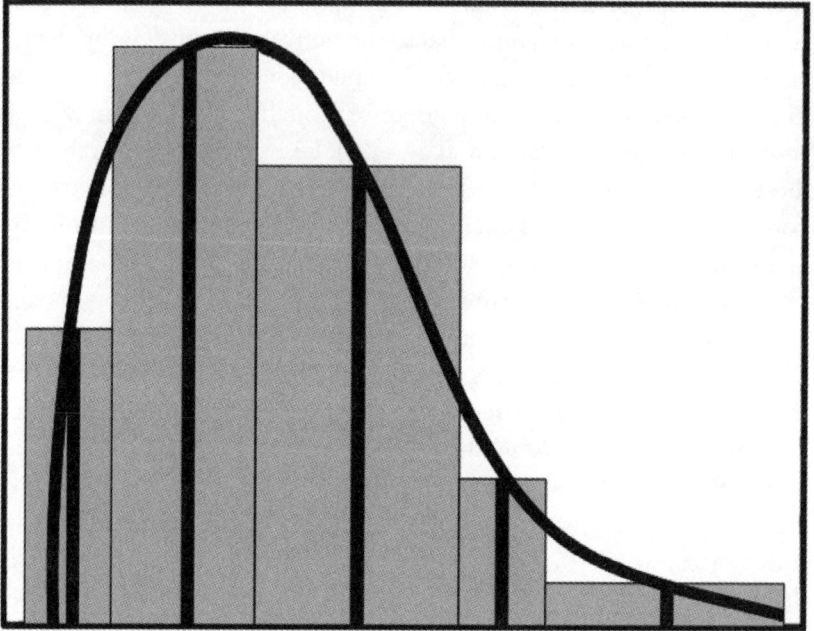

Figure 3.1. Heuristic sketch often cited in semiparametric group-based trajectory model literature

Source: Sterba et al., 2012, p. 592, Figure 2. Reprinted with permission from Taylor & Francis.

Note: Hypothesized semiparametric approximation of the probability density function of a single dimension random effect distribution. The locations of points of support correspond to class means; the heights of points of support correspond to class probabilities; the number of points corresponds to the number of classes.

histogram (here, $K = 5$). The location of the point of support for the kth class is determined by a class-specific growth coefficient (here, class-specific intercept). The proportion of individuals in class k determines the height (or mass) of the kth point of support. Together, these masses and locations define a discrete probability distribution for the SPGM. (pp. 592–593)

It is not always understood that this issue touches upon an important philosophical difference between SGBTM and GMM. As explicated in Shiyko, Ram, and Grimm (2012), SGBTM is intended as a means for discretely approximating a complex continuous distribution of growth trajectories for which the exact form is unknown, whereas GMM is a parametric technique that is designed to extract distinct normally distributed subpopulations with means and variances within a mixture (a nonparametric version of GMM that does not rely on any distributional assumption for the random effects has subsequently become available; see B. Muthén & Asparouhov, 2009). Furthermore, GMM is predicated on the assumption that these different distributions are linked to distinct underlying developmental processes. A nice graphical illustration of this philosophical difference between SGBTM and GMM is presented in Shiyko et al. (2012), reprinted in Figure 3.2. In both panels of Figure 3.2, the overall distribution of growth trajectories has an identical non-normal shape, represented by the solid line, but the model-fitting approaches undertaken by both techniques are different. Panel B shows how the continuous nonnormal distribution of slopes is discretely approximated with four points of support (SGBTM application); in contrast, Panel A shows how the same hypothetical nonnormal distribution is split into two normally distributed subpopulations (GMM application).

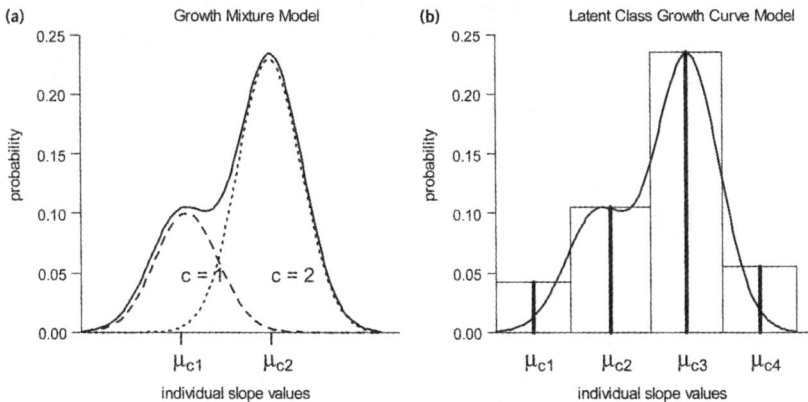

Figure 3.2. Conceptual differences between GMM and latent LCGCM
Source: Shiyko et al., 2012, p. 536, Figure 31.2. Reprinted with permission from Guilford Press.
Note: LCGCM is identical with the label "SGBTM" (Nagin, 2005) in the current book; c = latent trajectory class k; μ = trajectory class mean.

Shiyko et al. (2012) go on to note that

> to be clear, LCGCM [i.e., SGBTM] and GMM are similar in their aims to describe unobserved heterogeneity; however, the two approaches differ in how the heterogeneity is defined and estimated. Conceptually, LCGCM [i.e., SGBTM] finds clusters of individuals with similar and homogeneous developmental profiles, uncovering *between-class* heterogeneity. In contrast, GMM sets apart different developmental classes (*between-class* heterogeneity) and allows for interindividual differences within classes (*within-class* heterogeneity). . . . When making a decision about using LCGCM [i.e., SGBTM] or GMM, it is worth considering the theoretical and practical implications of each approach. (p. 537, emphasis in original)

Irrespective of this basic philosophical difference between SGBTM and GMM, much of the recent literature has concentrated on the question, under what conditions is it fruitful to apply these methods.

From a theoretical point of view (statistical considerations are discussed later), it is questionable whether SGBTM and GMM can be applied to taxonomic as well as nontaxonomic theories of development or whether their use is best restricted to taxonomic theories (e.g., Bauer, 2007; Nagin & Tremblay, 2005b). It is our belief that this spirited debate is intertwined with a fundamental discord on the utility of categorical versus dimensional models of human behavior that is evident in a multitude of scientific disciplines. The main question in this long-standing controversy is whether individuals differ by type (qualitatively distinct groupings) or linear gradation (degree on a continuum). Bauer (2007) asserts that individuals are more likely to differ by linear gradation given the multifaceted influences on human behaviors or outcomes. Within the fields of developmental psychopathology and psychiatry (see also Helzer, Kraemer, & Krueger, 2006; Pickles & Angold, 2003), there is "widespread recognition that many of the behaviors that we study are dimensionally distributed and do not show clear-cut points differentiating 'normality' and 'pathology'" (Maughan, 2005, p. 120). As mentioned earlier, this view is also encountered among criminologists (e.g., Nagin, 2005; Nagin & Tremblay, 2005b). That there can be any definitive resolution of this controversy is not clear. But it behooves SGBTM and GMM researchers well to remember that indirect applications can be incredibly useful and that they perhaps provide a more realistic representation of essential data features than their nonmixture counterpart techniques (Pastor & Gagné, 2013).

Model Selection and Class Enumeration

As discussed earlier, the application of SGBTM and GMM methodology is not straightforward and researchers must address multiple practical questions, such as how to select the best model for the data at hand. This section reviews controversies surrounding class enumeration and model selection in SGBTM and GMM analysis. Although they are presented in separate subsections, readers should keep in mind that these issues are often interrelated. Also, some controversial issues have been highlighted more in criminology relative to other fields such as psychology (and vice versa), partly because of limitations inherent to specific statistical software programs that are more commonly used for SGBTM and GMM analysis in the given scientific discipline.

STATISTICAL CRITERIA FOR CLASS ENUMERATION. First, there is considerable debate about the best way to apply the statistical criteria for identifying the number of latent trajectory groups that optimally represent the data. For the purposes of this discussion, it needs to be kept in mind that statistical criteria are not sufficient for selecting the optimal number of trajectory classes. Early SGBTM and GMM applications predominantly relied on penalized information-based criteria such as the Bayesian Information Criterion (Schwarz, 1978) as a basis for selecting the optimal number of trajectory classes. Other statistical criteria have become available in some statistical software packages in subsequent years (therefore, this discussion is an oversimplification contingent on the software being used), but Nagin's SGBTM methodology heavily relies on the Bayesian Information Criterion to this day (e.g., Nagin, Jones, Lima Passos, & Tremblay, 2018). Generally, the model that maximizes the Bayesian Information Criterion (i.e., has the smallest absolute Bayesian Information Criterion value) is chosen while also considering model adequacy, classification quality/uncertainty, and substantive issues.

There is not complete agreement on the usefulness of the Bayesian Information Criterion as a basis for model selection (e.g., Mulaik, 2009; Nagin, 2005; Preacher & Merkle, 2012; Vrieze, 2012). In some SGBTM and GMM applications, the Bayesian Information Criterion value simply continues to improve as the number of latent trajectory classes is increased (Nagin, 2005), without reaching a clear maximum value, that is then followed by a steady decline in the Bayesian Information Criterion. In these situations, the Bayesian Information Criterion does not clearly indicate a preferred number of trajectory classes. Another flaw is that the Bayesian Information Criterion tends to suggest too many classes in mixture modeling. Moreover, a simulation study from Preacher and Merkle (2012) revealed that model selection decisions based on the Bayesian Information Criterion are subject to sampling error (this is also a problem for other information-based criteria). In particular, it was found that assertions of model superiority based on the Bayesian Information Criterion can be highly unstable across repeated sampling and model selection uncertainty does not necessarily decrease with increases in sample size (sample sizes studied by Preacher & Merkle, 2012, ranged from $N = 80$–5,000). Given these results, some researchers have begun to explore bootstrap approaches as a possible means for alleviating model selection uncertainty in applications that rely on the Bayesian Information Criterion and other information-based criteria (Lubke et al., 2017).

In contrast, Nielsen et al. (2014) feel that the reliance on the Bayesian Information Criterion is problematic and proposed an alternative statistical software program, referred to as *crimCV*, to conduct group-based trajectory analyses. The *crimCV* package was developed for the open-source R program. It stands out from other statistical software in that it incorporates a cross-validation approach into the class enumeration process during group-based trajectory modeling. In particular, leave-one-out cross-validation statistics that can be used to decide on the optimal number of trajectory classes are calculated. It provides a useful statistic, the *cross-validation error*, to quantify the amount of error in the group-based modeling approach, which allows one to evaluate the given model's predictive ability. Generally, the final choice of K latent classes is based on the model that minimizes the cross-validation error value. In examinations conducted by Nielsen et al. (2014), the new cross-validation approach performed favorably in comparison to SAS PROC TRAJ and Mplus. The authors note that the cross-validation error statistic should be especially useful in situations in which the Bayesian

Information Criterion (as well as the Akaike Information Criterion) continues to improve without apparent limit as trajectory classes are added. A recent application of this approach can be found in Wheeler, Worden, and McLean (2016).

Fundamentally, both innovations (i.e., the bootstrap and cross-validation approaches) appear to be motivated by concerns about the Bayesian Information Criterion and other information-based criteria for class enumeration purposes. Both attempt to alleviate model selection uncertainty pertaining to the Bayesian Information Criterion during GMM and SGBTM analysis (although the strategies and technical details differ, of course). It is too early to know which of these alternative approaches will ultimately prevail in future SGBTM and GMM research.

DISTRIBUTIONAL ISSUES, MODEL MISSPECIFICATION, AND OVEREXTRACTION OF CLASSES. Second, the performance of SGBTM and GMM in correctly recovering the number of latent trajectory classes continues to be questioned. Class enumeration performance of GMM and SGBTM can be evaluated from both a Type 1 error and a Type 2 error control perspective (Peugh & Fan, 2012). Both scenarios are not well understood because of the scarcity of empirical research. In evaluations of Type 2 error control in the context of GMM, the simulated data represent a heterogeneous population with K (where $k > 1$ latent class; e.g., $k = 3$) latent growth trajectories. The aim is to determine to what extent GMM correctly indicates the K latent trajectory classes when the population consists of K unobserved heterogeneous subpopulations, each with its own unique growth trajectory. Peugh and Fan (2012) manipulated design conditions understudied in prior research (C. Enders & Tofighi, 2008; Nylund, Asparouhov, & Muthén, 2007; Tofighi & Enders, 2008) and concluded that the performance of GMM in terms of Type 2 error control was very questionable. Importantly, their simulation did not include covariates; other work found that class enumeration performance of GMM decreases as covariates are added to the model (Tofighi & Enders, 2008).

In evaluations of Type 1 error control in the context of GMM, the underlying population is defined as homogeneous with a single $k = 1$ latent growth trajectory. The goal is to examine the degree to which GMM correctly indicates that there is only a $k = 1$ latent trajectory in the sample (Peugh & Fan, 2012). Groundbreaking work on this issue was conducted by Bauer and Curran (2003a, 2003b). Findings from their simulation showed that nonnormal distributions of growth parameters (i.e., violations of within-class normality assumptions in GMM) can lead to incorrect conclusions about the number and even existence of latent trajectory classes. It is questionable whether trajectory groups that approximate a homogeneous nonnormal distribution can be reliably distinguished from trajectory groups that represent a true mixture of subpopulation distributions (Bauer, 2007; Bauer & Curran, 2003a). If there are substantial departures from normality in a homogeneous distribution, a multiple-latent class ($k > 1$) GMM model will almost always show a better fit than the correct single-group ($k = 1$) model, a problem known as *overextraction* (Bauer & Curran, 2003a, 2003b; see also Greenberg, 2016; Tofighi & Enders, 2008). Other model misspecifications, particularly of within-class correlations among measurement errors, can contribute to the uncovering of spurious latent classes (Bauer, 2007; Bauer & Curran, 2004). The overextraction of latent trajectory classes can adversely affect the estimation of predictor effects; the statistical power of such tests is likely reduced by parsing the total sample into smaller subgroups and spurious class-by-predictor interactions may be detected (Bauer & Curran, 2003a). Excellent summaries of this work, including prominent rebuttals (Cudeck & Henly, 2003; B. Muthén, 2003; Rindskopf, 2003), are available in prior texts (Erosheva et al., 2014; Peugh & Fan, 2012).

The existing controversy should not preclude informed applications of the GMM and SGBTM methodologies (Shiyko et al., 2012). In his *2004 Cattell Award Address*, Bauer (2007) observed that "latent trajectory classes are, in most cases, nothing more than artificial categories rendered from the true continuum of change. . . . I therefore believe that direct applications of GMM should be refrained from unless both the theory and data behind the analysis are uncommonly strong. . . . An alternative place for GMMs in psychological research is as an approximating device in indirect applications" (p. 777, 782). Somewhat relatedly, Greenberg (2016) builds on an earlier paper by Raudenbush (2005) when he advises that criminologists interested in studying the shape of distributions "should avoid assuming at the outset that criminal careers come in clusters. It would seem preferable to begin by recognizing that trajectories being modeled could be continuous, and look for clustering of trajectory parameters estimated under that assumption. If there is no evidence for the existence of discrete groups in a multilevel analysis, then the research might proceed using methods based on continuous distributions" (pp. 32–33). Greenberg's timely paper also reminds us that researchers need not limit themselves to a single statistical technique but should always consider potential alternatives (see also Warren, Luo, Halpern-Manners, Raymo, & Palloni, 2015). This availability of alternative methods implies that the challenge for applied researchers is to substantiate the adequacy and preferability of SGBTM and GMM approximations to a complex continuum of growth trajectories over more parsimonious techniques, such as hierarchical linear models and conventional growth curve modeling (Kreuter & Muthén, 2008a; Sterba et al., 2012).

A handful of simulation studies found that GMMs and SGBTMs with relatively few groups can discretely approximate complex continuous distributions of growth trajectories reasonably well (Brame, Nagin, & Wasserman, 2006; B. Muthén & Asparouhov, 2009; Nagin, 2005; Sterba et al., 2012). On the other hand, the errors in SGBTM approximations to complex continuous distributions have been shown to increase when the sample size is smaller, there are multiple random effects (e.g., random intercept, linear, and quadratic slopes dimensionality versus random intercept-only dimensionality), the random effects are uncorrelated, and/or binary outcome data are analyzed (Sterba et al., 2012). Also, "for the kind of data examined here–which mirrors developmental psychopathology applications–HLM [hierarchical linear modeling] and HGLM [hierarchical generalized linear modeling] performed adequately under a wider variety of circumstances than did SPGM [semiparametric group-based modeling]" (Sterba et al., 2012, p. 628), even in the presence of moderate departures from normality. These findings suggest that SGBTM may not always be the best choice when the objective is to approximate a complex continuous distribution of growth trajectories. That count outcome data, which are common in criminology, were not considered in the Sterba et al. (2012) study is noteworthy.

Other methodological SGBTM and GMM work has concentrated on the refinement of diagnostic tools and approaches for differentiating homogeneous nonnormal distributions from true mixtures of subpopulation distributions. Better scrutinizing of sample distribution properties (e.g., various normality checks, data transformations, Bayesian approaches), additional data, and relevant taxonomic theory may be necessary to distinguish between both possibilities (B. Muthén, 2003; Rindskopf, 2003). Latent class covariates and distal outcomes can aid in substantiating the utility of GMM models (e.g., Bauer & Curran, 2004; B. Muthén, 2003), and a handful of researchers have outlined construct validation approaches to support resultant trajectory classes (e.g., Morin et al., 2011; Petras & Masyn, 2010). Recent developments in skew t-distribution estimation methods (S. Lee & McLachlan, 2014; B. Muthén & Asparouhov, 2015) might offer a useful means to avoid overextraction of trajectory groups in GMM due to nonnormality (Newsom, 2015). C.-P. Wang, Brown, and Bandeen-Roche (2005) proposed ways of examining graphical residual diagnostics for GMM to detect model misspecifications of the growth trajectory parameters, the covariance structure, and the number of latent trajectory classes. Collectively, these methodological developments have opened new avenues for a more refined evaluation of SGBTM and GMM model adequacy in future applied research.

DEPENDENCY ON ANTECEDENTS OR COVARIATES. Third, the idea that trajectory group membership is predicated on a set of developmental risk factors that may be identified through analyses, such as multinomial regression, is not accepted by all scholars. From a conceptual standpoint, the absence of a clear and generally accepted specification of the causal mechanisms that link past events to later outcomes is a major limitation of the approach. Critics of the risk factor research also note that the common use of dichotomization of predictor and outcome variables results in an oversimplification of complex relationships (Case & Haines, 2009). This practice continues to have its defenders (Farrington & Loeber, 2000), even though the statistical literature has demonstrated that dichotomization can attenuate effects and often leads to sharp reductions of statistical power (J. Cohen, 1983; MacCallum, Zhang, Preacher, & Rucker, 2002).

As discussed previously, the inclusion of covariates in SGBTM and GMM analysis poses various challenges and researchers must decide between different modeling strategies, including the pseudo-class draw, single-step modeling, and three-step modeling approaches (e.g., Asparouhov & Muthén, 2014; Bandeen-Roche, Miglioretti, Zeger, &

Rathouz, 1997; Bolck, Croon, & Hagenaars, 2004; Vermunt, 2010; Wang et al., 2005; see also A. Piquero, 2008, on the so-called *classify/analyze* approach). Given that this is an active area of research and statistical software restrictions are a factor in the implementation of approaches, consensus on the preferred modeling strategy for the incorporation of covariates in SGBTM and GMM analysis has not yet emerged. Further complicating the situation, the performance of these approaches may also depend on other design factors. A recent simulation study found that the degree of class separation in GMM differentially impacted the accuracy of covariate effect estimates among four alternative modeling approaches (M. Li & Harring, 2016). Guidance on these decisions is likely forthcoming as the performance of alternative modeling approaches in estimating covariate effects is beginning to be studied across a broader range of real-data analytic GMM situations. For example, M. Li and Harring (2016) focused on time-invariant covariates in their simulation study, which is not very useful for researchers who need information on the performance of these alternative modeling approaches regarding the estimation of time-varying covariate effects. A somewhat related methodological challenge pertains to the potential impact of covariates on the uncovering of latent trajectory classes in SGBTM and GMM.

Just as with other types of latent class analysis, trajectory class membership of individuals in any given study may be affected by the presence of covariates, potentially leading to the uncovering of spurious latent classes, and this may be especially concerning when relations between predictors and trajectory parameters are nonlinear within classes (Bauer & Curran, 2004; Bauer, 2007). Thus, a key question for applied researchers throughout the years has been whether covariates should be included during the class enumeration process in GMM. In an influential simulation, Tofighi and Enders (2008) manipulated the number of repeated measures, sample size, class separation, class proportions, and within-class distribution, and found that the inclusion of covariates hampered correct GMM class enumeration, especially for sample sizes less than 1,000. Additional conditions, including model complexity (e.g., exclusion versus inclusion of within-class predictor effects, differing degrees of class invariance), type of covariate (e.g., active versus inactive, that is, whether a covariate has an impact on the model or no impact), and magnitude of correlation between covariates (e.g., low vs. moderate), have been varied in more recent simulations (Diallo, Morin, & Lu, 2017; L. Li & Hser, 2011). Unfortunately, results cannot always be directly compared across the three simulation studies and conclusions have occasionally been contradictory (see Diallo et al., 2017). Moreover, all recommendations to applied researchers on this issue must be tempered by a healthy dose of caution because they are necessarily restricted to the range of design conditions that have been studied thus far (e.g., time-varying covariates have typically not been considered). Currently, it appears to be advisable to conduct the GMM class enumeration process without covariates (Diallo et al., 2017), although further guidance is likely forthcoming in future years.

Last, overextraction of latent trajectory classes can adversely affect the estimation of predictor effects, including the reduced statistical power of such tests and the detection of spurious class-by-predictor interactions (Bauer & Curran, 2003a) even when the population is truly homogeneous. Our perception is that much of the applied SGBTM and GMM literature has given insufficient attention to this plausible alternative explanation of observed trajectory-specific predictor effects. For all these reasons, Newsom (2015) emphasizes the "need for thoroughly investigating plausible alternative models" (p. 286) in SGBTM and GMM analysis.

ROBUSTNESS OF THE NUMBER, SHAPE, AND GROUP MEMBERSHIP OF TRAJECTORY GROUPS. Other criticism or concerns about the trajectory methodology have focused on the degree to which the number, shape, and group membership of offender trajectory groups are robust across a wide range of methodological conditions, such as the length of follow-up, the age range, the number and spacing of time points, the sample size, the data source, the outcome operationalization, the coding of time versus age, and nonrandom attrition. Given that previous reviews included discussion of such conditions (e.g., Jennings & Reingle, 2012; A. Piquero, 2008; van Dulmen, Goncy, Vest, & Flannery, 2009), this review is not intended to provide an exhaustive coverage of all the available literature. Rather, it is meant to offer a sampling of five key findings, including newer contributions and methodological features that were not, or to a lesser extent, covered in earlier reviews.

As a prelude, it is important to take note of the fact that any SGBTM and GMM analysis can only be conducted post hoc, that is, after the criminal careers of individuals have unfolded. Although retrospective identification and classification of groups have a long tradition in the field of criminology, previous research with the 1945 Philadelphia Birth Cohort cautions that such groups do not always hold up prospectively (Wolfgang, Figlio, & Sellin, 1972), which poses significant challenges for public policy making (see Brame et al., 2012; A. Piquero, 2008). From this point of view, the trajectory methodology is less useful as a pure crime prevention approach, and it is no wonder that questions about the robustness of offender trajectory groups across varying methodological conditions have gained such prominence in the trajectory literature.

First, the *length of follow-up*, that is, the number of years included in statistical analysis, is highly relevant to this discussion. Indeed, the results of SGBTM and GMM analyses are dependent on the length of follow-up, and, related to this point, the results can change when additional follow-up years are added. Farrington, Piquero, and Jennings (2013) examined official convictions from age 10 to 56 for 404 men from the Cambridge Study in Delinquent Development (CSDD) and found that the number and shape of uncovered trajectory groups changed across age 10–16, 10–24, and 10–32 periods but stabilized when follow-ups beyond age 32 were added. In a very influential paper, Eggleston, Laub, and Sampson (2004) used data from the Gluecks' (1950) *Unraveling Juvenile Delinquency* study and analyzed the official crime counts of 500 men from age 7 to 70. A key finding was that trajectory shape and group membership varied with the length of follow-up, but the effect was not equally strong in all groups. Notably, trajectory group membership uncertainty was highest for men who were still engaged in high levels of offending at the end of the given observation period, and the trajectory shape for high-rate chronic offenders changed from approaching the peak age of offending to a declining pattern only from age 40 to 70. Overall, the strongest effects of length of follow-up were found for the most problematic group of high-rate offenders whose criminal career continued to unfold into middle and late adulthood. This result is not unexpected if we recall that "a statistical model is a characterization of collected, not uncollected, data" (Nagin & Tremblay, 2005b, p. 889). If SGBTM and GMM analysis is restricted to assessments up to, let's say age 32, then only data collected up to that point are used in the statistical analysis, and determining the subsequent pattern of crime for individuals whose criminal career has not yet terminated is impossible. In this sense, right-censoring of outcome data makes trajectory analysis results sample dependent.

A second influential methodological factor in trajectory research is what may be termed *data source* (i.e., self-report versus official records crime data). Criminologists have long known that both sources of data provide alternative windows on crime (Farrington, Jolliffe, et al., 2003), each fraught with its own limitations. Official records crime data capture only a small subset of all committed offenses, overrepresent more serious, violent crimes that are more likely to be reported to the authorities, receive a higher focus of police attention, are cleared at higher rates, and may be biased because of police patrolling and attorney and judicial discretion, among other factors. As well, self-report crime measures are affected by a variety of biases, such as memory recall, telescoping, and concealment problems, but capture a larger fraction of the true number of committed offenses (e.g., Ahonen, Loeber, Farrington, Hipwell, & Stepp, 2017; Farrington, Loeber, Stouthamer-Loeber, van Kammen, & Schmidt, 1996; Farrington, Jolliffe, et al., 2003; Federal Bureau of Investigation, 2001; Huizinga & Elliott, 1986; Lauritsen, 1998; Maxfield, Weiler, & Widom, 2000; Tarling & Morris, 2010; Thornberry & Krohn, 2003b). Given this situation, Piquero (2008) reasoned that the greater amount of information (i.e., higher offense frequencies) in self-report data should lead to the identification of more trajectory groups relative to studies with comparatively sparse official records data. Although this conclusion largely bears out in the literature (Jennings & Reingle, 2012; Piquero, 2008), not many longitudinal criminal career studies actually collect both official and self-report data (A. Piquero, Schubert, & Brame, 2014), which is a prerequisite for assessing the convergence of trajectory findings across both data sources for the same sample. Among the exceptions is the Oregon Youth Study data set. Wiesner, Capaldi, and Kim (2007) found three trajectory groups based on officially recorded arrests and six trajectory groups based on self-reported offending for the study men. However, the observation period for this analysis ended in the men's mid-20s, so replication that includes mid- and late adult years is indicated.

Much less attention has been given in the trajectory literature to the mounting evidence that self-reported *onset* of offending typically precedes officially recorded onset of offending by 3 to 5 years (Loeber et al., 2003; Moffitt, Caspi, Rutter, & Silva, 2001; Theobald & Farrington, 2014). Moreover, it has been found that the degree of concordance of self-reported and officially recorded onset of offending is unequal across offense types (concordance is higher for violent crimes than for property crimes) and particularly low for preadolescent offenders; just 16% of them also had official records that reflected preadolescent offending (Payne & Piquero, 2018). The impact of onset variability as a function of data source on the shape/number of trajectory groups is little understood beyond preliminary evidence that the inconsistently found adult-onset offender pathway may be more an artifact of overreliance on official records crime measures (McGee & Farrington, 2010; Payne & Piquero, 2018). Understanding when and why crime does not appear in official records data of individuals is a pressing need for trajectory group research, and we wholeheartedly concur with Payne and Piquero (2018) that "undoubtedly, the accurate measurement of when these trajectories begin is of paramount importance to developmental theory and crime policy" (p. 464).

A third relevant methodological feature in trajectory research is *attrition*. When mapping developmental courses of criminal behavior, attrition can arise for various reasons. In high-risk samples for criminal behavior, death may be a nontrivial source of attrition (Haviland, Jones, & Nagin, 2011). In the classic Gluecks' (1950) study, nearly half of the 500 males who had been incarcerated as juveniles had died by age 70 (Eggleston et al., 2004). Mortality thus becomes an issue for modeling crime trajectories over the life course. Another challenge is periods of criminal inactivity between crime events, commonly referred to as intermittency, which are related to offense seriousness and widen as offenders age (Baker, Metcalfe, & Piquero, 2015). Incarceration or exposure time (A. Piquero et al., 2001) becomes relevant when offenders are incarcerated, or institutionalized for other reasons, and thus without an opportunity to commit crimes in public. Although not extensively studied in SGBTM and GMM research, it has been demonstrated that for official records, crime data that neglect to include information on incarceration or exposure time (to avoid underestimating the level of crime and distorting the trajectory shape) and mortality (to avoid misclassifying zero offense counts resulting from death as desistance from crime) can alter trajectory results, especially among high-rate chronic offenders (Eggleston et al., 2004; A. Piquero et al., 2001; see also Bauer, 2007). It is important to recall that both data problems represent different forms of attrition, or missing data, that are generic challenges to all statistical analysis techniques of longitudinal data on human behavior (Nagin, 2004).

Haviland et al. (2011) proposed a generalization of SGBTM to accommodate *nonrandom* attrition or truncation due to death that varies across trajectory groups (intermittent missing data continue to be treated as missing at random). The intent is to address situations in SGBTM where there is a small trajectory group that is disproportionally prone to attrition (e.g., high-rate chronic offender groups), Analysis of simulation data (attrition was limited to the smaller of two groups) established that estimated trajectory group probabilities may be severely biased by differential attrition rates across groups if these groups are initially not well distinguished, and that estimated trajectory group probabilities will change over the observation window as a result of trajectory group-specific attrition rates. Additional simulation work is indicated that varies other data features (e.g., group sizes). To our knowledge, this extension of SGBTM has hardly been applied to crime data. It should be of great interest to researchers who wish to model crime trajectories up toward the end of the life course where accelerating death rates can be expected.

A fourth methodological aspect that needs to be considered is *coding on time versus age*. In longitudinal research, measurement occasion is often the metric of time, where Time 1 is equivalent to Wave 1, Time 2 to Wave 2, Time 3 to Wave 3, and so forth (for options to code the passage of time in SGBTM, see Nagin & Odgers, 2010b). However, it is not uncommon for longitudinal studies to recruit a cross section of adjacent birth cohorts (also referred to as an accelerated cross-sequential design), such as Grades 7 through 12 at Time 1 in the National Longitudinal Study of Adolescent Health. Lauritsen (1998) argued that ignoring heterogeneity in age within the time of assessment is problematic when modeling changes in offending over time because different individuals might be at different points of their crime trajectory at the first wave of assessment. Alternative metrics of time might be superior in such situations compared to modeling the passage of time based on measurement occasion (Bollen & Curran, 2006; Mehta & West, 2000). That is, researchers must then decide whether to model trajectories of offending based on the time of assessment or on the age at assessment. As noted by Bollen and Curran (2006), the latter approach often introduces another source of missing data for a given application. It is worthy to mention that some foundations for this modeling decision were developed within the conventional growth curve modeling literature (e.g., analysis of accelerated longitudinal designs; see S. Duncan & Duncan, 2012).

Although coding by the age at assessment has been used in SGBTM and GMM applications with such data sets (e.g., Windle, Mun, & Windle, 2005), a systematic investigation of the sensitivity of trajectory results to this modeling decision is almost nonexistent. We are aware of only one study that focused on this issue. For self-report offense variety counts, A. Piquero, Monahan, Glasheen, Schubert, and Mulvey (2012) examined SGBTM result concordance across both time metrics among male serious juvenile offenders from the Pathways to Desistance study. Coding by the time of assessment captured a 7-year period and the age at assessment, ages 14 to 25. Five trajectory groups were extracted with each metric, with exposure time taken into account, which differed in function and form between both time metrics. Trajectory group concordance across both time metrics was strong at high and low levels of offending variety but more limited between both ends of the spectrum. Last, there was high consistency in the covariates of trajectory groups across time metrics, although the magnitude of relations varied. These findings need to be replicated with a broader range of birth cohorts. Participants in the A. Piquero, Monahan, et al. (2012) study were 14 to 18 years old at baseline and, thus, might not have been different enough in terms of their locations on the age–crime curve at the start of the study. Replication is also indicated with population samples that might capture a larger share of less serious offenses and with official records data to study other methodological dimensions that are potentially confounded with this coding decision. Of course, the risk with age-based coding is that historical or other intervening processes that affect the underlying longitudinal growth patterns are not adequately reflected.

A fifth methodological dimension that needs to be considered is the sensitivity of trajectory results to *sample size*. Frankfurt, Frazier, Syed, and Jung (2016) surmised in a recent overview that the literature on procedures for assessing statistical power of SGBTM and GMM analyses is underdeveloped and lacks clear guidance for applied researchers on best practices for determining sufficient sample sizes. For SGBTM, a limited number of studies (D'Unger, Land, McCall, & Nagin, 1998; Sampson, Laub, & Eggleston, 2004) suggest that the number of extracted trajectory groups stabilizes beyond a minimum sample size of 200 to 500 individuals. In a simulation, Loughran and Nagin (2006) found good performance of a Poisson-based SGBTM in terms of its ability to estimate the group trajectories and mixing probabilities, even with sample sizes as small as 500. It is worthy to mention that they used a real data set of arrest histories of more than 13,000 individuals as their surrogate population for the simulation. Also, the authors caution that their findings may not generalize to situations where the trajectory groups are not well separated (e.g., as indexed by mediocre average posterior probabilities of group membership). For GMM, a handful of simulation studies have suggested that many real-life applications are likely underpowered, especially for samples sizes of fewer than 1,000 when covariates are included, which increases model complexity (e.g., Tofighi & Enders, 2008). In summary, our understanding of the sensitivity of trajectory results to sample size remains incomplete, and this is a critical issue that needs to be studied further in methodological work.

Notwithstanding the ongoing debate in the extant literature of these sorts of issues, the study of criminal trajectories remains an important approach to model and understand patterns of change and continuity in offending from a more person-oriented perspective. After all, Nagin (2016) continues to remind us that many of these controversies are not unique to SGBTM and GMM, mindful of Baumol's (1992) succinct observations nearly 30 years ago: "A well-designed model is, after all, a judiciously chosen set of lies, or perhaps more accurately put, partial truths about reality, which have been chosen so as to permit us to reason more effectively about some issues than we otherwise could. The model must be an oversimplification if it is to be tractable analytically. Optimality in model construction must be based on the trade-off between these two desiderata–accuracy of representation of reality and usability in analysis" (p. 55). Yet, we must not lose sight of the fact that accuracy is as much a function of the design of the data that are brought to bear on a particular problem as the statistical methodology that is used to analyze the data (Manski, 2007; Rubin, 2008).

Conclusion

This chapter has provided a backdrop for all substantive chapters of this book by synthesizing the main controversies and criticisms of the SGBTM and GMM methodology. As we have seen, many of the debates and criticisms are intertwined, although they have drawn differing levels of attention in the various scientific disciplines. In addition, innovative remedies for certain limitations of the trajectory methodology are increasingly being developed, including more refined model diagnostics, bootstrap approaches to address model selection uncertainty, cross-validation error index, and strategies for assessing the preferability of SGBTM and GMM over more parsimonious, conventional growth curve modeling techniques. The technical details of these proposed remedies differ among methodological frameworks and statistical software programs. Areas in need of further methodological research were also identified. The next chapter discusses major developmental models of crime.

Suggested Supplemental Readings

Authoritative papers from Bauer and colleagues (e.g., Bauer, 2007; Bauer & Curran, 2003a, 2003b, 2004) discuss potential pitfalls of GMM, such as conditions that contribute to the detection of spurious trajectory groups and spurious class-by-predictor interactions that had a huge impact on the evolution of best practices in the application of the trajectory methodology. Eggleston et al. (2004) raised awareness of the sensitivity of trajectory findings to factors such as the length of follow-up, incarceration, and mortality. Several papers provide helpful background on the limitations of the Bayesian Information Criterion and other information-based criteria during the process of class enumeration in trajectory modeling and lay the grounds for proposed remedies (e.g., Lubke et al., 2017; Nielsen et al., 2014; Preacher & Merkle, 2012). Last, important opinion pieces on SGBTM and GMM approaches were contributed by Brame et al. (2012), Erosheva et al. (2014), and Skardhamar (2010), while others forecast more refined future approaches to judging the adequacy and preferability of the SGBTM and GMM methodology (e.g., Diallo et al., 2017; Greenberg, 2016; Sterba et al., 2012).

4

Developmental and Life-Course Models of Crime

Two premises of this book are that criminal behavior is the product of developmental processes and that process models are essential for understanding crime in a developmental context. Theory plays a critical role in the articulation and evaluation of process models. Theory provides a road map for the steps that compose the process model. Theory also provides an outline of the relevant variables of the model and the purported direction of effects, in a sense, ordering the expected trail from risk factors to outcomes. Finally, theory also provides an explanation of the underlying causal mechanisms that link risk factors to outcomes. In the 1990s, developmental and life-course theories of crime have ascended as a major research paradigm. Since then, it has been argued by some scholars that the existing theories of crime needed to become age-graded (e.g., Cullen, 2011). However, it is not always clear to criminologists what a "developmental perspective" really is about, as illustrated in this excerpt from Sampson and Laub (2005c):

> In our view, however, a key misunderstood issue concerns the very meaning of development in developmental criminology. Lewontin has stated that "... the term *development* is a metaphor that carries with it a prior commitment to the nature of the process" (2000:5, emphasis in the original). Using the analogy of a photographic image, Lewontin argues that the way the term development is used is a process that makes the latent image apparent. This seems to be what developmental criminological theory is all about. For example, in Moffitt's theory of crime, the environment offers a "set of enabling conditions" that allow individual traits to express themselves. Although reciprocal interactions with the environment are allowed, life-course persistent offenders and adolescent-limited offenders follow a pre-programmed line of development in a crucial respect–an unwinding, an unfolding, or an unrolling of what is fundamentally "already there." The view of development as a predetermined unfolding is

linked to a typological understanding of the world–different internal programs will have different outcomes for individuals of a different type. As
Lewontin writes, "If the development of an individual is the unfolding
of a genetic program immanent in the fertilized egg, then variations in
the outcome of development must be consequences of variations in that
program" (2000:17). Debates about development in the social sciences
are not new. . . . Some developmentalists recognize social interactions,
but in the end most embrace a between-individual focus that emphasizes
the primacy of early childhood attributes that are presumed to be stable.
In our theory of crime, development is better conceived as the constant
interaction between individuals and their environment, coupled with
purposeful human agency and "random developmental noise." (p. 178)

Although we do not agree with the reductionist definition from
Sampson and Laub (2005c) of what a "developmental perspective" is all
about, the issues that they raise are fundamental to the objectives of this
chapter on developmental models of crime. Without a good understanding of what a "developmental perspective" entails among the leading life-
span developmental psychologists of our time, criminologists will fall
short in incorporating core developmental concepts in the explanation
of different developmental trajectories of criminal behavior.

This chapter expands material covered previously to provide a
theoretical backdrop for the substantive criminal trajectory literature
discussed in this book. It emphasizes theoretical models that aim to articulate the *processes* linking past events to future outcomes. The chapter
begins with an overview of major developmental and life-course theories of crime, including Moffitt's (1993, 1997) dual taxonomy theory of
antisocial behavior, Patterson's (1993, 1996; Patterson & Yoerger, 1993,
1997) coercion theory, Thornberry's (1987; Thornberry & Krohn, 2001,
2005) interactional theory, and Sampson and Laub's (Laub & Sampson,
1993, 2003; Sampson & Laub, 1993, 1997) age-graded theory of informal
social control. This section seeks to makes the point that major developmental and life-course theories of crime do not only limit themselves
to considering just early childhood attributes but also articulate predictions about the role of developmental successes and failures, age-graded
influences, and interactions between individual and environment in
the explanation of criminal behavior across the life span, although each

to a differing degree and in its own manner. The second section of the chapter summarizes the central tenets of contemporary developmental science. As we will see, early risk-factor and reductionist conceptualizations of human development have been replaced by dynamic developmental systems frameworks that emphasize dynamic transactions between multilayered, age-graded individual and contextual systems across the life span. We argue that these frameworks hold great promise to enrich criminological theorizing (e.g., on human agency).

Developmental and Life-Course Models of Offending

As stated previously, developmental and life-course theories of crime became prominent during the 1990s. The key reasons for the emergence of these theories, including changes in funding priorities of major U.S. funding agencies and a reevaluation of the merits of longitudinal panel research in criminology, are outlined by McGee and Farrington (2016). Since then, the British psychologist and criminologist David Farrington and his colleagues have been at the forefront of attempts to integrate developmental and life-course theories of offending. These efforts are highlighted in the 2002 Sutherland address (Farrington, 2003), the edited volume *Integrated Developmental & Life-Course Theories of Offending* (Farrington, 2005a), and the chapter "Building Developmental and Life-Course Theories of Offending" (Farrington, 2008). Building on this body of work, Farrington and Ttofi (2015) asserted that "developmental and life-course criminology (DLC) . . . is concerned mainly with three topics: (a) the development of offending and antisocial behavior from the womb to the tomb; (b) the influence of risk factors and protective factors at different ages; and (c) the effects of life events on the course of development" (p. 19). They note that more traditional criminological theories primarily sought to explain *between-individual differences* in offending, for example, as a function of individual levels of low self-control (Gottfredson & Hirschi, 1990). Developmental and life-course theories, in contrast, strive to explain *within-individual changes* in offending over time. Thus, developmental and life-course theories require the use of longitudinal individual-level data. Additionally, any developmental and life-course theory of offending must be able to explain 10 widely accepted conclusions about the development

TABLE 4.1. Ten Conclusions About the Development of Crime That Developmental and Life-Course Theories Must Explain

1. The prevalence of offending peaks in the late teenage years (i.e., between ages 15–19).

2. The peak onset age of offending is between 8 and 14; the peak age of desistance from offending is between 20 and 29.

3. Early onset age of offending is associated with longer criminal career duration and higher number of committed offenses.

4. Fairly high stability in the rank ordering of offenders across time (between-individual stability) does not preclude within-individual change in prevalence/rate of offending. There is also intergenerational transmission of criminal activity.

5. A small fraction of the population commits a disproportionally large fraction of all crimes.

6. Offending is versatile rather than specialized (but specialization increases with age).

7. Offenders often engage in multiple types of antisocial behavior (e.g., crime, heavy drinking, reckless driving, sexual promiscuity, bullying, truancy).

8. Co-offending predominates up to the late teenage years, whereas lone offending is more common from age 20 onward.

9. Offending up to the late teenage years is motivated by multiple reasons (e.g., utilitarian, excitement/enjoyment, anger); utilitarian motives become dominant from age 20 onward.

10. There is increasing diversification of offending up to age 20 (i.e., different offense types are initiated at distinctively different ages); after age 20, diversification decreases and specialization increases.

Note: Based on Farrington and Loeber (2013).

of individual criminal behavior that are shown in Table 4.1 (based on Farrington & Loeber, 2013). A comparison of how major developmental and life-course theories of offending address these core empirical and theoretical issues was undertaken by Farrington (2008).

Before we describe the essential features of four influential developmental and life-course theories, we note that life-course and developmental theories of crime are built on different preexisting frameworks. Laub and Sampson (1993) played a key role in introducing life-course theory to criminologists by integrating concepts from Glen Elder's life-course model of human development (Elder, 1974, 1998b) with elements of Hirschi's (1969) social control theory. Hereby, the life course is defined as "pathways through the age-differentiated life-span" (Elder, 1985b, p. 17). A central contention is that the quality of adolescent and adult social bonds, which are the basis for the exercise of informal social control, explains criminal behavior above and beyond the effects of early-life criminal propensity (e.g., childhood low self-control) and that age-graded changes in social bonds explain changes in crime (e.g., desistance), whereas continuity or persistence in crime across time mostly results from accumulated negative consequences of prior criminal behavior, such as school failure and incarceration (Laub & Sampson, 1993, 2003; Sampson & Laub, 1993, 1997). In short, life-course approaches are rooted in sociological research traditions and emphasize "variability and exogenous [social context] influences on the course of development over time that cannot be predicted by focusing solely on enduring individual traits (population heterogeneity) or even past experiences (state dependence)" (Laub & Sampson, 2003, p. 34).

Developmental theories of crime are mostly built on psychological life-span research traditions and seek to examine the development and dynamics of offending over time to identify risk factors that precede or co-occur with developmental patterns of offending and its associated deviant behaviors and to study processes that account for such linkages and temporal variations in offending across the life span. Apart from these general aims, the features of these theories are somewhat loosely defined (Benson, 2002), reflecting the fact that they encompass a fairly heterogeneous group of scholars who adopted specific developmental concepts (for examples, see Thornberry, 1997). Nevertheless, developmental theories of crime may be characterized by the following notions (Farrington, 2005a; Thornberry, 1997): (a) a strong focus on within-person variation in offending across the life span and the processes that account for intra-individual continuity and change across time; (b) the notion that offending may evolve in an orderly progression across the life span, with less serious precursors already occurring in childhood, thus stressing the need to broaden the studied age range (to include individuals' childhood years) in criminological research and to observe issues related to heterotypic and homotypic continuity; (c) the recognition that adaptive and maladaptive behavior is a function of multifactorial influences, which may themselves undergo change over time, and whose effects may be age- and time-dependent (e.g., factors linked to onset may not be linked to desistance) and result in the same or different outcomes across different persons; (d) an appreciation that developmental courses of offending are embedded in several ecological contexts and that these context factors, as well as person factors, jointly explain continuity and change of offending across the life span; and (e) the awareness that differing etiological models may be required to explain multiple distinctive offender pathways. In sum, while the commonalities with life-course approaches to crime are self-evident, developmental theories of crime tend to place a stronger emphasis than do life-course theories on biopsychosocial risk factor models of offending, thereby partially neglecting macro-societal and structural factors. In addition, multiple pathway models of offending occupy a more prominent role among developmental theories of crime.

Next, we introduce four influential developmental and life-course theories that aim to articulate the *processes* linking past events to future outcomes and represent a spectrum of theoretical arguments often encountered in group-based trajectory research on offending. Our presentation focuses on the essential features of these developmental and life-course theories that are relevant for the purposes of this book. Each of these theories is evolving in the sense that its versions differ slightly across different sources as its originators refined their propositions on consideration of study findings. Several other developmental and life-course theories of crime are not discussed due to space limitations but described in previous overviews (e.g., Farrington & Ttofi, 2015; McGee & Farrington, 2016). These include developmental and life-course theories from Catalano and Hawkins (1996; Catalano et al., 2005), Farrington (2005c), Lahey and Waldman (2003, 2005), Le Blanc (1997, 2005), Loeber and colleagues (1993; Loeber, Slot, & Stouthamer-Loeber, 2008), and Wikström (2005).

Developmental Taxonomy of Antisocial Behavior (Terrie Moffitt)

Moffitt (1993) proposed a widely referenced developmental taxonomy of antisocial behavior that distinguishes two qualitatively different groups of offenders, termed life-course-persistent (LCP) and adolescence-limited (AL) offenders, in addition to a group of nonoffenders. The offender groups are distinguished in terms of etiological factors, types of offenses in which each engages, onset age and length of criminal career, and adult outcomes. Moffitt's dual taxonomy implies that LCP and AL offenders differ in kind rather than in degree. LCP offenders, composing about 5% of the population, are posited to initiate offending at an early age, commit a broad range of offenses at a high rate, and persist in being criminally active through adulthood. The much larger AL offender group is hypothesized to initiate offending later in adolescence, exhibit a limited criminal career duration characterized by less versatility and severity in the types of committed offenses, and desist from offending by early adulthood.

Moffitt (1993, 1997) further postulated group-specific causal mechanisms to explain the offending trajectories of both groups. AL offenders are posited to experience relatively normal development until adolescence. The primary impetus for AL offending is contact with delinquent peers during the adolescent years whose antisocial lifestyle is mimicked by AL offenders to gain adult status and power. The subjective experience of a "maturity gap," that is, of being physically developed enough to look like adults but socially not allowed the rights and freedoms of adults, motivates AL offenders to commit relatively minor status and property offenses that resemble adultlike behaviors and freedoms, such as rule-breaking behavior, petty theft, and substance use. AL offenders are expected to "naturally" desist from offending when they reach adulthood, in which opportunities for postsecondary education and job prospects become available, and realize the societal penalties for continued engagement in crime.

In contrast to AL offenders, propensity factors play a prominent role for the LCP group. Specifically, childhood individual risks, such as difficult temperament, low impulse control, poor neurological functioning, and impaired cognitive abilities, interact with disadvantaged family environments, such as low socioeconomic status, poor parental mental health, parental criminality or drug abuse, and inept parenting, in a manner that leads to childhood onset of antisocial behavior. The crime repertoire of LCP offenders is varied and consistent across contexts, rather than specialized, and includes violent offenses. Their criminal careers are expected to last through the adult years because of myriad adverse consequences of early offending that limit future environmental options in multiple domains of life (referred to as *snares* or *cumulative consequences*) and the stability of their early individual characteristics that are carried forward into later periods of life in which they cause proximal adverse effects (referred to as *contemporary consequences*).

LCP offenders thus become ensnared in a criminal lifestyle and a life-long, persistent pattern of criminality.

Moffitt (2006a) conducted a systematic review of 10 years of research on her theory and concluded that, although many predictions of the taxonomy enjoyed support, additional offender groups needed to be considered, particularly low-level chronic offenders (posited to approximate LCP offenders in terms of being undercontrolled, with family adversity, parental psychopathology, and low intelligence) and adult-onset offenders (whose true existence she questioned). In a recent update, Moffitt (2018) called for testing polygenic scores as LCP-specific risk factors and raised the possibility that "a normative brain maturity gap" (p. 182) contributes to AL offending. Independent reviews concluded that the original taxonomy needed extension to match accumulating findings (DeLisi & Piquero, 2011), that the average ages of onset of offending behavior were similar for LCP and AL groups (Jolliffe, Farrington, Piquero, MacLeod, & van der Weijer, 2017), and that the differences between AL and LCP groups were much more quantitative than qualitative in nature (Assink et al., 2015; Fairchild, van Goozen, Calder, & Goodyer, 2013; Jolliffe, Farrington, Piquero, Loeber, & Hill, 2017; Skardhamar, 2009).

The Coercion Model (Gerald Patterson)

Patterson's coercion model draws on behavioral principles of conditioned learning, modeling, and contingent reinforcements to explain the mechanisms linking past events to future outcomes. Criminal behavior and its early precursors "are conceptualized as complex outcomes of a history of reinforcing exchanges with the immediate social environment. This process starts within the family context but takes place in several stages and settings across the life course. The most important mechanism for learning antisocial behavior within the family context is hypothesized to be negative reinforcement, wherein a young child learns to use aversive responses (termed 'coercive behaviors') to terminate the aversive behaviors of parents and siblings" (Wiesner, Capaldi, & Patterson, 2003, pp. 317–318). These coercive interaction styles are later reinforced within the peer group. Patterson (1993) coined the term "chimera effect" to refer to the orderly progression of relatively minor forms of antisocial behavior toward more severe forms across the life span. Patterson further proposed two offender groups in addition to a nonoffender group (Patterson, 1996; Patterson & Yoerger, 1993, 1997; Wiesner et al., 2003). In contrast to Moffitt (1993), Patterson's model is based on a linear gradation hypothesis. This means the posited offender and nonoffender groups are rank-ordered in levels of childhood risks that "represent variations on the same underlying theme" (Patterson & Yoerger, 2002, p. 155). Several differences between the two offender groups were posited regarding the age of onset, the length of criminal career, and the associated developmental processes.

The more severe offender trajectory group, labeled *early-onset offenders*, resembles earlier depictions of unsocialized aggressors and reflects a mix of temperamental risk and coercive parenting in childhood. Specifically, early-onset offenders become involved in early antisocial behaviors because of failed early childhood socialization. Poor parenting practices (e.g., displayed by antisocial parents) foster coercive interaction styles among family members through which children acquire a large repertoire of antisocial behaviors. This pattern of interaction is especially likely to happen for children with a difficult temperament. Failure to develop prosocial skills leads to rejection by conventional peers, followed by early involvement with deviant peers who are the driving force for rapid growth and escalation of covert antisocial behaviors toward an early arrest before age 14. Early starters are at high risk for chronic offending and continuation of criminal careers during the adult years because of their generalized coercive interaction styles, accumulated secondary problems and developmental failures (e.g., academic failure, substance abuse, incarceration), and continued engagement in high-risk contexts, sometimes because of active selection processes and, at other times, because of restricted environmental options (e.g., intimate relationships with antisocial partners, affiliation with delinquent peers in adulthood).

The less severe offender trajectory group, termed *late-onset offenders*, is hypothesized to begin delinquent behavior only in adolescence and to desist on entering the early adult years. Late-onset offenders experience marginally poor parenting behaviors (less than do early starters but more than do nonoffenders) and thus acquire a more limited repertoire of antisocial behaviors as well as average prosocial skills (hence, they have also been labeled "marginal offenders"). Late-onset offending primarily results from close association and interaction with deviant peers in the adolescent years because of disrupted parental supervision. They are more likely than early-onset offenders to turn away from criminal behavior as early adulthood approaches because of the experience of age-graded environmental discontinuities (e.g., establishment of a relationship with a prosocial romantic partner, starting a family of procreation), aided by their better developed prosocial skills and fewer accumulated negative consequences of prior offending.

Reid, Patterson, and Snyder (2002) provide a comprehensive account of the coercion model and its application for intervention purposes. Key predictions regarding the role of poor parenting practices, early antisocial behavior, and deviant peers were supported for the most part in empirical research (e.g., Dishion, Patterson, & Kavanagh, 1992; Dishion, Spracklen, Andrews, & Patterson, 1996; Patterson & Yoerger, 1999; Simons, Johnson, Conger, & Elder, 1998; Simons, Wu, Conger, & Lorenz, 1994). Capaldi and colleagues advanced the coercion model by delineating the processes hypothesized to account for persistence and desistance in crime during adulthood (Capaldi & Wiesner, 2009; Wiesner et al., 2003) and anchoring it within a broader and more integrative Dynamic Developmental Systems perspective (Capaldi. Kerr, Eddy, & Tiberio, 2016; Capaldi, Shortt, & Kim, 2005; Capaldi & Wiesner, 2009).

Interactional Theory (Terence Thornberry and Marvin Krohn)

Interactional theory, first introduced by Thornberry (1987) and extended by Thornberry and Krohn (2001, 2005), integrates concepts from interactional theory, social network theory, and Elder's (1974, 1998b) life-course theory to explain continuity and change in a broad spectrum of antisocial behaviors over time (Thornberry, Lizotte, Krohn, Smith, & Porter, 2003). It is based on the following three premises (Thornberry & Krohn, 2005). First, antisocial behavior follows a behavioral trajectory that unfolds over the life course, characterized by its onset, duration, and termination. Its causes vary systematically with individuals' developmental stages. Prior states and behaviors, successes or failures with which preceding developmental stages are negotiated, and opportunities that are opened and closed to individuals as a consequence of their behavior are causally related to later states and behaviors. Second, antisocial behavior and its causes are involved in mutually reinforcing causal loops across the individual's life course. This premise is a very distinctive feature of their interactional theory. In addition, antisocial behavior emerges from complex interactional processes between the individual and its immediate environment that vary by social structural factors (e.g., social class, race/ethnicity, and neighborhood). Third, the multiple causal forces of antisocial behavior vary considerably across individuals. As the magnitude of these causal forces increases, the individual's engagement in criminal activity becomes both more likely and increases in severity.

The authors do not distinguish distinctive types of offenders (Thornberry, Lizotte, et al., 2003) but suggest that the causes of antisocial behavior vary depending on the age of onset (Thornberry & Krohn, 2005). In the preschool years (birth to age 6), early manifestations of antisocial behavior emerge from the confluence of structural adversity (e.g., welfare dependency, disorganized neighborhood, poverty), ineffective parenting (e.g., low affective ties, physical punishment, inconsistent discipline), and the child's difficult temperament and neuropsychological deficits (e.g., poor emotion regulation, impulsiveness, greater fearlessness to noxious stimuli). Children who start early are more likely to continue engagement in antisocial behavior over time because of (a) the persistence of structural adversity, ineffective parenting, and difficult temperament and neuropsychological deficits and (b) the reciprocal consequences of their earlier antisocial behavior. In contrast, neuropsychological deficits are believed to be less prominent in children who initiate antisocial behavior at older ages. In childhood (at ages 6–12), neighborhood and family factors are most important for the initiation of antisocial behavior, whereas school and peer factors predominate in adolescence (at ages 12–18). Interestingly, late starters who initiate antisocial behavior in early adulthood (at ages 18–25) are posited to exhibit cognitive deficits (e.g., poor school performance, low IQ) that were buffered at earlier ages by a supportive family and school environment but diminish their chances for successful transitions into adult roles (e.g., employment, marriage). Compared to adolescent onsetters, late starters are expected to show more continuity in antisocial behavior over time because of their stronger cognitive deficits. Thornberry (2009) further extended this interactional theory to account for intergenerational continuity and discontinuity in antisocial behavior.

Age-Graded Theory of Informal Social Control
(Robert Sampson and John Laub)

Sampson and Laub proposed an expanded age-graded theory of informal social control (Laub & Sampson, 1993, 2003; Sampson & Laub, 1993, 1997) that combines core tenets of Elder's life-course model of human development (Elder, 1974, 1998b) and Hirschi's (1969) social control theory. Specifically, the life course is conceptualized as the "sequence of culturally defined age-graded roles and social transitions that are enacted over time" (Caspi, Elder, & Herbener, 1990, p. 15). It is further argued that "the important institutions of both formal and informal social control vary across the life span" (Sampson & Laub, 1997, p. 142). Age-graded informal social control, as indexed by the strength of social bonds to family, peers, schools, and adult institutions such as marriage and employment, is emphasized as a crucial crime-inhibiting factor. Conversely, offending is postulated to be more likely when an individual's social bonds are weak or broken.

The strength of social bonds depends on attachments to institutions of informal social control and parental socialization processes. Structural background factors (e.g., social class, broken families) and enduring individual differences (e.g., low intelligence, early conduct problems, difficult temperament) are presumed to exert indirect influences on crime through their effects on informal social control. A central contention of the theory is that stable individual characteristics (population heterogeneity) and past experiences (state dependence) are not sufficient for predicting individual criminal behavior over the life course (Laub & Sampson, 2003). Rather, the quality of age-graded informal social bonds in adolescence and adulthood is critical for understanding criminal behavior above and beyond the effects of early propensity factors. Thereby, age-graded changes in social bonds are important for the explanation of changes in offending (e.g., desistance from crime is linked to adult life events or turning points, such as marriage and stable employment, that help "knifing off" offenders from prior criminogenic social contexts), whereas continuity and persistence in crime is traced back to manifold negative consequences of prior offending that undermine later bonds of social control (e.g., incarceration, official labeling because of criminal justice contact), also referred to as processes of "cumulative disadvantage" (Laub & Sampson, 1993; Sampson & Laub, 1993, 1997, 2005c).

On one hand, the age-graded theory of informal social control may be viewed as a general theory of crime because the notion of distinctive offender types, such as life-course-persistent offenders, is explicitly rejected by the authors (e.g., Sampson & Laub, 2005c, 2009). On the other hand, the theory emphasizes the importance of dynamic factors (i.e., within-individual changes in age-graded informal social control) in the explanation of offending over the life course, which stands in marked contrast to static (i.e., between-individual) explanations offered by more traditional general theories of crime (e.g., Gottfredson & Hirschi, 1990). Static viewpoints assert that continuity in offending over the life course results from population heterogeneity in an underlying propensity toward criminal behavior that is established early in life and stable across the life course. Such "ontogenetic" (Dannefer, 1984) conceptualizations of human development were strongly debunked by Sampson and Laub (1997) for the explanation of offending over the life course.

In more recent articulations of their theory, Sampson and Laub (e.g., 2005a, 2005c) especially highlighted the role of "human agency," the purposeful execution of choice and individual will, in the decision to desist from criminal activity. They go on to note that "at a meta-theoretical level, our long-term follow-up data direct us to insist that a focus purely on institutional, or structural, turning points and opportunities is incomplete, for such opportunities are mediated by perceptions and human decision-making . . . the data make clear that agency is a crucial ingredient in causation and thus will be a first-order challenge for future work in life-course criminology" (Sampson & Laub, 2005c, p. 177).

In the next section, we describe the core tenets of a metamodel that undergirds the leading theories of human development of our time. As we will see, developmental science has a rich tradition of theorizing about the role of human agency and intentional self-regulation across the life course, including Brandtstädter's action theory of human development (e.g., Brandtstädter, 1998, 1999, 2006) and Baltes's Selection, Optimization, and Compensation (SOC) theory (e.g., Baltes & Baltes, 1990; Freund & Baltes, 2002). Most developmental scientists would subscribe to some form of systems approach that bridges multiple levels (P. Marshall, 2013).

Contemporary Developmental Science: The Relational Developmental Systems Metamodel (Richard Lerner and Willis Overton)

As mentioned previously, Sampson and Laub (2005c) observed that the meaning of the term *development* is not always clear and subject to continuing debate. They went on to assert that "developmentalists tend to believe that childhood and adolescent risk characteristics are what really matter–hence the rise of the 'early risk-factor' paradigm" (Sampson & Laub, 2005c, p. 179). We disagree with their characterization of modern developmental theories as being preoccupied with childhood and adolescent risk factors. In fact, our reading of the literature is that such conceptualizations of human development—as well as *reductionist (psychogenic or biogenic*; Lerner, Agans, DeSouza, & Hershberg, 2014, p. 256; see also Lerner, Hershberg, Hilliard, & Johnson, 2015; Overton, 2015) approaches—have fallen out of favor with developmental scientists. The leading theories of human development of our time are fundamentally different from the earlier reductionist approaches (Capaldi et al., 2016) in that they take longer term developmental perspectives, focus on intraindividual and interindividual change over time, regard mutually influential *person <-> context relations* across time as the primary unit of analysis, emphasize the role of human agency in ecological context and relative *plasticity* (the potential for systematic change) in development across the life span, and use more dynamic and theoretically integrative process models that include the potential for adaptive developmental regulations between individuals and ecological contexts. This paradigm shift in developmental science is astutely described by Lerner and colleagues (2015):

> Developmental science seeks to describe, explain, and optimize intraindividual (within-person) change and interindividual (between-person) differences in intraindividual change across the life span. . . . However, the meaning of the term *development* continues to engage scholars in philosophical and theoretical debate. . . . Past concepts of development were predicated on Cartesian philosophical ideas about the character of reality that separated, or "split," what was regarded as real from what was relegated to the derivative, "unreal," or epiphenomenal. . . . Major instances of

such splitting involved classic debates about nature versus nurture as "the" source of development, continuity versus discontinuity as an appropriate depiction of the character of the human (intraindividual) developmental trajectory, transformational versus variational change as the quality of developmental change, and stability versus instability as an adequate means to describe interindividual differences in developmental change. Today, most major developmental theories eschew such splits, and instead use concepts drawn from a process-related paradigm . . . and, in turn, from [relational developmental systems] RDS-based theories/models associated with this paradigm. . . . Compared to a Cartesian worldview, the process-relational paradigm focuses on process, becoming, holism, relational analysis, and the use of multiple perspectives and multiple explanatory forms. Within the process-relational paradigm, the organism is seen as inherently active, self-creating (autopoietic), self-organizing, self-regulating (agentic), nonlinear/complex, and adaptive. . . . Within the RDS metamodel, the integration of different levels of organization frames understanding of life-span human development. . . . The conceptual emphasis in RDS theories is placed on mutually influential relations between individuals and contexts, represented as individual <-> context relations. These relations vary across place and across time. . . . History is the broadest level within the ecology of human development and imbues all other levels with change. Such change may be stochastic (e.g., non-normative life or historical events) . . . or systematic, and the potential for systematic change constitutes a potential for (at least relative) plasticity across the life span. . . . Accordingly, framed by such conceptions, contemporary developmental science regards the basic process of development as involving the above-noted individual <-> context relations, which engage variables among levels of organization ranging from biology through individual and social functioning to societal, cultural, physical, ecological, and, ultimately, historical levels of organization. (pp. 3–4, emphasis in original)

The relational developmental systems metamodel represents the dominant paradigm in contemporary developmental science and its core tenets are summarized in Table 4.2. Detailed descriptions of the relational developmental systems metamodel are provided in prior work (Lerner et al., 2015; Overton, 2015). Its perhaps most distinctive feature for our

TABLE 4.2. Defining Features of the Relational Developmental Systems Metamodel

Relational Metatheory

Predicated on a philosophical perspective that transcends Cartesian dualism and atomism, theories derived from the relational developmental systems metamodel are framed by a process-relational paradigm for human development. This focus includes an emphasis on process and a rejection of all splits between components of the ecology of human development (e.g., between nature- and nurture-based variables, between continuity and discontinuity, and between stability and instability). Holistic syntheses replace dichotomies as well as reductionist partitions of the developing relational system through the integration of three relational moments of analysis: the identity of opposites, the opposites of identity, and the syntheses of wholes. Driving from the relational metatheory, relational developmental systems posit the organism as an inherently active, self-creating, self-organizing, and self-regulating nonlinear complex adaptive system, which develops through embodied activities and actions, as they coact with a lived world of physical and sociocultural objects.

The Integration of Levels of Organization

Relational thinking with the rejection of Cartesian splits is associated with the idea that all levels of organization within the ecology of human development are integrated, or fused. These levels range from the biological and physiological through the cultural and historical.

Developmental Regulation across Ontogeny Involves Mutually Influential Individual <-> Context Relations

As a consequence of the integration of levels, the regulation of development occurs through mutually influential connections across all levels of the developing relational system, ranging from genes and cell physiology through individual mental and behavioral functioning to society, culture, the designed and natural ecology and, ultimately, history. These mutually influential relations may be represented generically as Level 1 <-> Level 2 (e.g., Family <-> Community), and in the case of ontogeny may be represented as individual <-> context.

Integrated Actions, Individual <-> Context Relations, Are the Basic Unit of Analysis Within Human Development

The character of developmental regulation means that the integration of actions–of the individual on the context and of the multiple levels of the context on the individual (individual <-> context)–constitutes the fundamental unit of analysis in the study of the basic process of human development.

Temporality and Plasticity in Human Development

As a consequence of the fusion of the historical level of analysis–and therefore temporality–in the levels of organization comprising the ecology of human development, the developing relational system is characterized by the potential for systematic change, plasticity. Observed trajectories of intraindividual change may vary across time and place as a consequence of such plasticity.

Relative Plasticity

Developmental regulation may both facilitate and constrain opportunities for change. Thus, change in individual <-> context relations is not limitless, and the magnitude of plasticity (the probability of change in a developmental trajectory occurring in relation to variation in contextual conditions) may vary across the life span and history. Nevertheless, the potential for plasticity at both individual and contextual levels constitutes a fundamental strength of all human development.

(continued)

TABLE 4.2. Defining Features of the Relational Developmental Systems Metamodel (*continued*)

Intraindividual Change, Interindividual Differences in Intraindividual Change, and the Fundamental Substantive Significance of Diversity

The combinations of variables across the integrated levels of organization within the developmental system that provide the basis of the developmental process will vary at least in part across individuals and groups. This diversity is systematic and lawfully produced by idiographic, group differential and generic (nomothetic) phenomena. The range of interindividual differences in intraindividual change observed at any point in time is evidence of the plasticity of the developmental system and makes the study of diversity of fundamental substantive significance for the description, explanation, and optimization of human development.

Interdisciplinarity and the Need for Change-Sensitive Methodologies

The integrated levels of organization composing the developmental system require collaborative analyses by scholars from multiple disciplines. Interdisciplinary knowledge is a central goal. The temporal embeddedness and resulting plasticity of the developmental system require that research designs, methods of observation and measurement, and procedures for data analysis be change- and process-sensitive and able to integrate trajectories of change at multiple levels of analysis.

Optimism, the Application of Developmental Science, and the Promotion of Positive Human Development

The potential for and instantiations of plasticity legitimates an optimistic and proactive search for characteristics of individuals and of their ecologies that, together, can be arrayed to promote positive human development across life. Through the application of developmental science in planned attempts (interventions) to enhance (e.g., through social policies or community-based programs) the character of humans' developmental trajectories, the promotion of positive human development may be achieved by aligning the strengths of individuals (operationalized as the potentials for positive change) and contexts.

Source: Lerner et al. (2015, pp. 17–18, Table 1.1). Reprinted with permission from Taylor & Francis. Reformatted to fit within the page margins of this book.

purposes is that developmental systems are hypothesized to comprise multilayered, age-graded individual and contextual systems (e.g., biological, psychological, social, cultural-historical) that interact with each other across the life span and are integrated into a synthetic coactional system that is subject to change over time. In other words, the process of development is "conceptualized as the functioning of, and transactions across and within, biological, psychological, and social systems, with constant feedback and interaction over time" (Capaldi & Wiesner, 2009, p. 376). An example of such transactions and constant feedback and interaction over time is presented in Capaldi and Eddy (2005) in relation to the development of delinquent behavior that may continue into adulthood. During the childhood years, the focus of their model is on the reciprocal interactions of the characteristics of the developing child, such as temperament risk, including irritability and impulsivity, with the child's immediate social environment (e.g., parenting and peer association in the family and peer domains, respectively). These transactions occur within, and are affected by, larger contextual factors affecting the family (e.g., parental divorce, household income).

The use of the concepts *coaction* or *transaction* is not accidental but, rather, is meant to reflect the bidirectionality and mutual influences of the agentic individual on its contexts and of the multilayered contexts on the individual across the life span. The relational developmental systems metamodel is thus inherently dynamic in nature and explicitly rejects the notion that the developmental system as a whole can be neatly partitioned into additive individual and contextual components; rather, they are *fused*, closely intertwined with each other and interdependent, and jointly drive development across the life span. Because of this coalescence of individual and contextual systems, the term *interaction* is used only when referring to statistical interactions within the general linear model or quotes from other sources (Lerner et al., 2015). The intuitive appeal of the relational developmental systems metamodel is, at least to some degree, offset by the challenge of matching theory and analytical methodology, although dynamic systems and person-oriented approaches have gained more visibility in recent years (e.g., Granic & Hollenstein, 2006; Granic & Patterson, 2006; Hollenstein, 2011; P. Marshall, 2013; Sterba & Bauer, 2010).

In general, Lerner and colleagues (2015) argue that most leading theories of human development can be subsumed under the relational developmental systems metamodel, although there are differences in emphasis or focus. These theories include Lerner's developmental contextualism (e.g., Ford & Lerner, 1992; Lerner, 2002, 2004), Baltes's life-span developmental theory (e.g., Baltes 1987; Baltes & Baltes, 1990: Baltes, Lindenberger, & Staudinger, 2006; Freund & Baltes, 2002), Brandtstädter's action theory of human development (e.g., Brandtstädter, 1998, 1999, 2006), Elder's life-course theory (e.g., Elder, 1998b; Elder & Shanahan, 2006), Bronfenbrenner's bioecological model (e.g., Bronfenbrenner, 1979, 2005), and Magnusson's holistic person-context interaction theory (e.g., Magnusson 1995, 1999; Magnusson & Stattin, 2006). As mentioned previously, developmental science has a rich tradition of theorizing about the role of human agency and intentional self-regulation across the life course and offers protocols for testing these propositions (e.g., in experimental research). Developmental and life-course theories of crime can learn much from considering these strands of work. First and foremost, the SOC theory from Baltes (e.g., Baltes & Baltes, 1990; Freund & Baltes, 2002) stands as one of these important works, as we will see later.

Brandtstädter's action theory of human development (e.g., Brandtstädter, 1998, 1999, 2006) also has much to offer to developmental and life-course theories of crime. Although criminologists increasingly emphasize the important role of human agency (e.g., Sampson & Laub, 2005c), the construct often remains abstract and vaguely defined (Paternoster, 2017). The identity theory of desistance from crime (Paternoster & Bushway, 2009) represents an important exception in criminological theorizing but has been criticized for several reasons, including lacking a life-course perspective, envisioning the construct of human agency as being unmeasurable, and limiting itself to a rational choice theory perspective (Cullen, 2017). We submit that Brandtstädter's action theory has great potential for enriching criminological theorizing on human agency so that a broader view on these issues can evolve. First, it adopts a life-course perspective and emphasizes the individual's intentional self-development through regulatory actions that shape his or her behavior and development over the life span. Brandtstädter (1998) stated that "through action, and through experiencing the consequences of our actions, we construe representations of ourselves and of our material, social, and symbolic environments, and these representations guide and motivate activities by which we shape and influence our behavior and personal development" (p. 807). Put differently, actions serve as the means through which individuals influence their ecological contexts and, based on the feedback that results from their actions, organize their ideas about their ecological contexts and themselves and form intentions and goals for their future actions. At the same time, Brandtstädter's action theory recognizes that there are limits in the individual's developmental goals that can be actualized because of individual and contextual constraints on plasticity over the life span.

Action theory–guided research on intentional self-development over the life span thus focuses on three areas: "(1) the development of intentional action in general, and of cognitive and representational processes related to intentionality; (2) the formation of beliefs and competencies related to personal control over development; and (3) the development of the self (or self-concept) as a more or less coherent structure of self-referential values, beliefs, and standards that guides and directs self-regulatory processes" (Brandtstädter, 2006, p. 545). As such, Brandtstädter's action theory offers detailed theorizing and testable process models on various dimensions of intentional self-development through self-regulatory actions across the life span. In this sense, it provides a firm foundation on which developmental and life-course theories of crime can build on for developing more fine-grained notions of the construct and role of human agency.

Second, Brandtstädter's action theory offers measurement protocols for testing hypotheses about the means and effects of intentional self-development (e.g., concrete strategies that are used by individuals to overcome barriers and cope with constraints that they cannot overcome, respectively). For example, these protocols have been applied to examine how individuals negotiate age-related performance deficits in various domains of functioning (e.g., Rothermund & Brandtstädter, 2003). We submit that these protocols could be adapted for the purposes of criminological trajectory research. For example, having a history of contacts with the criminal justice system can block some opportunities for securing legal employment and lead to job instability (e.g., Sampson & Laub, 1993, 1997; Stoll & Bushway, 2008; Wiesner, Capaldi, & Kim, 2010), which, in turn, increases the risk of subsequent adult offending (e.g., Sampson & Laub, 1990). The agentic actions undertaken by offender trajectory groups to negotiate these barriers could be studied using Brandtstädter's measurement protocols and action theory as an organizing framework. This proposition dovetails nicely with Cullen (2017), who advocated for embracing a cognitive psychological approach to incorporating the role of human agency in criminological theorizing:

> A more promising strategy, I believe, would be to mirror the field of cognitive psychology by developing the field of *cognitive criminology*. Under this umbrella, the goal would be to map how offenders think and, in particular, to study which cognitions encourage and which prevent the choice of crime. These investigations could include, . . . theories of desistance, the decision making of active street and white-collar offenders, perceived certainty and severity of punishment, criminogenic thinking

errors and their amenability to rehabilitation, and how age-graded cognitions are involved in criminal development. (p. 378, emphasis in original)

Third, Brandtstädter's action theory includes a dual-process model of assimilative and accommodative coping, according to which

> attempts to avoid or diminish actual or anticipated losses by instrumental, self-corrective, and compensatory activities constitute an *assimilative* mode of coping. . . . *accommodative* processes involve a devaluation of, or disengagement from, blocked goals and a lowering of personal performance standards and aspirations. . . . Assimilative efforts should dominate as long as people feel able to actively change the situation or to enact sufficient compensatory or self-regulatory interventions; accommodative processes, by contrast, should become dominant when action-outcome expectancies have been eroded through repeated unsuccessful attempts to change the situation. (Rothermund & Brandtstädter, 2003, pp. 896–897, emphasis in original)

Again, we contend that these already existing process models provide a firm foundation that developmental and life-course theories of crime can build on to develop a more fine-grained lens with which to view the means and role of human agency in offender trajectory research. Many aspects of this dual-process model of coping have obvious similarities to Baltes's tripartite SOC theory (see Haase, Heckhausen, & Wrosch, 2013).

Conclusion

This chapter has described the core features of four influential developmental and life-course theories of crime. Collectively, these theories do not limit themselves to considering just early childhood attributes but, additionally, factor in the role of developmental successes and failures, age-graded influences, and interactions between individual and environment in the explanation of criminal behavior across the life course. An emergent theme in these theories is the need to more explicitly account for the role of human agency. Next, central tenets of modern developmental science were summarized. It was argued that older reductionist and early-risk-factor models of human development have been replaced by a relational developmental systems metamodel that emphasizes mutually influential dynamic transactions between multilayered, age-graded individual and contextual systems across the life span, holism, relative plasticity, temporality, and human agency. Examples of specific theories of human development were mentioned that have the potential to enrich criminological theorizing on human agency over the life course. The next chapter presents and synthesizes the results of studies on the number, shape, and nature of criminal trajectories.

Suggested Supplemental Readings

The edited volume from Morizot and Kazemian (2015) provides an excellent overview of emergent topics related to the field of developmental criminology, including developmental theories of offending (Farrington & Ttofi, 2015). Major developmental and life-course theories of offending are portrayed in the edited volume from Farrington (2005a). A detailed comparison of many of these theories is undertaken in Farrington (2008). Overton (2015) and Lerner et al. (2015) explicate how the life-course and life-span approaches from Elder and Baltes, along with other leading frameworks of human development, may be subsumed under a developmental systems theory metamodel that has become the dominant paradigm in contemporary developmental psychology. The article from Haase et al. (2013) offers a concise synthesis of three leading theories of developmental regulation across the life span, including Brandtstädter's action theory and Baltes's tripartite SOC theory. Outstanding rationales for matching developmental theory, method, and model are presented by Collins (2006) and Ram and Grimm (2007). Key design issues in developmental research are covered in Hartmann, Abbott, and Pelzel (2015). Excellent primers on the collection of data across the life span are available from major longitudinal studies of antisocial behaviors (e.g., Capaldi, Chamberlain, Fetrow, & Wilson, 1997; Stouthamer-Loeber, 2012; Stouthamer-Loeber & van Kammen, 1995). These practical considerations for carrying out long-term studies are rarely described but critical for testing developmental theories of crime and human behavior within well-designed studies.

5

Findings on the Number and Shape of Criminal Trajectories

In the introduction to his book *Group-Based Modeling of Development*, Nagin (2005) stated that investigating and charting the progression and causes of behavioral, biological, and physical phenomena over time represent some of "the most fundamental and empirically important research topics in the social and behavioral sciences and medicine" (p. 1). Nagin went on to make the point that most phenomena studied from a longitudinal perspective are not likely to unfold as a single growth trajectory; rather, individual differences within a population allow "for the possibility that there are meaningful subgroups that follow distinctive developmental trajectories" (2005, p. 1). This position is consistent with the second premise of this book, that offenders compose a heterogeneous population and that this heterogeneity extends to longitudinal patterns of offending behavior. For example, it is widely recognized that the age–crime curve, which describes the rapid increase in criminal behavior through adolescence, followed by a peak in late adolescence and a steady decline into adulthood, obscures variability in longitudinal growth patterns (Tahamont, Yan, Bushway, & Liu, 2015). This variability is reflected in differences in the shape, peak age, and length of the trajectories.

As noted previously, the aim of group-based trajectory modeling is to capture this heterogeneity and identify multiple growth trajectories from the individual profiles of the longitudinal data. The resulting latent classes are homogeneous within trajectories and heterogeneous across trajectories. Whether the different classes identified by trajectory analysis constitute distinct typologies of offenders, as in a taxonomy (e.g., Moffitt, 1993), or are dimensional in nature, differing by degree rather than kind (Walters, 2012), is a controversial topic that awaits further research (Walters, 2015). More work is needed to validate and clearly define the offender types derived from trajectory analyses to determine if they hold up to theoretical and empirical scrutiny as distinct groups

(Brame, Paternoster, & Piquero, 2012; Raudenbush, 2001). This type of research is important because trajectory groups are products of the data analyses and, as such, are statistical "approximations of a more complex reality" (Nagin, 2016, p. 365). In this sense, trajectories are useful as *descriptive* entities that provide summaries of the individual profiles composing the data set at hand. A next step in this line of investigation is to *explain* the observed patterns of behavior through theory and research (Mulvey, 2014).

This chapter presents the results of selected studies on criminal trajectories with the aim of highlighting the heterogeneity within general populations and several offender subpopulations. It describes and synthesizes the results in terms of the number of trajectory groups derived; their shape, peak, length, size (i.e., the proportion of individuals assigned to each class based on the highest posterior probability); and the crime mix and offers insights into the reasons for the variability across studies along these dimensions. The chapter thus contributes a state-of-the-art overview of what is known about criminal trajectories and what this work tells us about the nature and pattern of offending over time within and across individuals.

The chapter extends previous reviews by A. Piquero (2008) and Jennings and Reingle (2012) and includes findings from the general offender trajectory literature as well as from trajectory studies on several subpopulations, specifically, female offenders and sex offenders. As well, to highlight the range of topics to which group-based trajectory modeling has been applied within a criminology context, we selected three novel topic areas in which trajectory analysis has been used. These topics are (a) risk to reoffend, based on risk assessments (Hochstetler, Peters, & DeLisi, 2016); (b) code-of-the-streets beliefs (Moule, Burt, Stewart, & Simons, 2015); and (c) cross-national acts of terrorism (LaFree, Morris, & Dugan, 2010). The chapter concludes with an examination of the monetary costs associated with criminal trajectory groups, that is, the financial burden to society.

Given the focus of this book on criminal behavior, we do not present findings pertaining to externalizing behavior in childhood, including aggression and bullying, although there is a rich literature on these topics (e.g., see Nagin & Tremblay, 1999, 2001; Pepler, Jiang, Craig, & Connolly, 2008; Reijntjes et al., 2013). Indeed, some of the early, foundational studies on trajectory analysis by Daniel Nagin and Richard Tremblay concerned aggressive behavior in children. Also, this review is not meant as an exhaustive coverage of all the available studies. Rather it is meant to provide a sampling of the trajectory research on offenders and subpopulations of offenders, including topics that have not been covered in earlier reviews.

Criminal Trajectories of General Populations

Previous reviews of the criminal trajectory literature were conducted by A. Piquero (2004a, 2008) and Jennings and Reingle (2012). Reflecting the growth in trajectory modeling research, the number of studies included in these reviews increased from about 50 in 2004 (A. Piquero, 2004a) to 80 in 2008 (A. Piquero, 2008) to 105 in 2012 (Jennings & Reingle, 2012), and the progression shows no signs of slowing (Erosheva, Matsueda, & Telesca, 2014). Across studies, the data sources vary widely, from teacher-reported behavior (Broidy et al., 2003) to self-reported offending (Fergusson & Horwood, 2002), arrests and police contacts (D'Unger, Land, & McCall, 2002), and official records of convictions (Roeder, Lynch, & Nagin, 1999). The follow-up period generally extends from adolescence to the mid- to late 20s or 30s. Two studies followed-up offenders through their 70s (Blokland, Nagin, & Nieuwbeerta, 2005; Laub & Sampson, 2003) and one study up to age 56 (Farrington, Piquero, & Jennings, 2013).

In terms of the number of trajectory groups identified across studies, the figure ranges from two (e.g., Yessine & Bonta, 2009) to seven (e.g., Jennings, Maldonado-Molina, & Komro, 2010), with four being the modal number (Jennings & Reingle, 2012; A. Piquero, 2008). Generally, differences in the number of groups may be the result of methodological factors, such as sample size (larger samples yield more groups), sample characteristics (female samples yield fewer groups), and type of data used (self-reports yield more groups than official records; for further discussion see van Dulmen, Goncy, Vest, & Flannery, 2009). Commonly identified trajectory groups include high-rate, moderate-rate, low-rate, and nonoffender groups; early and late starters; early and late desisters; and adolescent-peaking and adult-peaking pathways. The five trajectory groups (and their size) of the Cambridge Study in Delinquent Development (CSDD) to age 40 are illustrative of the overall findings:

(1) nonoffenders (62.3%), (2) low-adolescence-peaked offenders (18.6%), (3) very low-rate chronic offenders (11.3%), (4) low-adolescence-peaked offenders (5.4%), and (5) high-rate chronic offenders (2.5%; A. Piquero, Farrington, et al., 2007).

The reader is reminded at this point that such group labels are meant as heuristic devices used to highlight key features of each extracted trajectory, such as its shape, peak age, and length. Indeed, L. Brennan and Shaw (2013) noted that the application of a label is subjective and arbitrary. For example, the terms *chronic* and *persistent* are both used to label a trajectory that extends the length of the follow-up period (and above the zero point), which can differ across studies, rendering the term specific to the given study. The same concern applies to the use of the label "desister." Brennan and Shaw also noted that there is no standard metric for the rate of antisocial behavior (or whatever the dependent variable is). Therefore, terms such as *high rate, moderate rate,* and *low rate* must be taken as relative, making it difficult to compare levels of offending across studies. Nonetheless, we will continue to use these terms and take their meaning at face value as they are applied in the trajectory literature.

Studies that have used community (rather than known offender) samples tend to identify a nonoffender group, which often comprises the majority of individuals in the sample (e.g., A. Piquero, Farrington, et al., 2007). Studies with offender samples typically identify a low-rate (e.g., near-zero) trajectory group, which often constitutes the largest group in the sample. For example, Bersani, Nieuwbeerta, and Laub (2009) found that 70% of the offenders in their sample fell into the lowest rate group (referred to as sporadic offenders). In addition to identifying a nonoffender or low-rate group, at the other end of the trajectory group spectrum is the high-rate trajectory group that shows persistence in offending. These high-rate chronic offenders (as they are typically labeled) generally constitute between 3% and 10% of the sample, irrespective of sample characteristics, but account for a disproportionate amount of the crimes committed by the sample. For example, A. Piquero, Farrington, et al. (2007) found that the high-chronic group from the CSDD composed only 2.5% of the sample but accounted for 20% of all convictions. Likewise, Day et al. (2012) found that their high-late group made up only 3.9% of the sample but were responsible for 15.8% of the unique court contacts. We will pick up this issue later when we examine the monetary costs associated with criminal trajectory groups.

Some studies have examined the crime mix of offense trajectories. The crime mix is an important consideration as it allows researchers to clarify the relationship among some of the defining features of the criminal career, such as the rate, type, and severity of offending (A. Piquero, Sullivan, et al., 2010) and, in the case of trajectory analysis, the *rate* of offending and the *type* of offenses committed. For example, the rate of offending may become *conflated* with the type of offender, such that high-rate chronic offenders are seen, perforce, as serious, violent offenders.

In brief, studies have found that individuals following a high-rate trajectory (i.e., assigned by the highest posterior probability) commit more nonviolent (e.g., theft, vandalism, burglary) than violent (e.g., assault, weapons, robbery) offenses. Likewise, individuals following a low-rate trajectory tend to commit more violent than nonviolent offenses (MacDonald, Haviland, & Morral, 2009; A. Piquero, Brame, Mazerolle, & Haapanen, 2002; A. Piquero, Sullivan, et al., 2010). For example, Blokland et al. (2005) examined the crime mix for five offense trajectories generated for a sample of 5,164 serious offenders from the Netherlands. They found that 70% of the convictions incurred by individuals on the high-rate-persistent trajectory were for nonviolent crimes and 11.9% were for violent crimes. By contrast, 53.6% of the convictions incurred by individuals on the low-rate-desister trajectory were for nonviolent crimes and 19.1% were for violent crimes. This result is consistent with the finding that offenders following a low-rate trajectory also tend to follow a low-variety offending trajectory (Monahan & Piquero, 2009), suggesting that they are more specialists than generalists. Monahan and Piquero also found that, although not as strong an effect, the same pattern held for individuals following a high-rate trajectory, who tended to follow a high-variety trajectory.

To summarize the findings on general populations, Blokland and Nieuwbeerta (2010) identified four key conclusions of the trajectory research in their review of the literature. First, there is evidence of considerable heterogeneity in the age–crime curves within the population of offenders, with trajectories differing in the age of onset, the peak age of offending, and the rates of ascendance and descendance. Second, desistance appears to be the rule rather than the exception. Indeed, A. Piquero

(2008) noted that it was not uncommon for all trajectory groups to show substantial declines in offending by the mid-30s. However, lower-rate trajectories tend to peak at an earlier age, and higher-rate chronic trajectories tend to peak at a later age, typically in the mid-30s. Predictors of desistance include good marriages in adulthood (Laub & Sampson, 2003). Third, most studies yield trajectories with a sharp peak of offending, approximating the age–crime curve. Many also find one or more chronic offense trajectories that manifest steady rates of offending over the follow-up period (at high, moderate, or low levels). Fourth, most studies identify trajectories not predicted by developmental theories of crime (e.g., Moffitt, 1993), including a low-level chronic (e.g., A. Piquero, Farrington, et al., 2007) and adult onset (F. Andersson & Levander, 2013) pattern, although the latter group may be an artifact of official records crime measures.

Further work is needed to identify and clarify the defining characteristics of each criminal trajectory to gain a clearer, more nuanced picture of what they mean, without being too reductionistic. Second, future investigations could tease apart other dimensions of the criminal career concept than those discussed earlier, including the age of onset and the length of trajectory, with offending frequency, seriousness, and type. Too little attention has been paid to providing such descriptive information about trajectory groups. Perhaps, at a minimum, researchers could routinely include a table on the frequency severity and types of offenses committed for each group.

Last, more research is needed to better understand the factors associated with the maintenance of the different trajectories once initiated. For example, it has been suggested that low- and moderate-rate persistent offenders may experience alcohol and drug use problems that keep them in a cycle of criminal activity (Laub & Sampson, 2003; Monahan & Piquero, 2009; A. Piquero, Sullivan, et al., 2010; A. Ward et al., 2010). These offenders represent an interesting and particularly challenging subgroup for the justice system, largely because of their persistence in offending. While not committing offenses at a high rate, these individuals appear to be holding firm to their active involvement in a criminal lifestyle. This effect may be the result of being "stuck" in a situation from which they cannot easily extricate themselves, perhaps because of the presence of such psychosocial problems as substance use and abuse, a low level of social support, and maladaptive coping rather than a hardened commitment to a criminal lifestyle (A. Ward et al., 2010). As such, this group may be a prime target for treatment interventions and rehabilitation programming by the justice system. However, this is a hypothesis in need of further investigation. The next section examines the criminal trajectory research on female offenders and sex offenders. Examining this literature allows us to delve deeper into the heterogeneity of offending trajectories within the heterogeneity of the offender population.

Criminal Trajectories of Offender Subpopulations

FEMALE SAMPLES. Much of the research on criminal trajectories has been conducted with male samples. In an effort to close the gender gap, a growing body of research on the longitudinal patterns of criminal activity among females has emerged over the past 15 years. Questions about the heterogeneity in their offense trajectories and proximity to the conventional (male) age–crime have framed the handful of studies conducted since the early 2000s. This is not to say that the study of offending behavior in girls and women has been neglected in the criminology literature (Hoyt & Scherer, 1998; Hubbard & Pratt, 2002), only that it has not been given the same attention as offending in boys and men (Steffensmeier & Allan, 1996). This paucity of research may be because of the lower levels in the rate, severity, and prevalence of offending among women, compared to men, and, hence, the lower social, personal, and financial impacts on society (Fontaine, Carbonneau, Vitaro, Barker, & Tremblay, 2009). At the same time, questions about potential gender differences in delinquent trajectories and the issue of gender-specific (vs. gender-neutral) theories that account for onset, course, and desistance from crime remain important considerations (L. Brennan & Shaw, 2013). From a life-course perspective, understanding the unique trajectories that characterize female offending also may lead to different approaches for early intervention and prevention approaches (Belknap & Holsinger, 2006).

Two contrasting theories on the developmental pathways to offending for girls and women have gained prominence in the literature. Based on a review of the research, Silverthorn and Frick (1999) concluded that the onset of antisocial behavior in girls tends to occur in adolescence because of biological changes and changes in the social environment. Moreover, those who do exhibit antisocial behavior also experience difficulties into adulthood, including alcohol addiction, arrests, psychiatric problems, and unstable employment. As a result, Silverthorn and Frick have put forth the argument that a single pathway, which they labeled the delayed-onset pathway, sufficiently accounts for the course of offending in females. Importantly, they posited that the same developmental risk factors seen in boys who follow the life-course-persistent (LCP) pathway of Moffitt's (1993) dual taxonomy model are also present in girls on the delayed-onset pathway. By contrast, Moffitt (1994, 2006b; Moffitt, Caspi, Rutter, & Silva, 2001) claimed that the dual taxonomy model (Moffitt, 1993) accounts for the onset and course of offending equally well in females as for males. Generally, within the trajectory literature, greater support has been found for the dual pathway model than the single pathway model (El Sayed, Piquero, & TenEyck, 2017; Fontaine et al., 2009).

Four points emerge from the trajectory research on female offenders. First, a review of the literature finds that, like the research with male offenders, there is considerable variability in the methodologies used in the studies. These pertain to four elements: (a) the nature of the samples, which include community (F. Andersson, Levander, Svensson, & Levander, 2012; Fergusson & Horwood, 2002; Murphy, Brecht, Huang, & Herbeck, 2012; Reingle, Jennings, & Maldonado-Molina, 2011), at-risk (S. Miller, Malone, Dodge, & Conduct Problem Prevention Research Group, 2010; Molero, Larsson, Tengström, & Eklund, 2015; Prendergrast, Huang, Evans, & Hser, 2010), and offender samples (Cauffman, Monahan, & Thomas, 2015; Jennings, 2011); (b) developmental ages periods covered, including adolescence only (S. Miller et al., 2010), childhood into adolescence (Jennings, Maldonado-Molina, & Komro, 2010; Odgers et al., 2008), childhood into adulthood (D'Unger et al., 2002), and adolescence into adulthood (Blokland & van Os, 2010; Molero et al., 2015; Murphy et al., 2012); (c) data sources, including self-report (Ahonen, Jennings, Loeber, & Farrington, 2016; F. Andersson et al., 2012; Miller et al., 2010; Murphy et al., 2012) and official records (Blokland & van Os, 2010; Molero et al., 2015; Prendergrast et al., 2010); and (d) follow-up lengths, which range from 3 years (Jennings, Maldonado-Molina, Piquero, et al., 2010) to 60 years (Blokland & van Os, 2010). As a result, drawing general conclusions from this research may be misleading and may obscure essential differences in the longitudinal nature and pattern of the offense trajectories. Also, whereas some studies used exclusively female samples (Ahonen et al., 2016), others used mixed-gender samples and compared findings for males and females (F. Andersson et al., 2012; D'Unger et al., 2002; Fergusson & Horwood, 2002; Molero et al., 2015; Murphy et al., 2012). Nonetheless, as A. Piquero (2008) noted in reference to the broader criminal trajectory literature, synthesizing the research with this caveat in mind is a valuable starting point to understand the longitudinal offending patterns of girls and women. Second, across studies, the number of trajectory groups identified ranges from two (Molero et al., 2105) to seven (Jennings, Maldonado-Molina, & Komro, 2010), with most studies identifying three or four. This finding is inconsistent with both Silverthorn and Frick's (1999) and Moffitt's (1994) theories.

Third, overall, the research finds support for both similarities and differences in comparisons of trajectories from male and female samples. Studies that have used mixed gender samples have found considerable similarities in the number, shape, and relative size of the resulting trajectories (e.g., Cauffman et al., 2015; S. Miller et al., 2010; Odgers et al., 2008; Prendergast et al., 2010), including identification of a high-rate chronic offense group. For example, Fergusson and Horwood (2002) identified four trajectory groups for each of the male and female subgroups in their New Zealand sample. These groups were labeled (with the size in parentheses) low-risk offenders (41.0% and 71.0% for male and females, respectively), early-onset adolescence-limited offenders (14.7% and 21.0% for male and females, respectively), intermediate-onset adolescence-limited offenders (10.3% and 3.7% for male and females, respectively), late-onset adolescence-limited offenders (24.9% and 2.4% for male and females, respectively), and chronic offenders (9.4% and 2.1% for male and females, respectively). Likewise, Murphy et al. (2012) found four comparable groups for the male and female subsamples in their study. The groups were labeled high (12.1% and 10.0% for male and females, respectively), decreased (25.2% and 21.6% for male and females, respectively), moderate (13.5% and 16.6% for male and females, respectively), and low (49.2% and 51.7% for male and females, respectively). In both these studies, the largest groups were the low-rate trajectories, and the smallest groups were the high-rate-chronic trajectories. Moreover, compared to males, females were more likely to be represented in the low-rate groups and less likely to be represented in the high-rate groups.

Fourth, in spite of these similarities, some studies have found differences in the number and shape of the trajectories for male and female samples (F. Andersson et al., 2012; D'Unger et al., 2002; Jennings, 2011; Loeber, Jennings, Ahonen, Piquero, & Farrington, 2017). For instance, D'Unger et al. (2002) used arrest data from the second Philadelphia Cohort Study (Tracy, Wolfgang, & Figlio, 1990), which covered the period from ages 8 to 26. Their trajectory results yielded five groups for the male subsample ($n = 1,000$) and three groups for the female subsample ($n = 3,000$). The male trajectory groups were labeled nonoffenders (60.8%), low-rate adolescence-peaked offenders (8.6%), high-rate adolescence-peaked offenders (1.0%), low-rate chronic offenders (21.3%), and high-rate chronic offenders (8.3%). The female trajectories were labeled nonoffenders (84.4%), low-rate adolescence-peaked offenders (10.4%), and high-rate adolescence-peaked offenders (5.3%). In their analyses of a Swedish cohort, F. Andersson et al. (2012) found three overlapping offense trajectories: nonoffenders (66.7% and 93.0% for males and females, respectively), low-rate desisters (27.0% and 4.5% for males and females, respectively), and high-rate chronic offenders (1.8% and 0.5% for males and females, respectively) and two trajectories that were unique to males and females. The trajectories unique to males were labeled low-level chronic (2.5%) and high adolescence peaked (1.9%), and the trajectories unique to females were labeled early-onset desisters (1.2%) and adult-onset offenders (0.8%).

To summarize, two general conclusions could be drawn from the literature about criminal trajectories and gender. First, compared to their male counterparts, females are more likely to be assigned to the nonoffender, low-rate, and early-onset adolescence-limited groups and less likely to be assigned to the high-rate and chronic/persistent groups. Second, female offenders tend to peak earlier than males and show lower levels of offending across all ages. These differences highlight the importance of performing separate trajectory analyses for male and female samples. Further work is needed to unpack the gender-specific trajectories to identify their similarities and differences with respect to predictors, correlates (e.g., crime mix), and outcomes. Because neither of the current theories maps well onto the empirical findings, these results could be related to theoretical formulations for further validation and refinement.

SEX OFFENDERS. Since McMillan, Hastings, Salter, and Skuse (2008) recommended the use of trajectory analysis to study sex offending, a handful of researchers have taken up their challenge. This small body of work has essentially addressed two questions: (a) Do sex offenders compose a homogeneous population (Freiburger, Marcum, Iannacchione, & Higgins, 2012; Ronis & Borduin, 2013; Tewksbury & Jennings, 2010), and (b) do sex offenders specialize in their preferred offense type, or do they fit into a broader syndrome of antisociality; that is, are they generalists (Lussier, 2005)?

Tewksbury, Jennings, and Zgoba (2012) addressed the former question, applying trajectory analysis in a unique way to test the impact of Sex Offender Registration and Notification (SORN) on sexual recidivism. Using official records over an 8-year period, they examined the sex offending trajectories in two matched samples of sex offenders in New Jersey, one released prior to the implementation of SORN ($N = 250$) and one released after the implementation of SORN ($N = 250$). Their results yielded two similar trajectory groups for both samples, which they labeled low risk (82.3% and 79.5% for the pre-SORN and post-SORN samples, respectively) and high risk (17.7% and 20.5% for the pre-SORN and post-SORN samples, respectively). Note that risk label refers to the risk of recidivism and relates to the estimated rate of offending over time for each trajectory group. Follow-up analyses indicated that more rapists and offenders with female and stranger victims were represented in the high-risk trajectory and that more child molesters were represented in the low-risk trajectory. Also, the authors concluded that SORN did *not* reduce the rate of sexual offender recidivism, a conclusion they also came to in two companion studies (Jennings, Zgoba, & Tewksbury, 2012; Tewksbury & Jennings, 2010).

Freiburger et al. (2012) addressed the diversity question in a sample of 500 sex offenders. They used police arrests for a sex offense between the ages of 19 and 33 as the dependent variable. Their trajectory analyses yielded three groups, referred to simply as Group 1 (18.0%), Group 2 (12.4%), and Group 3 (67.7%). Group 1 comprised individuals who began offending at around age 24 and were at low risk to reoffend sexually. Group 2 comprised individuals who peaked between the ages of 23 and

28 and desisted to age 33; they were identified as most likely to be one-time offenders. Group 3, the largest group, comprised individuals who began offending at age 23 and remained constant to age 33. They were the most likely to recidivate in other ways, that is, to be career criminal generalists (i.e., versatile offenders) rather than specialists. Based on these two studies, it can be reasonably concluded that, compared to general offender populations, there is only a modicum of diversity in the longitudinal offending patterns for sex offenders, particularly among those who specialize in sexual offending.

The finding that sex offenders who are at highest risk to recidivate are also most likely to be generalists (and persistent offenders) is consistent with several other findings in the literature. It is consistent with the observation that, contrary to popular belief, sex offenders, as a group, tend to have a lower rate of recidivism than other types of offenders (Sample & Bray, 2006), in the range of 11% to 19% (Hanson, Bourgon, Helmus, & Hodgson, 2009). It is also consistent with research on the relationship between sex offending and criminal trajectories based on general offense data. For example, Lussier, Tzoumakis, Cale, and Amirault (2010) examined trajectories of general criminal offending among a sample of 250 federally imprisoned sex offenders in British Columbia, Canada. The criminal data were derived from two sources: (a) self-reports collected during individual interviews, which covered the age period of 12 to 18 and (b) official records, which covered the age period of 19 to 35. Their trajectory analysis results yielded four groups, labeled very low-rate offenders (56%), low-rate desisters (26%), late bloomers (10%), and high-rate chronic offenders (8%). Further analyses revealed that, although the frequency of sex offenses did not differ across the four trajectory groups, the high-rate chronic offenders were more versatile in their sexual offending, and those in the low-rate group were the least versatile in sexual crimes (i.e., were the most specialized). Versatility in sexual offending included sexual assault, threatening sexual assault, sexual murder, incest, and indecent public acts. These results accord with Ronis and Borduin (2013), who also found that the prevalence of sex offenders across four general offending trajectories did not differ. In other words, sex offenders may be generalists who differ both in their rate of offending over time, like general offenders, and in the versatility of their sex offenses—some are more versatile, while others are more specialized.

In summary, on one hand, sex offenders, as a group, tend to be quite heterogeneous with respect to such characteristics as victim preferences (e.g., age, sex, relationship to offender) and type of offenses committed (e.g., exhibitionism, assault, sexual touching; Tewksbury et al., 2012). On the other hand, they tend to be more homogeneous in terms of their longitudinal patterns of recidivism, with only two or three classes identified in this small literature. By comparison, this number is the same or smaller than the number of trajectory classes identified in analyses of only violent or only property offenses (MacDonald et al., 2009; McCuish, Corrado, Hart, & DeLisi, 2015; A. Piquero et al., 2002). Also, specialists tend to have briefer trajectories and to be less likely to recidivate than sex offenders who also commit other types of offenses. In this regard, applying the label "sex offender" to samples used in this small body of trajectory research may be spurious, as many general offenders also have sex offenses on their rap sheets and many sex offenders also have non–sex offenses on their rap sheets. Further work is needed to examine the offense trajectories for distinct groups of sex offenders, including Internet sex offenders, that takes into consideration offender characteristics, such as victim preferences, offense types, and age of onset (i.e., adolescent versus adult onset). In the next section, we examine applications of the trajectory methodology to address novel research questions in three areas: risk assessments, code-of-the-street beliefs, and cross-national terrorism.

Other Trajectory Analysis Applications

We have observed the tremendous growth of trajectory research over the last 25 years. We have also marveled at the novel ways in which group-based trajectory modeling continues to be applied to address a wide array of exciting questions on a variety of topics within a criminal justice context. This work has been aided by the greater availability of longitudinal data and the motivation and resourcefulness of innovative researchers who have endeavored to create and share their data sets. We present research on three topic areas to illustrate some novel research questions addressed by the trajectory methodology in recent years.

RISK ASSESSMENTS. Risk assessment instruments are commonly used in the criminal justice system to assist in managing the risk of offenders and for making decisions about custody levels, treatment plans, and probation and parole. With what are called "fourth-generation" risk assessment tools, such as the Level of Service/Case Management Inventory (Andrews, Bonta, & Wormith, 2004), targets of treatment are identified for effective case management of offenders. In this regard, risk levels would be expected to be dynamic and decrease with subsequent administrations if treatment recommendations were followed. Few studies have examined change in risk scores over time. Day, Wilson, Bodwin, and Monson (2017) used a multilevel modeling approach to assess change in risk scores on the Level of Service Inventory–Ontario Revision (Girard & Wormith, 2004), one of the risk tools in the suite of Level of Service Inventory instruments. Data were available for 469 adult offenders in Ontario who had at least one assessment on the Level of Service Inventory–Ontario Revision over a 15-year period. Growth curve analysis indicated that the overall risk score increased at a rate of 0.11 points every year over the course of the follow-up period ($p = .014$). However, this result may obscure individual differences in the pattern of change that may be identified by a trajectory analysis approach. Moreover, individuals with more risk assessments, suggesting lengthier involvement with the justice system and higher risk scores, would contribute more to the overall growth trend than individuals with fewer risk assessments.

Hochstetler et al. (2016) applied trajectory modeling to data on 582 offenders in a midwestern state who had been paroled in 2010 and who had three ($N = 356$) or four ($N = 226$) risk assessments completed with the Level of Service Inventory-Revised (Andrews, Bonta, & Wormith, 1995). Separate analyses were performed for the two samples. Their results indicated that three trajectory groups provided the best fit to the data for both samples. The groups were labeled low risk (Class 1), high but declining (Class 2), and stable and high (Class 3). The group sizes for the three-assessment sample were 15.2%, 52.2%, and 32.6%, for Groups 1, 2, and 3, respectively; the group sizes for the four-assessment sample were 18.6%, 25.7%, and 55.8%, for Groups 1, 2, and 3, respectively. As expected, recidivism rates were highest for the Class 3 trajectory, followed by the Class 2 trajectory, and lowest for the Class 1 trajectory. While remaining cautious about these preliminary results, the authors concluded that, with further research, trajectories of risk scores that capture dynamic changes over time, rather than risk scores assessed at a single point, may be used to predict criminal outcomes.

CODE-OF-THE-STREETS BELIEFS. The notion of a code of the streets, based on the work of Elijah Anderson (1999), is concerned with the role of street culture on a person's involvement in criminal activity and a criminal lifestyle, particularly among African Americans. Within this framework, families may be characterized as either "decent" or "street," and socialization patterns within the family, and later the peer group, can perpetuate and strengthen one's adherence to a code of the street. As a result, code-of-the-street beliefs are thought to be stable over time into adulthood. Moreover, experiences of racial discrimination and exposure to criminal activity are thought to maintain belief in the code.

Moule et al. (2015) examined trajectories of code-of-the-street beliefs in a sample of 699 African Americans in Georgia and Iowa who were followed from ages 11 to 24. Their results identified five trajectory groups simply labeled Class 1 to Class 5. All but one of the groups showed a stable trajectory over time, although all had different starting points (i.e., intercepts). For example, Class 1 (7.1%) had the lowest starting point and a stable trajectory and may be considered "decent." By contrast, Class 5 (6.3%) had the highest starting point and a stable trajectory and be considered "street." Class 2 (34.2%) and Class 3 (40.8%) started somewhere in the middle. Last, Class 4 (11.6%) represented an unanticipated finding in that this trajectory started out as high as Class 5 at age 11 but declined over time to a point nearly in line with Class 1 at age 24. A comparison of the groups on several risk factors indicated that, although Class 4 experienced considerable racial discrimination, they also experienced supportive caregivers and moderate self-control and delinquent peer associations. These findings suggest that, for some, at least, beliefs in the street code are not as immutable as previously thought and may be sensitive to social conditions, perhaps because of targeted interventions.

CROSS-NATIONAL TERRORISM. Trajectory research has typically been based on the premise that crime is not evenly distributed across individuals. Less typical, a nascent body of research is emerging based on a comparable premise that crime is not evenly distributed across places, locations, and geographical spaces. In other words, paraphrasing Sherman (1995), most trajectory researchers have addressed the question of the *whodunit*; a handful of trajectory researchers have also addressed the question of the *wheredunit*.

Since the mid-2000s, trajectory methodology has been applied to investigate the underlying heterogeneity in longitudinal patterns of criminal activity (including terrorism) across geographical spaces, including street segments (i.e., street blocks) of a city—micro-places of crime (Weisburd, Bushway, Lum, & Yang, 2004), neighborhoods (Griffiths & Chavez, 2004), cities (McCall, Land, & Parker, 2011; Parker, Stansfield, & McCall, 2016), and countries (LaFree et al., 2010; N. Piquero & Piquero, 2006; N. Morris & Slocum, 2012). As Weisburd et al. (2004) noted, trajectory analysis has the dual advantage of identifying developmental trends in crime places over time and of identifying subgroups of places that reflect distinct longitudinal patterns (e.g., "hot spots"). The practical and policy implications of this work relate to the differential allocation of law-enforcement resources to where crime trends appear to be on an upward slope (LaFree et al., 2010). The focus here is on cross-national research and terrorism.

LaFree et al. (2010) examined country-level patterns of terrorist attacks between 1970 and 2006. *Terrorism* was defined as "acts of violence by nonstate actors, perpetrated against civilian populations, intended to cause fear, in order to achieve a political objective" (p. 624) and included both domestic acts, which accounted for the majority of attacks by as much as seven to one, and transnational acts. Data for the study were derived by combining several sources, including the Global Terrorism Database, the international RAND-MIPT database, and the international-domestic RAND-MIPT database. Separate analyses were conducted for (a) total terrorist attacks, (b) attacks attributed (by a media source) to a specific terrorist organization to reduce ambiguity and distinguish terrorist from nonterrorist attacks, and (c) fatal attacks, in which at least one life was lost and for which there would be a greater likelihood of media coverage.

Their results identified five groups for total attacks, four groups for attributed attacks, and three groups for fatal attacks, clearly underscoring the variability across countries over time that would be masked by a single trajectory for all countries. The smaller number of trajectory groups identified for the attributed and fatal attacks was not surprising given the fewer data points for these analyses. For the attributed attacks, the resulting groups reflected a considerable amount of clustering among the groups. Group 4 comprised only 8.6% of the countries, including Colombia, France, India, and Israel, but accounted for 67% of the attacks. This trajectory class showed an increase in events between 1970 and 1976, reaching a peak in 1989, followed by a very rapid decline after 1995. By contrast, Group 1 comprised only 5.3% of the countries and accounted for nearly 5% of the attacks. This trajectory had a very low profile throughout the follow-up period until 2001, at which point the trajectory spiked upward until 2004 when it surpassed all other trajectories. Group 2 had a stable low trajectory throughout the period, comprising 75% of the countries but only accounting for 9% of the attributed attacks. Last, Group 3 reflected a moderate rate trajectory that peaked in 1992 and fell to a very low level in the late 1990s. This group comprised 11% of the countries and accounted for 19.5% of the attacks.

In spite of the different number of groups identified in the three sets of analyses, similarities in results were noted. First, all analyses identified a group that consisted of only a few countries but experienced a large number of attacks. Second, low- or moderate-rate groups were also identified that comprised a small number of countries that experience an upsurge in attacks toward the end of the follow-up period. Finally, low-rate groups were generated that comprised a large number of countries but experienced only a few attacks. Just as we may cluster individuals based on their longitudinal rate of offending over time, we may similarly cluster countries based on their experience with terrorist activities.

Examining trajectories of terrorism over time also points to a group of countries that show a dramatic surge in the number of terrorist attacks experienced in the latter years of the study. This finding suggests these settings may be considered hot spots in the immediate future, where terrorist attacks have only recently become more frequent and where potentially destabilizing forces may impact the political, social, and economic circumstances of these countries as an outcome of this rise in terrorism. In terms of future work, although both domestic and transnational terrorist incidents were included in the analyses to increase the sample size, future investigations could perform separate analyses, given that they may have different political, social, and economic impacts (Enders, Sandler, & Gaibulloev, 2011). Also, as Morris and Slocum (2012) noted, additional theories are needed not only to account for the observed differences in terrorist incidents across countries but also to "predict different etiologies for different trajectory groups" (p. 128).

Monetary Costs Associated with Trajectory Groups

As a final topic for discussion, we consider the financial costs associated with trajectory groups derived from general offender populations. This work addresses the fascinating question of how the financial burden of crime on society may be distributed across offender groups. This line of investigation harkens back to our earlier discussions of the impact of the small group of serious and persistent offenders who are responsible for a disproportionate amount of crime. Such research also provides fodder for discussion about applying the findings of trajectory studies to policy and practice.

The previously reviewed literature makes clear that heterogeneity is a defining feature of criminal populations. For example, we observe that a small group of offenders is responsible for a disproportionate amount of crime over time and that most offenders desist in offending in adulthood, although some remain engaged in criminal activity over time, even at a low rate. Following from this important work, the question can be asked about how the monetary costs associated with different trajectory groups are distributed.

The last 20 years have seen a burgeoning interest in the economics of crime. This interest may be attributed, in part, to the significant methodological advances that have allowed researchers to generate more precise cost figures for the various domains and components associated with crime (e.g., victim costs, offender costs, and criminal justice costs), as well as both tangible (e.g., those associated with law enforcement, the youth and adult criminal justice systems, and loss of productivity and wages) and intangible (e.g., those associated with loss of life, trauma, pain, and the suffering of victims) costs. These advances include developments in the "bottom-up" and "top-down" methodologies, the two main approaches for determining costs estimates. The specific methods used to create the cost estimates for the bottom-up and top-down approaches are complex and beyond the scope of this chapter. The interested reader is directed to the seminal work of Mark Cohen (2005; M. Cohen & Bowles, 2011).

Overall estimates of the annual costs of crime in North America, including both tangible and intangible costs, have been as high as US$1.7 trillion when considering the aggregate costs on society (D. Anderson, 2012). For the costs of a single, high-risk individual, Mark Cohen and

Piquero (2009) estimated that the lifetime cost (to age 32) of a single career criminal was between US$2.6 and US$4.4 million (in 2007 dollars). Put another way, working effectively with a youth at high risk for a long-term criminal career to age 12 can save somewhere between US$2.6 and US$4.4 million.

We may also surmise that the costs of crime are not equally distributed across a population of offenders, much like the distribution of the rate of crime is not equally distributed across the offender population. In keeping with this premise, a handful of studies have estimated the financial burden of crime associated with trajectory groups. These studies have been conducted with data from the United States (M. Cohen, Piquero, & Jennings, 2010), England (A. Piquero, Jennings, & Farrington, 2013), Australia (Allard et al, 2014), and Canada (Day, Koegl, Rossman, & Oziel, 2015). In reviewing these studies, two considerations must be taken into account. One is the method for deriving the trajectory groups, including reference to the sample characteristics, the length of follow-up, the measure of crime, and so forth. The second is the method for deriving the cost estimates. For ease of comparison, this information is presented for each of the four studies in Table 5.1.

As indicated in Table 5.1, the age range covered by the follow-up period in all four studies extended from adolescence into adulthood. Nonetheless, there was some variability in terms of sample characteristics, particularly the sample composition, the sample size, and the length of follow-up. In terms of the number of trajectory groups identified across the studies, the figure ranged from four to seven. All studies found one or more high-rate chronic group, which comprised a small number of offenders. All studies also found one or more nonoffender or low-rate offender groups, which composed a large percentage of the sample. For example, A. Piquero et al. (2013) found that their high-rate chronic group ($n = 8$) made up 1.9% of the sample and that their nonoffender group ($n = 271$) made up 66% of the sample.

In terms of the cost estimates generated by the studies, in spite of the fact that each reported bottom-up estimates for their respective samples (Cohen et al., 2010 also reported top-down estimates), that there was a great deal of variability in the estimated values across the studies is of interest to note. This variability may be attributed to

TABLE 5.1. Sample Characteristics for Four Cost of Crime Studies

Study	Allard et al. (2014)	M. Cohen et al. (2010)	Day et al. (2015)	A. Piquero et al. (2013)
Country	Australia	U.S.	Canada	U.K.
Sample size	41,377	6,750	386	411
Sample type	Offender	Community	Offender	At-risk
No. of trajectory groups	5	4	7	5
Offense data	Admission, plea, or finding of guilt for an offense	Police contacts	Convictions	Convictions
Length of follow-up	16 years (age 10–25)	19 years (age 8–26)	15 years (age 12–26)	41 years (age 10–50)
Method of cost estimation	Bottom-up	Bottom-up and top-down	Bottom-up	Bottom-up
Currency, year	AUD, 2012	USD, 2007	CADCND, 2013	GBP and USD, 2003
Aggregate cost of crime	$1,136,000,000	$264,505,360 (bottom-up) $529,122,665 (top-down)	$2,260,152,620	$3,254,935 (£2,042,297)
Average cost per offender	$27,454	$165,342143,619[1a] (bottom-up) $330,753287,099[1a] (top-down)	$5,855,318	$23,250[1a]
Representation of sample and percentage of costs incurred by the high-rate chronic group	3.0% of sample; 28.7% of costs	3.1% of sample; 44% of costs	3.9% of sample; 11.3% of costs	1.9% of sample; 23% of costs

Note: [1a]Average figures excludes nonoffenders.

methodological differences, including sample characteristics (e.g., if males and females were included), the length of the follow-up (especially for persistent offenders), the number of offenses committed by the sample, the number of offense types included in the analyses, the number of criminal justice components included in the bottom-up estimates, jurisdictional differences in these costs, whether the estimates included only one offense per offender (e.g., index offense or most serious offense) or all offenses committed by the offender, and whether the cost estimate included undetected offenses, that is, the "dark figure" of crime. For example, excluding undetected crimes in the Day et al. (2015) study reduced the estimated cost from CN$2.26 billion (average per person was CN$5,855.318) to CN$671,321,758 (average per person was CN$1,739,176).

In all four studies, a small group of high-rate persistent offenders accounted for a disproportionate amount of the offending costs incurred by the sample (see Table 5.1). For example, Allard et al. (2014) found that the early-onset chronic group composed 3.0% of the sample but accounted for 28.7% of the total cost incurred by the sample. Similarly, A. Piquero et al. (2013) found that the average cost of the high-rate chronic group, which had only eight members, was more than double the average cost of the high-adolescence-peaked group, which had 21 members.

Further details about the relative costs of trajectory groups are presented for the Day et al. (2015) study in Table 5.2. Although the average cost per offender was CN$5.8 million, the distribution of costs was not equal across the sample. For example, the average cost for offenders on the high-late trajectory was nearly three times that amount. Furthermore, even though these group members composed only 3.9% of the sample, they were responsible for 8.7% of the convictions and incurred 11.3% of the costs. By contrast, those in the low-desister group composed nearly 30% of the sample, accrued 16.0% of the convictions but were responsible for only 18.0% of the costs, an average of CN$3.5 million per person. These figures highlight the large differences in the financial burden of crime imposed on society by the different trajectory groups. As noted earlier, these differences have important policy and practice implications in terms of the costs savings to be gained by implementing effective crime prevention and early intervention programs.

At the same time, given the imprecision in the estimates of the costs of crime, it may be rightfully argued that these studies underestimate the total economic burden on society. At present, there is no gold standard method for estimating the costs of crime, and every study is subject to its own limitations. Moreover, some social costs, such as the loss of social cohesion in a low-income neighborhood, personal costs of a child growing up with an incarcerated parent, and family costs of grieving the loss of a child to a life of crime are impossible to quantify, making the true cost of crime incalculable.

THE NUMBER AND SHAPE OF CRIMINAL TRAJECTORIES | 167

TABLE 5.2. Average Convictions and Costs for Trajectory Groups in Day et al. (2015) Study

Trajectory group	People		Convictions			Costs[a]		
	Sum	% Total	Sum	Average Per Person	% Total	Sum	Average Per Person	% Total
Low Desister	115	29.8%	787	6.84	16.0%	$407,807,667	$3,546,154	18.0%
Low Persister	125	32.4%	1061	8.49	21.5%	$474,140,398	$3,793,123	21.0%
Moderate Adolescence Peaked	45	11.7%	857	19.04	17.4%	$356,299,619	$7,917,769	15.8%
Moderate-Late Persister	14	3.6%	253	18.07	5.1%	$112,171,812	$8,012,272	5.0%
Moderate-Early Persister	55	14.2%	1081	19.65	21.9%	$444,709,320	$8,085,624	19.7%
High Early	17	4.4%	460	27.06	9.3%	$210,704,742	$12,394,397	9.3%
High Late	15	3.9%	427	28.47	8.7%	$254,319,062	$16,954,604	11.3%
Total All Offenders	386	100.0%	4,296	12.76	100.0%	$2,260,152,620	$5,855,318	100.0%

Note: From Table 8 in Day et al. (2015).
[a]Costs are in 2013 Canadian dollars.

Conclusion

This chapter has examined findings of trajectory analyses with a focus on the number, profile, and size of trajectory classes yielded by the research. The aim of the chapter was not to find the true number of trajectory groups, which has been noted to be highly problematic (Greenberg, 2016) but, rather, to highlight the variability and diversity that characterizes the general offender population, select subpopulations (female offenders and sex offenders), and various other related topics. We also examined the costs of crime associated with offender trajectories to shine a light on the differences in social and financial costs associated with different trajectory groups. The next chapter extends this work and presents findings on predictors and correlates of trajectory group membership with a particular focus on the small group of persistent and high-rate offender classes typically identified in studies.

Suggested Supplemental Readings

The chapter by A. Piquero (2008) holds up well as a comprehensive review of the criminal trajectory literature between 1993 and 2005. More recently, the edited 2015 volume by Morizot and Kazemian provides an excellent overview of a number of topics conceptually related to this chapter, including trajectories of aggression in young children (Tremblay, 2015), the age–crime curve (DeLisi, 2015), and developmental theories of offending (Farrington & Ttofi, 2015). Prepared as a tribute to Canadian criminologist Marc Le Blanc, in its 32 chapters, the book covers many important and emerging topics related to the field of developmental criminology. The book also covers a number of topics specifically discussed in this chapter, including criminal trajectories, in general (A. Piquero, Gonzalez, & Jennings, 2015); gender differences in offending trajectories (Lanctôt, 2015); and trajectories of sex offenders (Lussier, 2015).

6

Predictors and Correlates of Criminal Trajectory Groups

Between 1831 and 1854, London, England, was beset by four severe outbreaks of cholera, killing tens of thousands of people. The outbreak of 1853, for example, took the lives of more than 10,000. In the summer of 1854, London was hit by its fourth outbreak. In the Soho district the death rate reached just over 600. The significance of Soho is that it was in this neighborhood that the true cause of the disease was first identified. Nineteenth-century England saw a rapid growth in industrialization and urbanization. These circumstances gave rise to a host of poor, filthy, and squalid conditions in the cities and the surrounding districts. These conditions became breeding grounds for disease and widespread epidemics, such as cholera. For centuries, it had been believed that diseases like cholera were spread by a "miasma in the atmosphere" or foul or poisonous air from decaying matter (UCLA Fielding School of Public Health, n.d.). As a result, each new outbreak led to no meaningful developments to stem the tide of its mortal effects, as it continued to ravage the industrial cities.

During the outbreak of 1854, an astute and tenacious physician by the name of Dr. John Snow began meticulously gathering the necessary evidence to build his own ideas and challenge the accepted miasma theory in support of his belief that cholera was spread by bacteria through contaminated water. Through many interviews conducted with residents in the area and by examining water samples under a microscope and carefully monitoring the pattern of the disease on a map, he discovered that the source of the contaminated water, the epicenter of the epidemic, was a pump on the corner of Broad Street (now named Broadwick Street) and Cambridge Street (now named Lexington Street) in Soho. Removal of the handle of the pump led to a remarkable decrease in the spread of cholera (although the epidemic may have already been in decline). Although his findings were dismissed by the authorities and had been for some time to come, they eventually came to be accepted, leading to significant improvements in the sanitation facilities. The case of Dr. John Snow and his determined efforts to pinpoint the cause of the cholera epidemic illustrates both the scientific and practical utility of finding the *root causes* of diseases, as well as other afflictions, disorders, and social ills that affect our society, crime among them.

Causes, Correlates, and Risk Factors

Like modern-day John Snows, criminologists, psychologists, and sociologists have long been engaged in a relentless pursuit for the root cause of crime. Unlike cholera, however, which has a single cause, crime is multiply determined; that is, across and within individuals, myriad factors may be implicated as contributing to the onset, course, and desistance of criminal activity. Today, through the strident efforts of theorists and researchers, we know a great deal about the putative factors that give rise to the onset of crime. However, as a complex human behavior, the search for the root causes is an incredibly complex task.

How does one identify a variable as a cause of crime in the way Dr. Snow identified bacteria as the cause of cholera? How does a researcher separate cause from correlation? As we will see, these questions require clarity and specificity in the use of the terms *risk factor, correlate*, and *cause*. Research design also factors into the conclusions that may be drawn from studies about (potential) causal relations. Researchers have at their disposal a range of methodologies, including descriptive, correlational, experimental, and quasi-experimental, to answer empirical questions. Each has its own advantages and disadvantages (Farrington, 2013), and investigators need to acknowledge the strengths and limitations of their work. In this chapter, we discuss the methodological and terminological issues of risk factor research. We then review the research on correlates and predictors of criminal trajectory group membership, in particular, the high-rate and persistent trajectory, given its prominence in criminology. Studies of correlates and predictors are discussed in separate sections to maintain their essential distinction in this type of research. Finally, conclusions are drawn about the state of the knowledge on developmental risk factors of criminal trajectories.

LONGITUDINAL RESEARCH. As discussed in the introduction, the study of the causes of crime relies on the use of longitudinal research, particularly, *prospective* longitudinal designs (Farrington, 1997, 2007). In a prospective longitudinal study, starting at a given point in time and moving forward (as opposed to gathering data retrospectively), repeated observations are gathered from the same individuals over time. This method enables an unambiguous temporal ordering of the variables of interest (Farrington & Loeber, 2014). What this means is that the researcher can identify (within the limits of the research) whether a given variable X appears before, after, or at the same time as another variable, Y. For a variable to be properly identified as a potential causal variable, X must precede the onset of Y. For example, exposure to domestic violence has been identified as a contributing factor to the onset of delinquency (Eitle & Turner, 2002; Kitzmann, Gaylord, Holt, & Kenny, 2003). To be properly identified as a causal variable, the exposure must come before the onset of the antisocial behavior. However, simply establishing temporal precedence, although essential, is not sufficient for establishing causality. Causal relations imply change at the level of the individual; that is, the researcher must additionally demonstrate that a change in variable X leads to a change in variable Y. For a fulsome discussion of research methods to study causal relations in the field of criminology, see Farrington (1988). These methods include natural experimental studies of within-individual change, randomized clinical intervention experiments, and behavioral-genetic studies (Moffitt, 2005; A. Piquero & Weisburd, 2010; Shadish, Cook, & Campbell, 2002).

ROLE OF THEORY. The study of the causes of crime also relies on theory to guide the selection of variables of interest, that is, the predictor variables and the outcomes. As noted earlier, theory plays a critical role in providing an outline of and rationale for the relevant variables composing a purported theoretical pathway (i.e., causal chain) and the expected direction of effects among the variables, in a sense, ordering the expected trail of events from risk factors to outcomes (Cullen, Benson, & Makarios, 2012). Ultimately, developmental risk factors have the effect of undermining, interfering with, or thwarting normative developmental processes; in other words, taking a person off a normative track of psychological growth and development, which has the effect of interfering with the achievement of developmental tasks (leading to adaptational failure). The earlier the risk factor occurred in the person's life, the more deleterious the impact because of the cumulative effects of risk factors (Tackett, 2010).

Distinctions among Variables in Risk Factor Research

The search for the causes of crime has been aided by formalized distinctions among different *types* of variables that may factor into the equation. These variables include risk factors, causal risk factors, correlates, proxies, and markers. Distinctions among these variables have proved to be important as they provide key conceptual definitions of the different types of factors that may come into play in the study of crime from a developmental perspective. Definitions and distinctions have been discussed at length by Kraemer, Kazdin, Offord, and their colleagues (Kazdin, Kraemer, Kessler, Kupfer & Offord, 1997; Kraemer et al., 1997; Kraemer, Stice, Kazdin, Offord, & Kupfer, 2001), and an in-depth discussion is beyond the scope of this chapter. Suffice it to say that the term *risk factor* has been used inconsistently in the literature (Murray, Farrington, & Eisner, 2009), and some have called for the consistent use of standard definitions to avoid miscommunication and confusion and to accurately represent the nature of the relationship between the independent and dependent variables (Kazdin et al., 1997; Kraemer et al., 1997, 2001).

Further to this point, Kraemer and colleagues (1997; see also Kazdin et al., 1997) distinguish between a risk factor and a correlate. A *correlate* refers to a variable that shows a significant association with the outcome, that co-occurs with the outcome, or for which a temporal precedence has not been established. Although correlational findings raise questions about directionality and causality, identifying correlates is an essential first step in the search for risk factors and a good deal of the research on risk factors has been focused on identifying correlates (Derzon, 2007). The problem with identifying correlates, however, as Farrington (1997) observed, is that "literally thousands" (p. 362) of variables have been found that correlate with offending behavior. Identifying which of these variables might be causally related to crime is the next step in the research. However, Moffitt (2005) and others (e.g., Rutter, Pickles, Murray, & Eaves, 2001) have lamented that few studies use research designs that enable the evaluation of causal relations.

Researchers use the term *risk factor* to identify variables that may be causally related to an outcome. A variable is identified as a risk factor if it occurred before the onset of the outcome and shows a significant association with the outcome (Tanner-Smith, Wilson, & Lipsey, 2013). Kazdin et al. (1997) referred to a risk factor as an antecedent condition that increases the likelihood of a maladaptive outcome. Some key elements of a risk factor are that (a) the risk factor temporally precedes the outcome, (b) the presence of the risk factor puts an individual at increased risk for a maladaptive outcome compared with a randomly selected individual from a general population, and (c) the relation between a risk factor and an outcome is understood as probabilistic. Note that a risk factor does not have to be a cause of the outcome.

Some risk factors appear close in time to the event or onset of the criminal activity; some appear distant in time to the event. These variables are called *proximal* and *distal* risk factors, respectively. According to Sampson (2001), the relation between distal and proximal variables is thought to involve a mediating effect, such that the impact of a distal variable on an outcome is not so much "'called forth' from the distant past" (p. vi) as much as mediated by proximal influences. In this regard, distal and proximal risk factors operate as part of complex, developmental causal chains to influence outcomes. For example, early trauma exposure disrupts normative developmental processes and neurochemical functioning that may set into motion a cascade of negative events leading to mental health problems, involvement in antisocial behavior, and possibly incarceration (Coleman & Stewart, 2010). The pathway leading to these outcomes may be mediated in adolescence by association with a deviant peer group, whose activities and values are reinforced through the process of *deviancy training* (Dishion & Piehler, 2007). Such contact with antisocial peers may lead to involvement in property offenses, such as shoplifting or break and enters; in drug offenses, such as possession or trafficking; in weapons use; violence; gang activity; and other delinquent behaviors.

Researchers also distinguish between *static* risk factors, which are unchangeable (e.g., age at first conviction, history of out-of-home placements), and *dynamic* risk factors, which are changing over time and are malleable and amenable to change (e.g., antisocial attitudes, substance use; Bonta & Andrews, 2017). Intervention or prevention programs will target dynamic risk factors, and so this is a useful distinction to make. Static risk factors, although not amenable to change through intervention, are still important to consider for both basic research and for prevention/early intervention programming.

Last, Kraemer et al. (1997) and Kazdin et al. (1997) distinguish between a risk factor and a causal risk factor. A *causal risk factor* is a risk factor that has been empirically shown to produce an outcome. In other words, alteration of the risk factor alters the likelihood, nature, or severity of the outcome. For example, harsh and punitive parental discipline (Jaffee, Strait, & Odgers, 2012) has been called a causal risk factor (Kazdin et al., 1997). Establishing that a variable is a causal risk factor is the final step in identifying a risk factor and provides important clues about targets for intervention and prevention. As Kraemer and colleagues (2005, p. 16) noted, "causal risk factors are the 'gold' of risk estimation—they can be used both to identify those of high risk of the outcome and to provide the bases for interventions to prevent the outcome." The next task, then, is to identify the causal processes or mechanisms that explain the causal relation between the risk factor and the outcome. Note that all criminal trajectory studies to date that have sought to identify risk factors have focused on developmental precursors and correlates of offense trajectories. Systematic investigations of causal risk factors have yet to be conducted (Moffitt, 2005). Nonetheless, methodologists see great value in examining developmental precursors and correlates of (offense) trajectories because the use of such auxiliary information is relevant for the construct validation of the derived trajectory groups (Bauer & Curran, 2004; Morin et al., 2011; Petras & Masyn, 2010).

Research on Risk Factors and Criminal Trajectories

For more than 25 years, criminal trajectory research has contributed immensely to the study of risk factors of crime. In particular, trajectory research has opened new ways of empirically clustering individuals into groups whose longitudinal pattern of offending is statistically similar, thereby providing an important means of data reduction for subsequent analysis that removes the element of subjectivity (A. Piquero, 2008). This advance in research has also allowed for a more nuanced examination of risk factors of crime. For example, rather than simply asking whether a variable distinguishes offenders from nonoffenders, which has been the focus of much of the research over the past few decades, researchers can now fine tune the question to ask which factors discriminate among *a set* of offender types, based on differences in the rate of offending over time. For example, developmental variables could be identified that distinguish offenders on a high-rate offense trajectory from offenders on a moderate-rate or low-rate trajectory, as well as nonoffenders. This refinement of the key empirical question, although subtle, represents a significant advancement in the quest for risk factors of crime. In addition, as noted, the criminal trajectory methodology provides a valid, empirically derived, objective, and systematic approach to address the long-standing and vexing problem of identifying the small group of offenders who engage in a high-rate and persistent pattern of criminal activity. Previously, this distinction was based on subjective and largely arbitrary cutoff levels. Given the prominence within criminology of the finding by Wolfgang, Figlio, and Sellin (1972) that a small group of offenders accounts for a disproportionate amount of crime, it is no wonder that trajectory research on risk factors that distinguishes individuals on a high-rate persistent offense trajectory from other trajectory groups has dominated the literature. The main question examined is, Are there reliable and distinguishable (distinct) antecedents (etiologies) to particular criminal trajectories? Once identified, the next step is to search for developmental links between developmental risk factors and trajectory group membership to establish the causal mechanisms that connect these events and outcomes. It is a good reminder that, to do so, we need good developmentally informed theories of crime (Farrington, 2005).

CLASSIFY/ANALYZE METHOD. The studies discussed in this chapter use the *classify/analyze* approach (A. Piquero, 2008; Roeder, Lynch, & Nagin, 1999). In this method, individuals are first sorted into discrete trajectory groups through the statistical procedure of semiparametric group-based trajectory modeling. Researchers in the field of criminology have used either the SAS-based module Proc TRAJ developed by Jones, Nagin, and Roeder (2001) or Mplus (L. Muthén & Muthén, 2012) for the extraction of offender trajectory groups. Once sorted, regression analyses (or other statistical approaches, for example, see van der Geest, Blokland, & Bijleveld, 2009) are applied to identify the best set of developmental predictors or correlates that differentiates the groups (Nagin & Odgers, 2010b). The classify/analyze approach combines both person-centered and variable-centered statistical methodologies (Bates,

2000). A. Piquero (2008, p. 29) provides an excellent summary of the different methodological approaches that may be used by treating trajectory groups as nominal categories:

> First, the most common approach is to, after sorting individuals into the various trajectory classifications, treat the groups as nominal categories and then examine how an array of risk/protective factors vary across the groups. This is commonly referred to as the classify/analyze approach, and provides basic descriptive information regarding how the various trajectory groups differ along key variables of interest. Relatedly, researchers can use the trajectory groups as outcome variables in a multinomial logistic regression framework, where key independent variables are used to predict membership in the various groups. A second substantive analysis taken with the trajectory results is to use the group classifications as predictors, along with other key theoretical variables, in a regression-based framework to predict the outcome of interest (i.e., crime counts). This approach allows for an examination of how key theoretical variables, e.g., local life circumstances, relate to criminal offending after taking into consideration unobserved individual differences (measured through group membership).

FOCUS ON HIGH-RATE PERSISTENT OFFENDERS. The classify/analyze method combines person-centered and variable-centered approaches and so brings together multiple lines of research in criminology, such as the work of the Gluecks (Glueck & Glueck, 1950) and Wolfgang et al. (1972; Tracy, Wolfgang, & Figlio, 1990). Following from these early works, the next logical questions are, (a) Can the small group of high-rate persistent offenders that accounts for a disproportionate amount of crime be identified in childhood, and (b) if so, can an early intervention or prevention program effectively forestall this high-rate, persistent criminal activity? The first question is the topic of this chapter, and the answer appears to be a qualified yes (cf. Bersani, Niewbeerta, & Laub, 2009; Sampson & Laub, 2003). The second question pertains to the "practical mission" (Masten, 2006) of risk factor research, of applying basic science to the prevention of criminal behavior (i.e., to reduce the impact of risk factors and strengthen protective factors). From the perspective of developmental systems theory (Lerner, Hershberg,

Hilliard, & Johnson, 2015; Lerner, Lerner, von Eye, Bowers, & Lewin-Bizan, 2011), more generally, this practice involves optimizing within-person development across the life span.

Given the focus of the book on criminal behavior, the trajectory studies discussed in this chapter are based on adolescent and adult samples; studies that only assessed childhood samples are excluded. Although children as young as seven can be criminally prosecuted in some jurisdictions around the world (Bartol & Bartol, 2011), few studies include criminal offense data for children under the age of 10. More typically, trajectory studies involving children examine growth patterns on indicators of externalizing behavior, which broadly includes a range of antisocial acts (e.g., aggression, lying) and rule violations. The Child Behavior Checklist (Achenbach, 1991) is a commonly used as a measure of externalizing behavior problems in children and youth. For reviews of trajectory research of externalizing behavior problems in children see Tremblay (2012), Jennings and Reingle (2012), A. Piquero (2008), and van Dulmen, Goncy, Vest, and Flannery (2009).

TWO DISSENTING STUDIES. It needs to be acknowledged at the outset that not all researchers agree that criminal trajectories can be predicted by developmental risk factors. In spite of the abundance of research in support of developmental predictors/correlates of criminal trajectory groups, two studies have found null effects and their relevance needs to be recognized. The studies of Sampson and Laub (2003) and Bersani et al. (2009) both failed to identify any factors that distinguished among their identified trajectory groups, which raises a cautionary note about prospectively identifying individuals at risk for any given trajectory.

Sampson and Laub (2003) used data collected for the Gluecks' (1950) studies of 500 male delinquents, ages 10 to 17. Sampson and Laub conducted an extensive search of the criminal records for the original sample beyond age 32, when the last follow-up was conducted, up to age 70. This investigation became the longest follow-up study of crime in the field of criminology. Using the SAS platform, six trajectory groups were generated based on the total crime data (versus only alcohol/drug crime and violent crime). These groups were labeled (with percentages in parentheses) high-rate chronic (3.2%), moderate-rate desister (26.1%), classic desister (19.9%), moderate-rate chronic (19.4%), low-rate chronic I (24.4%), and low-rate chronic II (8.0%). With respect to risk factors, 13 childhood and adolescent predictors were selected from the Gluecks' (1950) data set for analysis. These predictors included individual (e.g., intelligence, aggressiveness, extroversion, early onset antisocial behavior, arrest frequency in adolescence) and parent (e.g., criminality, parental instability) variables. Comparing risk factors (high scores indicated the presence of the given risk factor) across trajectory groups, Sampson and Laub's results revealed no significant differences on any of the variables. In other words, the percentage of individuals in each trajectory group who presented with the risk factor was not statistically different across the trajectory groups, meaning that no group was over- or underrepresented on any of the childhood or adolescent variables. Acknowledging the uniqueness of their finding within the broader developmental criminology literature, and remaining skeptical of typological approaches in criminology and the ability to prospectively distinguish among subtypes based on of developmental risk factors, Sampson and Laub (2003) concluded, "Even if we remain agnostic on whether offender groups are valid in an ontological sense, we can say with some confidence that adult trajectories of offending among former delinquents cannot be reduced to the past. The fact, therefore, remains that there are important differences in adult criminal trajectories that cannot be predicted from childhood, contra the National Summits of the policy world, and apparently much yearning among criminologists" (p. 588). At the same time, A. Piquero (2008) and Moffitt (2006b; see also Nagin & Tremblay, 2005b) counter this claim and identify several methodological factors that provide an alternative explanation for the lack of an effect, including the uniformly high-risk nature of the sample, which results in a restriction of range on risk variables, and the small number of individuals composing the high-rate chronic group, which limits the statistical power to detect an effect.

Bersani et al. (2009) examined the composition of criminal trajectory groups and predictors of trajectory group membership in a sample of 4,615 male (91%) and female (9%) offenders from the Netherlands. Official records were obtained for juvenile and adult offenses from ages 12 to 79. Because of the small number of individuals with offense records at the oldest ages, the trajectory analysis was censored either at 55 years or at the time of death, whichever came first. The results yielded four trajectory groups labeled, chronic offender (4.2%), classic desister (10.6%), low-rate offender (14.0%), and sporadic chronic (71.2%). Risk factor data

included four variables assessed in adolescence: (1) early onset of offending, (2) chronic offending during adolescence, (3) low intelligence, and
(4) psychological instability. The latter two variables were available for
only a subset of $n = 689$ of the original sample. To test for differences on
the risk variables across the trajectory groups, Bersani et al. (2009) used
a cross-validation approach, a technique that is unique in the criminal
trajectory literature (Efron, 1983; Stone, 1974). Using a randomly selected
subsample, they first developed a predictive model based on multinomial regression analysis. The parameter estimates derived from the
model were then tested on a second subsample. Their results indicated
that the model yielded poor predictive power to differentiate the groups,
particularly between the low-rate and the chronic offender groups. For
example, they found that "of the 328 cases observed to be members of
the low-rate offender group, only 5 were predicted to be a member of
that trajectory groups" (Bersani et al., 2009, pp. 486–487). The model
was similarly poor at predicting the chronic offender group. Like the
Sampson and Laub (1993) study, these findings raise a note of caution to
the prevailing zeitgeist in the criminology literature that high-rate, serious chronic offenders can be prospectively identified by developmental
risk factors and adolescent correlates. Rather, Bersani et al. suggested
that the research agenda be shifted to focus on adolescent and adult
variables that are associated with *desistance* from crime.

With these two studies in mind, we now proceed to review the criminal
trajectory literature in support of the contention that high-rate persistent
offenders can be identified at an early age. A distinction is made here between correlates and predictors of trajectory group membership, with the
key distinction being whether the factor precedes the onset of the criminal
trajectory. Simply put, predictors come before, correlates come after or at
the same time (or the temporal precedence is unknown). We begin with
the research on correlates and then turn to the research on predictors.

Correlates of Trajectory Group Membership

Given space limitations, this review is selective and focuses on three
topics: (a) tests of Moffitt's (1993) dual taxonomy theory, (b) psychopathy
and criminal trajectories, and (c) psychosocial maturity and criminal
trajectories.

TESTING MOFFITT'S THEORY. In their seminal paper. Nagin and Land (1993) tested the validity of Moffitt's (1993) recently proposed dual taxonomy theory, using data from the Cambridge Study in Delinquent Development (CSDD; Farrington & West, 1990). Recall that Moffitt postulated two distinct groups of offenders, the life-course-persistent (LCP) group and the adolescence-limited (AL) group, and proposed that each had a unique developmental pathway. Following the classify/analyze approach, Nagin and Land first conducted trajectory analyses and then distinguished the groups based on childhood (ages 8–10) and adolescent (ages 16–19) variables. Findings for the childhood variables are discussed in the next section on predictors of trajectory group membership. Here we present findings for the adolescent variables.

The results of their trajectory analysis yielded four groups, labeled nonoffenders (40%), high-rate chronic offenders (12%), adolescent-limited offenders (17%), and low-rate chronic offenders (33%). In terms of adolescent, correlates, the high-rate chronic offenders were more likely to be heavy drinkers, to smoke marijuana, to lie chronically, to have delinquent siblings, and to experience job instability. Although not statistically significant, the adolescent-limited group was characterized by greater peer popularity than the remaining three groups.

Nagin, Farrington, and Moffitt (1995) extended the findings of Nagin and Land (1993) and examined adolescent (at ages 14 and 18) and adult (at age 32) correlates of the four trajectory groups identified in Nagin and Land (1993). The main finding of the Nagin et al. (1995) study was that individuals on the adolescence-limited trajectory showed a mixed pattern of outcomes in relation to Moffitt's (1993) theory; in some ways, they were similar to the high-rate chronic group, but they differed from the high-rate chronic group in other ways. At ages 14 and 18, in comparison to the low-rate chronic and nonoffender groups, both the adolescence-limited and high-rate chronic groups were more likely to have engaged in violent behavior and cigarette smoking and to have had sex. This finding is consistent with Moffitt's (1993) proposition that the LCP and AL groups will both engage in delinquent behavior during their teen years. However, it is inconsistent with Moffitt as the AL group also engaged in violence (see also A. Piquero & Brezina, 2001). Moffitt proposed that individuals in the AL group would primarily engage in property and status offenses. Also consistent with Moffitt, the adolescence-limited and high-rate-chronic trajectory groups differed with respect to employment status at age 32. Those in the adolescence-limited group was indistinguishable from the nonoffenders with respect to their success in obtaining gainful employment, whereas the high-rate chronic group showed a more unstable pattern of employment. Furthermore, those in the adolescence-limited group and high-rate chronic group differed with respect to the development of a strong, positive attachment with their spouse, in favor of the adolescence-limited group. Last, contrary to Moffitt, at age 32, both those in groups continued to use drugs and drink heavily, get into fights, and engage in property offending, which, in the case of the adolescence-limited group, was often from their employer. These results suggest that, in spite of having a more normative childhood and adolescent development than the persistent offenders, individuals on the adolescence-limited trajectory show a poorer outcome in adulthood than would be expected from Moffitt's theory and may also experience negative repercussions (i.e., snares) from their involvement in antisocial behavior during adolescence (Moffitt, Caspi, Harrington, & Milne, 2002).

In another test of Moffitt's (1993) theory, White, Bates, and Buyske (2001) examined the relationship among neuropsychological, environmental, and personality factors assessed in adolescence and trajectory group membership. Moffitt proposed that individuals on an LCP group, whose offending behavior is initiated in childhood, would show evidence of neuropsychological deficits relative to individuals in the adolescence-limited group. To test this proposition, self-reported delinquent behavior was gathered in a sample of 698 male participants from the Rutgers Health and Human Development Project, a 13-year prospective longitudinal study of adolescent development. To facilitate their study of development across adolescence, White et al. used a cross-sequential design, whereby study participants were recruited into three age-cohort groups, those who were age 12 (youngest cohort), 15 (middle cohort), and 18 (oldest cohort) at Time 1 of data collection. Four waves of offense data were collected at 3-year intervals from ages 12 to 31.

Two personality variables were assessed at Time 1, impulsivity and harm avoidance. Because of issues of reliability with younger adolescents, a third personality variable, disinhibition (related here to sensation-seeking), was assessed at Time 1 for the middle and oldest cohorts and at Time 2 for the youngest cohort. The neuropsychological variables were assessed at Time 3 and included verbal ability and executive functioning. A proxy measure of early neurological problems was created based on two variables, low birth rate and premature birth, as reported by mothers when the participants were between 12 and 18 years of age. Finally, three measures of environmental risk were assessed at Time 1, family socioeconomic status (SES), family structure (i.e., single- or two-parent), and parental hostility.

The results of their trajectory analysis yielded four groups, labeled nondelinquents (47%), adolescence-limited delinquents (33%), escalating delinquents (13%), and persistent delinquents (7%). Results of the prediction models indicated that, contrary to expectation, with the non-delinquent group as the reference category (thus comparing this group with the three delinquent groups), significant effects were found for higher impulsivity, lower harm avoidance, higher disinhibition, higher parental hostility, and one-parent family, with the three delinquent groups showing poorer outcomes on these variables than the nondelinquent group. In other words, the three offender groups were undifferentiated from each other but differed from the nonoffenders. At the same time, consistent with Moffitt's (1993) theory, a comparison of the persistent group with the adolescence-limited group showed a difference for disinhibition, with the persistent group showing greater disinhibition. This variable reflects poor self-control and executive cognitive functioning related to neuropsychological dysfunction. Because the assessment of disinhibition was in adolescence, however, its status as a predictor of the persistent delinquent group, based on the dual taxonomy model, cannot be determined. Moreover, Moffitt (2006b) noted that, based on inspection of the graphical presentation of the trajectory groups, the group identified as the persistent delinquent trajectory may have been mislabeled as it better resembled an adolescence-peaked group, with its characteristic peak in adolescence (albeit at a higher level than the group labeled adolescence-limited delinquent), followed by a decline into adulthood. Therefore, it is unclear how their findings may be interpreted with respect to Moffitt's (1993) theory.

Taken together, the empirical evidence in support of Moffitt's (1993) model has been mixed with respect to the correlates of trajectory group membership (see also van der Geest et al., 2009). First, although the studies identify trajectories that resemble both the LCP (i.e., often referred to as high-rate chronic or persistent offenders) and AL groups, additional groups not predicted by the model also are identified. These groups include a low-rate chronic group and late-starter group. In a revision of the theory in keeping with the mounting evidence, Moffitt (2006b) added a third group, low-level chronic offenders to her taxonomy. Second, with respect to expected correlates of the AL and LCP groups, Nagin et al. (1995) found that both the adolescence-limited and high-rate-chronic groups engaged in antisocial behavior as adolescents, consistent with the model. However, contrary to the model, those in the adolescence-limited group also fared poorly in some respects as adults. The study by White et al. (2001) also yielded mixed results. They found that the delinquent groups were not different from each other on all variables, except disinhibition, which differentiated the persistent from the adolescence-limited group.

PSYCHOPATHY. Another important question to consider in relation to criminal trajectories is the extent to which the personality trait of psychopathy factors into trajectory group membership. Psychopathy is a stable personality disorder that is characterized by a cluster of variables, including impulsivity, deceitfulness, callousness, lack of empathy, remorse, and stimulation-seeking. Compared to nonpsychopathic offenders, psychopathic offenders are at a greater risk of more serious offending, including violence (Patrick, Zempolich, & Levenson, 1997), and show a higher likelihood of criminal recidivism (Schmidt, Campbell, & Houlding, 2011). It would be expected, then, that individuals on a high-rate and persistent criminal trajectory would show more psychopathic traits than would individuals on a low- or moderate-rate trajectory. A number of studies support this contention with both adolescent and adult samples.

McCuish, Corrado, Lussier, and Hart (2014) examined the association between offense trajectories and adolescent psychopathy in a sample of 64 female and 243 male offenders from British Columbia, Canada. Official conviction data were gathered from ages 12 to 28. Psychopathic traits were determined by scores on the Psychopathy Checklist: Youth Version (Forth, Kosson, & Hare, 2003), considered the "gold standard" of assessment. The sample had been assessed on the Psychopathy Checklist: Youth Version when they were incarcerated at a custodial facility for juvenile offenders. The trajectory analysis was performed with SAS Proc TRAJ.

Their results yielded four trajectory groups, labeled high-frequency chronic (27.3%), high-rate slow desister (14.6%), explosive-onset fast desister (20.6%), and adolescence limited (27.5%). Examination of psychopathy scores across the four groups indicated that individuals on the high-rate slow-desister group had the highest scores. They were also 5 times as likely as individuals on the adolescence-limited or explosive-onset fast-desister groups to have a score of 30 or more on the psychopathy measure. Last, individuals on the high-frequency chronic trajectory were twice as likely as individuals on the adolescence-limited and explosive-onset fast-desister groups to score 30 or more on the Psychopathy Checklist: Youth Version (Forth et al., 2003). These results support the hypothesis that more serious and chronic offense trajectories are associated with a greater degree of psychopathy in youth (see also Salihovic, Özdemir, & Kerr, 2014).

In a follow-up study with a larger sample size and more controls for criminogenic risk factors (e.g., substance use, abuse history, school behavior problems), Corrado, McCuish, Hart, and DeLisi (2015) found that two of the four factors that define psychopathy, the antisocial and lifestyle factors (but not the interpersonal and affective factors), were related to the high-rate-chronic trajectory. Corrado et al. (2015) determined that persistence in general offending, without regard for the severity or types of offenses (e.g., more serious, violent crimes), is related to the behavioral markers of psychopathy and that the interpersonal and affective dimensions have less of an impact on more minor offenses that likely compose the crime mix of the high-rate-chronic offense trajectories. These results, however, are not entirely consistent with Salihovic and Stattin (2017), who used a community-based sample of 811 male and female youth in Sweden whose criminal offenses were followed from ages 10 to 18. The authors found that both impulsive-irresponsible traits (i.e., a behavioral dimension) and grandiosity and manipulative traits (i.e., an interpersonal dimension) predicted the high and stable offending trajectory. Differences in these results may be attributed to the sample characteristics, the length of follow-up, the measures used to assess psychopathy, and the conceptual definition of the psychopathy construct (i.e., two versus three factors). Clearly, more work is needed to disentangle the specific dimensions of psychopathy associated with high-rate and chronic offense trajectories. As well, the question remains whether the psychopathic characteristics precede the start of the criminal trajectory or whether serious offending gives rise to these manifestations of psychopathy.

A. Piquero, Farrington, et al. (2012) examined the relation between psychopathy, assessed at age 48, and criminal trajectories to age 40 (see A. Piquero, Farrington, et al., 2007) in the CSDD sample. Psychopathy scores, based on the Psychopathy Checklist: Screening Version (Hart, Cox, & Hare, 1995), were generated from information gathered in an interview conducted at age 48 as well as file data collected between 12 and 48 years of age. As expected, across five trajectory groups, nonoffenders (62.3%), low-adolescence-peaked offenders (18.6%), very-low-chronic offenders (11.3%), high-adolescence-peak offenders (5.4%), and high-rate chronic offenders (2.5%; see A. Piquero, Farrington, et al., 2007 for a complete description of these trajectory groups), individuals on the high-rate chronic trajectory scored the highest on the Psychopathy Checklist: Screening Version. Moreover, when regressing psychopathy on two childhood risk factors (environmental risk and individual risk) and offense trajectories, only environmental risk and trajectory groups predicted psychopathy scores, with "frequent and chronic styles of offending strongly related to psychopathy" (A. Piquero, Farrington, et al., 2007, p. 591). This study provides further evidence that serious offense trajectories are associated with a greater degree of psychopathy. No study, however, has examined psychopathy as a precursor to the serious offending trajectory by assessing this characteristic in children. Such an investigation is possible using the Antisocial Process Screening Device, a parent and teacher rating scale developed by Paul Frick and Robert Hare (2001), to assess psychopathic characteristics in children ages 6 to 13.

Also, although psychopathic traits predicted trajectory group membership, it would not be expected that all individuals on that trajectory were psychopathic (McCuish et al., 2014). Therefore, it would be important to examine the offending characteristics of individuals on a high-rate-chronic trajectory who show psychopathic traits in terms of their offense characteristics, including crime mix and the seriousness and types of crimes committed, and compare those with individuals on the same trajectory who do not show psychopathic traits. It may be that psychopaths are more prolific in their offending and commit offenses of a more serious (i.e., violent) nature. Examining the types and severity of offenses committed by psychopathic individuals on other trajectories, including the low- and moderate-rate chronic, would shed further light on the nature of their longitudinal offense patterns (McCuish, Corrado, Hart, & DeLisi, 2015). Based on the findings of the Salihovic and Stattin (2017) and Corrado et al. (2015) studies, one might predict that the affective dimension of psychopathy is associated with a lower rate but with more serious, violent crimes. Also, do psychopathic offenders show the same pattern of intermittency and desistance as nonpsychopaths? How are the various dimensions of psychopathy related to the severity and types of offending across trajectory groups? Addressing these questions could have implications for the conceptualization of psychopathy and its relation to criminal activity across the life course.

PSYCHOSOCIAL MATURITY. Monahan, Steinberg, Cauffman, and Mulvey (2009) examined the association between psychosocial maturity in adolescence and criminal trajectory membership in a sample of 1,105 male juvenile offenders participating in the Pathways to Desistance study (Mulvey et al., 2004). Drawing on Gottfredson and Hirschi's (1990) general theory of crime, the aim of the study was to examine the role of increasing psychosocial maturity on desistance of offending, particularly among individuals on an adolescence-limited trajectory (Moffitt, 1993). Psychosocial maturity comprises three elements, assessed by two indicators each: temperance (i.e., impulse control, suppression of aggression), perspective (i.e., consideration of others and future orientation), and responsibility (i.e., personal responsibility and resistance to peer influence). Psychosocial maturity was assessed by standardized measures first administered at baseline when the sample was between 14 and 18 years of age (average 16.5 years) and annually after that over the next 4 years. Offense data were gathered over five waves (including baseline) from ages 14 to 22 and were based on the self-reported involvement in 22 antisocial acts.

The results of the trajectory analysis yielded five groups, labeled low (37.3%), moderate (18.7%), adolescence peak (14.6%), desister (23.7%), and persister (5.7%). Growth curve analysis was used to model the longitudinal pattern of development on the six indicators of psychosocial maturity. Psychosocial maturity was then examined in relation to the five trajectory groups. The results indicated that, as expected, increases on indicators of psychosocial maturity were associated with decreases in antisocial behavior in the low-level, moderate-level, adolescence-peak, and desister groups. By comparison, individuals on the persister trajectory tended to show continued deficits in the expression of psychosocial maturity, in particular, in the areas of impulse control, suppression of aggression, and future orientation.

The authors concluded that these specific effects were related to maturation of the brain and, specifically, development of the cognitive control system. In their conclusion, Monahan et al. (2009) highlighted two regions of the brain associated with psychosocial maturity, one associated with the cognitive control system and one associated with the social-emotional system. They noted that maturation in the "medial areas of the prefrontal cortex and in connections between medial cortical and paralimbic areas" (Monahan et al., 2009, p. 1666) would be expected to lead to greater empathy, self-knowledge, and attentiveness to social information and decreased susceptibility to peer pressure, important elements of good social-emotional functioning. Interestingly, differences between the persister group and the remaining trajectory groups were not observed in the areas of social-emotional functioning. Rather, differences were seen for temperance behaviors, associated with the cognitive control system. Maturation in the regions of the dorsolateral prefrontal and parietal cortices (Steinberg, 2008) would be expected to lead to enhanced impulse control and the ability to engage in planful behavior, two important aspects of mature cognitive functioning. The different findings related to different regions of the brain is not inconsistent with Moffitt's theory (1993) in that youth who persisted in antisocial behavior showed neurological deficits in some areas but not others.

In a follow-up study, Monahan, Steinberg, Cauffman, and Mulvey (2013) continued to collect antisocial activity and psychosocial maturity data for the sample to age 25. Repeating the same analyses, their trajectory analyses also yielded five trajectory groups, labeled low (37.2%), moderate (13.5%), early desister (31.3%), late desister (10.5%), and persister (7.5%). A growth curve analysis was conducted on a global index of psychosocial maturity. The results indicated that, first, normative psychosocial maturity continued to develop well into the 20s. Second, consistent with their earlier study, the persistence of antisocial behavior across the follow-up period was associated with both lower levels of psychosocial maturity at age 16 and a deficit in the development of psychosocial maturity compared to the remaining four trajectories.

Taken together, all these studies highlight the ways in which persistence in antisocial behavior and more serious offending are associated with distinct differences in illicit behavior, disrupted employment opportunities, relationship difficulties, personality problems, and neurological deficits associated with problems of disinhibition and psychosocial maturity, all assessed in adolescence or adulthood. Although of interest, these findings do not speak directly to the potential unique etiologies and developmental pathways that set individuals off onto distinct criminal trajectories. In the next section, we review studies that examine predictors of criminal trajectory membership assessed prior to the onset of the criminal activity.

Predictors of Trajectory Group Membership

Like the previous section, this review is selective due to space constraints and focuses on a number of studies that generally highlight several critical topics in the research. These topics are (a) dose effects, (b) age-graded influence of risk factors, and (c) results with community or high-/at-risk samples and offender samples. Returning to Nagin and Land (1993), these researchers used official conviction data to age 32 from the CSDD and risk factor information collected prospectively from study participants to examine the relation between childhood risk factors (ages 8–11) and adolescent correlates (ages 12–15 and 16–19) and criminal trajectories. Recall that their trajectory analysis yielded four groups, labeled high-rate chronic offenders (12%), adolescent-limited offenders (17%), low-rate chronic offenders (33%), and nonoffenders (40%). Comparisons across the groups revealed that at age 8 to 11, the high-rate chronic offenders were more troublesome and were lacking in concentration than were those in the other groups, particularly compared to the nonoffenders. These results provide some support for Moffitt's (1993) theory, but the authors cautioned that the results were more suggestive than definitive.

For decades, the CSDD data set has provided rich fodder for the statistical analysis of developmental processes associated with criminal behavior and for testing theory. The fact that the conviction data of the

CSDD extend across major developmental periods, from adolescence into adulthood, enabled Nagin and Land (1993) to find support for the hypothesis that the familiar age–crime curve at the aggregate level belies an underlying heterogeneity in the pattern of offending at the individual level, as predicted by Moffitt (1993). Moreover, the wealth of childhood risk-factor data permitted an examination of the early developmental processes that lead to frequent, serious, and persistent offending.

The CSDD was used again by A. Piquero, Farrington, et al. (2007) to examine developmental risk factors for trajectory group membership. Gathering conviction data to age 40, their trajectory analysis yielded five groups, labeled nonoffenders (62.3%), low adolescence-peaked offenders (15.6%), very low-rate chronic offenders (11.3%), high adolescence-peaked offenders (5.4%), and high-rate chronic offenders (2.5%). Twenty-seven developmental risk factors located in four domains (individual, parent, family, and school) were selected for analyses. These 27 variables were collapsed into two broad variables, individual and environmental (parent, family, school). A series of logistic regression analyses and multinomial regression analyses were run to compare the risk variables across the five trajectory groups. Results indicated that individuals with high scores (reflecting the presence of more risk factors) on the aggregate environmental and individual risk variables were more likely to be in the high-rate-chronic group followed by the high-adolescence-peaked group. By and large, a similar pattern of results was found in another reanalysis of the CSDD that used conviction data to age 56 (Farrington, Piquero, & Jennings, 2013), leading Farrington et al. (2013) to conclude that "thus, unlike Laub and Sampson's analysis of the Glueck delinquents, our analysis of the Cambridge males shows that we can predict that 88.5% of the most at-risk males will *not* be non-offenders over the life course based solely on childhood risk factors and that we can identify/predict nearly 30% of the high rate chronic offenders from childhood risk factors alone" (p. 57, emphasis in original).

That a greater number of risk factors was associated with the most severe trajectory group is referred to as a "dose effect" and has been reported in other studies (Fergusson, Horwood, & Nagin, 2000; Maldonado-Molina, Piquero, Jennings, Bird, & Canino, 2009; van Domburgh, Loeber, Bezemer, Stallings, & Stouthamer-Loeber, 2009). For example, in a test of Moffitt's (1993) developmental taxonomy theory,

Fergusson et al. (2000) examined the relation between developmental risk factors and trajectory groups. These researchers used self-reported data of offending behavior from ages 12 to 16 years in a community sample of youth from the Christchurch Health and Development Study (CHDS) in New Zealand. Developmental risk factors included a range of variables within the individual (e.g., intelligence, early-onset conduct and attentional problems) and family domains (e.g., marital conflict, stressful life events, parental criminality, and parental drug use) up to age 12, and the peer domain (i.e., deviant peer affiliations) from ages 14 to 18. Their trajectory analysis generated four groups, which they labeled nonoffenders (55.3%), moderate offenders (30.8%), adolescent-onset offenders (7.6%), and chronic offenders (6.3%).

Comparing risk factors across the trajectory groups, Fergusson et al. (2000) reported that individuals on the chronic trajectory had experienced the least favorable set of childhood circumstances (i.e., the most risk factors). These findings included experiencing a greater likelihood of early conduct problems, family adversity, and social disadvantage. Interestingly, early conduct problems were the strongest predictor of between-group differences, providing support for Moffitt's (1993) theory. At the same time, testing whether neurological problems, in interaction with difficult environmental circumstances (i.e., family adversity), provided the impetus to initiate the onset of the trajectory for these chronic offenders, as predicted by Moffitt, was not possible.

Other studies have not reported dose effects but rather reported on differences for discrete variables such that specific risk factors were associated with particular trajectory groups (e.g., A, Ward et al., 2010; Wiesner & Windle 2004). Wiesner and Capaldi (2003), for example, examined the relation between childhood predictors/adolescent correlates and offending trajectories using a prospective longitudinal design. The study sample consisted of 204 at-risk male youth from the community enrolled in the Oregon Youth Study. Their offense trajectories were tracked for 12 years, from ages 12 to 24, using a self-report survey. Childhood risk factors were assessed when the boys were between 9 and 12 years of age from interviews with the boys and their parents. In addition, adolescent correlates were assessed across three waves of data when the boys were between 13 and 17 years of age. For both childhood and adolescent variables, averages were taken across the waves to derive composite scores. These variables were located within the individual (e.g., depressive symptoms, substance use, sensation-seeking), family (e.g., harsh and inconsistent discipline, parental criminality, SES), school (i.e., academic achievement), and peer (i.e., deviant peer associations) domains.

The results of their trajectory analysis yielded six trajectory groups, identified as chronic high-level offenders (15.7%), chronic low-level offenders (18.6%), decreasing high-level offenders (27.9%), decreasing low-level offenders (21.6%), rare offenders (11.3%), and nonoffenders (4.9%). To identify predictors of trajectory group membership, multinomial regression analyses were performed using the high-level chronic offenders as the reference group. Note that this approach differs from most other studies, which use the low-level offenders or nonoffenders as the reference category in such analyses. The difference is a matter of framing the research question in terms of either how do the trajectory groups differ from the nonoffenders (or low-level offenders) or how do the groups differ from the high-level chronic group. Either way, although comparisons with the extreme group (high or low) are the most robust with regard to finding group differences (e.g., Wiesner & Capaldi, 2003), such comparisons may also lead to an overestimation of the strength of the relationship for that risk factor (Farrington, 2005d).

Their findings indicated that, compared to very rare offenders (i.e., the nonoffenders and rare offenders combined), individuals on the chronic high-level trajectory were more likely to have had attention problems, depressive symptoms, and poor parental supervision and to have engaged in risky sexual behavior and substance use. Also, lower levels of substance use differentiated individuals in the decreasing high-level group from the high-level chronic offenders. Moreover, the chronic low-level group differed from the chronic high-level group on adolescent factors but not childhood factors. These factors included fewer risky sexual behaviors and less involvement with delinquent peers, both in favor of the chronic low-level group. Wiesner and Capaldi (2003) noted that delinquent peer group was the most consistent factor that discriminated among the groups. They concluded that, consistent with developmental theories of antisocial behavior (e.g., Moffitt, 1993; Patterson, DeBaryshe, & Ramsey 1989), childhood and adolescent factors exert their influence at different stages of development. For example, family factors in childhood, specifically punitive and inconsistent parenting and low parental supervision, and deviant peer associations in adolescence were both uniquely associated with a chronic-high-level offense trajectory suggesting that, whereas family factors in childhood were associated with the onset of criminality in the chronic high-level group, peer factors in adolescence were associated with the maintenance of this offense trajectory.

It is noteworthy that findings regarding associations of specific child-hood risk factors to particular trajectory groups were more mixed in a subsequent analysis in which trajectories of officially recorded arrests of the Oregon Youth Study males up to age 26 were linked to child-hood predictors and a time-varying covariate deviant-peer associations (Wiesner, Capaldi, & Kim, 2012). In this case, offense trajectories were *not* based on self-report data and were tracked across a longer time (17 years). Analyses were conducted using SAS Proc TRAJ and yielded three arrest trajectory groups (see Wiesner, Capaldi, & Kim, 2007, for a complete description of these groups). Although the high-level chronic trajectory group (9.2%) had the highest mean levels on some child-hood risk factors (notably harsh and inconsistent parental discipline) and the time-varying covariate deviant-peer affiliations (especially past the juvenile years), childhood risk factors did not differentially predict membership in the two chronic offense trajectories when the equality of predictive effects was statistically tested with Wald tests. At the very least, these results demonstrate that findings for childhood predictors of offense trajectories may not necessarily converge across official records and self-report measures of crime.

In two studies, Day and his colleagues (Day et al., 2012; A. Ward et al., 2010) examined the childhood predictors and adolescent correlates asso-ciated with the criminal trajectories in two subsamples of juvenile offend-ers from Toronto, Canada (n = 378 and n = 386). The combined sample comprised the entire population of 764 male offenders who had been incarcerated as youth between 1986 and 1997 to one of two open-custody facilities in Toronto. The studies used a retrospective longitudinal design.

For both samples, the criminal data for juvenile and adult offenses were obtained from the (Ontario) Ministry of Correctional Services, the Canadian Police Information Centre, and Predisposition Reports from the client files maintained by the children's mental health center. Three data sources were used to ensure a high degree of completeness and accuracy for the sequenced, longitudinal offending data. From these sources, counts by age of all their unique court contacts arising from a new set of charges were recorded to September 26, 2007, the end of the follow-up period. The criminal count data were adjusted for both time-at-risk (Eggleston, Laub, & Sampson 2004) and estimated age at the time of offense rather than at court contact (Farrington et al., 2006; see Day et al., 2007, for details on these adjustments). In the A. Ward et al. (2010) study, the criminal activity was followed for an average of 12 years. In the Day et al. (2012) study, the sample was followed for an average of 16 years.

The results of the trajectory analysis in the A. Ward et al. (2010) study, performed using SAS Proc TRAJ, yielded four trajectory groups, labeled moderate rate (21.7%), low rate (65.1%), high-rate adult peaked (7.7%), and high-rate adolescence peaked (5.6%). The results of the trajectory analysis, in the Day et al. (2012) study, performed using the R package *crimCV* (Nielsen et al., 2014), yielded seven trajectory groups, labeled moderate-late persister (3.6%), high-late offender (3.9%), high-early offender (4.4%), moderate adolescence-peaked offender (11.7%), moderate-early persister (14.2%), low desister (29.8%), and low persister (32.4%).

For both studies, developmental predictors/correlates were extracted from client files maintained by the agency that operated the facilities. Two sets of coding schemes were developed to differentiate the childhood (i.e., birth–12 years) and adolescent (i.e., 13–18 years) variables. The variables were selected based on a review of the literature for the major putative factors associated with the onset or maintenance of criminal activity. A total of 17 variables were identified that fell into four life domains: (1) individual (e.g., impulsivity, intelligence, early onset conduct problems), (2) family (e.g., parental psychopathology, parental criminality, harsh discipline, poor child-rearing methods, involvement with alternative care), (3) peer (i.e., antisocial associates, peer rejection), and (4) school (i.e., poor academic achievement).

Multinomial regression analyses were conducted in both the A. Ward et al. (2010) and Day et al. (2012) studies to identify the set of variables that differentiate the trajectory groups, using the low-rate/low-rate-desister group as the reference category. Results of Ward et al. indicated that, in childhood, broken home and involvement in alternative care (e.g., child welfare) differentiated the moderate- and high-rate groups from the

low-rate trajectory. In adolescence, criminal family members differentiated the moderate- and high-rate groups from the low-rate group and
involvement in alternative care characterized the high-rate group in comparison to the low-rate group. Last, the low-rate group was not immune
from risk factors as individuals in this trajectory group were characterized
in adolescence by poor peer relations, familial abuse, and a broken home.

The results of Day et al. (2012) indicated that the early onset of antisocial behavior before the age of 12 differentiated the high-late and
the moderate-adolescence-peaked groups from the low-rate-desister
group. Poor academic achievement differentiated the moderate-
adolescence-peaked group from the low-desister group. In adolescence,
family relationship problems differentiated the high-late, moderate-
adolescence-peaked, and moderate-early-persister groups from the low-
rate-desister group. As well, involvement in alternative care increased
the likelihood of being in the high-late, high-early, and moderate-
adolescence-peaked groups. Last, good academic achievement increased
the likelihood of being in the low-desister group compared with the
high-late, moderate-adolescence-peaked, and moderate-early-persister
groups. In both studies, adolescent variables more strongly differentiated
the trajectory groups than did childhood variables. This finding fits with
the meta-analysis by Leschied, Chiodo, Nowicki, and Rodger (2008),
which found that adolescent risk factors tend to be stronger predictors
than childhood risk factors of adult criminal offending, consistent with
the *longitudinal law* (Moffitt, 1993). As well, in both studies, no group
was immune to the presence of risk factors. This effect might be attributed to the high-risk nature of this offender sample in that all had been
sentenced as juveniles to a custodial sentence. As a result, they all would
have experienced some adversity in their childhood or adolescence.

Some Reflections on the Literature

This chapter reviewed the literature on correlates and predictors of
criminal trajectories of adolescents and adults with an emphasis on the
factors associated with membership in the high-rate persistent trajectory groups. Table 6.1 provides an overview of studies that is updated
and expanded from an earlier review by Day et al. (2012). The majority
of these studies were conducted in the United States (especially with

community and high-risk samples), but other countries included England (typically based on data from the CSDD study), Canada (especially using male offender samples), Australia, Germany, Netherlands, and New Zealand. Potential limitations to the generalizability of these findings to samples from other, or understudied, countries thus must be kept in mind. Although most researchers used frequency counts of criminal acts, some studies focused on modeling crime trajectories using variety, seriousness, and seriousness-frequency measures of offending. Lessons learned from criminal career paradigm research remind us that different dimensions of criminal activity (e.g., frequency, seriousness, duration) are not necessarily related to the same developmental risk factors and correlates. Moreover, whereas self-report measures of offending behavior predominated in studies with community samples, most analyses with high-risk and offender samples relied on official records measures of crime. The findings reported earlier for the Oregon Youth Study add a cautionary note that such methodological features might influence substantive findings on developmental precursors and correlates of offense trajectories. Not many longitudinal data sets include measures of both self-reported and officially recorded criminal behavior, but a more systematic exploration of such issues with other samples is highly desirable.

Other methodological features also influence the study results. These features include (a) the number of variables and range of life domains included in the analyses; (b) the nature of the sample, that is, whether community, high risk, or offender; and (c) whether the analyses were guided by a particular theory, such as Moffitt's (1993) dual taxonomy, Patterson's early-/late-starter model (Patterson & Yoerger, 1993, 1997), or the social development model (Catalano & Hawkins, 1996). On the latter point, analyses of a particular theory tended to influence the selection of variables in the prediction models. A number of studies included in the review drew on Moffitt's (1993) dual taxonomy model, which posits two trajectories, each initiated by a different set of predictors. Other theoretical models, such as the early-/late-starter model from Patterson (Patterson & Yoerger, 1993, 1997), are less explicit in positing unique etiological factors and rely more on a linear gradation hypothesis, although there are differences among the offender groups in the posited developmental processes (Wiesner, Capaldi, & Patterson, 2003). Systematic tests of competing predictions from these different theoretical frameworks for the same sample are highly

TABLE 6.1. Trajectory Studies That Identify a High-Rate Chronic Group and Associated Childhood Predictors and/or Adolescent Correlates

Author(s)	Year	Data Set[a]	Sample Country N (gender[b])	Analysis[c] (software package)	No. Groups	High-Rate Group (offense variable[d])	Risk Factors
Fergusson, Horwood, & Nagin	2000	CHDS	Community New Zealand N = 936 (M/F)	LCA (PAN-MARK)	4	Chronic (6.3%) (S/O; variety[e])	Early conduct problems; family adversity; social disadvantage
McDermott & Nagin	2001	NYS	Community United States N = 835 (M)	SGBTM (GAUSS)	3	Group 3 (4.6%) (S; frequency[f])	Delinquent peers; negative labels of the child by parents
White, Bates, & Buyske	2001	HHDP	Community United States N = 698 (M)	MMLCR (Splus)	4	Persistent delinquents (7.0%) (S; frequency)	Disinhibition
Chung, Hill, Hawkins, Gilchrist, & Nagin	2002	SSDP	Community United States N = 808 (M/F)	SGBTM (SAS)	5	Chronic (7.0%) (S; seriousness[g])	Aggressive behavior; poor family management; antisocial peers; poor academic achievement; community availability of drugs
Wiesner & Silbereisen	2003	—	Community Germany N = 318 (M/F)	GMM (Mplus)	4	High level (14.0%) (S; frequency)	Male gender; older age at Wave 1 of data collection; low parental monitoring and empathy; high peer tolerance of deviance
Wiesner & Windle	2004	MAVS	Community United States N = 1,218 (M/F)	GMM (Mplus)	6	High-level chronic (6.4%) (S; frequency)	Poor academic achievement; adjustment problems; unsupportive family; negative life events

(*continued*)

TABLE 6.1. Trajectory Studies That Identify a High-Rate Chronic Group and Associated Childhood Predictors and/or Adolescent Correlates (*continued*)

Author(s)	Year	Data Set[a]	Sample Country N (gender[b])	Analysis[c] (software package)	No. Groups	High-Rate Group (offense variable[d])	Risk Factors
Nagin & Land	1993	CSDD	High risk England N = 403 (M)	SGBTM (GAUSS)	4	High-rate chronic (12.0%) (O; frequency)	Troublesome and poor concentration in childhood; job instability; delinquent siblings; marijuana use
Nagin, Farrington, & Moffitt	1995	CSDD	High risk England N = 403 (M)	SGBTM	4	High-rate chronic (12.0%) (O; frequency)	Weak attachment to spouse
Sampson & Laub	2003	GG	High risk United States N = 500 (M)	SGBTM (SAS)	6	High-rate chronic (3.2%) (O; frequency)	None was found
Wiesner & Capaldi	2003	OYS	At risk United States N = 204 (M)	GMM (Mplus)	6	Chronic high level (15.7%) (S; frequency)	Attention problems; poor parental supervision; depressive symptoms; risky sexual behavior; substance use; deviant peer group
Davis, Banks, Fisher, & Grudzinskas	2004	—	High risk United States N = 131 (M/F)	SGBTM (SAS)	3	High rate (12.1%) (O; frequency)	Male gender; substance abuse/ dependence disorder
A. Piquero, Farrington, & Blumstein	2007	CSDD	High risk England N = 411 (M)	SGBTM (SAS)	6	High-rate chronic (2.5%) (O; frequency)	High level on composite environmental and individual risk factors
Ryan, Hernandez, & Herz	2007	—	High risk United States N = 294 (M)	SGBTM (SAS)	3	Chronic (27.0%) (O; frequency)	Poor school achievement

(*continued*)

TABLE 6.1. Trajectory Studies That Identify a High-Rate Chronic Group and Associated Childhood Predictors and/or Adolescent Correlates (*continued*)

Author(s)	Year	Data Set[a]	Sample Country N (gender[b])	Analysis[c] (software package)	No. Groups	High-Rate Group (offense variable[d])	Risk Factors
Hoeve, Blokland, Semon Dubas, Gerris, & van der Laan	2008	PYS	High risk United States N = 849 (M)	SGBTM (SAS)	5	Serious persisting (24.2%) (S/O; seriousness)	Authoritarian parenting style
A. Piquero, Farrington, et al.	2012	CSDD	High risk England N = 411 (M)	SGBTM (SAS)	5	High-rate chronic (2.5%) (O; frequency)	Psychopathy scores
Wiesner, Capaldi, & Kim	2012	OYS	At risk United States N = 203 (M)	SGBTM (SAS)	3	High-level chronics (9.2%) (O; frequency)	Mixed evidence
Farrington, Piquero, & Jennings	2013	CSDD	High risk England N = 404 (M)	SGBTM (SAS)	5	High-rate chronic (5.2%) (O; frequency)	High level on composite environmental and individual risk factors
J. Marshall	2006	SABC	Offender Australia N = 3,343 (M/F)	SGBTM (SAS)	6	Very high (0.9%) (O; frequency)	Indigenous status
Livingston, Stewart, Allard, & Ogilvie	2008	—	Offender Australia N = 4,470 (M/F)	SGBTM (SAS)	3	Chronic (11.0%) (O; frequency)	Indigenous status; male
Bersani, Nieuw-beerta, & Laub	2009	CCLCS	Offender The Netherlands N = 4,615 (M/F)	SGBTM (SAS)	4	Chronic (4.0%) (O; frequency)	None was found
Mac-Donald, Haviland, & Morral	2009	AOP	Offender United States N = 419 (M/F)	SGBTM (SAS)	3 (violent) 3 (non-violent)	High-rate chronic (5.9%) (S; frequency) High-rate chronic (14.0%) (S; frequency)	Delinquent peers delinquent peers; sub-stance abuse

(*continued*)

TABLE 6.1. Trajectory Studies That Identify a High-Rate Chronic Group and Associated Childhood Predictors and/or Adolescent Correlates (*continued*)

Author(s)	Year	Data Set[a]	Sample Country N (gender[b])	Analysis[c] (software package)	No. Groups	High-Rate Group (offense variable[d])	Risk Factors
Monahan, Steinberg, Cauffman, & Mulvey	2009	PDS	Offender United States N = 1,105 (M)	SGBTM (SAS)	5	Persister (5.7%) (S; variety)	Future orientation; impulse control; suppression of aggression
van Domburgh, Vermeiren, Blokland, & Doreleijers	2009	—	Offender The Netherlands N = 287 (M)	SGBTM (SAS)	3	High rate (7.0%) (O; seriousness-frequency[h])	Older at first offense; non-Western ethnicity
van der Geest, Blokland, & Biljeveld	2009	—	Offender The Netherlands N = 274 (M)	SGBTM (SAS)	5	High-frequency chronic (5.9%) (O; frequency)	Criminal family members; suicide attempts; delinquent peers
Yessine & Bonta	2009	—	Offender (Aboriginal) Offender (non-Aboriginal) Canada N = 439 (M)	GMM (Mplus)	2 2	Chronic high (18.7%) (O; seriousness-frequency) Chronic high (12.3%) (O; seriousness-frequency)	Delinquent peers; family dysfunction; substance use problems with accommodation
A. Ward et al.	2010	—	Offender Canada N = 378 (M)	SGBTM (SAS)	4	High-rate adult peaked (7.7%) (O; frequency)	Alternative care involvement; criminal family members
Day et al.	2012	—	Offender Canada N = 386 (M)	SGBTM (*crimCV*)	7	High late (3.9%) (O; frequency)	Alternative care involvement; early onset problem behavior
Monahan, Steinberg, Cauffman, & Mulvey	2013	PDS	Offender United States N = 1,105 (M)	SGBTM (SAS)	5	Persister (7.5%) (S; variety)	Deficit in the development of psychosocial maturity

(*continued*)

TABLE 6.1. Trajectory Studies That Identify a High-Rate Chronic Group and Associated Childhood Predictors and/or Adolescent Correlates (*continued*)

Author(s)	Year	Data Set[a]	Sample Country N (gender[b])	Analysis[c] (software package)	No. Groups	High-Rate Group (offense variable[d])	Risk Factors
McCuish, Corrado, Lussier, & Hart	2014	ISVYOS	Offender Canada N = 307 (M/F)	SGBTM (SAS)	4	High-frequency chronic (27.4%) (O; frequency)	Psychopathy scores

Note: Name of data set and software package are listed when identified by the authors of the given study.
[a] AOP = RAND Adolescent Outcomes Project; CCLCS = Criminal Career and Life-Course Study; CHDS = Christchurch Health and Development Study; CSDD = Cambridge Study of Delinquent Development; GG = Glueck and Glueck study; HHDP = Rutgers Health and Human Development Project; ISVYOS = Incarcerated Serious and Violent Young Offender Study; MAVS = Middle Adolescent Vulnerability Study; NYS = National Youth Survey; OYS = Oregon Youth Study; PDS = Pathways to Desistance Study; PYS = Pittsburgh Youth Study; SABC = South Australia Birth Cohort; SSDP = Seattle Social Development Project.
[b] M = Male; F = Female.
[c] GMM = latent growth mixture modeling; LCA = latent class analysis; MMLCR = mixed-mode latent class regression; SGBTM = semiparametric group-based trajectory modeling.
[d] S = Self-report measure of offending; O = official-records measure of offending.
[e] Variety refers to the number of different antisocial/criminal behaviors committed at each period.
[f] Frequency refers to the total number of criminal behaviors/convictions at each period.
[g] Seriousness refers to the seriousness level of the most serious offense committed at each period.
[h] Seriousness-frequency uses a combination of frequency counts and seriousness ratings.

desirable to advance our knowledge on precursors and correlates of offense trajectories (for an example, see Wiesner et al., 2012).

In addition, recent theoretical approaches framed within a development and life-course perspective, such as cascade models (Masten & Cicchetti, 2010) propose testable hypotheses about the complex transactions and interactions among risk factors across multiple levels and systems within and outside the individual. More research is needed to further develop and test these models. Further work is also needed to understand the role and impact of protective and promotive factors on the development of adaptive and maladaptive outcomes (Loeber, Farrington, Stouthamer-Loeber, & White, 2008; Lösel & Bender, 2003). The modest success in using childhood risk factors to identify/predict future high-rate chronic offenders (nearly 30% in the CSDD; Farrington et al., 2013) fits with contemporary developmental systems theory that recognizes the *relative* plasticity of human development across the life span (e.g., Lerner et al., 2015). For example, some of these frameworks study ecological and developmental assets of the developing person that are posited to foster positive develop-ment and reduce the likelihood of problem behaviors (Lerner et al., 2011). Integration of such thinking into criminology is in its early stages.

There is now a greater understanding of the role and impact of key risk factors in the lives of individuals on the development of antisocial and criminal behavior. No single variable in childhood or adolescence consistently stood out as a predictor of high-rate persistent offending. Rather, as seen in Table 6.1, a number of variables from multiple life do-mains contribute to the high-rate-chronic offense trajectory. Individual risk factors included early conduct problems and attention problems, aggressive behavior, adjustment problems, sensation seeking, depres-sion, suicidality, substance abuse/dependence, risky sexual behavior, and psychosocial immaturity. Family factors included family adversity, authoritarian parenting, poor parental monitoring and supervision, low parental empathy, negative labels applied by the parents to the child, family contact with a child welfare agency, and criminal family mem-bers. Peer factors included association with a delinquent or deviant peer group and high peer tolerance of deviance. The school factor was poor academic achievement. Environmental factors included social disadvan-tage, exposure to community violence, and availability of drugs.

It remains to be seen whether these variables, which cut across mul-tiple life domains, fit into a neat, theoretically cohesive developmental model that can collectively account for high-rate persistent offending or whether the variables reflect the principle of *equifinality* (Cicchetti & Rogosch, 1996), whereby, across individuals, exposure to a range of vari-ables converge to result in a common outcome. Moreover, if research finds that a set of predictors fit a theoretical model, the factors may also be *developmentally sequenced* such that their influence is exerted at dif-ferent periods of development (e.g., early, middle, or late childhood, or early or late adolescence). For example, during childhood, family factors (e.g., harsh parenting or family structure) are more influential as predic-tors of crime, whereas, during adolescence, peer factors (e.g., antisocial peers or peer substance use) are more salient (Tanner-Smith et al., 2013; Wiesner & Capaldi, 2003).

Last, further research is needed to examine potential causal mecha-nisms linking risk factors to criminal outcomes (Farrington et al., 2013). For example, involvement with alternative care (e.g., living in a foster home) has been found to be an important risk factor for high-rate criminal offending (Day et al. 2012; Leschied et al., 2008; Nicol et al., 2000; Ryan & Testa, 2005). Questions remain about the developmental processes involved in the life experiences associated with child welfare involvement that would either create its own risk factor or exacerbate existing risk factors, for later contact with the justice system (Corrado, Freedman, & Blatier, 2011). Some have suggested that limited educational opportunities, placement instability, unreliable or nonexistent support from family, and low-wage employment contribute to the difficulties foster care youth encounter as they exit the system, which further increases the likelihood they will become involved in the justice system (Alltucker, Bullis, Close, & Yovanoff, 2006; Ryan, Hernandez, & Herz, 2007).

At the same time, Ryan et al. (2007) noted that not all foster care youth have contact with the justice system. Their trajectory analysis indicated that 52% of the sample were identified as nonoffenders. These individuals were more likely to be in school than those who had criminal offenses. Consistent with a developmental and life-course perspective, further investigations could examine the developmental risk factors associated with family breakdown and child maltreatment that initiate a pathway to child welfare involvement, program instability, poor academic achievement, and other challenges facing dependent youth in order to better understand the mechanisms underlying the child welfare–delinquency link (Alltucker et al., 2006; Ryan et al., 2007; Ryan, Testa, & Zhai, 2008). This research could then inform the development of support systems to assist youth as they transition out of foster care and of programs that help children and youth experience educational success while in the care of the child welfare system. The next chapter reviews the literature on associations between criminal trajectories and later life outcomes, including poor health outcomes and success or failure in various later life domains, and the role of turning points and an explanation of desistance from crime, considering such factors as marriage, parenthood, and employment.

Conclusion

John Snow was successful in finding the cause of cholera. Criminology scholars still have a way to go. Specifying and delineating the key variables involved in the quest provide greater conceptual clarification for the task at hand. Greater availability of longitudinal databases and advances in statistical analyses, including trajectory group modeling, conducted within a risk factor research framework, allow researchers to address more complex questions with greater precision. In the end, although identifying the root causes of a complex phenomenon such as crime is difficult, perhaps unending (Blomberg, Mestre, & Mann, 2013), with perseverance and good science, we hold the optimistic view that researchers will establish causality through explanatory models that are rooted in developmental and multidisciplinary discourses and are well supported by research across diverse populations across the life course. It is the hope that these models will inform the development of effective strategies to bring about meaningful change in the lives of individuals through prevention and intervention. We also acknowledge that, unlike cholera, with its single pathogen that can be kept in check, crime, as a social phenomenon, represents more of a "moving target."

Suggested Supplemental Readings

An overview of leading theories of causation is provided in Shadish and Sullivan (2012). Haviland and Nagin (2005) lay out how more confident causal inferences, for example, regarding the effects of turning points on offense trajectories, can be drawn during the analysis of nonexperimental longitudinal data by combining semiparametric group-based trajectory modeling with propensity score matching. Kraemer et al. (1997) and Kazdin et al. (1997) provide thorough discussions of the different types of variables mentioned earlier.

7

Later Life Outcomes, Turning Points, and Desistance

The explanation of desistance from crime, that is, the process through which criminal "'careers' fizzle out and eventually end" (Rocque, 2017, p. 1), has been an enduring goal of criminological research. This chapter mostly focuses on quantitative work on this topic and explore how this literature can be tied more closely to group-based criminal trajectory research. Desisting offender trajectories have been identified in several studies (e.g., Bushway, Sweeten, & Nieuwbeerta, 2009; Sampson & Laub, 2003), but trajectory researchers have paid little heed to the extant literature on theories of desistance from crime. We submit that better integration of these independent strands of criminological research is needed to advance our understanding of desisting offender trajectory groups. Moreover, the incorporation of cornerstones of leading developmental frameworks on self-regulatory strategies across the life course would serve to sharpen the construct and role of human agency in desisting versus persisting offender trajectories and their later life outcomes. To this end, the following excerpt of life-history narratives from Laub and Sampson's (2003) classic volume *Shared Beginnings, Divergent Lives* serves as a useful backdrop for the rest of the chapter:

> At the time of our interview, Leon's major turning point, at least in his own mind, was marriage. He met his wife when he was 1/. . . . His wife knew he was in trouble as an adolescent, but she decided to take a chance on him anyway. During our interview with Leon, she stated, . . . "It wasn't unusual in those days for kids to be in that kind of trouble and for some reason . . . if my daughter took up with anybody like that, I'd go through the roof! We had so many strikes against us. He had no education, he drank. Not when we were together . . . When you think of it, you know, I can't get over how well we've done with how little we had. He had no occupation. He was a baker. And luckily he learned to bake and then he learned to manage, and he was a go-getter, and actually that's all we had going. And I was a

fighter and go-getter. Even though I had a little bit more education, we got so much in common, that's why we get along so well, we like the same things" . . . As a married man, Leon worked every day, did not go out with the guys, and was home every night. . . . Leon insisted to us that he would have continued getting into trouble if he had not married. Indeed, some fifty years earlier, when asked for the reasons behind his reformation, Leon stated emphatically, "My wife straightened me out." Even before his actual marriage, Leon's parole officer remarked that he had given up drinking and gambling when he became interested in a 17-year-old woman who would later become his wife. (Laub & Sampson, 2003, pp. 120–121)

Leon's story shows how a good marriage can promote desistance from crime, in this case primarily through a change in routine activities (i.e., working every day in legal employment, staying home in the evenings, and no longer spending leisure time with deviant peers). As we will see later, his story echoes one major theme in the explanation of desistance.

The next two excerpts from other researchers highlight the importance of human agency, identity shifts, and cognitive transformations, representing a second major theme in understanding the desistance process. "So I got another chance and I'm gonna do it this time, because I want to change. I want to go home and be with my kids. I want to live a drug-free life. I want to be able to be an abiding citizen and do what I need to do and not always be in trouble and be bad-ass. That is not me" (Opsal, 2012, p. 388).

Another individual remarks, "You get tired of bein' tired, you know. I got tired of hustlin', you know. I got tired of livin' the way I was livin', you know. Due to your body, your body, mentally emotionally, you know. Everybody's tryin' to get over. Everybody will stab you in your back. Nobody gives a fuck about the next person. And I used to have people talkin' to me, 'You know, you're not a bad lookin' girl. You know, why you don't get yourself together?'" (Baskin & Sommers, 1998, p. 129).

Extant trajectory research has mostly focused on the description and prediction of criminal trajectories. By comparison, later life outcomes of criminal trajectories (e.g., problem behaviors, health outcomes, employment) are understudied, although this issue has drawn more interest in recent years. Trajectory research has paid even less attention to the investigation of turning points that can redirect trajectories away from criminal activity or the processes that lead to the eventual termination of criminal behavior. To overcome these gaps, trajectory researchers need to interface more systematically with these independent strands of the criminological literature. For example, trajectory studies can shed light on whether everyone desists from crime, making it a normative event, and the possible forces that reorient offenders toward a desisting pathway (e.g., psychosocial maturation, identity change, brain maturation, life events such as starting a family of procreation). All these issues have important implications for policy making and the prevention of crime, but a systematic review and research agenda within the criminal trajectory modeling literature is lacking. To move trajectory research toward this direction, the chapter synthesizes what we know about relations of criminal trajectories to later life outcomes, turning points, and desistance from crime and seeks to make the case for a programmatic agenda that ties trajectory research on these topics more closely to developmental science.

The chapter begins with a discussion of key features of the concepts of desistance and turning points that occupy an important role in the field of criminology, including their definitions, explanations, and methodological issues in studying these phenomena. Next, the results of studies that have examined later life outcomes of criminal trajectories, including adverse health outcomes, psychopathy, various forms of problem behaviors, and success or failure in various adult life domains, are reviewed. A related but emerging area is to examine the risk of recidivism for different criminal trajectories. This is followed by a discussion of the handful of studies that investigated turning point hypotheses and explanations of desistance within the group-based trajectory modeling approach. Last, the chapter makes the case for better integration of this line of research with developmental frameworks, such as incorporating the Selection, Optimization, and Compensation (SOC) theory from Paul Baltes (e.g., Baltes & Baltes, 1990) to refine the role of human agency in trajectories of crime in a developmentally sensitive manner.

Desistance from Crime: Definitions, Methodological Issues, and Explanations

To provide a backdrop for the findings of trajectory studies on later life outcomes, turning points, and desistance, we first draw on the broader criminological literature on these concepts. The term *desistance* from crime refers to the process by which individuals cease committing criminal acts (e.g., Bushway & Paternoster, 2013; Kazemian, 2015; Laub & Sampson, 2001). This important feature of a criminal career has received renewed attention in recent years. Bushway and Paternoster (2013) observe in their review of this topic that "once people start offending, society is very interested in findings ways to encourage them to stop or desist. The study of change is potentially both methodologically and theoretically interesting from an academic perspective. However, the problem becomes simplistic if desistance is an inevitable, predetermined part of life for every person who engages in crime (Sampson & Laub, 2003). Therefore, we start by verifying that there are in fact people who offend throughout their life-course, and that desistance is not 'normative'" (pp. 213–214). Consistent with their claim, group-based trajectory analyses indicate that most offenders appear to have desisted from crime by mid- to late adulthood (Bushway & Paternoster, 2013; Sampson & Laub, 2003), with a relatively small subset of individuals committing crimes lifelong (Bushway et al., 2009) and that there are substantial differences in the timing of desistance among trajectory groups (Farrington, Piquero, & Jennings, 2013; Sampson & Laub, 2003). The resultant need to better understand *when* and *why* specific offender trajectory groups stop engaging in criminal behavior has undoubtedly contributed to the renewed interest in desistance research.

Nevertheless, the definition and measurement of the construct of desistance remain challenges. There is widespread consensus among criminologists that desistance from crime is best conceptualized as a gradual behavioral *process* (e.g., Bottoms, Shapland, Costello, Holmes, & Muir, 2004; Bushway, Piquero, Broidy, Cauffman, & Mazerolle, 2001; Fagan, 1989; Laub & Sampson, 2001; Le Blanc & Fréchette, 1989; Loeber & Le Blanc, 1990; Maruna, 2001), not an *event* of instantaneously moving from a state of committing crime to a state of nonoffending. This position is held for several reasons. First, the cessation of criminal activity is unlikely to occur abruptly, especially for individuals with early-onset high-rate offending patterns, although some scholars have argued that it is possible, perhaps after a traumatic event (e.g., Cusson & Pinsonneault, 1986; Shover, 1996). Second, periods of criminal inactivity between crime events (i.e., intermittency) do occur over the course of criminal careers and widen as offenders age (Baker, Metcalfe, & Piquero, 2015). These temporary lulls in offending may be falsely interpreted as desistance and difficult to distinguish from the permanent cessation of criminal activity (Kazemian, 2007, 2015; Laub & Sampson, 2001, 2003; A. Piquero, 2004b; A. Piquero, Farrington, & Blumstein, 2003). Findings from a qualitative study in Sweden further caution that intermittency periods can represent different underlying dynamics, including a temporary stop of criminal activity without a commitment to long-term change and a second form of temporary inactivity that involves "the will to desist" (Carlsson, 2013, p. 924). Third, criminal careers of individuals who cease all criminal activity at the same age may be distinguished by very different pathways (in terms of variety, frequency, seriousness, and length), rendering single-parameter measures of desistance inadequate. Rather, integrating multiple criminal career parameters (i.e., frequency, seriousness, and versatility of offending) to better capture the dynamic changes occurring during the process of desistance from crime (Kazemian, 2012) appears preferable.

Consistent with these changes in the conceptualization of desistance from crime, the use of dichotomous measures of desistance has significantly decreased. Such measures represent *static* definitions of desistance and fail to capture information on changes in rates of offending over time. Instead, measurement approaches that emphasize process views of desistance have become more common. These approaches adopt *dynamic* definitions of desistance and focus on the pathways by which individuals reach the state of nonoffending (Bushway, Thornberry, & Krohn, 2003). Not surprisingly, process models of desistance from crime require longitudinal data so that intra-individual changes in criminal activity over time can be tracked. However, criminologists have offered quite different dynamic definitions of desistance and consensus on the best analytic strategies has yet to emerge. More than 25 years ago, Le Blanc and Fréchette (1989, followed by Loeber & Le Blanc, 1990) asserted that before individuals permanently terminate all criminal activity, the frequency of offending (as indexed by the parameter lambda) declines, offense specialization increases with greater engagement in more minor offenses, and a culmination point is reached. In an influential paper, Bushway and colleagues (2001) defined desistance as the "process of reduction in the rate of offending from a nonzero level to a stable rate empirically indistinguishable from zero" (p. 500). More recently, Bushway and Paternoster (2013) drew a useful analogy to stochastic time series models and distinguished the following four nonstationary time series processes that map on different theories of desistance from crime.

Model 1 is a *time series with a trend parameter* that is based on the passage of time. The posited inevitable aging of the organism in the general theory of crime (Gottfredson & Hirschi, 1990) is a key example of this explanation of desistance from crime. Model 2 consists of a *cointegrated time series*, in which a time-varying covariate is added to the model specification, whereby the coefficient on the covariate is time-constant. Examples of such explanations of desistance from crime include several maturational and developmental theories (e.g., Gove, 1985) in which the covariate is theorized to peak and decline over time in the same manner as offending propensity changes over the life course. Model 3 represents a *times series with a structural break*, which implies that there are two more sets of parameters (i.e., the causal process is different across periods). Bushway and Paternoster (2013) assert that elements of this time-series specification are present in many desistance theories that focus on the notion of age-graded causal factors, especially frameworks that are predicated on the assumption of an interaction between age-graded life events and individual characteristics (e.g., Giordano, Cernkovich, & Rudolph, 2002). Model 4 consists of a *time series with a random walk*, in which current behavior is simply a function of behavior in the preceding time interval plus a constant and a shock (where the shock is permanently incorporated into the time series). This model is most consistent with Laub and Sampson's (2003) notion of random events or macro-societal life events (e.g., war, natural disasters, the Great Depression).

In summary, desistance researchers continue to lament the multitude of operational definitions of desistance (see Kazemian, 2007, 2015; Laub & Sampson, 2001; Maruna, 2001; Rocque, 2017, for further discussion); "because of the lack of clear, consistent definitions and measurement strategies, many ambiguities persist in the literature and several issues must be examined when seeking to make sense of this literature" (Rocque, 2017, p. 52). To this end, the four models introduced by Bushway and Paternoster (2013) provide a critical tool for advancing desistance research. Although it may not be possible to neatly map every theory of desistance onto one of the four processes, we concur with the authors that their models should prove very fruitful for the task of sharpening the theorizing in existing frameworks. In the end, it is likely that several different mechanisms account for desistance from crime, many of which are captured in the described nonstationary time-series models, rendering the search for the one and only operational definition of desistance a fool's errand.

The *explanation of desistance from crime* has been an enduring goal of criminological research (e.g., Bushway & Paternoster, 2013). A rather simplistic explanation was offered by criminologists Gottfredson and Hirschi (1990), who claimed that the process of moving from the state of offending to the state of not offending is rather uniform and the biological consequence of age (the "inexorable aging of the organism"; p. 141). Hence, criminal career parameters such as onset, persistence, and desistance are all traced back to the latent propensity toward crime. Other scholars disagreed with the notion of a single underlying cause of all criminal career dimensions (e.g., the concept of "asymmetrical causation"; Uggen & Piliavin, 1998). Moreover, making accurate long-term predictions about desistance from crime based on early risk factors (e.g., Kazemian, Farrington, & Le Blanc, 2009; Laub & Sampson, 2003; Morizot & Le Blanc, 2007) has proved difficult. Thus, many explanatory models emphasize changes in adult life circumstances or experiences as key mechanisms, above and beyond early risk factors, the age of onset of offending, and the mere chance effects (e.g., Laub & Sampson, 2003). Social processes related to adult social bonds or age-graded environmental discontinuities have drawn much attention (see Leon's vignette presented earlier). In contrast, individual processes related to adult identity formation, maturation, and human agency have only recently emerged as another critical theme (see the second and third vignettes presented earlier). A discussion of the entire literature on desistance from crime is beyond the scope of this book, but excellent reviews continue to appear (e.g., Bersani & Doherty, 2017; Bushway & Paternoster, 2013; Farrall & Calverley, 2006; Farrall, Hunter, Sharpe, & Calverley, 2014; Kazemian, 2015; Laub & Sampson, 2001, 2003; Paternoster, Bachman, Bushway, Kerrison, & O'Connell, 2015; Rocque, 2017). Here, we simply intend to synthesize emerging trends and major theories in desistance research and provide a sampling of key findings. Studies that applied the group-based trajectory methodology in desistance research are discussed in a later section of this chapter.

Age-graded environmental discontinuities that lead to processes that shape or reinforce changes in behavior play a key role in the pathway to desistance from crime according to many scholars (e.g., Laub & Sampson, 2003; Sampson & Laub, 1993, 2005a). The transition from adolescence to adulthood marks several psychosocial transitions and contextual changes, such as entering the labor force, starting postsecondary education, going to the military, establishing a relationship with a romantic partner, starting a family of procreation, and obtaining stable employment. These age-graded environmental discontinuities can lead to desistance from crime by limiting access to salient reinforcers of criminal activity and reducing the payoffs of offending behavior (Wiesner, Capaldi, & Patterson, 2003). According to informal social control theory, normative psychosocial transitions such as marriage, parenthood, or employment constitute powerful informal social controls that can, under the right conditions, act as turning points by impacting routine activities and opportunities for crime and reducing the motivation to continue committing crimes (e.g., Laub & Sampson, 2003; Sampson & Laub, 2005).

MARRIAGE AND COHABITATION. Marriage is often regarded as a key turning point in the pathway to desistance from crime and has indeed been linked to reduced criminal activity (e.g., Bersani, Laub, & Nieuwbeerta, 2009; Craig & Foster, 2013; Doherty & Ensminger, 2013; Farrington & West, 1995; Horney, Osgood, & Marshall, 1995; McGloin, Sullivan, Piquero, Blokland, & Nieuwbeerta, 2011; Sampson & Laub, 1993), although nil results have also been found (e.g., Kruttschnitt, Uggen, & Shelton, 2000). Adopting a counterfactual approach, Sampson, Laub, and Wimer (2006) found that marriage accounts for an average reduction of 35% in the probability of offending. Analyses of intra-individual change over time showed that men committed fewer crimes when married than when not (e.g., Kerr, Capaldi, Owen, Wiesner, & Pears, 2011; Sampson & Laub, 2005), although there were no differences in criminal activity over time when men were cohabitating versus single (Kerr et al., 2011, but see Savolainen, 2009, on stronger cohabitation effects). In addition, the link between marriage and desistance from crime appears to be qualified by relationship quality or stability (e.g., Bersani & Doherty,

2013; see also Capaldi, Kim, & Owen, 2008, on romantic relationships), developmental timing of the marriage or cohabitation (e.g., Ouimet & Le Blanc, 1996; Theobald & Farrington, 2009), and characteristics of the partner (e.g., Skardhamar, Monsbakken, & Lyngstad, 2014; van Schellen, Poortman, & Nieuwbeerta, 2012).

The interpretation of these effects can be complicated. It is unclear whether the mechanism underlying the marriage–desistance association is related to attachment or bonding to a partner per se (Capaldi, Kerr, Eddy, & Tiberio, 2016). Rather, marriage lessens the amount of leisure time spent with deviant peers (e.g., Warr, 1998), who provide positive reinforcement of criminal behavior (Patterson, Reid, & Dishion, 1992), and increases pressure to spend time with and support the family. Notwithstanding these findings, there also is fairly strong evidence that the selection of intimate partners is a nonrandom process (Boutwell, Beaver, & Barnes, 2012; Krueger, Moffitt, Caspi, Bleske, & Silva, 1998; van Schellen et al., 2012). Offenders are often paired with antisocial partners, either because of rejection by prosocial romantic partners or because offenders actively select intimate partners with whom they can engage in behaviors they enjoy (e.g., drug use, partying) or who are similar to them (Capaldi & Crosby, 1997; Wiesner et al., 2003). These "assortative mating" effects imply that the relation of marriage to desistance from crime may, at least to some extent, be spurious and reflective of self-selection effects. Moreover, results from a Norwegian study call into question whether marriage per se acts as a causal agent in the pathway to desistance because the drop in criminal activity among married participants was observed in the years preceding marriage (i.e., during the courtship period; Lyngstad & Skardhamar, 2013). Upon consideration of such findings, Skardhamar, Savolainen, Aase, and Lyngstad (2015) concluded in a very comprehensive review that "claims about the restraining influence of marriage are overstated. . . . The criminological literature has been insensitive to the reality that entering a marital union is increasingly unlikely to signify the point at which a committed, high-quality relationship is formed" (p. 385).

PARENTHOOD. In a recent review of the crime desistance literature Capaldi et al. (2016) noted that "parenthood increases pressure for social conformity—including stable employment and stable intimate relationships—both of which are incompatible with crime and other problem behaviors, such as heavy drinking and drug use. Consistent with theories of differential association and social learning, the fathers' greater involvement with children, partners, and family may reduce the time available to socialize with male peers in contexts that support crime" (p. 786). The basic mechanisms linking parenthood to desistance from crime are thus presumed to be fairly similar to what was described earlier regarding the effects of marriage, but the parenthood–desistance link has been studied less frequently by comparison. Because the pattern of empirical findings parallels those for marriage in many ways, only a brief overview is offered. Kreager, Matsueda, and Erosheva (2010) found that the transition to motherhood was linked to decreased delinquency among women from disadvantaged communities in Denver, and this effect was even more substantial than that of marriage. For a sample of at-risk men from Oregon, Kerr et al. (2011) reported that occurrence of first fatherhood was related to accelerated decreases in criminal activity, even after controlling for effects of marriage and cohabitation. A considerable portion of this association was explained by father's co-residence with children. Second, some research suggests that associations may be moderated by the developmental timing of parenthood. The older men were when they became fathers, the more pronounced were the decreases in criminal behavior that followed the birth of a child (Kerr et al., 2011). In contrast, Monsbakken, Lyngstad, and Skardhamar (2013) found that most of the decline in offending took place before the birth of a child. To a varying degree, the drop was contingent on gender and relationship status. This observation is similar to what Lyngstad and Skardhamar (2013) described for the marriage–desistance link in the same Norwegian sample.

EMPLOYMENT. Many criminologists subscribe to the view that employment and job stability promote desistance from crime (e.g., Laub & Sampson, 2003; Sampson & Laub, 1993). The empirical evidence has yielded mixed results, with some studies finding nil effects (e.g., Giordano et al., 2002). Qualitative narratives suggest that obtaining a satisfying job was an important accomplishment in the lives of men who desisted from crime (Shover, 1996), with employment perhaps being most critical for sustaining the process of desistance (Laub & Sampson, 2003). Tripodi, Kim, and Bender (2010) found in a study with male parolees in Texas that employment was not related to a decreased likelihood of reincarceration but was associated with longer time lags to reincarceration (i.e., lengthier time intervals of being crime-free in the community). The authors concluded that the desistance process for ex-prisoners might be better conceptualized as a gradual behavioral change process that encompasses various stages. The developmental timing of employment also plays a role. Using data from the National Supported Work Demonstration Project, Uggen (2000) found that the crime reduction effect of work was stronger among individuals over 26 years of age. Morizot and Le Blanc (2007) reported that employment promoted desistance from crime only at specific developmental periods among adjudicated French Canadian males.

With regard to mechanisms that underlie the work–desistance association, employment is presumed to promote desistance from crime through four processes (Laub & Sampson, 2003): (a) employer and employee partake in a reciprocal exchange of social capital, (b) the restriction of opportunities for crime resulting from more structured routine activities (especially under full-time legal employment) and thus a reduced "probability that criminal propensities will be translated into action" (Laub & Sampson, 2003, p. 47), (c) the exertion of direct informal social control in the work context (e.g., employer supervision helps keep employees in line), and (d) the formation of a "sense of identity and meaning" (Laub & Sampson, 2003, p. 47) to one's life. Results from empirical research are not always fully congruent with these propositions. Wright and Cullen (2004) observed that employment increased contact with prosocial coworkers, which "restructure friendship networks by diminishing contact with delinquent peers" (p. 185). The authors concluded that employment promotes desistance from crime through increased associations with prosocial coworkers rather than through the acquisition of increased social capital. It was less the quality of the job that conditioned this effect (as argued by Sampson & Laub, 1993) but, rather, the "*quality of peer associations* that occur within the context of work" (Wright & Cullen, 2004, p. 200, emphasis in original). In addition, Laub and Sampson (2003) cautioned that the work–desistance association may be partially spurious: "It is likely that selection contamination is even greater for employment, if for no other reason than that there are sorting mechanisms (for example, applications, interviews) for work that are not found in informal marriage markets" (pp. 47–48).

In summary, the extant literature documents complex associations between major adult transitions (e.g., marriage, parenthood, employment) and desistance from crime that are often contingent on qualitative features of the transition and its timing. For example, precocious entry into adult social roles typically does not exhibit crime-reduction effects but, rather, contributes to continued offending (e.g., Farrall & Calverley, 2006; Ouimet & Le Blanc, 1996). Theobald and Farrington (2009) found that the crime-reduction effect of marriage was less pronounced for late marriages relative to early or midrange marriages. Lageson and Uggen (2013) concluded in a review that the effect of work on crime appears to change over the life course. These findings reaffirm the critical role that the timing of life events plays in shaping individual's trajectories according to Elder's sociological life-course perspective (e.g., Elder, 1998a; George, 2009).

Adult transitions such as *residential relocation* (Kirk, 2012) and *military service* (Bouffard, 2005; Craig & Foster, 2013; Sampson & Laub, 1993) might also function as turning points but are understudied in desistance research. The effects of *incarceration* on recidivism rates or desistance from crime have been studied more widely, but evidence for its crime-deterrence role is hard to come by (Bales & Piquero, 2012; Gendreau, Goggen, & Cullen, 1999; Maruna & Toch, 2005; Nagin, Cullen, & Jonson, 2009; Weatherburn, 2010), and this field of study would benefit from better integration with prisoner reentry research (see Blumstein & Nakamura, 2009; Bushway, Nieuwbeerta, & Blokland, 2011; Kazemian, 2015).

There is growing recognition among desistance researchers that many putative turning points are interdependent. For example, work is closely interfaced with family life in multiple ways (Han & Moen, 1999; Osgood, Ruth, Eccles, Jacobs, & Barber, 2005), and the period of mid-adulthood is characterized by a significant increase in the number of social roles (Helson & Soto, 2005). Desistance researchers increasingly focus on understanding the relative impact of differing turning points (e.g., parenthood versus cohabitation/marriage; Farrington & West, 1995) and studying joint effects between multiple turning points (e.g., the "respectability package" of marriage and job stability; Giordano et al., 2002; Sampson & Laub, 1993; Savolainen, 2009). Findings from Scandinavian studies (e.g., Monsbakken et al., 2013; Savolainen, 2009) have also raised awareness that the oftentimes complex associations between major adult transitions and desistance from crime are influenced by societal context (e.g., welfare system, social safety net, treatment of convicted offenders). A final point worthy of mention is that, compared to prior generations, transitions into adult social roles have become more variable and occur over relatively longer periods in individuals' lives (Arnett, 2004; Furstenberg, Kennedy, McLoyd, Rumbaut, & Settersten, 2004). This issue raises the question of whether the driving forces behind desistance from crime remain the same for today's emergent adults (J. Hill, Blokland, & van der Geest, 2016). Certain transitions have become more challenging for youth from at-risk backgrounds, such as the acquisition of stable employment given the increased educational demands and the decreasing want for unskilled labor in the job market (Osgood, Foster, Flanagan, & Ruth, 2005). These historical changes can limit the ecological validity of research on desistance from crime across birth cohorts (see also Sampson & Laub, 2016, pp. 328–329).

A second major theme in the explanation of desistance from crime is the individual processes related to adult identity formation, maturation, and human agency. In contrast to Laub and Sampson (2003), who considered internal cognitive or psychological changes during the path to desistance to be a byproduct of entering normative adult social roles, this set of theories emphasizes cognitive, emotional, identity, or other maturational shifts within individuals as necessary for desistance from crime to occur (see Paternoster et al., 2015).

Within criminology, this set of theories mostly emerged from ethnographic studies and analyses of life history narratives (e.g., Giordano et al., 2002; Maruna, 2001). Arguably, the best-known theories in this area (see Kazmian, 2015, for an overview) are the theory of cognitive and emotional transformation (e.g., Giordano et al., 2002; Giordano, Schroeder, & Cernkovich, 2007) and the identity theory of desistance (e.g., Bushway & Paternoster, 2013; Paternoster & Bushway, 2009; Paternoster et al., 2015). Giordano's theory of cognitive and emotional transformation states that several cognitive transformations must occur for the process of desistance from crime to commence and be carried out: (a) The offender must be more open to change, (b) the offender must perceive the turning points ("hooks for change") to be salient and important for him or her, (c) the offender must change his or her perception of a deviant lifestyle (i.e., become more aware of its negative consequences), and (d) the offender must form a new noncriminal identity ("replace-ment self"). These cognitive shifts are complemented by emotional transformations that occur within the context of new prosocial bonds (i.e., changes in the way anger is understood and managed). The identity theory of desistance from Paternoster and Bushway (2009), in contrast, is grounded in a rational choice perspective. Specifically, human agency is theorized to consist of four properties: intentionality, forethought, reflexivity, and power. Once agentic offenders (i.e., those who possess these four properties) realize that their criminal activity is more costly than beneficial, the result of their own actions or failures, and these fail-ures and costs are thus likely to continue in the future, the process of changing their own identity is initiated. Specifically, a shift must occur from the "feared self" (an image of what the person does not want to be or fears becoming) to the "positive possible self" (a new, more positive image of what the person wants to become), which, in turn, triggers be-havioral changes away from deviant activities or lifestyles toward more conventional roles or "hooks." In both theories, then, turning points or "hooks for change" can be involved in the pathway to desistance, but this gradual process must be launched first by internal or subjective trans-formations. Paternoster et al. (2015) discuss the differences among these desistance theories in greater detail and present preliminary empirical support from qualitative and quantitative data. Despite these advance-ments, there is a need for greater elaboration of concepts such as human agency in this line of research (e.g., Bersani & Doherty, 2017; Carlsson, 2016; Healy, 2013).

Parallel to this literature, other fields (e.g., psychology, neuroscience) came to realize that even individual differences once thought to be sta-ble, such as personality traits, are better framed in a life-course dynamic approach. In a meta-analysis, Roberts, Walton, and Viechtbauer (2006) found a clear pattern of normative change across the life course, with people becoming more socially dominant, conscientious, and emotion-ally stable with age. Steinberg et al. (2008) found that individuals report less sensation seeking in the late than in the early 20s. Several authors have noted a normative trend toward personality structures that reflect greater self-control and risk avoidance as people reach adulthood (e.g., W. Johnson, Hicks, McGue, & Iacono, 2007; see Na & Paternoster, 2012, on the malleability of self-control). Multiple dimensions of psychosocial maturity are posited to show growth in this period (Monahan, Steinberg, Cauffman, & Mulvey, 2009) and changes in personality traits over time are indeed correlated with decreases in offending (Morizot, 2015).

Major brain development, including myelinization, reaches a mature stage by early adulthood (Casey, Tottenham, Liston, & Durston, 2005; Giedd et al., 1999) and relates to the maturity of inhibitory control systems (M. Welsh, Pennington, & Groisser, 1991) and self-regulation (Steinberg, 2008). More recently, Steinberg (2008, 2010a) and others (Casey, Getz, & Galvan, 2008) proposed a dual systems hypothesis of adolescent risk-taking, which relates increases in reward-seeking and risk-taking during adolescence to a sharp increase in dopaminergic activity in the limbic and paralimbic areas of the brain (the so-called socioemotional system). The rise in reward-seeking is presumed to occur before the structural maturation of the cognitive control system and its interconnections to the socioemotional system. Others have suggested that peers may influence adolescent risk-taking through the sensitization of brain regions linked to the anticipation of rewards (Chein, Albert, O'Brien, Uckert, & Steinberg, 2011).

In summary, this body of work offers intriguing possibilities for the development of more integrative theories of desistance that include maturational factors. Kazemian (2015) observes in a recent review that, "few studies have explored the role of genetic and biological factors in desistance research" (p. 306) and stresses the need for more exploration of complex interplays between genes and the environment in the desistance process (e.g., Barnes & Beaver, 2012; Beaver, Wright, DeLisi, & Vaughn, 2008). Other theoretical work focuses on the interplay between social process and individual change in the explanation of desistance from crime (e.g., LeBel, Burnett, Maruna, & Bushway, 2008). Thereby, it is important to keep in mind that any observed relations between social, individual, and maturational (biological, neurological, genetic, and so forth) processes and desistance from crime must be evaluated within the context of possible self-selection effects that reflect underlying criminal propensities. As Laub and Sampson (2001) noted, "selection is thus a threat to the interpretation of any desistance study" (p. 23). Moreover, establishing the temporal or causal order between these processes can be challenging because they are often interdependent and occur simultaneously. "Some potential variables may occur in such close proximity to desistance that, for all practical purposes, it is impossible to measure which comes first; moreover, they may have reciprocal influences" (Le Blanc, 1993, p. 56). Up to this point, we have drawn on the broader criminological literature on desistance from crime to provide a backdrop for the remainder of the chapter. As mentioned previously, we submit that criminal trajectory research needs to connect more explicitly with this literature. As a first step toward this end, we next discuss how hypotheses about putative causal effects of turning points can be examined in group-based trajectory research.

Turning Points and Studying Causal Effects in Group-Based Trajectory Modeling

In criminal career research, the term *turning points* usually refers to well-defined events, such as marriage, parenthood, and employment, that are followed by subsequent gradual changes in offending (e.g., Sampson & Laub, 1993, 2005a). Rooted more in sociological life-course theory, George (2009) delineates the concept of turning points as follows:

[Turning points are] specific events or milestones that substantially alter the direction and/or slope of a trajectory. In personal biography, turning points are often described as "defining moments" or "watershed experiences." There is a general expectation that turning points affect specific outcomes. . . . First, and most important, turning points can only be identified retrospectively; that is, it is not possible to know whether an event or experience will be a turning point until there are long-term data afterward that permit the investigator to link a change in the form of the trajectory of the dependent variable to an earlier event or experience. . . . Second, turning points can be observed in either age- or time-dependent trajectories. In general, developmental turning points are more easily identified in age-dependent trajectories, and turning points triggered by external events are more visible in time-dependent trajectories. Third, because nondevelopmental turning points are relatively rare (i.e., they are not experienced by a large portion of the population or at a specific age), between-person analyses are unlikely to reveal them, which is additional evidence of the utility of trajectories that measure intraindividual patterns of stability and change. (pp. 169–170)

This description illuminates the many facets of the concept of turning points, which are rarely explicitly articulated in theories of desistance from crime, and highlights the notion that within-individual analyses are better suited to test turning point hypotheses than are between-person analyses. It comes then as no surprise that Paternoster and Bushway (2009) explicitly recommend the use of group-based trajectory modeling to test theories of desistance. This is not to say that is group-based trajectory modeling the best method for studying these issues. Desistance researchers continue to use multiple techniques—multilevel modeling, group-based trajectory modeling, propensity score matching, counterfactual methods, hazard models—that do not necessarily lead to identical conclusions (e.g., Brame, Bushway, & Paternoster, 2003; Bushway et al., 2003; Bushway & Paternoster, 2013; Kerr et al., 2011; Kurlychek, Bushway, & Brame, 2012; Lussier, McCuish, & Corrado, 2015; Nagin, 2005; Paternoster, Bachman, Kerrison, O'Connell, & Smith, 2016; Paternoster & Bushway, 2009; Sampson et al., 2006; Theobald & Farrington, 2009; Wimer, Sampson, & Laub, 2008). Several texts provide excellent expositions to innovative ways of testing turning point hypotheses (C. Cohen, 2008; Osgood, 2010; Singer & Willett, 2003).

Some general comments on studying causal effects in desistance research are in order. Apel and Sweeten (2010, p. 543) succinctly summarize the main issues when they write that

> researchers in the discipline of criminology have long been interested in the "treatment effect" of discrete events on an individual's delinquent and criminal behavior. Is stable employment associated with less delinquency and crime? What is the effect of marriage to a noncriminal spouse on desistance? Is high school dropout related to a higher rate of offending? Notice the conspicuous absence of explicitly causal terminology in the way that these questions are posed. Criminological research is typically reliant on nonexperimental data, or data in which the treatment of interest (e.g., employment, marriage, dropout) is often not randomized for ethical or practical reasons. Yet this creates a situation known as the selection problem–a situation in which individuals are free to exercise some degree of discretion or choice with regard to the event(s) that they experience. The selection problem arises when there is something peculiar to the choice set, the choice maker, or some

combination thereof, which partially determines the individual's choice as well as his or her behavioural response to that choice. . . . In the absence of randomization, researchers interested in point identification of causal effects are forced to approximate the conditions of a controlled experiment. The evaluation literature is replete with examples of different quasi-experimental techniques, so called because they attempt to create a situation in which treatment is "as good as randomly assigned."

These issues of causal inference also arise for the application of group-based trajectory methodology in tests of desistance theories. Turning first to situations in which randomization of the treatment is possible, such as in randomized intervention trials, multigroup growth mixture modeling (GMM) capabilities can be used to study treatment effects (B. Muthén, Brown, Hunter, Cook, & Leuchter, 2011; B. Muthén et al., 2002), whereas semiparametric group-based trajectory modeling (SGBTM) can partially approximate treatment effect heterogeneity estimation through the use of propensity score matching methodology (Na, Loughran, & Paternoster, 2015, Footnote 7). However, turning points such as marriage or parenthood are typically observed in passive longitudinal panel studies, which record only naturally occurring variation in this type of explanatory variables. In contrast to the gold standard of experiments, passive longitudinal panel studies are inherently subject to threats to internal validity and selection bias and can never yield definitive proof of causality (Rubin, 2008). The careful designing of passive prospective studies can "offer means of ruling out several important types of competing explanations and thereby strengthening the plausibility of a causal interpretation" (Osgood, 2010, p. 376). Analytic approaches that improve the internal validity of passive longitudinal designs include fixed effects regression, instrumental variables, propensity score methods, and pseudo-randomized and discontinuity designs (P. Miller, Henry, & Votruba-Drzal, 2016; see also Foster, 2010; Rubin, 2008).

Turning-point effects are a central theme in criminology and causal inference issues have risen to the forefront in Nagin's work after the publication of his book on SGBTM in 2005. His collaboration with Amelia Haviland was essential for combining SGBTM with propensity score matching methods to strengthen inferences about the impact of putative causal factors (Haviland & Nagin, 2005; Haviland, Nagin, &

Rosenbaum, 2007; Haviland, Nagin, Rosenbaum, & Tremblay, 2008; Nieuwbeerta, Nagin, & Blokland, 2009). Haviland et al. (2008) describe the basic idea behind the use of propensity score matching techniques in developmental trajectory modeling as follows (for information about propensity score techniques in general, see Apel & Sweeten, 2010; Shadish, 2013):

> Making causal inferences with nonexperimental data is fraught with ambiguity in almost all problem contexts. In developmental studies much of this ambiguity takes a particular form, namely, the prior trajectory of the behavior under study predicts both the likelihood of the turning-point event and the future trajectory of the behavior. The approach described here is designed to address this form of the problem by trying to take full advantage of the rich set of measurements that are a hallmark of modern longitudinal studies. Group-based trajectory modeling is used to stratify the data into clusters of individuals with similar trajectories of behavior prior to their experiencing the turning-point event. Stratification by trajectory group also provides a means for identifying developmentally meaningful subgroups in the population for whom treatment effects may vary. Propensity score matching is used to insure balance on the large numbers of measured covariates present in these data that might otherwise bias the treatment effect estimate. . . . Although trajectory groups, propensity scores, and optimal matching have some technical details, the end product is simply presented and understood–treated and control groups that are comparable at baseline, prior to treatment, with respect to observed covariates. (pp. 433–435)

The situation is different for GMM, which is embedded in a latent variable framework and does not lend itself easily to integration with propensity score matching techniques (Muthén, 2010). However, this framework offers other means for strengthening causal inferences. First, instrumental variables (e.g., Angrist, Imbens, & Rubin, 1996; Bushway & Apel, 2010; Foster & McLanahan, 1996; Miller et al., 2016) can be used for increasing confidence in causal inferences. There is limited work focused on the incorporation of instrumental variable approaches into GMM to improve causal inferences in clinical trials (e.g., Jo, Wang, & Ialongo, 2009). It may be possible to adapt these techniques at a future point in time for the examination of turning point hypotheses, such as the impact of incarceration on offender trajectories among parolees. Second, another line of work concentrates on the development of piecewise latent growth mixture models with unknown knots (e.g., Kohli, Harring, & Hancock, 2013; Zopluoglu, Harring, & Kohli, 2014). Turning points, referred to as knots by methodologists, may not always be observable, and the timing of knots or change points may differ among individuals. These GMM techniques appear to hold promise for addressing substantive questions about the process of desistance (e.g., in prisoner reentry research) but perhaps more for exploratory, curve-fitting purposes. Third, GMM offers greater flexibility in studying covariate effects than SGBTM because covariates can additionally predict variation in growth parameters within trajectory classes (Na et al., 2015). It also allows for easy combination with other statistical techniques, which broadens the range of substantive questions that can be studied. Substance use research offers interesting applications of potential interest to criminologists.

For example, Huh, Huang, Liao, Pentz, and Chou (2013) derived groups with different adult role constellations via latent class analysis, thus simultaneously capturing adult roles in multiple life domains, and related them to substance use trajectory classes. Witkiewitz and Masyn (2008) modeled the time to first relapse after receiving a community alcohol treatment via discrete-time survival analysis, extracted postlapse drinking trajectory groups via GMM, and examined relations of covariates with both time to relapse and postlapse drinking trajectories. Wiesner, Silbereisen, and Weichold (2008) examined both concurrent and lagged relations of a time-varying covariate (deviant peer affiliation) to alcohol use levels within each trajectory group after controlling for background factors. Significant lagged effects can be interpreted more confidently because of the unambiguous temporal ordering of variables. This last set of applications is much weaker in terms of causal inferences than the extensions discussed earlier (i.e., propensity score matching, instrumental variable approaches). Nonetheless, our hope is that they serve as an inspiration to the kinds of questions the next generation of desistance researchers might aspire to address. Next, we discuss findings from a handful of group-based trajectory modeling studies on later life outcomes and desistance from crime.

Later Life Outcomes of Criminal Trajectories

Many scholars anticipate that high-rate chronic or life-course-persistent offenders will also experience significant failure and poorer outcomes in multiple life domains compared to lower-level or adolescent-limited offenders (e.g., Moffitt, 1993; A. Piquero, Shepherd, Shepherd, & Farrington, 2011; Wiesner, Capaldi, & Kim, 2011). That is, these scholars expect distinctive offender trajectories to be related to differential outcomes later in life, and such relations should be maintained after controlling for early propensity factors and prior levels of the outcome. Conversely, theorists such as Gottfredson and Hirschi (1990) would argue that these associations are spurious, merely reflecting stable individual differences in antisocial behavior or shared underlying propensity factors such as low self-control. No matter which of these positions is adopted by the researcher, temporal ordering is a critical design feature of trajectory studies on this issue (i.e., measurement of the later life outcomes should commence *after* the last time point that is used for the trajectory modeling of criminal behavior).

This section synthesizes the conclusions of group-based trajectory modeling studies on outcomes of offender trajectories. Given the focus of this book, studies that used subjective classification criteria for creating trajectory groups (e.g., Jennings, Rocque, Fox, Piquero, & Farrington, 2016; Moffitt, Caspi, Harrington, & Milne, 2002; A. Piquero, Daigle, Gibson, Piquero, & Tibbetts, 2007) are not included in this review. Table 7.1 shows an overview of the studies on this issue that used SGBTM or GMM methodology to extract offender trajectory groups.

As can be seen, a sizable number of studies used data from the seminal Cambridge Study in Delinquent Development (CSDD) that was conducted with a high-risk sample of 411 men in London, England. This study is uniquely suited for research on life outcomes of offender trajectory groups because the study participants were followed up into their mid- and late adult years. With one exception (N. Piquero, Piquero, & Farrington, 2010), all CSDD studies controlled for a large set of childhood individual and environmental risk factors, which means that differential outcomes are not merely a function of shared early risk factors. At the same time, the proportion of high-rate chronic offenders is very small (e.g., 2.5%) in most of these CSDD studies, so caution must be exercised

TABLE 7.1. Trajectory Studies That Examined Outcomes of Offender Trajectories (in Chronological Order)

Authors (Year)	Sample Data Set[a], Country N Analysis Sample (Gender[b])	No. Trajectory Groups (offense variable[c])	Outcomes
Nagin, Farrington, & Moffitt (1995)	High risk CSDD, England N = 403 (M)	4 groups to age 32 (O; frequency[d])	Outcomes at age 32: Adolescence-limited (AL) offenders indistinguishable from never-convicted and better than chronic offenders in the work domain; AL had better spousal relationships than chronic offenders; however, AL continued to drink heavily, use drugs, get into fights, and commit crimes. Weak differences among offender trajectories in terms of impulsivity.
Wiesner, Kim, & Capaldi (2005)	At risk OYS, United States N = 204 (M)	6 groups to age 23/24 (S; frequency)	Outcomes thru age 25/26: Chronic high-level, and, to a lesser extent, chronic low-level offenders, had higher levels for drug use, alcohol use, and depression
Wiesner & Windle (2006)	Community MAVS, United States N = 724 (M/F)	6 groups to age 17 (S; frequency)	Outcomes at age 23.8: All active offender trajectories showed poorer outcomes in alcohol and illicit drug use (but not depression); scant differential outcomes among the four most active offender trajectories
S. Miller, Malone, Dodge, & Conduct Problems Prevention Research Group (2010)	At risk Fast Track Project, United States N = 754 (M/F)	4 groups to Grade 12 (S; frequency)	Outcomes at age 19: Chronic delinquency and increasing trajectory groups had poorer outcomes for risky sexual behavior, partner violence, and depression (but not for reported pregnancy)
A. Piquero, Farrington, Nagin, & Moffitt (2010)	High risk CSDD, England N = 365 (M)	5 groups up to age 40 (O; frequency)	Outcome at age 48: Both chronic offender groups with highest life-failures and more convictions
N. Piquero, Piquero, & Farrington (2010)	High risk CSDD, England N = 365 (M)	5 groups up to age 40 (O; frequency)	Outcome at age 48: High-rate chronic offenders least likely to hold prestigious white-collar jobs

(continued)

TABLE 7.1. Trajectory Studies That Examined Outcomes of Offender Trajectories (in Chronological Order) (*continued*)

Authors (Year)	Sample Data Set[a], Country N Analysis Sample (Gender[b])	No. Trajectory Groups (offense variable[c])	Outcomes
A. Piquero, Shepherd, Shepherd, & Farrington (2011)	High risk CSDD, England N = 365 (M)	5 groups up to age 40 (O; frequency)	Outcomes at age 48: High-rate chronic offenders with highest risk for being registered disabled; hospitalization (no significant differences in illness, injury, and death)
Wiesner, Capaldi, & Kim (2011)	At risk OYS, United States N = 197 (M)	3 groups up to age 26/27 (O; frequency)	Outcomes thru age 29/30: Both chronic groups had poorer outcomes for deviant peer affiliation, education, and work domains than rare offenders; high-level chronic offenders had the poorest levels for mental health problems and physical aggression to partner; no differences found for antisocial partnering, alcohol & drug use, psychological aggression to partner
A. Piquero, Farrington, et al. (2012)	High risk CSDD, England N = 304 (M)	5 groups up to age 40 (O; frequency)	Outcome at age 48: High-risk chronic offenders with highest psychopathy levels
Brook, Lee, Finch, Brown, & Brook (2013)	Community African American & Puerto Ricans from East Harlem in New York City, United States N = 838 (M/F)	4 groups to age 24 (S; frequency)	Outcomes at age 29: High-persistent and moderate-persistent groups showed more violence, more marijuana abuse/dependence, more discard with partner, had more drug using peers; moderated persistent offenders also resided in higher crime neighborhoods
Yonai, Levine, & Glicksohn (2013)	Offender National population of juvenile offenders, Israel N = 17,176 (M/F)	2 groups up to age 26 (pre-first conviction) (O; variety[e])	Number of months (1–156 months) from first conviction to second conviction: Versatility group at increased risk of recidivism compared to specialization group
A. Piquero, Farrington, Shepherd, & Auty (2014)	High risk CSDD, England N = 411 (M)	5 groups up to age 40 (O; frequency)	Outcome at age 57: High-rate chronic offenders with the highest risk of death

(*continued*)

TABLE 7.1. Trajectory Studies That Examined Outcomes of Offender Trajectories (in Chronological Order) (*continued*)

Authors (Year)	Sample Data Set[a], Country N Analysis Sample (Gender[b])	No. Trajectory Groups (offense variable[c])	Outcomes
A. Piquero, Theobald, & Farrington (2014)	High risk CSDD, England N = 212, 319 (M)	5 groups up to age 40 (O; frequency)	Outcomes at age 32, 48, 50: High-rate chronic offenders with increased odds of intimate partner violence and criminal violence
Verbruggen, van der Geest, & Blokland (2016)	High risk Youth in judicial treatment institution, Netherlands N = 251 (M/F)	4 groups before age 34 (O; frequency)	Outcome at age 34: Low-rate chronic and high-rate chronic offenders with lower levels of general adult life adjustment

Note: Name of data set listed when identified by the authors of the given study.
[a]CSDD = Cambridge Study of Delinquent Development; MAVS = Middle Adolescent Vulnerability Study; OYS = Oregon Youth Study.
[b]M = Male; F = Female.
[c]S = Self-report measure of offending; O = Official-records measure of offending.
[d]Frequency refers to the total number of criminal behaviors/convictions at each period.
[e]Variety refers to utilization of a versatility index that captures the extent to which offenders demonstrate a proclivity toward specialization or versatility in offending at each period.

in interpreting findings for this trajectory group. The analytical sample sizes vary across CSDD studies due to missing values, as do the ages at which the outcomes were assessed (i.e., age 32, 48, 50, and 57). All CSDD studies used the five offender trajectory groups that were uncovered by A. Piquero, Farrington, et al. (2007) in an analysis of official records crime data up to age 40. For the sake of brevity, these CSDD study features are not mentioned again during the following description of findings.

The outcomes that were assessed in all studies shown in Table 7.1 were grouped into five domains: (1) adverse health outcomes and death, (2) psychopathy, (3) problem behaviors, (4) success or failure in multiple adult life domains, and (5) risk of recidivism. A small subset of these studies could have fit with more than one domain. Seven of the 14 studies were conducted in the United Kingdom, all with data from the CSDD study (Nagin, Farrington, & Moffitt, 1995; A. Piquero, Farrington, Fontaine, Vincent, Coid, & Ullrich, 2012; A. Piquero, Farrington, Nagin, & Moffitt, 2010; A. Piquero, Farrington, Shepherd, & Auty, 2014; A. Piquero, Shepherd, Shepherd, & Farrington, 2011; A. Piquero, Theobald, & Farrington,

228 | LATER LIFE OUTCOMES, TURNING POINTS, DESISTANCE

2014; N. Piquero, Piquero, & Farrington, 2010). The remaining studies were conducted in the United States (Brook, Lee, Finch, Brown, & Brook, 2013; S. Miller, Malone, Dodge, & Conduct Problems Prevention Research Group, 2010; Wiesner, Capaldi, & Kim, 2011; Wiesner, Kim, & Capaldi, 2005; Wiesner & Windle, 2006), Netherlands (Verbruggen, van der Geest, & Blokland, 2016), and Israel (Yonai, Levine, & Glicksohn, 2013). Out of the 14 studies, only five (Brook et al., 2013; S. Miller et al., 2010; Verbruggen et al., 2016; Wiesner & Windle, 2006; Yonai et al., 2013) included females. Eight of the 14 studies were conducted with high-risk samples, two with community samples, three with at-risk samples, and one with an offender sample. The age at which later life outcomes were assessed varied considerably among the studies, ranging from emerging/ early adulthood (S. Miller et al., 2010; Wiesner & Windle, 2006), late 20s (Brook et al., 2013; Wiesner et al., 2011; Wiesner et al., 2005), to mid-adult and late adult years (Nagin et al., 1995; A. Piquero et al., 2011; A. Piquero, Farrington, et al., 2010, 2012, 2014; A. Piquero, Theobald, et al., 2014; N. Piquero et al., 2010; Verbruggen et al., 2016; Yonai et al., 2013).

ADVERSE HEALTH OUTCOMES AND DEATH. A. Piquero et al. (2011) focused on several health outcomes at age 48, including death, for the offender trajectory groups from the CSDD. As expected, the high-rate chronic offenders had the significantly highest risk for hospitalization and being registered disabled. On the other hand, no significant differences among offender trajectory groups were observed in terms of illness, injury, and death by age 48. In a subsequent study, A. Piquero, Farrington, et al. (2014) followed up the CSDD participants to age 57 and uncovered a mortality rate of over 7.5% for the London men, with an average age of death of 42 years. In contrast to the prior study, the high-rate chronic offenders now had the highest risk of death, even after controlling for childhood risks as well as analogous behaviors (drug use, heavy drinking, excessive smoking), illnesses, and injuries.

PSYCHOPATHY. Using data from the CSDD, A. Piquero, Farrington, et al. (2012) compared the average levels of psychopathy at age 48 among the offender trajectory groups. They reported that the high-rate chronic offenders had the highest average levels of psychopathy, whereas the nonoffenders were characterized by the lowest levels.

PROBLEM BEHAVIORS. A. Piquero, Theobald, et al. (2014) examined the relation of offender trajectory groups from the CSDD with intimate partner violence at age 32, age 48, and at a combined age 32 and 48, as well as criminal violence up to at age 50. Their study is interesting because it speaks to the degree to which criminal behavior may spill over into violence in other domains of life. They found that high-rate chronic offenders had significantly heightened odds of intimate partner violence and criminal behavior in the mid-adult years. In a study with 754 youth from the Fast Track Project in the United States, S. Miller et al. (2010) found that youth in the chronic delinquency and increasing trajectory groups showed poorer outcomes at age 19 in terms of risky sexual behavior, partner violence, and depression; no differences were found among delinquency trajectory groups for reported pregnancy. The associations were controlled for demographic background factors and were not moderated by gender. Wiesner et al. (2005) used data from 204 males in the Oregon Youth Study and investigated the associations of six self-report offender trajectories with young adult (i.e. through age 25/26) alcohol use, drug use, and depressive symptoms. Controlling for childhood and adolescent proxies of the given outcome, parents' socioeconomic status, parental criminality, and antisocial propensity, chronic high-level offenders fared significantly worse than the other trajectory groups in terms of drug use and depressive symptoms. Results for alcohol use pointed in the same direction, but the differences were not significant for contrasts with other more active offender trajectory groups. By comparison, there were fewer differential outcomes in these three domains when less active offender trajectory groups were contrasted with chronic low-level offenders. Last, Wiesner and Windle (2006) used data from a community sample of 724 young women and men in the United States. Six middle-adolescent self-report offender trajectories were linked to young adult (average age 23.8 years) depression, alcohol, and illicit drug use. Each outcome was measured in the form of lifetime rate of psychiatric disorder, annual rate of psychiatric disorder, and elevated level of problematic behavior. Findings showed that, after controlling for low parental education, gender, and baseline level of the outcome, all active offender trajectory groups showed significantly poorer outcomes in the domains of young adult alcohol and illicit drug use (but not depression) relative to the rare offender trajectory group. However, there was scant evidence of differential outcomes among the four most active offender trajectory groups.

SUCCESS OR FAILURE IN MULTIPLE ADULT LIFE DOMAINS. We refrain from discussing the results of a very early study with the CSDD (Nagin et al., 1995) because it covered a much shorter time span (offender trajectories to age 32) than the subsequent CSDD studies, there was no temporal ordering of offender trajectories and outcomes (outcomes at age 32), and associations were not controlled for prior levels. In a subsequent analysis of the CSDD data, A. Piquero, Farrington, et al. (2010) examined the relation of offender trajectories to a composite construct of life failure at age 48 that encompassed the following dimensions: unsatisfactory accommodation, unsatisfactory cohabitation, unsatisfactory employment, involved in fights, unsatisfactory alcohol use, drug use, self-reported offenses, convicted, and unsatisfactory mental health. Their results differ slightly from those of other CSDD studies insofar as both chronic trajectory groups, very low-rate chronic offenders and high-rate chronic offenders, had the highest levels of life failures at age 48. In addition, both groups accumulated a higher number of convictions between ages 41 and 50. Interestingly, these findings were mirrored in a more recent study with 251 youth institutionalized in a Dutch judicial treatment institution (Verbruggen et al., 2016). Here, the authors investigated the association of offender trajectories with a general adult life adjustment construct. It was composed of the following domains: regular accommodation, employment, intimate relationship, regular contact with children, satisfactory health, alcohol abuse, drug abuse, and self-reported crime. The authors found that low-rate chronic and high-rate chronic trajectory offender groups showed significantly lower levels of general adult life adjustment at age 34 than did the other trajectory groups, even controlling for employment pathways, background, and childhood characteristics. In another CSDD study, N. Piquero et al. (2010) focused specifically on relations between offender trajectory groups and occupational prestige at age 48. The main finding was that high-rate chronic offenders were least likely to hold prestigious white-collar jobs (defined as managerial or professional positions) at age 48, whereas nonoffenders were the most likely to hold such positions. This study did not control for early propensity or risk factors, so the interpretation of these findings is not as straightforward as those of the other CSDD studies.

The study by Brook et al. (2013) stands out because it was conducted with 838 African American and Puerto Ricans youth from East Harlem in New York City. These ethnic/racial groups are understudied in extant trajectory research on this topic. The authors identified four trajectory groups of self-reported offending to age 24 and linked them to various outcomes at age 29, adjusted for gender, ethnicity, and prior levels of the given outcome. Among other results, high-persistent and moderate-persistent trajectory groups were significantly related to more frequent violence toward others, more marijuana abuse/dependence, more discord with partner, and having more drug-using peers. In addition, the moderate-persistent group was significantly more likely to reside in high-crime neighborhoods. However, the high-persistent offender trajectory group consisted of just 18 study participants, and results for this group thus must be interpreted with caution. Last, Wiesner et al. (2011) used data from 197 at-risk Oregon Youth Study men to examine the relations of three official records offender trajectories to age 26/27 with young adult outcomes. The outcomes were assessed to age 29/30 in the areas of education and work, mental health problems, drinking and drug use, antisocial partnering, deviant peer affiliation, and aggression toward a partner. All predictive effects were controlled for childhood antisocial propensity and childhood and adolescent proxies of the outcome. An earlier study with the Oregon Youth Study data (Wiesner et al., 2005) had used self-report measures of offending, covered a shorter time span, and focused on fewer adult life domains. The findings revealed that both chronic offender trajectory groups had significantly poorer outcomes for deviant peer affiliation, education, and work domains than did the rare-offenders group. Also, the high-level chronic offenders stood out from both other groups in terms of significantly higher levels of mental health problems and physical aggression toward a partner. Differential adult life outcomes among the three trajectory groups were not observed for the remaining domains (antisocial partnering, psychological aggression toward a partner, and alcohol and drug use).

RISK OF RECIDIVISM. Yonai et al. (2013) merged two national databases to examine the relation of age–versatility curve offender trajectories to timing of recidivism for a national population of 17,176 Israeli juvenile offenders. Using official records measures of offending variety (i.e., the diversity index), the authors identified two trajectory groups up to age 26 that characterized the age–versatility curve of police contacts before first conviction. The juvenile offenders were followed up from 1996 to 2008 (the average follow-up period was 11.19 years, with a maximum of 13 years), and recidivism was operationalized as the number of months that elapsed from the first conviction to the second conviction. A Kaplan–Meier analysis revealed that the survival time to recidivism was significantly shorter for the versatility group than it was for the specialization group (31 vs. 39 months). After controlling for multiple demographic, familial, and criminogenic risk factors, Cox proportional hazards models showed that juvenile offenders in the versatility group were at significantly heightened risk of recidivism compared to those in the specialization group. The authors interpreted their findings as being more congruent with developmental taxonomic theories of crime than with competing theoretical frameworks (e.g., a pattern characterized by gradual specialization in the offense repertoire with age was not found for this sample). To our knowledge, this is the only study that linked age–versatility curve offender trajectory groups to the time to recidivism.

In sum, this body of work suggests that chronic high-level offenders are characterized by significantly poorer outcomes in a broad range of adult life domains, especially in comparison to rare or nonoffenders. This finding is consistent with propositions from developmental taxonomies of crime (e.g., Moffitt, 1993). In contrast, findings are mixed for chronic low-level (a group that was not anticipated in original formulations of developmental taxonomies) and adolescence-limited offenders (a group that was anticipated but is not consistently uncovered in group-based trajectory research). In some cases, both groups show elevated levels of problematic outcomes (nearly reaching levels found for chronic high-level offenders but not necessarily for as broad a range of outcomes), whereas they are indistinguishable from less active offender trajectories in other studies. Further investigation is warranted because half of the small set of studies are based on data from a single sample (the CSDD), offender and community samples, as well as ethnic/racial minorities, are underrepresented, and the number of countries for which this has been examined is limited. The predominant focus has been on studying maladaptive outcomes or failures for the most active offender trajectories (guided by concepts such as cumulative disadvantage, adaptational failures in normative developmental tasks, and developmental cascades). As we assert at the end of this chapter, a stronger focus on adaptive functioning (e.g., self-regulatory strategies that foster successful aging) would enhance our understanding of later life outcomes of offender pathways.

Turning Points and Desistance from Crime in Criminal Trajectory Research

This section reviews group-based trajectory studies that examined how changes in adult life circumstances (e.g., marriage, parenthood, employment) are related to persisting versus desisting offender trajectories. Given this focus, we do not include the well-known study from Nagin, Pagani, Tremblay, and Vitaro (2003) on the impact of grade retention on physical aggression trajectories in this synthesis. Table 7.2 shows an overview of quantitative studies on desistance from crime that used SGBTM and GMM methodology to extract offender trajectory groups. As can be seen, the handful of studies typically used data from male offender or high-risk samples (except for Blokland & Nieuwbeerta, 2005) and in a limited number of countries (the Netherlands, Norway, and the United States). Their findings were sorted into the following domains: marriage/cohabitation, parenthood, employment, stakes in conformity, and imprisonment.

MARRIAGE/COHABITATION. In their seminal study with 480 men from the Gluecks' (1950) Boston area delinquent subsample, Laub, Nagin, and Sampson (1998) examined the association between marriage and offending up to age 32, controlling for age, juvenile arrests, and offender trajectory group membership. The authors theorized that the quality of the marriage was a decisive factor and that its effect on criminal behavior would be gradual over time. Importantly, their study also attended to the possibility of romantic bonds being formed before marriage (during courtship). Consistent with their main argument, the study results revealed a gradual reduction in officially recorded offending at each time point during the postmarriage period among men with

TABLE 7.2. Trajectory Studies That Examined Desistance From Crime (in Chronological Order)

Authors (Year)	Sample Data Set[a], Country N Analysis Sample (Gender[b])	No. Trajectory Groups (offense variable[c])	Impact on Desistance
Laub, Nagin, & Sampson (1998)	High risk GG, United States N = 480 (M)	4 groups to age 32 (O; frequency[d])	Good marriage has a gradual crime-reducing effect
Piquero, Brame, Mazerolle, & Haapanen (2002)	Offender CYA, United States N = 524 (M)	4 groups of joint trajectories to age 28 (O; frequency)	Stakes in conformity mostly unrelated to crime
Blokland & Nieuw-beerta (2005)	(A) Offender CCLCS, Netherlands N = 4,615 (M/F) (B) General population National Crime Survey, Netherlands N=2,244 (M/F)	(A) 4 groups to age 72 (O; frequency) (B) 2 groups to age 72 (S; frequency)	(A) Marriage has a crime-reducing effect in two groups (low-rate and moderate-rate offenders); separation boosts crime in all four groups; parent-hood boosts crime among sporadic offenders (B) Marriage, separation, and parenthood are unre-lated to changes in crime
Nieuwbeerta, Nagin, & Blokland (2009)	Offender CCLCS, Netherlands N = 2,790 (M)	3 pre-imprisonment groups up to age 37 (O; frequency)	First-time imprisonment between age 18–38 related to increased conviction rate in the 3 years following release
van der Geest, Bij-leveld, & Blokland (2011)	High-risk Residential treat-ment sample, Netherlands N = 263 (M)	5 groups to age 32 (O; frequency)	Employment has a crime-reducing effect in all groups except adolescent-limited serious offenders; type of job makes a differ-ence; job stability has no additional effect
Skardhamar & Savolainen (2014)	Offender Sample of recidivist males, Norway N = 783 (M)	5 groups to mid-adulthood (O; prevalence[e])	No crime-reducing effect of entering stable legitimate employment, except for a small group (< 2%)

Note: Name of the data set listed when identified by the authors of the given study.
[a]CCLCS = Criminal Career and Life-Course Study; CYA = California Youth Authority; GG = Glueck and Glueck study.
[b]M = Male; F = Female.
[c]S = Self-report measure of offending; O = Official-records measure of offending.
[d]Frequency refers to the total number of criminal behaviors/convictions at each period.
[e]Prevalence (1= one or more offense committed, 0= zero offense committed).

strong marital attachment ("good marriages"), whereas no such crime-reduction effect was found for the existence of marriage itself (i.e., good and not-good marriages combined). Romantic bonds during the court-ship period were unrelated to the rate of offending. Separate analyses for each offender trajectory group revealed similar results (except for one group characterized by an early decrease in criminal activity), although some effects were weaker. This early work set an important precedent for subsequent group-based trajectory research on desistance from crime.

In another study, Blokland and Nieuwbeerta (2005) examined the relation between marriage and crime for different offender trajectory groups followed to age 72. Effects were adjusted for between-individual differences in the propensity to be in a certain life-course state. Measures of attachment to the partner were not available, so their results cannot be compared easily with the findings from Laub et al. (1998). The study was unique insofar as analyses were conducted both with official records data on convictions from the Criminal Career and Life Course Study, which was composed of a large representative offender sample from the Netherlands ($N = 4{,}615$), and self-reported crime levels from a Dutch National Crime Survey with a large representative general population sample ($N = 2{,}244$). At the within-individual level, marriage was significantly linked to a decrease in convictions among offenders in the low- and moderate-rate offender groups of the Criminal Career and Life Course Study but not for the sporadic and high-rate offender groups. At the same time, separation was significantly related to an increase in convictions in all four trajectory groups of the Criminal Career and Life Course Study. In contrast, neither marriage nor separation had signifi-cant effects on crime for all trajectory groups in the general population sample. This result might be partly attributed to the low level of offend-ing in the sample, which left little room for the posited crime-inhibiting effect of marriage to be exerted.

PARENTHOOD. In a study described earlier with two representative Dutch samples, Blokland and Nieuwbeerta (2005) also examined the effects of parenthood on crime for several offender trajectory groups. Unfortunately, measures of the quality of social bonds with their off-spring were not available. Overall, results were nonsignificant in both samples after accounting for the effects of marriage and separation. The only exception was that, at the within-individual level, parenthood was significantly related to a heightened conviction rate for sporadic offenders in the Criminal Career and Life Course Study, which was against expectations. The authors note that the overall conviction rate among sporadic offenders was low, which decreased the chance to detect a crime-inhibiting effect of parenthood for this offender group.

EMPLOYMENT. Building on earlier work (van der Geest, Blokland, & Bijleveld, 2009), van der Geest, Bijleveld, and Blokland (2011) explored the relation of employment, type of job (regular vs. temporary), and job stability with crime for five offender trajectory groups followed to age 32. All relations were statistically controlled for between-individual differences in stable personality and background factors. Official records data on convictions were collected for a Dutch high-risk sample of 263 men who had undergone residential treatment for serious behavioral problems in a juvenile justice institution. The authors observed that, "after release, 85 percent offended at least once and 87 percent never held a job" (van der Geest et al., 2001, p. 1197) and that the men "had difficulties in keeping their job for longer than 2 years" (van der Geest et al., 2001, p. 1224). At the within-individual level, employment was significantly associated with a decrease in convictions for four out of five trajectory groups (the effect was non-significant for adolescent-limited serious offenders). Interestingly, the crime-reducing effect of employment was achieved through temporary jobs among high-frequency chronic offenders, whereas regular jobs were beneficial for other trajectory groups (especially high-frequency desisters) in addition to holding temporary jobs. Job stability did not have an additional effect on conviction rates, except among high-frequency chronic offenders for whom the effect was unexpectedly positive. This finding is noteworthy because "'stability' is the most common attribute used to identify jobs with potential to reorient criminal trajectories" (Skardhamar & Savolainen, 2014, p. 287). The level of job stability might have been too low in this high-risk sample for the effect to emerge.

Another study was conducted by Skardhamar and Savolainen (2014) using official records crime data from 783 recidivist males in Norway. The men were born between 1960 and 1974, had accumulated a minimum of five felonies during the period from 1992 to 2000, and held marginal labor market status (in 1998–2000) prior to entering stable legitimate employment (in 2001–2006), defined as a job lasting a minimum duration of 6 months. The data did not contain information on the type of jobs. A key objective was to find out whether the expected reduction in crime occurred after entering stable employment or preceded the transition while adjusting for the effects of marital status and demographic covariates. Modeling changes in crime before and after entry into employment, it was found that most men had desisted from crime prior to obtaining a stable job and that this transition was not associated with subsequent reductions in crime. The expected crime-reducing effect of the employment transition was detected only for a very small group of offenders (<2%). These findings suggest that, in most cases, stable legitimate employment is a consequence, not a cause, of desistance from crime.

STAKES IN CONFORMITY. The study by A. Piquero, Brame, Mazerolle, and Haapanen (2002) stands out in its focus on the effects of time-varying local life circumstances on joint trajectories of violent and nonviolent offending over time. This extension of the group-based trajectory approach accounts for shared longitudinal covariation across both crime types. The term *stakes in conformity* refers to the combination of the life events of marriage and full-time employment. Social ties in both domains are deemed most effective in inhibiting crime based on Sampson and Laub (1993). However, the data set did not contain information on qualitative dimensions of both life events. The study included two other time-varying covariates, heroin dependence and alcohol dependence, not of interest here because they are assumed to be related to recidivism. Official records crime data on 524 male serious offenders from the California Youth Authority followed for a 7-year postparole period (to maximum age 28) were used. Cumulative stakes in conformity were unrelated to offending rates within trajectory groups, except in one group for which a significant inverse relation with nonviolent (but not violent) offending was found.

IMPRISONMENT. Nieuwbeerta, Nagin, and Blokland (2009) combined group-based trajectory modeling with risk set matching, a generalized form of propensity score matching, to examine the effect of first-time imprisonment between age 18 and 38 on conviction rates in the 3 years following release. Research on this topic is loosely connected with the desistance literature due to select theoretical traditions that assume a crime-reducing effect of imprisonment, an assertion that is not shared by other frameworks (for an overview of these competing positions, see Nieuwbeerta et al., 2009). Selection effects are a major concern in research on this topic and the authors went to great length to maximize the internal validity of their study (e.g., imprisoned offenders were matched to those not imprisoned based on pre-imprisonment trajectories of offending as well as time varying imprisonment propensity scores). The authors drew on official records conviction data from a subsample of the Criminal Career and Life Course Study (N = 2,790; women were excluded from the analysis sample). The mean age of first-time imprisonment in the analysis sample was 22 years (median age = 20 years). Serious chronic offenders, who were unmatchable because nearly all of them are sentenced to prison in the Netherlands, had to be excluded from statistical analysis. Findings are thus not generalizable to the entire population of imprisoned offenders. The main result was that first-time imprisonment is linked to an increased conviction rate in the 3 years postrelease, but its effect size declined with increasing age (as do crime levels in general). Most of these crime-amplifying effects of first-time imprisonment were also observed within each offender trajectory group. In conclusion, "on balance the criminogenic effects of imprisonment on the imprisoned are larger than any preventive effect that might stem from special deterrence" (Nieuwbeerta et al., 2009, p. 251).

Morris and Piquero (2013; not shown in Table 7.2) used a similar methodological approach to examine the treatment effect of first-time arrest on subsequent criminal behavior. Their analyses revealed that first-time arrest had a crime-amplifying effect in the most chronic offender trajectory group and, to a lesser extent, among the medium-risk offender trajectory group, whereas no such effect was found for the low-risk offender trajectory group. We refrain from further discussion of this study because it was carried out in a much younger developmental period and thus does not contribute much to our main topic at hand. These types of studies represent intriguing applications of the group-based trajectory approach and have enormous potential for informing public policy makers on the impact of criminal justice sanctions.

In sum, no clear pattern emerged from this small set of group-based trajectory studies regarding the association of changing adult life circumstances with desisting versus persisting offender trajectories, especially in the employment domain. This conclusion stems, in part, from the difficulty of choosing event indicators that are equally meaningful across historical periods, macro-societal contexts, and types of samples (e.g., high risk, offender, general population). As noted earlier, transitions into adult social roles have become more variable and nowadays occur over relatively longer periods compared to prior generations. Entering a marital union is less likely to signify the point at which a committed intimate relationship is formed among contemporary adult samples (Skardhamar et al., 2015). Regular employment may be a meaningful marker for less active offender trajectories, whereas temporary employment might be best suited for chronic high-level offenders (van der Geest et al., 2011; see also Skardhamar & Savolainen, 2014). It will be critical for further research on this issue to pay careful attention to selecting markers that are meaningful for the sample and developmental period at hand (e.g., different employment features might be indicated for young adult versus middle adult developmental periods) and to include more than just one marker variable into statistical analysis. The next section offers suggestions for better integration of this literature with developmental science.

The Case for Better Integration with Developmental Frameworks on Self-Regulation

Our central assertion throughout this book is that group-based criminal trajectory research would benefit from incorporating knowledge from leading developmental frameworks on aspects that are underdeveloped in criminological theorizing. We describe here how the tripartite Selection, Optimization, and Compensation (SOC) theory (e.g., Baltes & Baltes, 1990; Freund & Baltes, 2002) may be used to refine criminological thinking about the role of human agency in desisting and persisting trajectories of crime and their later life outcomes.

As mentioned previously, the construct of human agency has been increasingly viewed as an important concept in theories of desistance from crime (e.g., Sampson & Laub, 2005c) but remains abstract and vaguely defined to this day (Paternoster, 2017). For instance, Paternoster (2017) asserted that the construct of human agency is unmeasurable. In contrast, Cullen (2017) stressed the need for a life-course perspective on the role of human agency in the development of criminal behavior, argued that the field of criminology should not limit itself to a rational choice conceptualization of human agency, and suggested that criminologists should borrow from psychological frameworks to "study which cognitions encourage and which prevent the choice of crime . . . and how age-graded cognitions are involved in criminal development" (p. 378). Broadly speaking, we concur with Cullen's (2017) assessment but focus here on developmental science instead of the cognitive psychology framework envisioned by Cullen.

To recapitulate from our earlier discussion, SOC theory provides a comprehensive framework that encompasses three self-regulatory processes of life management across the life span (e.g., Baltes & Baltes, 1990; Baltes, Lindenberger, & Staudinger, 1998; Freund & Baltes, 2002), namely, selection, optimization, and compensation. *Selection* pertains to the identification and selection of personal goals and goal priorities. Selection processes may be guided by personal preferences and desired states (i.e., *elective selection*: goal specification, including the avoidance of specific outcomes such as the undesired self, setting up a goal hierarchy) or loss experiences (i.e., *loss-based selection*: giving up or devaluing a blocked goal, developing new goals or lowering standards, restructuring a goal hierarchy). *Optimization* refers to the acquisition and investment of internal and external resources (i.e., means) necessary for achieving one's personal goals. *Compensation* specifies the use of compensatory (i.e., alternative) means to maintain functioning in a goal domain when means to achieve one's initial goals are no longer available or blocked. Importantly, SOC theory is advanced as a metamodel and its application to specific domains of functioning requires domain- and context-contingent elaboration (Freund & Baltes, 2002). This means that the concrete strategies exemplifying the three SOC processes depend on the domain of functioning (for illustrative examples, see Baltes et al., 1998, p. 1058) and the opportunities or barriers for goal attainment (e.g., Haase, Heckhausen, & Wrosch, 2013). The SOC model has served as an influential paradigm for investigating intentional self-regulation (Gestsdóttir & Lerner, 2008) from early adolescence through the 10th decade of life (Baltes et al., 2006). We argue that incorporating key findings from this literature is fruitful to complement extant criminological theorizing on the role of human agency in criminal development.

First, findings from some studies (e.g., Zimmerman, Phelps, & Lerner, 2007) suggest that, consistent with predictions of Freund and Baltes

(2002), "SOC processes move from a single, undifferentiated factor [in early adolescence] to a more differentiated, tripartite structure of selection, optimization, and compensation during adolescence" (Geldhof, Bowers, Gestsdóttir, Napolitano, & Lerner, 2015, p. 216). This means that intentional self-regulation, as operationalized by the SOC model, undergoes significant development during the second decade of life, with the three SOC processes being clearly differentiable in adult samples (Freund & Baltes, 2002). Criminological theorizing ought to be sensitive to differences between adolescents and adults in the factor structure of intentional self-regulation and use age-appropriate measures of SOC processes in empirical studies.

Second, there are indications that the capacity for intentional self-regulation increases and becomes more salient for adaptive functioning during adolescence (Gestsdóttir & Lerner, 2008). This increased capacity is, in part, the result of normative brain development over the adolescent years, which enhances cognitive control, especially as it relates to long-term goals (Steinberg, 2010b). In addition, the importance of a sense of personal future increases throughout adolescence (Schmid & Lopez, 2011), and the formation of a more developed identity aids adolescents in selecting goals about their personal future, which contributes to the application of goal-relevant strategies as postulated in the SOC model (Brandtstädter, 2006; Schmid, Phelps, & Lerner, 2011). It is, therefore, not surprising from this vantage point that cross-sectional data from Freund and Baltes (2002) showed that endorsements of all SOC processes increased from young adulthood (18–43 years) to a peak in middle adulthood (43–67 years), followed by a decline into older adulthood (67–89 years) for all SOC processes except elective selection, which continued to ascend into older adulthood. From a developmental perspective, it would be expected that, based on this literature and in line with Baltes's focus on successful or adaptive functioning, an increase in the three SOC processes would be associated with a greater likelihood of desisting trajectories of crime.

Third, Baltes et al. (1998) noted that, according to SOC theory,

> successful development is defined as the conjoint maximization of gains (desirable goals or outcomes) and the minimization of losses (avoidance of undesirable goals or outcomes) . . . the nature of what constitutes gains

and losses, and of the dynamic between gains and losses, is conditioned by cultural and personal factors as well as the lifetime of individuals. Thus, a given developmental outcome achieved through SOC can at a later ontogenetic time or in a different context be judged as dysfunctional. Moreover, what constitutes a gain and what a loss is also dependent on whether the methods used to define are subjective or objective. (p. 1054)

With increasing age, the ratio of gains to losses becomes more unfavorable; thus, goal orientation is posited to change from a predominant orientation toward gains in young adulthood to a stronger orientation toward the prevention of loss in older adulthood (Depping & Freund, 2011). This change implies that compensation should become a stronger motivational factor for self-regulatory action as individuals age. Ebner, Freund, and Baltes (2006) indeed observed this shift in goal orientation and suggested that it may be adaptive for older adults but perhaps less so for younger adults who are faced with restrictions of resources. Depping and Freund (2011) concluded from these results that, "for younger adults, having to prevent losses might constitute the exception to the rule of maximizing gains. As a consequence, they might react even more strongly to losses than older adults for whom losses are expected and more common. . . . For younger adults having to prevent losses might be a stronger signal of something going wrong because losses are rather unexpected during this phase of the life span" (p. 355; see also Heckhausen, Wrosch, & Schulz, 2010). This conclusion implies that the salience and adaptive function of the SOC process of compensation might differ between younger and older offenders.

At the same time, applications of SOC theory to group-based criminal trajectory research ought to be cognizant of the myriad structural barriers that are encountered by offenders (see Bersani & Doherty, 2017). Given these well-documented constrained opportunities, the potential for human agency to influence or redirect trajectories of offending should not be overstated. Interestingly, SOC theory is also informative for criminological theorizing on self-regulatory strategies for adjusting to structural barriers. Intentional self-regulation research generally suggests that disengagement from unattainable goals is adaptive for individual well-being (e.g., Brandtstädter, 2009; Haase et al., 2013; Heckhausen et al., 2010; Tomasik & Silbereisen, 2012; Wrosch, Scheier,

Carver, & Schulz, 2003), especially under highly constrained opportunities. It has been speculated that adolescents and young adults might interpret the "loss" component of loss-based selection of goals as indicative of personal failure rather than as normative developmental decline as is more typical in older age (Baltes et al., 2006; Geldhof et al., 2015). Heckhausen et al. (2010) observed that "self-protective strategies of control (e.g., avoiding self-blame by attributing failure to external factors, comparing with less fortunate others) need to be activated to minimize the long-term damage that failure could have on motivational resources (e.g., self-esteem and hope for success in future actions)" (p. 41). We submit that this line of SOC research might be particularly informative for rehabilitation efforts aiming to minimize adverse psychological consequences among life-course-persistent offenders, who often experience blocked goals by late adolescence or early adulthood (e.g., barriers to securing stable legal employment because of entrapment in illicit drug use, low educational attainment, and history of criminal justice sanctions). More broadly, SOC theory provides an organizing framework and established protocols for exploring hypotheses on the role of self-regulatory actions across the life span. With few exceptions (e.g., Rühs, Greve, & Kappes, 2017), criminologists have yet to realize what developmental science has to offer to help open the black box of human agency in the development of offending.

Conclusion

This chapter has synthesized research on the relations of criminal trajectories to later life outcomes, turning points, and desistance from crime. Collectively, these issues have received insufficient attention in the group-based criminal trajectory literature, with important foundational studies appearing only in recent years. To move trajectory research toward addressing these issues more comprehensively, the chapter first drew on the broader criminological literature to describe how these phenomena (i.e., desistance, turning points) can be defined, assessed, and explained. A case was made for the development of more integrative theories of desistance from crime. Next, existing and emergent strategies for testing hypotheses about causal effects (of turning points) in group-based trajectory studies were discussed. This material was followed by a synthesis of the findings on relations of criminal trajectories to later life outcomes, turning points, and desistance from crime. Gaps in knowledge that need to be addressed in future trajectory research were identified. The chapter ended with a presentation of ideas of how criminal trajectory research can be enriched by drawing on major developmental theories of human agency across the life span. The next chapter examines the policy and practice implications of criminal trajectory research.

Suggested Supplemental Readings

The classic volume from Laub and Sampson (2003), *Shared Beginnings, Divergent Lives*, contains fascinating retrospective reflections of offenders on their reasons for desisting from crime. The seminal review from Laub and Sampson (2001) summarizes the desistance literature before 2001. Excellent contemporaneous reviews of the state-of-the-art knowledge and theorizing about desistance from crime are provided by several authors (e.g., Bersani & Doherty, 2017; Kazemian, 2015). Paternoster et al. (2015) offer a very detailed and useful comparison of four influential theories of desistance from crime. The reader from C. Cohen (2008) provides excellent demonstrations of innovative quantitative techniques for assessing the effects of turning points on various outcomes. Excellent overviews of SOC theory and closely related frameworks are provided by Baltes et al. (1998, 2006), Brandtstädter (2006), Freund and Baltes (2002), Haase et al. (2013), and Heckhausen et al. (2010).

8

Implications for Policy and Practice

This chapter examines the policy and practice implications of criminal trajectory research. We consider the applied relevance of criminal trajectory research both *within* the criminal justice system (e.g., to assessment, treatment, and rehabilitation) and *outside* the criminal justice system (e.g., to early intervention and prevention). However, before we can answer the main question, *What* are the policy and practical implications of criminal trajectory research? we need to ask a more basic question, *Is* criminal trajectory research even relevant, as a method of inquiry to the formulation of policy and practice? In addressing this question, we approach the issue from both a narrow perspective and a broad perspective. A narrow perspective focuses strictly and narrowly on the methods and findings of criminal trajectory research, while a broad perspective focuses more broadly on the conceptual and theoretical frameworks in which criminal trajectory research may be situated.

A NARROW PERSPECTIVE. There are scholars skeptical of the applied relevance of criminal trajectory research and we can appreciate the origins of this skepticism. In fact, the practical utility of criminal trajectory research is a highly contentious issue in the literature (DeLisi, 2005). The debate centers on the ecological validity of uncovered trajectory groups and the validity of predicting criminal trajectories from developmental risk factors (Sampson & Laub, 2016). As noted previously, the output of group-based trajectory modeling is largely descriptive and derived through retrospective analyses of the data. Equally important, the standard (classify/analyze) methodology for identifying predictors of trajectory group membership is correlational, although extensions that allow for stronger causal inferences are available, such as propensity score matching (Haviland & Nagin, 2005; Haviland, Nagin, & Rosenbaum, 2007; Haviland, Nagin, Rosenbaum, & Tremblay, 2008; Nieuwbeerta, Nagin, & Blokland, 2009) and instrumental variable approaches (e.g., Angrist, Imbens, & Rubin, 1996; Bushway & Apel, 2010; Foster & McLanahan, 1996; P. Miller, Henry, & Votruba-Drzal, 2016). Group-based trajectory modeling is a data-driven technique that, like cluster analysis, may generate results that only bear a modest resemblance to reality (K. Monahan, Steinberg, Cauffman, & Mulvey, 2009). Of particular relevance for the objectives of this chapter, group-based trajectory modeling can lead to the detection of spurious class-by-predictor interactions (Bauer, 2007; Bauer & Curran, 2004). Viewed through a narrow lens, then, these validity caveats suggest that criminal trajectory research does not lend itself easily or readily to the development of policy or practice (cf. A. Piquero, Farrington, Welsh, Tremblay, & Jennings, 2009). Nonetheless, we assert that further methodological refinements and research are needed to advance an agenda that capitalizes on the trajectory research methodology for policy purposes.

More optimistically, we draw on the positions of several renowned researchers that lead us to the position that trajectory research *does* have a role to play to inform policy and practice. Marc Le Blanc (2012), for example, noted, in reference to the variability in the timing (i.e., onset and offset) and height (i.e., in terms of frequency and seriousness) of the age–crime curve, that "the task of criminology is to identify the mechanisms that create the form of this trajectory, and the mechanisms that influence quantitative and qualitative changes on that trajectory along the life course" (p.125). We agree with this statement and extend it to include the multiple trajectories identified through the trajectory methodology. Similarly, Peter Greenwood (2006) lamented the state of prevention programming: "Rarely have prevention efforts been framed in our understanding of the life-course trajectory of antisocial behavior and of the stages of child and adolescent development that contribute to the onset and persistence of delinquent behavior" (p. 5). More direct to the point, Darrick Jolliffe and colleagues (Jolliffe, Farrington, Piquero, MacLeod, & van de Weijer, 2017) asserted that, "from a policy perspective, it is important to distinguish between different 'types' of offenders so that the criminal justice responses to their behavior can be appropriately tailored to prevent or reduce subsequent offending" (p. 4). At present, however, we feel such a policy objective is largely aspirational. As we will see, several recent reviews of the literature suggested that it has been difficult to identify specific risk factors that differentiate life-course-persistent (LCP) from adolescence-limited (AL) offenders and to prospectively predict who will be on an LCP trajectory (Assink, van der Put, Hoeve, de Vries, Stams, & Oort, 2015; Jolliffe et al., 2017). However, trajectory research is still in its early stages, and further work is needed to more fully utilize this approach.

A BROAD PERSPECTIVE. Broadly viewed, we can expand our focus of criminal trajectory research to address the question of policy and practical implications and remain cautiously optimistic that it does have something to contribute. Viewed through a wider lens, we may situate criminal trajectories, as a concept and statistical technique, within the developmental systems, developmental and life-course criminology, and criminal career frameworks. These broad perspectives provide our starting point for discussing the policy and practice implications.

Developing this notion, that current sentencing and incarceration practices fail individuals is evident (Cullen, Jonson, & Nagin, 2011; Lambie & Randell, 2013). Although there may be many reasons for this outcome, one reason may be that they fail to promote normative developmental processes that enable offenders to be set back onto a normative or typical developmental pathway. From a developmental perspective, what is needed is a criminal justice system with policies and programs that are sensitive to developmental processes across the life span, including processes pertaining to criminal behavior and its desistance. This position is anchored in research on the importance of the successful negotiation of age-appropriate developmental tasks to promote positive development over the life course (Ouwehand, Ridder, & Bensing, 2007; Skeem, Scott, & Mulvey, 2014). There is growing interest in this viewpoint (Farrington, Loeber, & Howell, 2012; Steinberg, Chung, & Little, 2004), which dovetails nicely with the premises of criminal trajectory research (e.g., a focus on development).

In the next two sections, we develop the position that criminal trajectory research has relevance to the formulation of policy and practice within and outside the criminal justice system. We begin with a discussion of the applications and implications to early intervention and prevention and then turn to assessment, treatment, and rehabilitation within the criminal justice system.

Policy and Practice Implications outside the Criminal Justice System

Outside the justice system, there is ample evidence that early intervention and prevention programs work to mitigate the developmental precursors of criminal behavior. Developing evidence-based early intervention and prevention programs would constitute good practice, and findings from trajectory research may help inform these efforts. In their book *Saving Children From a Life of Crime*, Farrington and Welsh (2007) state that preventing crime is neither easy nor impossible, but is achievable. We agree with this position and use it as a jumping-off point to explore further the policy and practice implications. To set the stage for the discussion, we present a case study of Tyler.

TYLER'S TROUBLED LIFE. Tyler had a difficult start in life. At age 4, his mother brought him to the hospital emergency room with a broken arm. Earlier that day his father, in anger, had thrown him against the wall for breaking the television remote control. His father tended to use harsh and punitive discipline. He also had been involved in property crimes, primarily theft and possession of stolen property, for which he had served time in prison, including during Tyler's lifetime. Tyler was often left in the care of his father while his mother worked as a waitress to cover the bills. After the hospital incident, Child and Family Services became involved, and Tyler was removed from the home and taken into the care of the Children's Aid Society. At age 5, he was sent to live with his first foster family. His oppositional and aggressive behavior, however, made him difficult to manage and, over the next 5 years, he found himself in four different foster homes.

Throughout his life, Tyler did poorly in school and experienced learning and behavioral problems. He had difficulty making friends and by middle childhood was often involved in schoolyard brawls. After one particularly vicious fight, the principal suspended him from school. At age 12, he found his way into the company of other like-minded youth in his neighborhood. They began smoking cigarettes and using alcohol and marijuana. He had his first contact with the law at age 14 for breaking and entering and theft. The judge ordered him to pay restitution and apologize to the victim. Noncompliance with the order led to a subsequent charge and a sentence of probation.

Tyler dropped out of school at age 17. He began using alcohol and drugs daily and found it increasingly difficult to abide by the rules of his foster family. In the years that followed, difficulty with emotional self-regulation and a tendency to use drugs and alcohol to cope with life stressors and difficult feelings all too often led Tyler into drunken brawls, resulting in further assault charges and more time in prison. By age 18 (i.e., as a youth), he had been in prison on five separate occasions. Given his aggressive behavior and antisocial tendencies, deviant peer associations, and missed opportunities to turn his life around, he would subsequently find himself in a vicious cycle of surviving on the streets and spending time in prison.

Tyler is a fictional person. He was created for a report titled *Tyler's Troubled Life: The Study of One Young Man's Path Towards a Life of Crime* (Public Safety Canada [PSC], 2016) for PSC, a branch of the Canadian government. The objectives achieved by the report were threefold. First, it illustrated the myriad risk factors and one hypothetical developmental pathway that can lead a young person into a life of crime. Second, it highlighted the missed opportunities to intervene in the life of a young person to alter that course of development. Last the report provided an estimate of the high financial (not to mention personal and social) costs associated with a life of crime and the savings to be gained by implementing developmentally appropriate and evidence-based early intervention and prevention policies and programs. At the end of Tyler's story, at age 30, he had incurred a total cost to society of CN$1,403,476. This figure includes the costs for child and family services, hospital visits, foster care placements, psychological assessments, and special education placements, and the costs for the crimes he committed and the response of the criminal justice system (e.g., court personnel, incarceration in youth and adult facilities).

THE PROMISE OF EARLY INTERVENTION AND PREVENTION. What is clear from this case study is that the burden of suffering from crime is enormous. From a public health perspective, it is incumbent on relevant stakeholders to apply what is known about the etiology, developmental course, and consequences of crime to prevent its onset (Farrington & Welsh, 2007; Vaughn et al., 2011). On the programming side, we know that an investment in empirically validated services can yield dividends over time. According to the *Tyler* report (PSC, 2016), at a cost of CN$6,700 per child, if Tyler had received the Stop Now and Plan (SNAP®) program for children ages 6 to 10 years, the potential cost savings could have been as high as CN$1,197,706.65. The Youth Inclusion Program for young people between the ages of 11 to 14 years costs about CN$8,485 per youth and could have yielded savings of up CN$1,133,738.50 had Tyler been enrolled. Last, Multisystemic Therapy for youth 15 to17 years of age is provided at a cost of US$4,743 per youth and could have saved CN$887,735.79 if offered to Tyler.

These programs represent a few of the many interventions across developmental periods that are widely available throughout North America and the United Kingdom shown to be effective and cost efficient (Greenwood, 2006; McCollister, French, & Fang, 2010; Tremblay & Craig, 1995; Welsh, Farrington, & Gowar, 2015). A meta-analysis of 200 studies by Mark Lipsey and David Wilson (1998), which covered a broad range of programs, found that the average effect sizes for programs for noninstitutionalized and institutionalized juvenile offenders were .14 ($p < .05$; range from −.03 to .52) and .10 ($p < .05$; range from −.01 to .41), respectively. Although these mean figures represent small effect sizes (J. Cohen, 1988), C. Hill, Bloom, Black, and Lipsey (2008) suggest interpreting effect sizes in keeping with expected outcomes. Put another way, these figures reflect a reduction in criminal recidivism of about 6 percentage points, or a change from 40% to 34%. It could also be pointed out that there was considerable variability in the results of studies included in the meta-analysis. Programs with better outcomes focused on interpersonal skills and behavioral change (e.g., social skills) rather than scared-straight tactics and discipline-focused approaches (e.g., wilderness/challenge programs). Last, programs with a high degree of treatment integrity or fidelity, that is, the degree to which the program was implemented as intended, generated larger effect sizes.

For programs designed to *prevent* the onset of aggressive, delinquent, and antisocial behavior in children and youth, there is substantial evidence of their effectiveness, as well (Farrington, Gaffney, Lösel, & Ttofi, 2017; Nation et al., 2003; A. Piquero et al., 2009; A. Piquero, Jennings, Farrington, Diamond, & Gonzalez, 2016). For example, a meta-analysis of the long-term (i.e., up to 1 year) effects of 34 prevention programs for children and youth at risk for antisocial behavior yielded an average effect size of .25 (Sawyer, Borduin, & Dopp, 2015). Programs that comprised more components, included booster sessions, and were based on a child-focused theory showed better outcomes than programs that comprised fewer components, did not include booster sessions, and were based on other theories. As well, in an update to their earlier meta-analysis of early family/parenting programs for antisocial behavior (A. Piquero et al., 2009), Piquero and colleagues (A. Piquero, Jennings, Diamond, et al., 2016) found an average effect size of .37 across 78 studies. This figure corresponds to a reduction in recidivism of 15 percentage points, for example, from 60% in the control group to 45% in the treatment group. This average effect size was slightly larger than the average effect size obtained in their 2009 paper (.35). As well, the larger effect size than that obtained in the Sawyer et al. (2015) study is likely due to the more focused nature of the programs included in the A. Piquero, Jennings, Diamond, et al. (2016) analysis.

In terms of cost savings, a growing body of research has shown that prevention programs can bring a considerable return on investment (Manning, Smith, & Homel, 2013). For example, for every US$1.00 spent on the High/Scope Perry Preschool Program, an early childhood education program in Ypsilanti, Michigan, the program repaid US$16.14, including a cost savings for criminal activity (Nores, Belfield, Barnett, & Schweinhart, 2005; Schweinhart 2007). In other words, participation in this program yielded participants higher lifetime earnings, a lower burden on welfare support, and a lower rate of criminal activity compared to participants in a control group. Further evidence of the savings from investing in prevention comes from the systematic reviews by Steven Aos (e.g., Aos, Phipps, Barnoski, & Lieb, 2001) of the Washington State Institute for Public Policy. Information about the costs and benefits of a wide range of social programs is found on the institute's website (www.wsipp.wa.gov). Programs are grouped by type, including juvenile justice, adult criminal justice, children's mental health, child welfare, adult mental health, and substance abuse. For example, according to the website (as of October 2017), the Triple P Positive Parenting Program (Level 4), an intensive program for parents of children with conduct problem behaviors (Sanders, 1999), costs $992 per parent to implement in Washington State and can yield benefits of $3,331. This figure equates to a cost–benefit ratio of 3.36 to 1, or a cost savings of $3.36 for every $1.00 spent on the program.

Generally, prevention programs aim to reduce the impact of risk factors on developmental processes and strengthen protective factors in a person's life (Farrington, 2007). They may target individuals, families, or schools and could be universal (i.e., for everyone) or selective or indicated (i.e., for high-risk individuals; Mrazek & Haggerty, 1994). Although many have been shown to be effective, as noted earlier, the literature reveals considerable variability in the effectiveness of programs (Pardini, 2016). Clearly, more work is needed to build the armamentarium of resources and programs to effectively address the complex and "wicked" problem (Head, 2008; Rittel & Webber, 1973) of reducing crime.

CRIMINAL TRAJECTORY RESEARCH. What are the policy and practice implications of the group-based trajectory approach? From a narrow perspective, the implications concern the early identification and prevention of individuals on a developmental pathway toward a high-rate and persistent offense trajectory. Indeed, trajectory researchers (ourselves included) have expounded on the practical implications of their work in the closing paragraphs of research articles, based on the observed, statistically significant predictors (and correlates) of trajectory group membership. These statements typically include recommendations for early intervention and prevention programs to target particular variables associated with children on a pathway toward chronic offending (e.g., Reingle, Jennings, & Maldonado-Molina, 2012; D. Shaw, Hyde, & Brennan, 2012; Yessine & Bonta, 2009). For example, based on the results of their study, Chung, Hill, Hawkins, Gilchrist, and Nagin (2002) suggested that prevention programs target delinquent peer associates, school bonding, and availability of drugs in the neighborhood. Similarly, Shaw et al. (2012) suggested focusing on early parenting and other family factors that might affect caregiving quality and maternal depression.

There are challenges in translating research into practice, however. As Dodge (2008) noted, "psychologists have recently become enamored with public policy implications of their work and are too often willing to make sweeping recommendations to any legislator or policymaker who will listen" (p. 587). Additionally, researchers may make statements that go beyond the data at hand, for example, drawing causal conclusions based on correlational findings: "Because factor X was observed to predict trajectory class Y and not trajectory class Z, even when controlling for factors A, B, and C, policymakers might focus on changing X when wanting to prevent the onset of the Y trajectory." These reflect some of the dangers to guard against.

Either way, many groups that have a stake in the issue agree that research has an important role to play in translating developmental findings for policy makers (Lochman, 2006; Shonkoff & Balers, 2011). Science, particularly the science of prevention (B. Welsh & Farrington, 2012), has a great deal to offer the development of crime prevention and crime control programs and policies (B. Welsh, Braga, & Bruinsma, 2013). In the words of Jennifer Skeem, and colleagues (Skeem, Scott, & Mulvey, 2014), "because the crime problem is complex and potential solutions are politically sensitive, science should be used to inform policy changes" (p. 710). In regards to outcome research and program evaluation, which are important topics for crime prevention and reduction efforts, science has much to offer in addressing the question: "*What* treatment, by *whom*, is most effective for *this* individual with *that* specific problem, and under *which* set of circumstances" (Paul, 1967, p, 111, emphasis in original). Within the field of developmental psychopathology, Ann Masten (2006) speaks of the "practical mission" of developmental psychopathology "to prevent or ameliorate behavioral problems and disorders and to promote positive development" (p. 47). A parallel "practical mission" within the field of developmental criminology is *translational criminology*, which is designed to "prevent, reduce, and manage crime" (Laub, 2016, p. 631).

The position that trajectory research is applicable to policy and practice is offset by the countervailing viewpoint that trajectory research cannot and should not be used to inform early intervention and prevention efforts, largely for the reasons noted earlier. Prediction and prevention of crime are predicated on understanding the causes of crime. Although considerable efforts in both theory and research over the last 80 years have contributed greatly to elucidating these causes, as in understanding any human behavior, positing an account of the causes of crime is an extraordinarily complex task. The complexity lies, in part, in the multiplicity of factors that may influence the onset, course, and desistance of the behavior within individuals.

Taking this opposing view, Sampson, Winship, and Knight (2013; see also Case & Haines, 2009; Rein & Winship, 2000) attest that there is insufficient evidence to make claims about causal relations (e.g., what causes crime) on which to base sound policy and practice. Therefore, it is premature, perhaps even reckless (Blomberg, Mestre, & Mann, 2013), to use the current state of knowledge to inform policy and practice. In particular, Sampson et al. (2013) argue that there is a need for more research on the causal mechanisms that link variables of interest. This means not just identifying that one variable leads to another but also asking "how and why," that is, to address the "black box" problem. Research on causal mechanisms, they note, serves to advance the needs of policy "to achieve an outcome *via a certain route*" (Sampson et al., 2013, p. 596, emphasis in original).

We do not disagree with the position that further research is needed before we can make statements *with certainty* about the causes of crime, particularly research on causal mechanisms. But we also feel that we cannot wait until such time that stronger evidence than is currently available is gathered before embarking on ways to prevent crime (see also Latessa, Cullen, & Gendreau, 2002). There is no need to wait until the root causes of crime have been identified to develop and implement programs to address putative risk factors. A great deal is known about the risk factors associated with the onset and maintenance of offending and about programs that can effectively address some of these risk factors, if implemented with fidelity (Blomberg et al. 2013; Farrington & Welsh, 2007). This is not to say that there is no room for improvement with further study and more research. In other words, we need to move cautiously and not overly optimistically when intervening in the lives of individuals, particularly young children who, by virtue of experiencing some putative risk factors, may be "treated" for a condition they have not developed and, in fact, may never develop (Robins, 1966). However, as Sampson et al. (2013) concede, theory, research, and practice are mutually informing. To wait until such time that we have perfect prediction, as some might suggest (Carlsson & Sarnecki, 2016), is simply unrealistic and, perhaps, ultimately unachievable.

PREDICTING TRAJECTORY GROUP MEMBERSHIP. Early research on developmental predictors of crime sought to identify variables that differentiate offenders from nonoffenders. This led to veritable laundry lists of risk factors (Allard, Chrzanowski, & Stewart, 2012). Fortunately, this work has been summarized with meta-analyses (e.g., Lipsey &

Derzon, 1998), which allow for a relative and comparative analysis of the strength of association of a predictor with an outcome variable (e.g., crime). Based on this work, research suggests that early identification of children at risk of long-term offending can be achieved "with relative accuracy" (National Research Council, 2013, p. 22). With the advent of group-based trajectory modeling, however, there has been a shift toward studies that attempt to identify variables that make more fine-grained discriminations among "types" of offenders based on criminal trajectories. This research was described previously, with a particular focus on predictors/correlates of a high-rate and persistent criminal trajectory.

Where does the literature stand with respect to predicting trajectory group membership? Two recent studies offer insights into this question. Assink et al. (2015) conducted a meta-analysis of the literature on predictors of life-course-persistent (LCP) and adolescence-limited (AL) groups. Although not exclusively focused on trajectory studies, their review sheds light on the developmental risk factors that are differentially associated with LCP and AL offenders by combining the results from a large number of studies (in this case, 48 studies on 55 different samples). This research is an important step in identifying a robust set of variables that may be used to inform early intervention and prevention programs and policies that target specific trajectory groups. Their results indicated that differences between the LCP and AL groups across 14 risk domains (e.g., antisocial attitude, family, and school/employment) were found for a number of areas, notably, criminal history, aggression, and alcohol/drug abuse. However, the authors concluded that differences between the groups were more quantitative than qualitative. In other words, both LCP and AL groups experience risk factors; however, the prevalence of risk factors was greater in the LCP group than the AL group (see also Fairchild, van Goozen, Calder, & Goodyer, 2013).

Jolliffe, Farrington, Piquero, Loeber, and Hill (2017) conducted a systematic review of the literature to test a modified version of Moffitt's (1993) dual taxonomy theory. In a systematic review, all the available studies are identified that fit a set of defined criteria. In this case, Jolliffe, Farrington, Piquero, Loeber, et al. (2017) identified 14 studies that used a prospective longitudinal methodology to differentiate LCP offenders from AL offenders, in addition to a third group, late-onset (LO) offenders, on developmental risk factors. LO offenders have been identified in a number of (nontrajectory) studies (e.g., McGee & Farrington, 2010; Zara & Farrington, 2009). The array of risk factors fell into three domains: personality/individual, family, and socio-demographic. Similar to the Assink et al. (2015) study, Jolliffe, Farrington, Piquero, Loeber, et al. (2017) concluded that the three groups differed more in the strength of the associations than on any specific risk factor: "While specific risk factors did not seem to differentiate LCP, AL, and LO offending, there was an indication that the different offending types were associated with different strengths of association, and with the number of key risk factors" (p. 8). They also called for further research, in particular, studies that include low birthweight and prenatal problems as predictors, variables that are consistent with Moffitt's (1993) conceptualization of the LCP group. Aside from these two excellent reviews, we feel there is a still need for a synthesis of the literature (i.e., a meta-analysis or systematic review) that focuses exclusively on criminal trajectory research.

If no specific risk factor or set of factors emerges as a defining feature of either LCP or AL offenders, where does that leave us with respect to informing policy and practice? We feel that trajectory research can contribute to the development of early intervention and prevention programs. To make our case, we begin with the position that, to make a significant and meaningful impact on the prevention of crime, programs need to target individuals who are at the greatest risk of becoming high-rate persistent offenders (i.e., following high-rate, persistent offense trajectories; Baglivio, Jackowski, Greenwald, & Howell, 2014; M. Cohen & Piquero, 2015; Moffitt, 2018; Welsh & Farrington, 2007). As Tolan and Gorman-Smith (2002, p. 715) observed, "prevention will be more effective if focused on this small percentage of high-risk youth and that different prevention efforts will be needed for this population than the rest of the population." The question of how to identify these individuals remains. In spite of the shortcomings of prediction and prevention work as noted earlier, three areas of research could provide important foundations for achieving this agenda: (a) research on cumulative risk, (b) research on age of onset as a predictor of long-term offending, and (c) research on risk assessment instruments for predelinquent children.

CUMULATIVE RISK. Prevention programs could target children exposed to multiple risk factors. This position is consistent with an abundance of research on the deleterious impact of *cumulative risk* (Evans,

Li, & Whipple, 2013), also known as a dose-response effect (Baglivio, Wolff, Piquero, Howell, & Greenwald, 2017; Loeber, Burke, & Pardini, 2009). Cumulative risk refers to exposure to multiple risk factors and the cumulative impact of that exposure over time. Simply put, "the more risk factors [children] are exposed to the worse the outcome" (Evans et al., 2013, p. 1343). For example, using data from the Pittsburgh Youth Study, Stouthamer-Loeber, Loeber, Wei, Farrington, and Wikstrom (2002) found that 70% of children in their oldest sample who had a risk score of five were subsequently identified as persistent offenders. This result compares with only 10% of children with a risk score of zero. In their youngest sample, 71% of those with a risk score of five were subsequently identified as persistent offenders, compared to only 2% of those with a zero-risk score. Similarly, Herrenkohl and colleagues (Herrenkohl, Maguin, Hill, Hawkins, Abbott, & Catalano, 2000) found that, at ages 10, 14, and 16, youth exposed to six or more risk factors had a 7, 10, and 11 times greater odds, respectively, of committing violent crimes at age 18 than did youth exposed to fewer than two risk factors at each age. Returning to the case of Tyler, individuals who grow up with the kinds of experiences he had would be identified as a high priority for early intervention and prevention programs.

AGE OF ONSET. Considerable evidence supports the notion that an early age of onset for antisocial behavior portends a lengthy criminal career (X. Chen, 2016; DeLisi, 2006; Greenwood, 2006). An age of onset prior to 12 to 15 increases the likelihood that an individual will continue to offend, diversify his or her offending behavior, and be represented among the 5% to 10% of youth who become chronic offenders (cf. Whitten, McGee, Homel, Farrington, & Ttofi, 2017). Frechette and Le Blanc (1987) found that boys who committed their first offense prior to age 12 or 13 committed twice as many offenses, based on an annual rate of self-reported offending, than did those who started at a later age. Similarly, Moffitt, Caspi, Dickson, Silva, and Stanton (1996) found that 43% of males in their New Zealand sample had an age of onset for conduct problems during childhood (i.e., the LCP group) had a court record by age 18, and that 25% had been convicted for a violent offense. In contrast, 20% of males with an age of onset for conduct problems during adolescence (i.e., the AL group) had a court record by age 18, and 8% had been convicted for a violence offense. Last, in a review of the literature, Krohn, Thornberry, Rivera, and Le Blanc (2001) found that early-onset youth were two to three times more likely to be chronic offenders than were late-onset youth and had committed more offenses than did late-onset youth. As we know, age of onset has been incorporated into several prominent developmental theories of antisocial behavior (i.e., Moffitt, 1993; Patterson, Capaldi, & Bank, 1991) and the most recent version of the *Diagnostic and Statistical Manual of Mental Disorders* (*DSM-5*) distinguishes between early- and late-onset types of the conduct disorder psychiatric diagnosis (American Psychiatric Association [APA], 2013).

However, there is considerable variability in the definition of early and late onset. Moffitt (1993) stated that the LCP group initiates their conduct problem behavior in childhood (i.e., before puberty) and that the AL group starts in the adolescent years (i.e., alongside puberty). Patterson et al. (1991) stated that late-onset offenders begin around age 15, whereas early-onset offenders initiate their antisocial behavior by age 8. The *DSM-5* (APA, 2013) uses the age of 10 to differentiate the childhood and adolescent onset types of conduct disorder. Differences in definition also may arise when using official records versus self-reported behavior. Research suggests that an official criminal record is often preceded by involvement in antisocial behavior (Le Blanc & Frechette, 1989). Loeber, Farrington, and Waschbusch (1998) found that, based on self-report data, the onset for serious offending begins about seven years prior to a first recorded conviction. Therefore, with an age of first court contact of 15 years, serious misbehavior could have occurred as early as 8 years of age. This distinction is consistent with clinical evidence that conduct problems that do not abate by age 8 might be considered a chronic condition, which, like diabetes, would need to be managed over time with supports (Kazdin, 1995). The policy implication for the age-of-onset variable speaks to the need for early intervention for children in middle to late childhood who display high levels of conduct problem behaviors. Again, Tyler serves as an exemplar of a child who would be identified as in need of intervention and who presents with an array of needs that programs could address.

RISK ASSESSMENT INSTRUMENTS. The early identification of children at greatest risk for long-term criminal involvement could be enhanced by combining risk factors into index scores (Appleyard,

Egeland, Dulmen, & Sroufe, 2005) or standardized risk assessment instruments (Farrington, & Loeber, 2013). Creating psychometrically sound scales could provide useful tools for predicting antisocial and criminal behavior in children. Several examples from the literature illustrate their potential usefulness. In the first example, using data from the Cambridge Study in Delinquent Development (CSDD), Farrington, Piquero, and Jennings (2013) created a cumulative risk index comprising 27 risk factors, assessed at ages 8 and 10, across two broad domains, individual and environmental. They used the index to predict criminal trajectory group membership up to age 56. Results indicated that higher index scores were associated with the two trajectories with the highest volume and/or duration of offenses, high adolescence-peaked and high-rate chronic. Moreover, of the 26 individuals in the top 5% on the childhood risk factor index (i.e., with at least 15 risk factors), 88.5% were later identified as offenders (vs. nonoffenders), and 30% were found to be on a high-rate chronic offense trajectory. In the second example, using a similar approach to Farrington et al. (2013), Sivertsson and Carlsson (2014) created a cumulative index score from 26 risk indicators, assessed when their sample of 187 boys was 11 to 15 years. They then used the index score to predict later criminal offending to age 59. Their results yielded "a clear association between childhood risk factors and offending in adulthood" (Sivertsson & Carlsson, 2014, p. 404). For example, they found that 33.3% of the highest risk boys were in the highest frequency offender group, based on the number of officially recorded offenses per year from ages 15 to 59. By contrast, only 3.5% of the lowest risk boys were in the highest frequency offenders. It should be noted that, although the results of both these studies were statistically significant, the effects were only moderately strong.

In addition to these screening tools, researchers have begun to develop structured risk assessment tools for making decisions about the prediction and management of risk for violent behavior in children. Three such measures are the Cracow instrument (Corrado, 2002; Lussier, Corrado, Healey, Tzoumakis, & Deslauriers-Varin, 2011) and the Early Assessment Risk List for boys (EARL-20B) and for girls (EARL-21G; Augimeri, Enebrink, Walsh, & Jiang, 2010). Risk assessments are common in the criminal justice system for making decisions about risk to reoffend and for treatment planning. Risk assessment instruments are designed to be theory-driven, empirically based, and psychometrically sound (Le Blanc, 2002; Lösel & Bender, 2006). Some examples of risk assessment measures for justice-involved youth are the Youth Level of Service/Case Management Inventory (Hoge, Andrews, & Leschied, 2002), Structured Assessment of Violence Risk in Youth (Borum, Bartel, & Forth, 2002), and the Washington State Juvenile Assessment (Barnoski, 2002).

The purpose of a risk assessment is risk management. In other words, a risk assessment tool should set out guidelines for managing an individual's level of risk with supports and services. According to the risk, need, and responsivity model (Bonta & Andrews, 2017), the level of risk should match the level of service intensity; in other words, high-intensity services should be provided to high-risk individuals, and low-intensity services should be provided to low-risk individuals. As well, services should target the criminogenic needs identified by the risk assessment instrument and be responsive to the individual's level of functioning.

The Cracow instrument was developed out of a research workshop held in Cracow, Poland, in 2000, funded by the Scientific Affairs Division of the North Atlantic Treaty Organization. The workshop brought together more than 30 researchers from 16 countries (Corrado, Roesch, Hart, & Gierowski, 2002). The Cracow instrument is a comprehensive, 34-item risk/needs management tool that assesses risk for serious violence (e.g., physical attack causing injury) in youth. This instrument is unique in that is takes a development approach and assesses risk factors for four age periods: birth/infancy (0–1 year), early childhood (2–5 years), middle/late childhood (6–12 years), and adolescence (13–17 years). For example, early childhood risk factors include two risk domains specific to that age period (psychological functioning and parenting skills) and three risk domains carried over from birth/infancy (pre-/perinatal, socioeconomic situation, and family environment). Carrying over prior risk factors is consistent with the notion of cumulative risk, as discussed earlier. Indeed, risk factors experienced early in life (e.g., during the prenatal and perinatal periods of development) confer the most detrimental effects over the life span (Lussier, Healey, Tzoumakis, Deslauriers-Varin & Corrado, 2010). These factors not only include maternal substance use and birth complications but also include abuse and neglect experienced in the first five years of life (Osofsky & Lieberman, 2011). On the Cracow instrument, risk factors in the parenting skills domain include hostile parenting, a lack of consistent discipline, and the presence of inadequate norms or rule. Each item is rated on a 3-point scale from *absent* (0), *somewhat present* (1), or *definitely present* (2), based on a parent interview. For each developmental period, the Cracow instrument also provides areas to target for high-intensity intervention based on coding of critical items.

Studies of the psychometric properties (i.e., reliability and validity) of the Cracow instrument are limited. In one study with 100 preschool children (58 boys and 42 girls) in Vancouver, Canada, the 26 items composing the early childhood period yielded an adequate level of internal reliability (coefficient alpha = .77; Lussier et al. 2011). The measure was also found to be effective at postdicting the most physically aggressive children in the sample, assessed in the previous year. In general, although the Cracow instrument is a work in progress, it looks promising as a research and clinical tool for the early identification of those at greatest risk for a persistent criminal trajectory.

The EARL-20B and EARL-21G are structured risk assessment tools developed by researchers at the Child Development Institute, in Toronto, Canada. The tools were designed for children between the ages of 6 and 12. The structure of the tools is similar to the Historical/Clinical/Risk Management instrument for adults (Webster, Douglas, Eaves, & Hart, 1997). (Chris Webster was involved in developing both the Historical/Clinical/Risk Management instrument and the EARL tools.) The EARL tools comprise 20 items for boys and 21 items for girls in three risk domains: family, child, and responsivity. The EARL-21G consists of the same items as the EARL-20B except for the addition of two items, Caregiver–Daughter Interaction and Sexual Development, and omission of the Authority Contact item on the EARL-20B. Items are rated by clinical staff on a 3-point scale from *absent* (0), *partially present* (1), or *definitely present* (2). The sum of the items generates a total risk score to predict antisocial and criminal behavior in children and adolescence. Using a structured professional judgment (SPJ) approach, rather than a straight actuarial approach (de Rutier & Augimeri, 2012), individuals also may be classified into risk categories of "low," "moderate," or "high." Last, the EARL tools include a Case Planning Form to assist clinicians to link the assessment results with clinical risk management strategies (de Rutier & Augimeri, 2012).

Using Canadian and Swedish samples, the EARL-20B has been found to be reliable and valid (Augimeri, Jiang, Koegl, & Carey, 2006; Enebrink, Långström, & Gumpert, 2006; Enebrink, Långström, Hultén, & Gumpert, 2006; Webster, Augimeri, & Koegl, 2002). Interrater reliability was reported to be good, with correlation coefficients between three raters ranging from .79 to .97 (Webster et al., 2002). The three-factor structure for both the boys and girls measures was supported with confirmatory factor analyses (Augimeri, Pepler, Walsh, Jiang, & Dassinger, 2010). The EARL-20B was shown to predict aggression in children at 6-month and 30-month follow-up (Enebrink et al., 2006), and the EARL-20B and EARL-20G predicted criminal activity, health outcomes, and mental outcomes in a sample of 379 boys and 67 girls with conduct problem behavior, referred to the SNAP® treatment program in Toronto (Koegl, 2011). For example, Koegl (2011) found that 87.6% of boys who scored in the "high risk" level on the EARL-20B had a conviction by age 21 compared to 69.5%, 66.1%, and 53.5% for the boys in the "moderate-high risk," "low-moderate risk," and "low risk" levels, respectively (note these risk-level categories differ from those indicated earlier). The pattern was somewhat different for girls, however. Whereas 72.2% of the "high risk" girls had a conviction by age 21, only 25.0% of the girls in the "moderate-high risk" level had a conviction. By contrast, 31.3% of the girls in the "low risk" level had a conviction, and 35.3% of the girls in the "low-moderate risk" level had a conviction. Note that Type 1 (false-positive) and Type 2 (false-negative) errors may be a problem that can compromise the utility of a risk assessment instrument. At the same time, the task in trajectory analysis is not to predict who will or will not offend but to detect at what *rate* a person will offend over time, that is, to follow a "high"-, "moderate"-, or "low"-rate trajectory, for example.

Last, and of most relevant to this book, Augimeri and colleagues conducted two studies that used EARL scores to predict trajectory group membership. First, Augimeri et al. (2006) predicted trajectory group membership in a sample of 38 SNAP®-referred boys. Using three data points (pretreatment, posttreatment, and 6-month follow-up) of parent-report scores on the Delinquency scale of the Child Behavior Checklist (now called the Achenbach System of Empirically Based Assessment; Achenbach & Rescorla, 2001) Augimeri et al. (2006) generated three trajectory groups, labeled high, medium, and low levels of delinquency. Results indicated that the EARL-20B scores differentiated boys in the high (vs. low) delinquency classes and boys in the medium (vs. low) delinquency classes. Second, with a larger sample of children referred to the SNAP® program ($n = 573$ boys and $n = 380$ girls), Augimeri, Pepler, et al. (2010) examined the association between EARL scores and trajectory groups over four waves of data (pretreatment, posttreatment, and 6- and 12-month follow-up) using the Externalizing and Conduct Disorder scales of the Achenbach System of Empirically Based Assessment. Results indicated that, for girls but not boys, higher EARL scores were associated with membership on both the high-externalizing trajectory group and the high–conduct disorder trajectory group. Although yielding mixed results, these studies provide preliminary evidence for the use of structured risk assessment tools for children to predict trajectory group membership. Further research is needed with longer follow-up periods and with criminal offense data to generate the trajectory groups to make more definitive statements about the validity of structured assessment tools to predict those at greatest risk for high-rate and persistent offending.

In conclusion, when we take a narrow view of criminal trajectory research, there is little direct applied relevance to policy and practice. However, drawing back a bit, we can envision a program of research that capitalizes on robust findings in three lines of research to predict individuals at greatest risk to eventuate a high-rate and persistent offense trajectory. Putting the pieces together, further research could investigate the use of structured risk assessment instruments with children who have an early age of onset for serious antisocial behavior (such as those referred to a clinical program such as SNAP®) and who have experienced multiple risk factors from an early age (e.g., prenatal) to predict subsequent criminal trajectory assignment. The case of Tyler provides an example of a child whose circumstances and early-life experiences could warrant assessment and early intervention. In the next section, we examine the applied relevance of criminal trajectory research within the criminal justice system.

Policy and Practice Implications within (vs. outside) the Criminal Justice System

To begin our discussion, we note that one of the prominent findings of the criminal trajectory research is that offenders in low-rate trajectory groups constitute the largest proportion of offenders in study samples, typically about 60%, with high-rate and chronic offenders composing between 5% to 10% of samples (e.g., A. Piquero, Farrington et al., 2007). Nonetheless, government policies and practices are often framed as if high-rate groups compose the largest proportion of offender populations, with government expenditures allocated accordingly. Building more prisons and setting harsher penalties for offenders are at odds with the data and constitute a waste of limited resources. We raise this observation as an example of how criminal trajectory research might inform policy.

We may also take a broad view of criminal trajectory research and situate criminal trajectories, as a concept and a statistical technique, within a developmental systems, developmental and life-course criminology, and criminal career framework and use them as anchors for a fulsome discussion of the policy and practice implications. To contextualize our position, we concur with Sullivan and Piquero (2016b, p. 428) who state in a review of the criminal career concept that

> given human beings' penchant for telling and attempting to understand stories, . . . it is not at all surprising that connecting terms like "careers," "pathways," and "turning points," and "developmental trajectories" to questions about crime and criminal behavior would be embraced by a significant subgroup of criminologists. Our thinking about causality, which is endemic in human cognition (Sloman, 2005) is inherently tied to questions about what preceded that which we currently observe and what might follow from it. Unravelling these stories—whether in ethnographies or quantitative summaries of longitudinal data—is one interesting way of learning about and explaining crime and criminal behavior.

In addition to "learning about and explaining crime," we would add *preventing* and *reducing* crime. Indeed, the case study of Tyler sparks the imagination to speculate how we might apply what we know about a criminal trajectory not yet realized to prevent its onset in the first place or to provide an appropriate response for its desistance once initiated. We believe that framing the issue within a developmental perspective, and, like Sullivan and Piquero, drawing on concepts of a trajectory, pathway, and turning point, provide a viable standpoint to advance strategies for both crime prevention (outside the justice system) and crime reduction (within the justice system).

In doing so, we place a particular emphasis on the role of adaptive functioning and successful achievement of developmental tasks across the life span. It is well established that the psychological struggles associated with adaptational failure (i.e., the failure to achieve developmental milestones) are associated with a lower level of psychological well-being (Schulenberg, Bryant, & O'Malley, 2004), difficulty transitioning into adult roles and responsibilities (Schulenberg, Sameroff, & Cicchetti, 2004; Steinberg et al., 2004), and an increased likelihood of antisocial and criminal behavior (Grisso & Schwartz, 2000; Skeem et al., 2014; Williams, Guerra, & Elliot, 1997; Zara & Farrington, 2016). According to Williams et al. (1997, p. 28), "violence is seen as a negative developmental outcome—one of many tragic consequences resulting from unmet development needs." Conversely, research suggests that *achievement* of developmental tasks is associated with criminal desistance (National Research Council, 2013). On this point, we end the chapter by connecting developmental tasks to *sense of agency*, which has been identified as a critical factor in the pathway to desistance (Bersani & Douherty, 2017; Laub, Sampson, & Sweeten 2006; Loeber & Ahonen, 2014; Maruna, 2001; Neill, 2006; Sampson & Laub, 2005a; Sivertsson & Carlsson, 2014; Sullivan, 2013).

DEVELOPMENTAL TASKS. In the introduction chapter, we discussed the importance of developmental tasks to the achievement of healthy psychosocial development, adjustment, and competence. We also discussed the cumulative impact of adaptational failure on the development of maladaptive outcomes. Third, we described the process of adaptation as hierarchical in nature in that successful adaptation at one developmental stage increases the likelihood (but not the certainty) of successful resolution of subsequent stage-salient tasks. To this point, Cicchetti and Rogosch (2002, p. 15) contend that "a major common theme that should undergird prevention efforts is how best to promote competent resolution of the primary developmental tasks of adolescence." Last, we presented the work of developmental psychologist, Paul Baltes, to illustrate how adaptation is a lifelong process, meaning that successful achievement of developmental milestones is salient throughout the life course. We use these principles to develop our case that trajectory research, broadly viewed (i.e., situated within a developmental context) can be applied to the formulation of criminal justice policy and practice.

In 1997, Kirk Williams, Nancy Guerra, and Delbert Elliot wrote a report proposing a comprehensive policy framework to prevent violence in youth. Their proposal was based on what they called an *Ecological Model of Life Course Development*. Their report recommended that programs and services pay attention to three key, individual-level concepts: (1) developmental stages, (2) transitions and pathways, and (3) and nested social contexts. In essence, their model emphasized that violence-prevention programs should be sensitive to developmental needs and achievement of developmental tasks to support healthy human development. Williams et al. proposed that *existing* programs for children, youth, and their families (vs. proposing that new programs be developed) be delivered in a way that is consistent with their model to foster adaptive functioning in young people and their successful transition into adulthood.

APPLICATION OF DEVELOPMENTAL TASKS TO THE CRIMINAL JUSTICE SYSTEM. We propose an approach to treatment and rehabilitation services for offenders within the justice system that, like the Williams et al. (1997) model, emphasizes successful achievement of developmental tasks across the life span. However, whereas Williams et al. discussed their model only with respect to youth, we extend our policy approach to adulthood, including long-term offenders and lifers (Kazemian & Travis, 2015). We argue that the risk of criminal recidivism would be reduced if offenders were able to make the kinds of psychological, psychosocial, and personal changes that enable them to alter the course of their criminal trajectory (Rocque, 2014). As stated earlier, we propose that the justice system be sensitive to the developmental needs of individuals across their life span. More specifically, the justice system should provide opportunities to allow individuals to achieve resolution of developmental tasks at any stage of development. This position is consistent with the *stage-environment fit* theory of development (Eccles et al., 1993) in which a mismatch between the needs of the individual and the opportunities available in the social context (including the justice system) will undermine the positive growth and development of the individual (Cauffman, Cavanaugh, Donley, & Thomas, 2016). It is also consistent with Skeem et al. (2014, p. 733), who contend that, with respect to adolescents in the juvenile justice system:

> Interventions should be structured to respond to the developmental needs of youth . . . Correctional programs constitute the social context for juveniles in the justice system and should be designed to provide, to the extent possible, the elements that are important for healthy development—authoritative parent figures, structured and limited contact with antisocial peers and opportunities for interaction with prosocial peers, and educational and extracurricular programs that prepare youths for adult employment and social roles.

Our position is that, from a life-course developmental perspective, the goal of the criminal justice system, while addressing the need to hold individuals to account for their crimes, is to alter the criminal trajectory of individuals, facilitate their positive growth and development, and support their return to a normative developmental track. This position is grounded in a main tenet of developmental science: that understanding (and correcting) nonnormative or atypical development requires an understanding of normative or typical development.

These aims could be achieved by providing developmentally informed programming and treatment or alternative sentencing options to enable offenders, juvenile and adult alike, to achieve the developmental tasks of acquiring social skills, basic educational and vocational skills, and temperance skills to behave in a socially mature and responsible manner (Cauffman, 2012; Cauffman, Cavanagh, Donley, & Thomas, 2016; National Research Council, 2013). To ensure individuals' developmental needs are met, developmentally sensitive, structured risk assessment tools are needed to assess such factors as the level of psychosocial competence, including attachment and readiness for healthy intimate relations and positive peer relations, psychosocial maturity, and academic and vocational achievement (see Prior et al., 2011, for examples of measurement tools). Failure to attend to the developmental needs of individuals will compromise the effectiveness of efforts to reduce the risk of recidivism (National Research Council, 2013).

With further research, studies on criminal trajectories may serve as a basis for sorting out the heterogeneity among offender populations as a guide to address the developmental needs of individuals. With its focus on within-individual variation, trajectory research also may shed light on the timing of developmentally appropriate services, particularly if more studies examined developmental trajectories of phenomena other than crime, such as psychosocial functioning (e.g., psychosocial maturity, self-regulation skills, mental health symptoms; Rocque, 2014), including during periods of incarceration (Kazemian & Travis, 2015).

To conclude this chapter, we review the concept of agency and discuss its relevance to the process of criminal desistance. We draw a parallel between sense of agency and psychological autonomy, one of the developmental tasks of adolescence that leads to a successful transition to adulthood. We present this material to further bolster our rationale for attending to developmental tasks and adaptive functioning across the life span within the criminal justice system.

SENSE OF AGENCY. Sense of agency refers to "the purposeful execution of choice and individual will" (Sampson & Laub, 2005a, p. 37). Sense of agency engenders the notion that a person has the capability and motivation to make life decisions and actively take control of and shape his or her destiny and life course. Having a sense of agency allows a person to be future-oriented and goal-directed, bringing oneself toward a determined future self. From a developmental psychopathology perspective, sense of agency, or "psychological autonomy," relates to the development of a coherent sense of self, one of the developmental tasks of adolescence. Formation of a sense of agency prepares one to transition to adulthood, to assume the roles and responsibilities of adulthood, and to develop a sense of adult identity (C. Lee & Berrick, 2014). According to Cicchetti and Rogosch (2002), psychological autonomy is a multidimensional construct that comprises three dimensions: (1) psychological autonomy, which refers to emotional autonomy, for example, from childhood dependency on parents; (2) behavioral autonomy, for example, self-reliance; and (3) cognitive autonomy, for example, self-confidence in making decisions.

From a criminology perspective, sense of agency relates to the sense of identity described by Bushway and Paternoster (2011; Paternoster & Bushway, 2009) as part of the process that leads an individual toward criminal desistance. According to their *identity theory* of criminal desistance, moving toward desistance requires a shift in identity from "criminal" to "noncriminal." Like the notion of desistance itself, this identity shift is a *process* undertaken by a person who makes a conscious, deliberate, and intentional decision to disengage from criminal activity when it becomes no longer satisfactory. Just as the youth begins to integrate an "adult" sense of self into her or his current sense of self as a "youth," so, too, does the criminal integrate a sense of self (i.e., a "possible self") as a "non-criminal" and all that entails into her or his current sense of self.

We draw a parallel here between the process of forming a sense of adult identity as an adolescent, as a necessary developmental task leading to a successful transition to adulthood, and the process of forming a sense of noncriminal identity, as a necessary task that leads to the transition toward criminal desistance. Moreover, as the study of desistance requires individual-level longitudinal data, Paternoster and Bushway (2009; see also Bushway, Piquero, Broidy, Cauffman, & Mazerolle, 2001) explicitly recommend the use of group-based trajectory models to test their theory. With more emphasis on process-related variables and associated factors (e.g., environmental influences), criminal trajectory research also may help identify the most opportune time along a given offense trajectory to initiate the process of moving toward desistance.

The criminal justice system can provide opportunities to facilitate a sense of agency and enable the person to make an identity shift through the provision of supports and services and by creating an environment that facilitates a growth model. For details about such as model, we draw on Positive Youth Development and its strength-based approaches to intervention (L. Benson, Scales, Hamilton, & Sesma, 2006). Positive Youth Development is a field of research and an approach to practice that is concerned with promoting competency and fostering personal and social assets in young people (Roth & Brooks-Gun, 2003). Assets refer to four types: (1) physical development (e.g., good health habits), (2) intellectual development (e.g., knowledge of essential vocational skills, school success, good decision making), (3) psychological and emotional development (e.g., good coping skills, good emotional self-regulation skills, a commitment to good use of time), and (4) social development (e.g., connectedness, attachment to prosocial/conventional institutions). Broadly,

PYD [Positive Youth Development] seeks to promote one or more of the following: bonding, resilience, social competence, emotional competence, cognitive competence, behavioral competence, moral competence, self-determination, spirituality, self-efficacy, positive identity, belief in the future, recognition for positive behavior, opportunities for prosocial involvement, and prosocial norms. (L. Benson et al., 2006, p. 897)

As a strength-based approach to youth development, Positive Youth Development falls in line with other related approaches within the criminal justice system for reducing risk of recidivism by promoting psychological well-being. These approaches include positive criminology (Ronel & Elisha, 2011, 2014), strength-based approaches to working with offenders (Burnett & Maruna, 2006; Kewley, 2017), therapeutic jurisprudence (Wexler, 2014) and developmental jurisprudence (Buss, 2016), the Good Lives Model (T. Ward, Mann, & Gannon, 2007), and human rights approaches, procedural justice theory, and the recovery movement in the treatment of offenders with mental illness (Vandevelde et al., 2017).

Conclusion

This chapter has concerned the applications of criminal trajectory research to policy and practice within and outside the criminal justice system. We framed the discussion in terms of a narrow perspective and a broad perspective. Viewing criminal trajectory research from a broad perspective provides the best footing from which to consider the policy and practice relevance. Outside the criminal justice system, applications concern the prevention of crime and could capitalize on the work on early predictors of a high-rate and persistent criminal activity, with a particular focus on three areas: (a) cumulative risk, (b) early age of onset, and (c) risk assessment tools. Further work in criminal trajectory research can incorporate these areas to advance knowledge to tailor early intervention and prevention efforts. Within the criminal justice system, responses to reduce crime should be sensitive to developmental processes and incorporate a developmental perspective to enable achievement of developmental tasks across the life span. Criminal trajectory research that examines trajectories of process-related variables, such as self-regulation, psychosocial maturity, and sense of agency, and other factors that promote adaptive functioning, could facilitate this work. In the end, we agree with Farrington and Loeber (2013, p. 245) "that it is 'never too early, never too late' . . . to intervene successfully to reduce offending. In other words, it is highly desirable to focus not only on early intervention to prevent the adolescent onset of offending but also on later programs to prevent adult onset and to prevent continuation and encourage early desistance."

Suggested Supplemental Readings

The book *Changing Lives: Delinquency Prevention and Crime Control*, by Peter Greenwood (2006), offers a comprehensive and detailed account of the historical developments of policy-relevant research for crime prevention and crime control in the United States. Greenwood also presents specific examples of research designed to evaluate programs in terms of both effectiveness (e.g., reduced antisocial and delinquent behavior or recidivism) and efficiency (i.e., through cost benefit analysis). Last, he discusses the challenges faced by researchers and policymakers in translating findings into application. Laub's (2016) chapter in the *Handbook of the Life Course (Vol. 2)* outlines the role of life-course research in informing public policy. He also provides a personal account of his experiences as the director of the National Institute of Justice (NIJ) between 2010 and 2013 and his efforts to bring "translational criminology" to the fore to advance criminal justice policy within the NIJ. Finally, the book by Farrington and Welsh (2007), *Saving Children From a Life of Crime*, is a thorough discussion of the two parallel research streams to be applied toward crime prevention efforts: (a) studies of developmental risk factors for crime and (b) evaluation studies of early intervention programs to address putative risk factors.

Conclusion

We end this book as we began, with a call for a developmental perspective with which to frame the research on criminal trajectories. We call on researchers investigating criminal trajectories to integrate a developmental framework into their work and their research questions. Our intention here is not to replace extant developmental and life-course theories of crime but, rather, to complement them by incorporating meta-theoretical propositions from developmental science, with a focus on process models, causal models, explanation, and dynamic transactions. Researchers have typically characterized criminal trajectories as descriptive summaries (e.g., as clusters) of longitudinal data (Nagin & Odgers, 2010a, 2010b; A. Piquero, 2008; Osgood, 2005; Skardhamar, 2010). Moving beyond description to explanation, however, requires theory (Brame, Paternoster, & Piquero, 2012), and we have argued that a developmentally informed theoretical perspective provides a critical lens through which to understand and explain trajectory research findings and the onset, course, and desistance from crime. Tracing the course of a growth trajectory is one important objective. Another objective is to explain (and subsequently test in empirical studies) the observed longitudinal patterns of change and continuity across multiple latent trajectory classes, using theoretically derived causal mechanisms and developmental processes based on expected, typical, or normative patterns of growth and maturity.

The application of developmental theories also may inform practice and policy and provides guidance for remediation and corrective action (Decker, 2016). For example, as discussed earlier, developmental systems theory aims not only to describe and explain human functioning in a manner that is sensitive to the individual's developmental stage but also to optimize within-person development across the life span (Lerner, Hershberg, Hilliard, & Johnson, 2015; Lerner, Lerner, von Eye, Bowers, & Lewin-Bizan, 2011), for example, by capitalizing on effective self-regulatory strategies of life management (i.e., human agency). Although we are partial to developmental systems theory, we remain agnostic with respect to the selection of which developmental theories are best suited to trajectory research; we leave that to the particular affinities and objectives of the individual researchers. As Dr. James Billington, Librarian of Congress Emeritus, has noted, "stories unite people, theories divide them." To be sure, in spite of the plethora of candidate theories, there is a clear need for more work on theory development, testing, and refinement to inform criminal trajectory research.

Suggestions for Future Research

We present here 12 suggestions for future research on criminal trajectories. The first two suggestions focus on methodological issues. The remaining suggestions highlight substantive research needs, many of which arise from incorporating developmental science frameworks into criminal trajectory research.

First, there is a need for trajectory researchers to be more consistent and adhere to stricter reporting standards when reporting the findings from a latent growth mixture modeling or semiparametric group-based trajectory modeling analysis. This move toward consistent reporting standards will bolster the methodological rigor of future group-based trajectory studies and facilitate comparison of substantive findings across data sets and analyses. Frankfurt, Frazier, Syed, and Jung (2016) noted in a review of applications of group-based trajectory modeling methods within the clinical literature, "We believe that adopting consistent reporting standards will facilitate the comparison of psychotherapy process and outcome research across samples and settings" (p. 654). More consistent reporting standards will also be beneficial for a future meta-analysis on results of criminal trajectory studies. As an example of reporting guidelines, van de Schoot, Sijbrandij, Winter, Depaoli, and Vermunt (2017) put forth a comprehensive set of Guidelines for Reporting on Latent Trajectory Studies (GRoLTS-Checklist).

Second, there is an abundance of methodological challenges in the group-based trajectory modeling methodology that awaits further refinement and resolution. These challenges include, but are not limited to, the need for greater consistency and rigor in model selection approaches (e.g., incorporation of bootstrap and cross-validation approaches into the class enumeration process; Lubke et al., 2017; Nielsen et al., 2014), simulation work to deepen our understanding of class enumeration performance and sensitivity to nonnormal distributions (e.g., Bauer, 2007; Erosheva, Matsueda, & Telesca, 2014; Peugh & Fan, 2012), the refinement of model-building strategies to substantiate the adequacy and preferability of the group-based trajectory modeling methodology over more parsimonious techniques (e.g., Greenberg, 2016; Sterba, Baldasaro, & Bauer, 2012), and the evolution of firm guidelines for state-of-the-art modeling approaches to the inclusion of antecedents and covariates (e.g., Diallo, Morin, & Lu, 2017; M. Li & Harring, 2016). The latter point poses unique challenges for explanatory purposes when class sizes are small. Other ongoing work focuses on expanding innovative approaches for assessing treatment effects and putative causal effects of turning points in group-based trajectory modeling (e.g., integration with propensity score matching methodology; Haviland, Nagin, Rosenbaum, & Tremblay, 2008; Na, Loughran, & Paternoster, 2015), which opens new avenues for testing hypotheses about turning points within group-based criminal trajectory modeling.

Third, there is a need to combine individual-level analyses with environment-level analyses, such as through multilevel modeling (Leve & Cicchetti, 2016; G. Zimmerman & Messner, 2012). This suggestion is in keeping with developmental systems theory and developmental psychopathology frameworks, which stress the role of dynamic transactions between multilayered, age-graded individual and contextual systems across the life span (e.g., Capaldi & Wiesner, 2009; Granic & Patterson, 2006).

Fourth, there is a need to study trajectories of psychopathic offenders, as psychopathy is considered an enduring trait that may begin early in life. Moreover, this subpopulation of offenders comes with especially high costs to society. Although progress has been made in this area (McCuish, Corrado, Lussier, & Hart, 2014; A. Piquero, Farrington, Fontaine, Vincent, Coid, & Ullrich, 2012), more work is needed to better understand the underlying heterogeneity in the longitudinal course of psychopathic traits, particularly in relation to criminal offense trajectories and trajectories of relevant psychosocial domains (e.g., interpersonal relationships and substance abuse).

Fifth, there is a need to explore biological variables and processes associated with different trajectory groups. As Shanahan, Sulloway, and Hoffer (2000, p. 424) asserted, "a full conceptualization of development will require analytical strategies that examine the joint role that genes and context play in behavioural development." Recent work has elucidated the biological underpinnings of antisocial and criminal behavior and their interaction with the environment (see, e.g., F. Chen et al., 2016; Eme, 2015). For example, results of meta-analyses have determined that about "half of the variance in antisocial behavior is attributable to genetic influences with the remaining variance being attributable to environmental influences" (Barnes, Beaver, & Boutwell, 2011, p. 925). Loeber and Pardini (2008) reviewed the literature to identify the neurobiological underpinnings of violent behavior. They identified three broad characteristics that "underlie individual differences in the propensity for violent behavior within the population" (Loeber & Panrdini, 2008, p. 2495): (1) emotional and behavioral dysregulation, (2) cognitive impairments related to intellectual ability and working memory, and (3) deficits in emotional responses to aversive stimuli (e.g., fearlessness). Related to this, there is a need for more work to understand the relation between brain maturation and criminal trajectories (Capaldi & Wiesner, 2009; Moffitt, 2018). Last, the study by Barnes et al. (2011) provides a good example of research that contributes to a greater understanding of the biological basis of trajectory groups. Using sibling pair data (N = 2,284) from the National Longitudinal Study of Adolescent Health, they examined the genetic influence associated with Moffitt's (1993) life-course-persistent (LCP) and adolescence-limited (AL) offender groups as well as a third group of abstainers. They found that genetic factors accounted for between 56% and 70%, respectively, of the variance in being assigned to the LCP and abstainer groups and only 35% in being assigned to the AL group. These results suggest that the antisocial behavior of the more normative AL group is better accounted for by environmental factors than by genetics and that the antisocial behavior of the two nonnormative groups, LCP and abstainer, is better accounted for by genetics than by the environment. Unfortunately, this study did not use the group-based trajectory modeling methodology to extract the groups but, rather, constructed them based on the presence (or absence) of self-reported antisocial behavior over three waves of data.

Sixth, there is a need to examine links between joint trajectories, for example, aggression and victimization (e.g., Higgins, Kirchner, Ricketts, & Marcum, 2013; Jackson, Sher, & Schulenberg, 2005); violent and nonviolent criminal behaviors (e.g., MacDonald, Haviland, & Morral, 2009); victim–offender overlap (Mulford et al., 2018); crime and analogous or health-risking behaviors, such as drug use and precocious sexual activity (Nagin, Jones, Lima Passos, & Tremblay, 2018); or depression and delinquency (Wiesner & Kim, 2006). Do the trajectories in two or more domains of interest evolve in lockstep, and are they linked to shared or unique risk factors? Such work is not only useful for the construct validation of criminal trajectories, but also for the explanation of comorbidity, which is a central concept in developmental psychopathology (e.g., Angold, Costello, & Erkanli, 1999).

Seventh, guided by developmental cascades models (Masten & Cicchetti, 2010), which are also proffered in various criminological theories (e.g., Wiesner, Capaldi, & Patterson, 2003), there is a need to study *prospective* relations between criminal trajectories and trajectories of distinct behaviors, such as adult work trajectories and adult intimate partner violence trajectories (see also Doherty, Laub, & Sampson, 2009). Such work allows for examination of more dynamic relations of criminal trajectories with secondary consequences and later life outcomes, as well as questions related to heterotypic continuity (Nagin & Tremblay, 2001), which is a concept of key interest to developmental psychopathologists (e.g., Caspi, 1998; Sroufe, 2009).

Eighth, there is a need to examine the responsiveness of trajectory groups to treatment and rehabilitation programming (Nagin & Odgers, 2010b). Are low- and moderate-rate offenders more amenable to treatment than high-rate offenders? Do the results of risk assessment instruments accord with the rates of offending based on trajectory group membership? Moreover (and related to the fifth point earlier), Schwartz (2016) asserted that "variation in response to intervention may be explained, in part at least, by individual-level genetic variation" (p. 678). This point speaks to the need, more generally, for a greater investment in translational research (Beauchaine, Neuhaus, Brenner, & Gatzke-Kopp, 2008; Viding, Larsson, & Jones, 2008) to explore the broader implications of biosocial criminology for criminal trajectory research and to examine the interplay among theory, research, and practice.

Ninth, there is a need to move beyond a solely deficit-based approach in criminal trajectory research to examine the relation of protective and promotive factors to different trajectory groups. For example, are youth with more ecological developmental assets in the family, school, or community settings of the young person more likely to follow nonoffender or low-rate offender trajectories, as would be expected by positive youth developmental frameworks (Lerner et al., 2011)? Developmental systems theory has much to contribute on this front (e.g., ecological developmental assets, goal-optimization; Bowers, von Eye et al., 2011).

Tenth, there is a need to expand the investigation of turning points and desistance from crime within the trajectory approach. Leading frameworks of human development that emphasize the role of human agency, such as the Selection, Optimization, and Compensation (SOC) theory from Paul Baltes (e.g., Freund & Baltes, 2002) and related models of self-regulation across the life span (e.g., Haase, Heckhausen, & Wrosch, 2013), have strong potential to enrich criminological thinking about the process of desistance from crime. Are life-course-persistent, adolescent-limited, low-level chronic, and nonoffender trajectory groups rank-ordered in terms of aggregate SOC measures, consistent with a linear gradation hypothesis, or are the patterns of associations nonlinear? Which specific SOC processes (i.e., loss-based selection, optimization, compensation) are most effective for fostering desistance from crime, and are these effects moderated by developmental period (e.g., desistance in early adulthood versus at the beginning of middle adulthood)? SOC theory also provides measurement protocols and an organizing framework for studying which concrete optimization or compensatory strategies offenders choose to negotiate structural barriers, such as those encountered when attempting to secure high-quality, legal employment. Concrete strategies might include obtaining a GED to improve one's educational attainment, enrolling in computer literacy classes to acquire required computer skills, and going to the public library to complete online job application paperwork if individuals lack the financial means to afford purchasing the necessary hardware, and SOC theory could be used to determine the function of each concrete strategy (e.g., as compensatory self-regulatory actions). Finally, SOC theory could also be informative for rehabilitation efforts that aim to minimize adverse effects of blocked goals on the well-being and life satisfaction of life-course-persistent offenders by promoting adaptive strategies for disengaging from unattainable goals.

Eleventh, there is a need to expand the study of criminal trajectories to other countries around the world besides the United States, the United Kingdom, Canada, New Zealand, and the Netherlands (Eisner & Nivette, 2012). As a major public health concern, addressing the problem of crime, in all its manifestations, is a critical global issue. As we have argued, results from trajectory research may be used to contribute to the development of crime prevention and reduction strategies; they also may have relevance for worldwide efforts. However, as Eisner and Nivette (2012) emphasize, there is a need for more research to assess the transferability of research findings from the developed world to other parts of the world. Cross-cultural trajectory research is an area that is ripe for further investigation (e.g., Maldonado-Molina, Piquero, Jennings, Bird, & Canino, 2009).

Twelfth, advances in machine learning methods have enabled researchers, including in criminology, to develop algorithms to predict outcomes with greater precision, as an alternative to regression-based approaches (Bushway, 2013b; Rhodes, 2013). For example, Berk and Bleich (2013) have advocated for the use of machine learning to develop better models for offender risk prediction. Within the classify/analyze paradigm, prediction of trajectory group membership has been integral to trajectory research. Although no criminal trajectory studies have used machine learning, this might be a fruitful area for future work. As J. Franklin et al. (2017) observed in their meta-analysis on predicting suicidal thoughts and behaviors, this line of investigation would represent a "shift from a focus on risk *factors* to a focus on risk *algorithms*" (p. 218, emphasis in original).

Conclusion

More than 25 years have passed since the criminal trajectory methodology was first introduced to the scientific community. As Blumstein (2005) noted, novel analytical approaches, such as group-based trajectory analysis at the time of its inception, afford opportunities to reexamine old data and to generate new empirical insights into existing theoretical questions and controversies. In the case of criminal trajectory research, we can confidently conclude that the study of trajectories as "clusters in a trajectory space" (Maldonado-Molina et al., 2009) has intrigued life-course criminology researchers because of the potential it offers to proffer new insights into the pattern of criminal offending across the life span. The fact that trajectory analysis has captured the attention of researchers has sparked important debates about the merits of the group-based trajectory modeling approach. A comprehensive synthesis of the findings from myriad criminal trajectory studies was, thus, long overdue to expand on prior reviews (e.g., Jennings & Reingle, 2012; A. Piquero, 2008). At the same time, the group-based trajectory modeling methodology has matured since it was first introduced, and scientists from multiple disciplines have arrived at a much more balanced view of its strengths and shortcomings. We are excited about the prospects for the further evolution of the methodology and hope that this book starts a thoughtful dialogue. We also hope that our advocacy for interfacing more with developmental science frameworks will eventually take hold to allow the investigation of criminal trajectories to continue to flourish. The more we understand about the developmental progression of criminal behavior over the life course and its variations in topography across different trajectory classes, the better informed we might be about possible means of preventing its onset or at least tempering its course.

ACKNOWLEDGMENTS

We wish to thank Naomi Koerner, Chris Koegl, and Ray Corrado for their insightful and thoughtful comments on draft chapters of this book. We also thank Allyson Aritcheta for her assistance with the references and Carson Pun for his assistance with the Figures. We are especially grateful to Jennifer Hammer and Amy Klopfenstein of New York University Press for their patience and support in our writing of this book. On a personal note, many people have shaped our understanding of the importance of a developmental perspective, none more than my wife, Jean (D. M. D.), and former mentors, such as Deborah Capaldi, from the Oregon Social Learning Center, and the late Margaret Baltes (M. W.). This publication was supported by a grant provided by the Office of the Dean of Arts, Ryerson University.

REFERENCES

Achenbach, T. M. (1974). *Developmental psychopathology*. New York, NY: Ronald Press.

Achenbach, T. M. (1991). *Manual for the Child Behavior Checklist/4-18 and 1991 Profile*. Burlington: University of Vermont.

Achenbach, T. M., & Rescorla, L. A. (2001). *Manual for the ASEBA school-age forms & profiles*. Burlington: Research Centre for Children, Youth and Families, University of Vermont.

Ahonen, L., Jennings, W. G., Loeber, R., & Farrington, D. P. (2016). The relationship between developmental trajectories of girls' offending and police charges: Results from the Pittsburgh Girls Study. *Journal of Developmental and Life-Course Criminology, 2,* 262–274.

Ahonen, L., Loeber, R., Farrington, D. P., Hipwell, A. E., & Stepp, S. D. (2017). What is the hidden figure of delinquency in girls? Scaling up from police charges to self-reports. *Victims & Offenders: An International Journal of Evidence-based Research, Policy, and Practice, 12,* 761–776.

Allard, T., Chrzanowski, A., & Stewart, A. (2012). *Targeting crime prevention: Identifying communities which generate chronic and costly offenders to reduce offending, crime, victimisation, and Indigenous over-representation in the criminal justice system* (Trends & Issues in Crime and Criminal Justice No. 445). Canberra: Australian Institute of Criminology. Retrieved from http://crg.aic.gov.au

Allard, T., Stewart, A., Smith, C., Dennison, S., Chrzanowski, A., & Thompson, C. (2014). The monetary cost of offender trajectories: Findings from Queensland (Australia). *Australian & New Zealand Journal of Criminology, 47,* 81–101.

Alltucker, K. W., Bullis, M., Close, D., & Yovanoff, P. (2006). Different pathways to juvenile delinquency: Characteristics of early and late starters in a sample of previously incarcerated youth. *Journal of Child and Family Studies, 15,* 475–488.

American Psychiatric Association. (2013). *Diagnostic and statistical manual of mental disorders* (5th ed.). Arlington, VA: Author.

Anderson, D. A. (2012). The cost of crime. *Foundations and Trends in Microeconomics, 7,* 209–265.

Anderson, E. (1999). *Code of the street: Decency, violence, and the moral life of the inner city*. New York, NY: W. W. Norton.

Andersson, F., & Levander, M. T. (2013). Adult onset offending in a Swedish female birth cohort. *Journal of Criminal Justice, 41,* 172–177.

Andersson, F., Levander, S., Svensson, R., & Levander, M. T. (2012). Sex differences in offending trajectories in a Swedish cohort. *Criminal Behaviour and Mental Health, 22*, 108–121.

Andrews, D. A., Bonta, J., & Wormith, J. S. (1995). *Level of Service Inventory–Ontario Revision (LSI-OR): Interview and scoring guide.* Toronto, Canada: Ontario Ministry of the Solicitor General and Correctional Services.

Andrews, D. A., Bonta, J., & Wormith, J. S. (2004). *Level of Service/Case Management Inventory (LS/CMI‾): An offender assessment system.* Toronto, Canada: Multi-Health Systems.

Angold, A., Costello, E. J., & Erkanli, A. (1999). Comorbidity. *Journal of Child Psychology and Psychiatry, 40*, 57–87.

Angrist, J. D., Imbens, G. W., & Rubin, D. B. (1996). Identification of causal effects using instrumental variables. *Journal of the American statistical Association, 91*, 444–455.

Aos, S. Phipps, P., Barnoski, R., & Lieb, R. (2001). *The comparative costs and benefits of programs to reduce crime, Version 4.0.* Olympia: Washington State Institute for Public Policy. Retrieved from www.wsipp.wa.gov

Apel, R. J., & Sweeten, G. (2010). Propensity score matching in criminology and criminal justice. In A. R. Piquero & D. Weisburd (Eds.), *Handbook of quantitative criminology* (pp. 543–562). New York, NY: Springer.

Appleyard, K., Egeland, B., Dulmen, M. H., & Sroufe, L. A. (2005). When more is not better: The role of cumulative risk in child behavior outcomes. *Journal of Child Psychology and Psychiatry, 46*, 235–245.

Arnett, J. J. (2004). *Emerging adulthood: The winding road from the late teens through the twenties.* Oxford, England: Oxford University Press.

Asparouhov, T., & Muthén, B. (2014). Auxiliary variables in mixture modeling: Three-step approaches using M*plus. Structural Equation Modeling: A Multidisciplinary Journal, 21*, 329–341.

Assink, M., van der Put, C. E., Hoeve, M., de Vries, S. L., Stams, G. J. J., & Oort, F. J. (2015). Risk factors for persistent delinquent behavior among juveniles: A meta-analytic review. *Clinical Psychology Review, 42*, 47–61.

Augimeri, L. K., Enebrink, P., Walsh, M., & Jiang, D. (2010). Gender-specific childhood risk assessment tools: Early Assessment Risk Lists for Boys (EARL-20B) and Girls (EARL-21G). In R. K. Otto & K. S. Douglas (Eds.), *Handbook of violence risk assessment* (pp. 43–62). Oxford, England: Routledge.

Augimeri, L. K., Jiang, D., Koegl, C. J., & Carey, J. (2006). *Differential effects of the Under 12 Outreach Project (ORP) associated with client risk and treatment intensity* (Final report to the Provincial Centre of Excellence for Child and Youth Mental Health at CHEO, Ottawa, Ontario, Program Evaluation Grant # PEG162606–101). Ontario, Canada: Child Development Institute. Retrieved from www.excellencefor childandyouth.ca

Augimeri, L. K., Pepler, D. J., Walsh, M. M., Jiang, D., & Dassinger, C. R. (2010). *Aggressive and antisocial young children: Risk prediction, assessment, and clinical risk management* (Final report to the Provincial Centre of Excellence for Child and Youth Mental Health at CHEO, Ottawa, Ontario, Program Evaluation Grant #RG-976). Ontario, Canada: Child Development Institute. Retrieved from www .excellenceforchildandyouth.ca

Baglivio, M. T., Jackowski, K., Greenwald, M. A., & Howell, J. C. (2014). Serious, violent, and chronic juvenile offenders. *Criminology & Public Policy, 13,* 83–116.

Baglivio, M. T., Wolff, K. T., Piquero, A. R., Howell, J. C., & Greenwald, M. A. (2017). Risk assessment trajectories of youth during juvenile justice residential placement. *Criminal Justice and Behavior, 44,* 360–394.

Baker, T., Metcalfe, C. F., & Jennings, W. G. (2013). What are the odds? Predicting specialization in offending over the life course. *Criminal Justice and Behavior, 40,* 909–932.

Baker, T., Metcalfe, C. F., & Piquero, A. R. (2015). Measuring the intermittency of criminal careers. *Crime & Delinquency, 61,* 1078–1103.

Bales, W. D., & Piquero, A. R. (2012). Assessing the impact of imprisonment on recidivism. *Journal of Experimental Criminology, 8,* 71–101.

Baltes, P. B. (1987). Theoretical propositions of life-span developmental psychology: On the dynamics between growth and decline. *Developmental Psychology, 23,* 611–626.

Baltes, P. B., & Baltes, M. M. (1990). Psychological perspectives on successful aging: The model of selective optimization with compensation. In P. B. Baltes & M. M. Baltes (Eds.), *Successful aging: Perspectives from the behavioral sciences* (pp. 1–34). New York, NY: Cambridge University Press.

Baltes, P. B., Lindenberger, U., & Staudinger, U. (1998). Life-span theory in developmental psychology. In W. Damon & R. M. Lerner (Eds.), *Handbook of Child Psychology, Vol. 1: Theoretical models of human development* (5th ed., pp. 1029–1143). New York, NY: Wiley.

Baltes, P. B., Lindenberger, U., & Staudinger, U. M. (2006). Life span theory in developmental psychology. In W. Damon (Editor-in-Chief) & R. M. Lerner (Volume Editor), *Handbook of Child Psychology, Vol. 1: Theoretical models of human development* (6th ed., pp. 569–664). New York, NY: Wiley.

Baltes, P. B., Reese, H. W., & Lipsitt, L. P. (1980). Life-span developmental psychology. *Annual Review of Psychology, 31,* 65–110.

Bandeen-Roche, K., Miglioretti, D. L., Zeger, S. L., & Rathouz, P. J. (1997). Latent variable regression for multiple discrete outcomes. *Journal of the American Statistical Association, 92,* 1375–1386.

Barnes, J. C., & Beaver, K. M. (2012). Marriage and desistance from crime: A consideration of gene-environment correlation. *Journal of Marriage and Family, 74,* 19–33.

Barnes, J. C., Beaver, K. M., & Boutwell, B. B. (2011). Examining the genetic underpinnings to Moffitt's developmental taxonomy: A behavioral genetics analysis. *Criminology, 49,* 923–954.

Barnett, A., Blumstein, A., & Farrington, D. P. (1987). Probabilistic models of youthful criminal careers. *Criminology, 25,* 83–108.

Barnoski, R. (2002). Monitoring vital signs: Integrating a standardized assessment into Washington States' juvenile justice system. In R. R. Corrado, R. Roesch, S. D. Hart, & J. K. Gierowski (Eds.), *Multi-problem violent youth: A foundation for comparative research on needs, interventions, and outcomes* (pp. 219–231). Amsterdam, The Netherlands: IOS Press.

Bartol, C. R., & Bartol, A. M. (2011) *Criminal behavior: A psychological approach* (9th ed.). Upper Saddle River, NJ: Prentice Hall.

Baskin, D. R., & Sommers, I. B. (1998). *Casualties of community disorder: Women's careers in violent crime.* Boulder, CO: Westview Press.

Bates, M. E. (2000). Integrating person-centered and variable-centered approaches in the study of developmental courses and transitions in alcohol use: Introduction to the special section. *Alcoholism: Clinical and Experimental Research, 24*, 878–881.

Bauer, D. J. (2007). Observations on the use of growth mixture models in psychological research. *Multivariate Behavioral Research, 42*, 757–786.

Bauer, D. J., & Curran, P. J. (2003a). Distributional assumptions of growth mixture models: Implications for overextraction of latent trajectory classes. *Psychological Methods, 8*, 338–363.

Bauer, D. J., & Curran, P. J. (2003b). Overextraction of latent trajectory classes: Much ado about nothing? Reply to Rindskopf (2003), Muthén (2003), and Cudeck and Henly (2003). *Psychological Methods, 8*, 384–393.

Bauer, D. J., & Curran, P. J. (2004). The integration of continuous and discrete latent variable models: Potential problems and promising opportunities. *Psychological Methods, 9*, 3–29.

Bauer, D. J., & Shanahan, M. J. (2007). Modeling complex interactions: Person-centered and variable-centered approaches. In T. D. Little, J. A. Bovaird, & N. A. Card (Eds.), *Modeling contextual effects in longitudinal studies* (pp. 255–283). Mahwah, NJ: Erlbaum.

Baumol, W. J. (1992). On my attitudes: Sociopolitical and methodological. In M. Szenberg (Ed.), *Eminent economists: Their life philosophies* (pp. 51–59). Cambridge, England: Cambridge University Press.

Beauchaine, T. P., Neuhaus, E., Brenner, S. L., & Gatzke-Kopp, L. (2008). Ten good reasons to consider biological processes in prevention and intervention research. *Development and Psychopathology, 20*, 745–774.

Beaver, K. M., Wright, J. P., DeLisi, M., & Vaughn, M. G. (2008). Desistance from delinquency: The marriage effect revisited and extended. *Social Science Research, 37*, 736–752.

Belknap, J., & Holsinger, K. (2006). The gendered nature of risk factors for delinquency. *Feminist Criminology, 1*, 48–71.

Benson, M. L. (2013). *Crime and the life course: An introduction* (2nd ed.). New York, NY: Routledge.

Benson, P. L., Scales, P. C., Hamilton, S. F., & Sesma, A. (2006). Positive youth development: Theory, research, and applications. In R. M. Lerner (Ed.), *Handbook of Child Psychology, Vol 1: Theoretical models of human development* (pp. 894–941). Hoboken, NJ: Wiley.

Bergman, L. R. (1998). A pattern-oriented approach to studying individual development: Snapshots and processes. In R. B. Cairns, L. R. Bergman, & J. Kagan (Eds.), *Methods and models for studying the individual* (pp. 83–121). Thousand Oaks, CA: Sage.

Berk, R. A., & Bliech, J. (2013). Statistical procedures for forecasting criminal behavior. *Criminology & Public Policy, 12*, 513–544.

Bersani, B. E., & Doherty, E. E. (2013). When the ties that bind unwind: Examining the enduring and situational processes of change behind the marriage effect. *Criminology, 51*, 399–433.

Bersani, B. E., & Doherty, E. E. (2017). Desistance from offending in the twenty-first century. *Annual Review of Criminology*. Advanced online publication. Retrieved from https:// doi.org/10.1146/annurev-criminol-032317-092112

Bersani, B. E., Laub, J. H., & Nieuwbeerta, P. (2009). Marriage and desistance from crime in the Netherlands: Do gender and socio-historical context matter? *Journal of Quantitative Criminology, 25*, 3–24.

Bersani, B. E., Nieuwbeerta, P., & Laub, J. H. (2009). Predicting trajectories of offending over the life course: Findings of a Dutch cohort. *Journal of Research in Crime and Delinquency, 46*, 468–494.

Biesanz, J. C., Deeb-Sossa, N., Papadakis, A. A., Bollen, K. A., & Curran, P. J. (2004). The role of coding time in estimating and interpreting growth curve models. *Psychological Methods, 9*, 30–52.

Block, T., Brettfeld, K., & Wetzels, P. (2009). Jugendliche Mehrfach- und Intensivtäter in Hamburg: Neue Wege zur Beschreibung eines alten Problems [Young multiple and intensive offenders in Hamburg: New ways to describe an old problem]. *Zeitschrift für Jugendkriminalrecht und Jugendhilfe, 20*, 129–140.

Blokland, A. A. J., Nagin, D., & Nieuwbeerta, P. (2005). Life span offending trajectories of a Dutch conviction cohort. *Criminology, 43*, 919–954.

Blokland, A. A. J., & Niewbeerta, P. (2005). The effects of life circumstances on longitudinal trajectories of offending. *Criminology, 43*, 1203–1240.

Blokland, A. A. J., & Nieuwbeerta, P. (2010). Life course criminology. In S. G. Shoham, P. Knepper, & M. Kett (Eds.), *International handbook of criminology* (pp. 51–92). Boca Raton, FL: CRC Press.

Blokland, A. A. J., & van Os, R. (2010). Life span offending trajectories of convicted Dutch women. *International Criminal Justice Review, 20*, 169–187.

Blomberg, T. G., Mestre, J., & Mann, K. (2013). Seeking causality in a world of contingency: Criminology, research, and public policy. *Criminology & Public Policy, 12*, 571–584.

Blumstein, A. (2005). An overview of the symposium and some next steps. *The ANNALS of the American Academy of Political and Social Science, 602*, 242–258.

Blumstein, A., Cohen, J., & Farrington, D. P. (1988). Criminal career research: Its value for criminology. *Criminology, 26*, 1–35.

Blumstein, A., Cohen, J., Roth, J. A., & Visher, C. A. (Eds.). (1986). *Criminal careers and "career criminals"* (Vol. 1). Washington, DC: National Academies Press. Retrieved from www.nap.edu.

Blumstein, A., & Nakamura, K. (2009). Redemption in the presence of widespread criminal background checks. *Criminology, 47*, 327–359.

Boker, S., Neale, M., Maes, H., Wilde, M., Spiegel, M., Brick, T., . . . Fox, J. (2011). OpenMx: An open source extended structural equation modeling framework. *Psychometrika, 76*, 306–317.

Bolck, A., Croon, M. A., & Hagenaars, J. A. P. (2004). Estimating latent structure models with categorical variables: One-step versus three-step estimators. *Political Analysis, 12*, 3–27.

Bollen, K. A., & Curran, P. J. (2006). *Latent curve models: A structural equation perspective.* Hoboken, NJ: Wiley.

Bonta, J., & Andrews, D. A. (2017). *The psychology of criminal conduct* (6th ed.). New York, NY: Routledge.

Borum, R., Bartel, P., & Forth, A. E. (2002). *Manual for the Structured Assessment of Violence Risk in Youth. Consultation version.* Tampa: University of South Florida, Florida Mental Health Institute.

Bottoms, A., Shapland, J., Costello, A., Holmes, D., & Muir, G. (2004). Towards desistance: Theoretical underpinnings for an empirical study. *The Howard Journal of Criminal Justice, 43*, 368–389.

Bouffard, L. A. (2005). The military as a bridging environment in criminal careers: Differential outcomes of the military experience. *Armed Forces and Society, 31*, 273–295.

Boutwell, B. B., Beaver, K. M., & Barnes, J. C. (2012). More alike than different: Assortative mating and antisocial propensity in adulthood. *Criminal Justice and Behavior, 39*, 1240–1254.

Bowers, E. P., Gestsdóttir, S., Geldhof, G. J., Nikitin, J., von Eye, A., & Lerner, R. M. (2011). Developmental trajectories of intentional self regulation in adolescence: The role of parenting and implications for positive and problematic outcomes among diverse youth. *Journal of Adolescence, 34*, 1193–1206.

Bowers, E. P., von Eye, A., Lerner, J. V., Arbeit, M. R., Weiner, M. B., Chase, P., & Agans, J. P. (2011). The role of ecological assets in positive and problematic developmental trajectories. *Journal of Adolescence, 34*, 1151–1165.

Bozdogan, H. (1987). Model selection and Akaike's Information Criterion (AIC): The general theory and its analytical extensions. *Psychometrika, 52*, 345–370.

Brame, B., Nagin, D. S., & Tremblay, R. E. (2001). Developmental trajectories of physical aggression from school entry to late adolescence. *Journal of Child Psychology and Psychiatry, 42*, 503–512.

Brame, R., Bushway, S. D., & Paternoster, R. (2003). Examining the prevalence of criminal desistance. *Criminology, 41*, 423–448.

Brame, R., Nagin, D. S., & Wasserman, L. (2006). Exploring some analytical characteristics of finite mixture models. *Journal of Quantitative Criminology, 22*, 31–59.

Brame, R., Paternoster, R., & Piquero, A. R. (2012). Thoughts on the analysis of group-based developmental trajectories in criminology. *Justice Quarterly, 29*, 469–490.

Brandtstädter, J. (1998). Action-perspectives on human development. In W. Damon & R. M. Lerner (Eds.), *Handbook of Child Psychology, Vol. 1: Theoretical models of human development* (5th ed., pp. 807–863). New York, NY: Wiley.

Brandtstädter, J. (1999). The self in action and development: Cultural, biosocial, and ontogeneity bases of intentional self-development. In J. Brandtstädter & R. M. Lerner (Eds.), *Action and self-development: Theory and research through the life-span* (pp. 37–65). Thousand Oaks, CA: Sage.

Brandtstädter, J. (2006). Action perspectives on human development. In R. M. Lerner (Ed.), *Handbook of Child Psychology, Vol. 1: Theoretical models of human development* (6th ed., pp. 516–568). Hoboken, NJ: Wiley.

Brandtstädter, J. (2009). Goal pursuit and goal adjustment: Self-regulation and intentional self-development in changing developmental contexts. *Advances in Life Course Research, 14*, 52–62.

Brennan, L. M., & Shaw, D. S. (2013). Revisiting data related to the age of onset and developmental course of female conduct problems. *Clinical Child and Family Psychology Review, 16*, 35–58.

Brennan, T., & Breitenbach, M. (2009). The taxonomic challenge to general theories of delinquency: Linking taxonomic development to delinquency theory. In O. Sahin & J. Maier (Eds.), *Delinquency: Causes, reduction and prevention* (pp. 1–39). Hauppauge, NY: Nova Science Publishers.

Brennan, T., Breitenbach, M., & Dieterich, W. (2008). Towards an explanatory taxonomy of adolescent delinquents: Identifying several social-psychological profiles. *Journal of Quantitative Criminology, 24*, 179–203.

Brim, O. G. (1976). Theories of the male mid-life crisis. *The Counseling Psychologist, 6*, 2–9.

Broidy, L. M., Nagin, D. S., Tremblay, R. E., Bates, J. E., Brame, B., Dodge, K. A., . . . Vitaro, F. (2003). Developmental trajectories of childhood disruptive behaviors and adolescent delinquency: A six-site, cross-national study. *Developmental Psychology, 39*, 222–245.

Bronfenbrenner, U. (1979). *The ecology of human development: Experiments by nature and design.* Cambridge, MA: Harvard University Press.

Bronfenbrenner, U. (2005). *Making human beings human.* Thousand Oaks, CA: Sage.

Brook, J. S., Lee, J. Y., Finch, S. J., Brown, E. N., & Brook, D. W. (2013). Long-term consequences of membership in trajectory groups of delinquent behavior in an urban sample: Violence, drug use, interpersonal, and neighborhood attributes. *Aggressive Behavior, 39*, 440–452.

Brown, S. A., McGue, M., Maggs, J., Schulenberg, J., Hingson, R., Swartzwelder, S., . . . Murphy, S. (2008). A developmental perspective on alcohol and youths 16 to 20 years of age. *Pediatrics, 121*, S290–S310.

Burnett, R., & Maruna, S. (2006). The kindness of prisoners: Strengths-based resettlement in theory and action. *Criminology and Criminal Justice, 6*, 83–106.

Bushway, S. D. (2013a). Life-course-persistent offenders. In F. T. Cullen & P. Wilcox (Eds.), *The Oxford handbook of criminological theory* (pp. 189–204). New York, NY: Oxford University Press.

Bushway, S. D. (2013b). Is there any logic to using logit: Finding the right tool for the increasingly important job of risk prediction. *Criminology & Public Policy, 12,* 563–567.

Bushway, S. D., & Apel, R. J. (2010). Instrumental variables in criminology and criminal justice. In A. R. Piquero & D. Weisburd (Eds.), *Handbook of quantitative criminology* (pp. 595–612). New York, NY: Springer.

Bushway, S. D., Nieuwbeerta, P., & Blokland, A. (2011). The predictive value of criminal background checks: Do age and criminal history affect time to redemption? *Criminology, 49,* 27–60.

Bushway, S., D & Paternoster, R. (2011). Understanding desistance: Theory testing with formal empirical models. In J. MacDonald (Ed.), *Measuring crime and criminality: Advances in criminological theory* (Vol. 17, pp. 299–333). London, England: Transaction Publishers.

Bushway, S. D., & Paternoster, R. (2013). Desistance from crime: A review and ideas for moving forward. In C. L. Gibson & M. D. Krohn (Eds.), *Handbook of life-course criminology: Emerging trends and directions for future research* (pp. 213–231). New York, NY: Springer.

Bushway, S. D., Paternoster, R., & Brame, R. (2003). Examining the prevalence of criminal desistance. *Criminology, 41,* 423–448.

Bushway, S. D., Piquero, A. R., Broidy, L. M., Cauffman, E., & Mazerolle, P. (2001). An empirical framework for studying desistance as a process. *Criminology, 39,* 491–516.

Bushway, S. D., Sweeten, G., & Nieuwbeerta, P. (2009). Measuring long term individual trajectories of offending using multiple methods. *Journal of Quantitative Criminology, 25,* 259–286.

Bushway, S. D., Thornberry, T. P., & Krohn, M. D. (2003). Desistance as a developmental process: A comparison of static and dynamic approaches. *Journal of Quantitative Criminology, 19,* 129–153.

Buss, E. (2016). Developmental jurisprudence. *Temple Law Review, 88,* 741–768.

Cairns, R. B., & Cairns, B. D. (1995). Social ecology over time and space. In P. Moen, G. H. Elder Jr., & K. Lüscher (Eds.), *Examining lives in context: Perspectives on the ecology of human development* (pp. 397–421). Washington, DC: American Psychological Association.

Campbell, D. T. (1963). From description to experimentation: Interpreting trends as quasi-experiments. In C. W. Harris (Ed.), *Problems in measuring change* (pp. 212–242). Madison: The University of Wisconsin Press.

Capaldi, D. M., Chamberlain, P., Fetrow, R. A., & Wilson, J. E. (1997). Conducting ecologically valid prevention research: Recruiting and retaining a "whole village" in multimethod, multiagent studies. *American Journal of Community Psychology, 25,* 471–492.

Capaldi, D. M., & Crosby, L. (1997). Observed and reported psychological and physical aggression in young, at-risk couples. *Social Development, 6,* 184–206.

Capaldi, D. M., & Eddy, J. M. (2005). Oppositional defiant disorder and conduct disorder. In T. P. Gullotta & G. R. Adams (Eds.), *The handbook of adolescent behavioral problems: Evidence-based approaches to prevention and treatment* (pp. 283–308). New York, NY: Springer.

Capaldi, D. M., Kerr, D. C. R., Eddy, J. M., & Tiberio, S. S. (2016). Understanding persistence and desistance in crime and risk behaviors in adulthood: Implications for theory and prevention. *Prevention Science, 17,* 785–793.

Capaldi, D. M., Kim, H. K., & Owen, L. E. (2008). Romantic partners' influence on men's likelihood of arrest in early adulthood. *Criminology, 46,* 267–299.

Capaldi, D. M., & Patterson, G. R. (1987). An approach to the problem of recruitment and retention rates for longitudinal research. *Behavioral Assessment, 9,* 169–177.

Capaldi, D. M., Shortt, J. W., & Kim, H. K. (2005). A life span developmental systems perspective on aggression toward a partner. In W. M. Pinsof & J. Lebow (Eds.), *Family psychology: The art of the science* (pp. 141–167). New York, NY: Oxford University Press.

Capaldi, D. M., & Wiesner, M. (2009). A dynamic developmental systems approach to understanding offending in early adulthood. In J. Savage (Ed.), *The development of persistent criminality* (pp. 374–388). New York, NY: Oxford University Press.

Carlsson, C. (2012). Using 'turning points' to understand processes of change in offending: Notes from a Swedish study on life courses and crime. *The British Journal of Criminology, 52,* 1–16.

Carlsson, C. (2013). Processes of intermittency in criminal careers: Notes from a Swedish study on life courses and crime. International Journal of Offender Therapy and Comparative Criminology, 57, 913–938.

Carlsson, C. (2016). Human agency, criminal careers, and desistance. In J. Shapland, S. Farrall, & A. Bottoms (Eds.), *Global perspectives on desistance: Reviewing what we know and looking to the future* (pp. 28–49). New York, NY: Taylor & Francis.

Carlsson, C., & Sarnecki, J. (2016). *An introduction to life-course criminology.* Thousand Oaks, CA: Sage.

Case, S., & Haines, K. (2009). *Understanding youth offending: Risk factor research, policy, and practice.* Portland, OR: Willan Publishing.

Casey, B. J., Getz, S., & Galvan, A. (2008). The adolescent brain. *Developmental Review, 28,* 62–77.

Casey, B. J., Tottenham, N., Liston, C., & Durston, S. (2005). Imaging the developing brain: What have we learned about cognitive development? *Trends in Cognitive Sciences, 9,* 104–110.

Caspi, A. (1998). Personality development across the life course. In W. Damon & N. Eisenberg (Eds.), *Handbook of Child Psychology, Vol. 3: Social, emotional, and personality development* (pp. 311–388). New York, NY: Wiley.

Caspi, A., & Elder, G. H., Jr. (1988). Childhood precursors of the life course: Early personality and life disorganization. In E. M. Hetherington, R. M. Lerner, &

M. Perlmutter (Eds.), *Child development in life-span perspective* (pp. 115–142). Hillsdale, NJ: Erlbaum.

Caspi, A., Elder, G. H. Jr., & Herbener, E. S. (1990). Childhood personality and the prediction of life-course patterns. In L. Robins & M. Rutter (Eds.), *Straight and devious pathways from childhood to adulthood* (pp. 13–35). Cambridge, England: Cambridge University Press.

Catalano, R. F., Fagan, A. A., Gavin, L. E., Greenberg, M. T., Irwin, C. E., Jr., Ross, D. A., & Shek, D. T. (2012). Adolescent health 3: Worldwide application of prevention science in adolescent health. *The Lancet, 379*, 1653–1664.

Catalano, R. F., & Hawkins, J. D. (1996). The social development model: A theory of antisocial behavior. In J. D. Hawkins (Ed.), *Delinquency and crime: Current theories* (pp. 149–197). New York, NY: Cambridge University Press.

Catalano, R. F., Park, J., Harachi, T. W., Haggerty, K. P., Abbott, R. D., & Hawkins, J. D. (2005). Mediating the effects of poverty, gender, individual characteristics, and external constraints on antisocial behavior: A test of the Social Development Model and implications for developmental life-course theory. In D. P. Farrington (Ed.), *Integrated developmental and life-course theories of offending* (Advances in Criminological Theory, Vol. 14, pp. 93–123). New Brunswick, NJ: Transaction.

Cauffman, E. (2012). Aligning justice system processing with developmental science. *Criminology & Public Policy, 11*, 751–758.

Cauffman, E., Cavanagh, C., Donley, S., & Thomas, A. G. (2016). A developmental perspective on adolescent risk-taking and criminal behavior. In A. Piquero (Ed.), *The handbook of criminological theory* (pp. 100–120). Hoboken, NJ: Wiley-Blackwell.

Cauffman, E., Monahan, K. C., & Thomas, A. G. (2015). Pathways to persistence: Female offending from 14 to 25. *Journal of Developmental and Life-Course Criminology, 1*, 236–268.

Cauffman, E., & Steinberg, L. (2012). Emerging findings from research on adolescent development and juvenile justice. *Victims and Offenders, 7*, 428–449.

Cesaroni, C. (2015). Young adults: An overlooked population in Canadian correctional policy and legislation. *Canadian Criminal Law Review, 19*, 115–128.

Chaiken, M. R., & Chaiken, J. M. (1984). Offender types and public policy. *Crime & Delinquency, 30*, 195–226.

Chassin, L., Curran P. J., Hussong, A. M., & Colder, C. R. (1996). The relation of parent alcoholism to adolescent substance use: A longitudinal follow-up study. *Journal of Abnormal Psychology, 105*, 70–80.

Chein, J., Albert, D., O'Brien, L., Uckert, K., & Steinberg, L. (2011). Peers increase adolescent risk taking by enhancing activity in the brain's reward circuitry. *Developmental Science, 14*, F1–F10.

Chen, F. R., Gao, Y., Glenn, A. L., Niv, S., Portnoy, J., Schug, R., . . . Raine, A. (2016). Biosocial bases of antisocial and criminal behavior. In A. R. Piquero (Ed.), *The handbook of criminological theory* (pp. 356–379). West Sussex, England: Wiley.

Chen, X. (2016). Childhood onset of behavioral problems and violent victimization among serious juvenile offenders: A longitudinal study. *Youth Violence and Juvenile Justice, 14,* 243–256.

Christenson, S. L., & Thurlow, M. L. (2010). School dropouts: Prevention considerations, interventions, and challenges. In K. A. Dodge (Ed.), *Current directions in child psychopathology for abnormal psychology* (pp. 148–155). Boston, MA: Allyn & Bacon. (Reprinted from Christenson, S. L., & Thurlow, M. L., 2004, *Current Directions in Psychological Science, 13,* 36–39).

Chung, I.-J., Hill, K. G., Hawkins, J. D., Gilchrist, L. D., & Nagin, D. S. (2002). Childhood predictors of offense trajectories. *Journal of Research in Crime and Delinquency, 39,* 60–90.

Cicchetti, D. (1984). The emergence of developmental psychopathology. *Child Development, 55,* 1–7.

Cicchetti, D. (Ed.). (2016). *Developmental psychopathology* (3rd ed.). New York, NY: Wiley.

Cicchetti, D., & Rogosch, F. A. (1996). Equifinality and multifinality in developmental psychopathology. *Development and Psychopathology, 8,* 597–600.

Cicchetti, D., & Rogosch, F. A. (2002). A developmental psychopathology perspective on adolescence. *Journal of Consulting and Clinical Psychology, 70,* 6–20.

Cicchetti, D., & Sroufe, L. A. (2000). Reflecting on the past and planning for the future of developmental psychopathology. *Development and Psychopathology, 12,* 255–550.

Cohen, C. (2008). *Applied data analytic techniques for turning points research.* New York, NY: Routledge.

Cohen, J. (1983). The cost of dichotomization. *Applied Psychological Measurement, 7,* 249–253.

Cohen, J. (1988). *Statistical power analysis for the behavioral sciences* (2nd ed.). Hillsdale, NJ: Erlbaum.

Cohen, M. A. (2005). *The costs of crime and justice.* New York, NY: Routledge.

Cohen, M. A., & Bowles, R. (2011). Estimating costs of crime. In A. R. Piquero & D. Weisburd (Eds.), *Handbook of quantitative criminology* (pp. 143–162). New York, NY: Springer.

Cohen, M. A., & Piquero, A. R. (2009). New evidence on the monetary value of saving a high risk youth. *Journal of Quantitative Criminology, 25,* 25–49.

Cohen, M. A., & Piquero, A. R. (2015). Benefits and costs of a targeted intervention program for youthful offenders: The YouthBuild USA Offender Project. *Journal of Benefit-Cost Analysis, 6,* 603–627.

Cohen, M. A., Piquero, A. R., & Jennings, W. G. (2010). Studying the costs of crime across offender trajectories. *Criminology & Public Policy, 9,* 279–305.

Coleman, D., & Stewart, L. M. (2010). Prevalence and impact of childhood maltreatment in incarcerated youth. *American Journal of Orthopsychiatry, 80,* 343–349.

Collins, L. M. (2006). Analysis of longitudinal data: The integration of theoretical model, temporal design, and statistical model. *Annual Review of Psychology, 57,* 505–528.

Corrado, R., Freedman, L., & Blatier, C. (2011). The over-representation of children in care in the youth criminal justice system in British Columbia: Theory and policy issues. *International Journal of Child, Youth, and Family Studies, 1 & 2*, 99–118.

Corrado, R. R. (2002). An introduction to the risk/needs case management instrument for children and youth at risk of violence: The Cracow Instrument. In R. R., Corrado, R. Roesch, S. D. Hart, & J. K. Gierowski (Eds.), *Multi-problem violent youth: A foundation for comparative research on needs, interventions, and outcomes* (pp. 295–301). Amsterdam, The Netherlands: IOS Press.

Corrado, R. R., & Freedman, L. (2011). Risk profiles, trajectories, and intervention points for serious and chronic young offenders. *International Journal of Child, Youth & Family Studies, 2*, 197–232.

Corrado, R. R., McCuish, E. C., Hart, S. D., & DeLisi, M. (2015). The role of psychopathic traits and developmental risk factors on offending trajectories from early adolescence to adulthood: A prospective study of incarcerated youth. *Journal of Criminal Justice, 43*, 357–368.

Corrado, R. R., Roesch, R., Hart, S. D., & Gierowski, J. K. (Eds.). (2002). *Multi-problem violent youth: A foundation for comparative research on needs, interventions, and outcomes*. Amsterdam, The Netherlands: IOS Press.

Costello, D. M., Swendsen, J., Rose, J. S., & Dierker, L. C. (2008). Risk and protective factors associated with trajectories of depressed mood from adolescence to early adulthood. *Journal of Consulting and Clinical Psychology, 76*, 173–183.

Craig, J., & Foster, H. (2013). Desistance in the transition to adulthood: The roles of marriage, military, and gender. *Deviant Behavior, 34*, 208–233.

Cudeck, R., & Henly, S. J. (2003). A realistic perspective on pattern representation in growth data: Comment on Bauer and Curran (2003). *Psychological Methods, 8*, 378–383.

Cullen, F. T. (2011). Beyond adolescence-limited criminology: Choosing our future—The American Society of Criminology 2010 Sutherland Address. *Criminology, 49*, 287–330.

Cullen, F. T. (2017). Choosing our criminological future: Reservations about human agency as an organizing concept. *Journal of Developmental and Life-Course Criminology, 3*, 373–379.

Cullen, F. T., Benson, M. L., & Makarios, M. D. (2012). Developmental and life-course theories of offending. In B. C. Welsh & D. P. Farrington (Eds.), *The Oxford handbook of crime prevention* (pp. 23–45). New York, NY: Oxford University Press.

Cullen, F. T., Jonson, C. L., & Nagin, D. S. (2011). Prisons do not reduce recidivism: The high cost of ignoring science. *The Prison Journal, 91*(Suppl.), 48S–65S.

Curran, P. J. (2003). Have multilevel models been structural equation models all along? *Multivariate Behavioral Research, 38*, 529–569.

Curran, P. J., & Hussong, A. M. (2003). The use of latent trajectory models in psychopathology research. *Journal of Abnormal Psychology, 112*, 526–544.

Curran, P. J., & Willoughby, M. T. (2003). Implications of latent trajectory models for the study of developmental psychopathology, *Development and Psychopathology, 15*, 581–612.

Cusson, M., & Pinsonneault, P. (1986). The decision to give up crime. In D. B. Cornish & R. V. Clarke (Eds.), *The reasoning criminal: rational choice perspectives on offending* (pp. 72–82). New York, NY: Springer.

Dannefer, D. (1984). Adult development and social theory: A paradigmatic reappraisal. *American Sociological Review, 49,* 100–116.

Davis, M., Banks, S., Fisher, W., & Grudzinskas, A. (2004). Longitudinal patterns of offending during the transition to adulthood in youth from the mental health system. *The Journal of Behavioral Health Services & Research, 31,* 351–366.

Day, D. M., Bevc, I., Duchesne, T., Rosenthal, J. S., Rossman, L., & Theodor, F. (2007). Comparison of adult offense prediction methods based on juvenile offense trajectories using cross-validation. *Advances and Applications in Statistics, 7,* 1–46.

Day, D. M., Bevc, I., Theodor, F., Rosenthal, J. S., & Duchesne, T. (2008). *Change and continuity in criminal offending: Criminal trajectories of the "Toronto" sample* (Final report submitted to the Ministry of Children and Youth Services). Toronto, Ontario, Canada: Ministry of Children and Youth Services. Retrieved from http://www.arts.ryerson.ca/dday/docs/Final%20Report.pdf

Day, D. M., Koegl, C. J., Rossman, L., & Oziel, S. (2015). *The monetary cost of criminal trajectories for an Ontario sample of offenders* (Research report: 2015-R011). Ottawa: Public Safety Canada. Retrieved from www.publicsafety.gc.ca

Day, D. M., Nielsen, J. D., Ward, A. K., Rosenthal, J. S., Sun, Y., Bevc, I., . . . Samuels, S. (2010). *Criminal trajectories of two subsamples of adjudicated Ontario youths* (Research report submitted to Public Safety Canada's National Crime Prevention Centre). Retrieved from www.bpiepc-ocipep.gc.ca

Day, D. M., Nielsen, J. D., Ward, A. K., Sun, Y., Rosenthal, J. S., Duchesne, T., . . . Rossman, L. (2012). Long-term follow-up of criminal activity with adjudicated youth in Ontario: Identifying offence trajectories and predictors/correlates of trajectory group membership. *Canadian Journal of Criminology and Criminal Justice, 54,* 377–413.

Day, D. M., Wanklyn, S. G., & Yessine, A. K. (2014). A review of terminological, conceptual, and methodological issues in the developmental risk factor literature for antisocial and delinquent behavior. *Child & Youth Care Forum, 43,* 97–112.

Day, D. M., Wilson, H. A., Bodwin, K., & Monson, C. M. (2017). Change in Level of Service Inventory–Ontario Revised (LSI-OR) risk scores over time: An examination of overall growth curves and subscale-dependent growth curves. *International Journal of Offender Therapy and Comparative Criminology, 61,* 1606–1622.

Decker, S. H. (2016). From theory to policy and back again. In A. R. Piquero (Ed.), *The handbook of criminological theory* (pp. 380–394). West Sussex, England: Wiley.

DeLisi, M. (2005). *Career criminals in society.* Thousand Oaks, CA: Sage.

DeLisi, M. (2006). Zeroing in on early arrest onset: Results from a population of extreme career criminals. *Journal of Criminal Justice, 34,* 17–26.

DeLisi, M. (2015). Age-crime curve and criminal career patterns. In J. Morizot & E. Kazemian (Eds.), *The development of criminal and antisocial behavior: Theory, research and practical applications* (pp. 51–63). New York, NY: Springer.

DeLisi, M., & Piquero, A. R. (2011). New frontiers in criminal careers research, 2000–2011: A state-of-the-art review. *Journal of Criminal Justice, 39,* 289–301.

Depping, M. K., & Freund, A. M. (2011). Normal aging and decision making: The role of motivation. *Human Development, 54,* 349–367.

Derzon, J. H. (2007). Using correlational evidence to select youth for prevention programming. *The Journal of Primary Prevention, 28,* 421–447.

de Rutier, C., & Augimeri, L. K. (2012). Making delinquency prevention work with children and adolescents: From risk assessment to effective management. In C. Logan, & L. Johnstone (Eds.), *Managing clinical risk: A guide to effective prevention* (pp. 199–224). New York, NY: Routledge.

Diallo, T. M. O., Morin, A. J. S., & Lu, H. (2017). The impact of total and partial inclusion or exclusion of active and inactive time invariant covariates in growth mixture models. *Psychological Methods, 22,* 166–190.

Dishion, T. J. (2000). Cross-setting consistency in early adolescent psychopathology: Deviant friendships and problem behavior sequalae. *Journal of Personality, 68,* 1109–1126.

Dishion, T. J., Patterson, G. R., & Kavanagh, K. A. (1992). An experimental test of the coercion model: Linking theory, measurement, and intervention. In J. McCord & R. Tremblay (Eds.), *The interaction of theory and practice: Experimental studies of intervention* (pp. 253–282). New York, NY: Guilford Press.

Dishion, T. J., & Piehler, T. F. (2007). Peer dynamics in the development and change of child and adolescent problem behavior. In A. S. Masten (Ed.), *Multilevel dynamics in developmental psychopathology: Pathways to the future. The Minnesota Symposia on Child Psychology* (Vol. 34, pp. 151–180). Mahwah, NJ: Taylor & Francis Group/Erlbaum.

Dishion, T. J., Spracklen, K. M., Andrews, D. W., & Patterson, G. R. (1996). Deviancy training in male adolescent friendships. *Behavior Therapy, 27,* 373–390.

Dmitrieva, J., Monahan, K. C., Cauffman, E., & Steinberg, L. (2012). Arrested development: The effects of incarceration on the development of psychosocial maturity. *Development and Psychopathology, 24,* 1073–1090.

Dodge, K. A. (2008). Framing public policy and prevention of chronic violence in American youths. *American Psychologist, 63,* 573–590.

Doherty, E. E., & Ensminger, M. E. (2013). Marriage and offending among a cohort of disadvantaged African Americans. *Journal of Research in Crime and Delinquency, 50,* 104–131.

Doherty, E. E., Laub, J. H., & Sampson, R. J. (2009). Group-based trajectories in life course criminology. In G. H. Elder, Jr., & J. Z. Giele (Eds.), *The craft of life course research* (pp. 187–210). New York, NY: Guilford Press.

Dumas, J. E., & Nilsen, W. J. (2003). *Abnormal child and adolescent psychology.* Boston, MA: Allyn & Bacon.

Duncan, S. C., & Duncan, T. E. (2012). Accelerated longitudinal designs. In B. Laursen, T. D. Little, & N. A. Card (Eds.), *Handbook of developmental research methods* (pp. 31–45). New York, NY: Guilford Press.

Duncan, T. E., Duncan, S. C., & Strycker, L. A. (2006). *An introduction to latent variable growth curve modeling: Concepts, issues, and applications* (2nd ed.). Mahwah, NJ: Erlbaum.

D'Unger, A. V., Land, K. C., & McCall, P. L. (2002). Sex differences in age patterns of delinquent/criminal careers: Results from Poisson latent class analyses of the Philadelphia cohort study. *Journal of Quantitative Criminology, 18*, 349–375.

D'Unger, A. V., Land, K. C., McCall, P. L., & Nagin, D. S. (1998). How many latent classes of delinquent/criminal careers? Results from mixed Poisson regression analyses of the London, Philadelphia, and Racine cohort studies. *American Journal of Sociology, 103*, 1593–1630.

Ebner, N. C., Freund, A. M., & Baltes, P. B. (2006). Developmental changes in personal goal orientation from young to late adulthood: From striving for gains to maintenance and prevention of losses. *Psychology and Aging, 21*, 664–678.

Eccles, J. S., Midgley, C., Wigfield, A., Buchanan, C. M., Reuman, D., Flanagan, C., & Mac Iver, D. (1993). Development during adolescence: The impact of stage-environment fit on young adolescents' experiences in schools and in families. *American Psychologist, 48*, 90–101.

Efron, B. (1983). Estimating the error rate of a prediction rule: Improvement on cross-validation. *Journal of the American Statistical Association, 78*, 316–331.

Eggleston, E. P., Laub, J. H., & Sampson, R. J. (2004). Methodological sensitivities to latent class analysis of long-term criminal trajectories. *Journal of Quantitative Criminology, 20*, 1–26.

Eisner, M., & Nivette, A. (2012). How to reduce the global homicide rate to 2 per 100,000 by 2060. In R. Loeber & B. C. Walsh (Eds.), *The future of criminology* (pp. 219–226). Oxford, England: Oxford University Press.

Eitle, D., & Turner, R. J. (2002). Exposure to community violence exposure to community violence and young adult crime: The effects of witnessing violence, traumatic victimization, and other stressful life events. *Journal of Research in Crime and Delinquency, 39*, 214–237.

Elder, G. H. (1974). *Children of the great depression: Social change in life experience.* Chicago, IL: University of Chicago Press.

Elder, G. H. (Ed.). (1985a). *Life course dynamics: Trajectories and transitions, 1968–1980.* Ithaca, NY: Cornell University Press.

Elder, G. H. (1985b). Preface. In G. H. Elder (Ed.), *Life course dynamics: Trajectories and transitions, 1968–1980* (pp. 15–20). Ithaca, NY: Cornell University Press.

Elder, G. H. (1985c). Perspectives on the life course. In G. H. Elder (Ed.), *Life course dynamics: Trajectories and transitions, 1968–1980* (pp. 23–49). Ithaca, NY: Cornell University Press.

Elder, G. H. (1986). Military times and turning points in men's lives. *Developmental Psychology, 22*, 233–245.

Elder, G. H. (1987). War mobilization and the life course: A cohort of World War II veterans. *Sociological Forum, 2*, 449–472.

Elder, G. H. (1998a). The life course as developmental theory. *Child Development, 69*, 1–12.

Elder, G. H., Jr. (1998b). The life course and human development. In W. Damon & R. M. Lerner (Eds.), *Handbook of Child Psychology, Vol. 1: Theoretical models of human development* (5th ed., pp. 939–991). New York, NY: John Wiley.

Elder, G. H., & Rockwell, R. C. (1979). The life-course and human development: An ecological perspective. *International Journal of Behavioral Development, 2,* 1–21.

Elder, G. H., Jr., & Shanahan, M. J. (2006). The life-course and human development. In R. M. Lerner (Ed.), *Handbook of Child Psychology, Vol. 1: Theoretical models of human development* (6th ed., pp. 665–715). Hoboken, NJ: Wiley.

Elliott, D. S. (2013). Crime prevention and intervention over the life course. In C. L. Gibson & M. D. Krohn (Eds.), *Handbook of life-course criminology: Emerging trends and directions for future research* (pp. 297–315). New York, NY: Springer.

El Sayed, S. A., Piquero, A. R., & TenEyck, M. (2017). Differentiating between Moffitt's developmental taxonomy and Silverthorn and Frick's delayed-onset models of female offending. *Criminal Justice and Behavior, 44,* 631–650.

Eme, R. (2015). Beauchaine ontogenic process model of externalizing psychopathology a biosocial theory of crime and delinquency. *Journal of Criminal Justice, 43,* 443–449.

Enders, C. K., & Tofighi, D. (2008). The impact of misspecifying class-specific residual variances in growth mixture models. *Structural Equation Modeling: A Multidisciplinary Journal, 15,* 75–95.

Enders, W., Sandler, T., & Gaibulloev, K. (2011). Domestic versus transnational terrorism: Data, decomposition, and dynamics. *Journal of Peace Research, 48,* 319–337.

Enebrink, P., Långström, N., & Gumpert, C. H. (2006). Predicting aggressive and disruptive behavior in referred 6- to 12-year-old boys: Prospective validation of the EARL-20B Risk/Needs Checklist. *Assessment, 13,* 356–367.

Enebrink, P., Långström, N., Hultén, A., & Gumpert, C. H. (2006). Swedish validation of the Early Assessment Risk List for Boys (EARL-20B), a decision aid for use with children presenting with conduct-disordered behaviour. *Nordic Journal of Psychiatry, 60,* 438–446.

Erosheva, E. A., Matsueda, R. L., & Telesca, D. (2014). Breaking bad: Two decades of life-course data analysis in criminology, developmental psychology, and beyond. *Annual Review of Statistics and Its Application, 1,* 301–332.

Evans, G. W., Li, D., & Whipple, S. S. (2013). Cumulative risk and child development. *Psychological Bulletin, 139,* 1342–1396.

Fagan, J. (1989). Cessation of family violence: Deterrence and dissuasion. In L. Ohlin & M. Tonry (Eds.), *Crime and justice: An annual review of research* (Vol. 11, pp. 377–425). Chicago, IL: University of Chicago Press.

Fairchild, G., van Goozen, S. H., Calder, A. J., & Goodyer, I. M. (2013). Research review: Evaluating and reformulating the developmental taxonomic theory of antisocial behaviour. *Journal of Child Psychology and Psychiatry, 54,* 924–940.

Farkas, G., & Beron, K. (2004). The detailed age trajectory of oral vocabulary knowledge: Differences by class and race. *Social Science Research, 33,* 464–497.

Farrall, S., & Calverley, A. (2006). *Understanding desistance from crime.* Maidenhead, England: Open University Press.

Farrall, S., Hunter, B., Sharpe, G., & Calverly, A. (2014). *Criminal careers in transition: The social context of desistance from crime.* Oxford, England: Oxford University Press.

Farrington, D. P. (1986). Stepping stones to adult criminal careers. In D. Olweus, J. Block, & M. Radke-Yarrow (Eds.), *Development of antisocial and prosocial behavior: Research, theories, and issues* (pp. 359–384). Cambridge, MA: Academic Press.

Farrington, D. P. (1988). Studying changes within individuals: The causes of offending. In D. P. Farrington & M. Rutter (Eds.), *Studies of psychosocial risk: The power of longitudinal data* (pp. 158–183). Cambridge, England: Cambridge University Press.

Farrington, D. P. (1997). Human development and criminal careers. In M. Maguire, R. Morgan, & R. Reiner (Eds.), *The Oxford handbook of criminology* (pp. 361–408). Oxford, England: Oxford University Press.

Farrington, D. P. (2002). Multiple risk factors for multiple problem violent boys. In R. R. Corrado, R. Roesch, S. D. Hart, & J. K. Gierowski (Eds.), *Multi-problem violent youth: A foundation for comparative research on needs, interventions, and outcomes* (pp. 23–34). Amsterdam, The Netherlands: IOS Press.

Farrington, D. P. (2003). Developmental and life-course criminology: Key theoretical and empirical issues—The 2002 Sutherland award address. *Criminology, 41,* 221–255.

Farrington, D. P. (Ed.). (2005a). *Integrated developmental and life-course theories of offending: Advances in criminological theory.* New Brunswick, NJ: Transaction Publishers.

Farrington, D. P. (2005b). Introduction. In D. P. Farrington (Ed.), *Integrated developmental and life-course theories of offending: Advances in criminological theory* (Vol. 14, pp. 1–14). New Brunswick, NJ: Transaction Publishers.

Farrington, D. P. (2005c). The integrated cognitive antisocial potential (ICAP) theory. In D. P. Farrington (Ed.), *Integrated developmental and life-course theories of offending* (Advances in Criminological Theory, Vol. 14, pp. 73–92). New Brunswick, NJ: Transaction Publishers.

Farrington, D. P. (2005d). The importance of child and adolescent psychopathy. *Journal of Abnormal Child Psychology, 33,* 489–497.

Farrington, D. P. (2007). Childhood risk factors and risk-focussed prevention. In M. Maguire, R. Morgan, & R. Reiner (Eds.), *The Oxford handbook of criminology* (4th ed., pp. 602–640). Oxford, England: Oxford University Press.

Farrington, D. P. (2008). Building developmental and life-course theories of offending. In F. C. Cullen, J. P. Wright, & K. R. Blevins (Eds.), *Taking stock: The status of criminological theory* (Advances in Criminological Theory, Vol. 15, pp. 335–364). New Brunswick, NJ: Transaction Publishers.

Farrington, D. P. (2013). Longitudinal and experimental research in criminology. In M. Tonry (Ed.), *Crime and Justice 1975–2025* (pp. 453–527). Chicago, IL: University of Chicago Press.

Farrington, D. P., Coid, J. W., Harnett, L. M., Jolliffe, D., Soteriou, N., Turner, R. E., & West, D. J. (2006). *Criminal careers up to age 50 and life success up to age 48: New findings from the Cambridge Study in Delinquent Development.* London, England: Home Office.

Farrington, D. P., Gaffney, H., Lösel, F. A., & Ttofi, M. M. (2017). Systematic reviews of the effectiveness of developmental prevention programs in reducing delinquency, aggression, and bullying. *Aggression and Violent Behavior, 33,* 91–106.

Farrington, D. P., Jolliffe, D., Hawkins, J. D., Catalano, R. F., Hill, K. G., & Kosterman, R. (2003). Comparing delinquency careers in court records and self-reports. *Criminology, 41,* 933–958.

Farrington, D. P., Kazemian, L., & Piquero, A. R. (Eds.). (2018). *The Oxford handbook of developmental and life course criminology.* Oxford, England: Oxford University Press.

Farrington, D. P., & Loeber, R. (2000). Some benefits of dichotomization in psychiatric and criminological research. *Criminal Behaviour and Mental Health, 10,* 100–122.

Farrington, D. P., & Loeber, R. (2013). Two approaches to developmental/life-course theorizing. In F. T. Cullen & P. Wilcox (Eds.), *The Oxford handbook of criminological theory* (pp. 226–252). New York, NY: Oxford University Press.

Farrington, D. P., & Loeber, R. (2014). Establishing causes of offending in longitudinal and experimental studies. In G. J. N. Bruinsma & D. Weisburd (Eds.), *Encyclopedia of criminology and criminal justice* (pp. 1368–1377). New York, NY: Springer-Verlag.

Farrington, D. P., Loeber, R., & Howell, J. C. (2012). Young adult offenders: The need for more effective legislative options and justice processing. *Criminology & Public Policy, 11,* 729–750.

Farrington, D. P., Loeber, R., Stouthamer-Loeber, M., van Kammen, W. B., & Schmidt, L. (1996). Self-reported delinquency and a combined delinquency seriousness scale based on boys, mothers, and teachers: Concurrent and predictive validity for African-Americans and Caucasians. *Criminology, 34,* 493–517.

Farrington, D. P., Loeber, R., & Welsh, B. C. (2010). Longitudinal-experimental studies. In A. R. Piquero & D. Weisburd (Eds.), *Handbook of quantitative criminology* (pp. 503–518). New York, NY: Springer.

Farrington, D. P., Piquero, A. R., & Jennings, W. G. (2013). *Offending from childhood to late middle age: Recent results from the Cambridge Study in Delinquent Development.* New York, NY: Springer.

Farrington, D. P., Snyder, H. N., & Finnegan, T. A. (1988). Specialization in juvenile court careers. *Criminology, 26,* 461–488.

Farrington, D. P., & Ttofi, M. M. (2015). Developmental and life-course theories of offending. In J. Morizot & L. Kazemian (Eds.), *The development of criminal and antisocial behavior: Theory, research and practical applications* (pp. 19–38). New York, NY: Springer.

Farrington, D. P., & Welsh, B. C. (2007). *Saving children from a life of crime: Early risk factors and effective interventions.* New York, NY: Oxford University Press.

Farrington, D. P., & West, D. J. (1990). The Cambridge Study in Delinquent Development: A long-term follow-up of 411 London males. In H.-J. Kerner & G. Kaiser (Eds.), *Criminality: Personality, behavior and life history* (pp. 115–138). New York, NY: Springer.

Farrington, D. P., & West, D. J. (1995). Effects of marriage, separation, and children on offending by adult males. In Z. S. Blau & J. Hagan (Eds.), *Current perspectives on aging and the life cycle* (Vol. 4, pp. 249–281). Greenwich, CT: JAI Press.

Federal Bureau of Investigation. (2001). *Crime in the United States 2001: Uniform Crime Reports.* Washington, DC: Government Printing Office.

Feng, X., Shaw, D. S., & Silk, J. S. (2008). Developmental trajectories of anxiety symptoms among boys across early and middle childhood. *Journal of Abnormal Psychology, 117,* 32–47.

Ferdinand, T. N. (1966). *Typologies of delinquency: A critical analysis.* New York, NY: Random House.

Fergusson, D. M., & Horwood, L. J. (2002). Male and female offending trajectories. *Development and Psychopathology, 14,* 159–177.

Fergusson, D. M., Horwood, L. J., & Nagin, D. S., (2000). Offending trajectories in a New Zealand birth cohort. *Criminology, 38,* 525–552.

Fontaine, N., Carbonneau, R., Vitaro, F., Barker, E. D., & Tremblay, R. E. (2009). Research review: A critical review of studies on the developmental trajectories of antisocial behavior in females. *Journal of Child Psychology and Psychiatry, 50,* 363–385.

Ford, D. L., & Lerner, R. M. (1992). *Developmental systems theory: An integrative approach.* Thousand Oaks, CA: Sage.

Forth, A. E., Kosson, D. S., & Hare, R. D. (2003). *Hare Psychopathy Checklist: Youth Version.* New York, NY: Multi-Health Systems.

Foster, E. M. (2010). Causal inference and developmental psychology. *Developmental Psychology, 46,* 1454–1480.

Foster, E. M., & McLanahan, S. (1996). An illustration of the use of instrumental variables: Do neighborhood conditions affect a young person's chance of finishing high school? *Psychological Methods, 1,* 249–260.

Frankfurt, S., Frazier, P., Syed, M., & Jung, K. R. (2016). Using group-based trajectory and growth mixture modeling to identify classes of change trajectories. *The Counseling Psychologist, 44,* 622–660.

Franklin, J. C., Ribeiro, J. D., Fox, K. R., Bentley, K. H., Kleiman, E. M., Huang, X., . . . Nock, M. K. (2017). Risk factors for suicidal thoughts and behaviors: A meta-analysis of 50 years of research. *Psychological Bulletin, 143,* 187–232.

Frechette, M., & Le Blanc, M. (1987). *Délinquances et délinquants* [Delinquency and delinquents]. Chicouitami, Canada: Gaetan Morin.

Freiburger, T. L., Marcum, C. D., Iannacchione, B. M., & Higgins, G. E. (2012). Sex offenders and criminal recidivism: An exploratory trajectory analysis using a Virginia sample. *Journal of Crime and Justice, 35,* 365–375.

Freund, A. M., & Baltes, P. B. (2002). Life-management strategies of selection, optimization and compensation: Measurement by self-report and construct validity. *Journal of Personality and Social Psychology, 82,* 642–662.

Frick, P. J. (2004). Developmental pathways to conduct disorder: Implications for serving youth who show severe aggressive and antisocial behavior. *Psychology in the Schools, 41,* 823–834.

Frick, P. J., & Hare, R. D. (2001). *Antisocial Process Screening Device (APSD)*. Toronto, Canada: Multi-Health Systems.

Furstenberg, F. F. Jr., Kennedy, S., McLoyd, V. C., Rumbaut, R. G., & Settersten, R. A., Jr. (2004). Growing up is harder to do. *Contexts, 3*, 33–41.

Geldhof, G. J., Bowers, E. P., Gestsdóttir, S., Napolitano, C. M., & Lerner, R. M. (2015). Self-regulation across adolescence: Exploring the structure of selection, optimization, and compensation. *Journal of Research on Adolescence, 25*, 214–228.

Gendreau, P., Goggen, C., & Cullen, F. T. (1999). *The effects of prison sentences on recidivism*. Ottawa: Corrections Research Branch, Solicitor General of Canada.

George, L. K. (2009). Conceptualizing and measuring trajectories. In G. H. Elder & J. Z. Giele (Eds.). *The craft of life course research* (pp. 163–186). New York, NY: Guilford.

Gestsdóttir, S., & Lerner, R. M. (2007). Intentional self-regulation and positive youth development in early adolescence: Findings from the 4-H Study of Positive Youth Development. *Developmental Psychology, 43*, 508–521.

Gestsdóttir, S., & Lerner, R. M. (2008). Positive development in adolescence: The development and role of intentional self-regulation. *Human Development, 51*, 202–224.

Gestsdóttir, S., Lewin-Bizan, S., von Eye, A., Lerner, J. V., & Lerner, R. M. (2009). The structure and function of selection, optimization, and compensation in middle adolescence: Theoretical and applied implications. *Journal of Applied Developmental Psychology, 30*, 585–600.

Gibbons, D. C. (1975). Offender typologies-two decades later. *British Journal of Criminology, 15*, 140–156.

Gibson, M. (2002). *Born to crime: Cesare Lombroso and the origins of biological criminology*. Westport, CT: Praeger.

Giedd, J. N., Blumenthal, J., Jeffries, N. O., Castellanos, F. X., Liu, H., Zijdenbos, A., . . . Rapoport, J. L. (1999). Brain development during childhood and adolescence: a longitudinal MRI study. *Nature Neuroscience, 2*, 861–863.

Giordano, P. L., Cernkovich, S. A., & Rudolph, J. L. (2002). Gender, crime, and desistance: Toward a theory of cognitive transformation. *American Journal of Sociology, 107*, 990–1064.

Giordano, P.C., Schroeder, R.D., & Cernkovich, S.A. (2007). Emotions and crime over the life course: A Neo-Meadian perspective on criminal continuity and change. *American Journal of Sociology, 112*, 1603–1661.

Girard, L., & Wormith, J. S. (2004). The predictive validity of the Level of Service Inventory-Ontario Revision on general and violent recidivism among various offender groups. *Criminal Justice and Behavior, 31*, 150–181.

Glueck, S., & Glueck, E. T. (1950). *Unraveling juvenile delinquency*. Cambridge, MA: Harvard University Press.

Goldstein, H. (1995). *Multilevel statistical models* (2nd ed.). London, England: Edward Arnold.

Gorman-Smith, D., & Loeber, R. (2005). Are developmental pathways in disruptive behaviors the same for girls and boys? *Journal of Child and Family Studies, 14*, 15–27.

Gottfredson, M., & Hirschi, T. (1986). The true value of Lambda would appear to be zero: An essay on career criminals, criminal careers, selective incapacitation, cohort studies, and related topics. *Criminology, 24*, 213–234.

Gottfredson, M., & Hirschi, T. (1988). Science, public policy, and the career paradigm. *Criminology, 26*, 37–55.

Gottfredson, M. R., & Hirschi, T. (1990). *A general theory of crime.* Stanford, CA: Stanford University Press.

Gove, W. R. (1985). The effect of age and gender on deviant behavior: A biopsychosocial perspective. In A. S. Rossi (Ed.), *Gender and the life course* (pp. 115–144). New York, NY: Aldine de Gruyter.

Graber, J. A., & Brooks-Gunn, J. (1996). Transitions and turning points: Navigating the passage from childhood through adolescence. *Developmental Psychology, 32*, 768–776.

Granic, I., & Hollenstein, T. (2006). A survey of dynamic systems methods for developmental psychopathology. In D. Cicchetti & D. J. Cohen (Eds.), *Developmental Psychopathology, Vol. 1. Theory and method* (2nd ed., pp. 889–930). Hoboken, NJ: Wiley.

Granic, I., & Patterson, G. R. (2006). Toward a comprehensive model of antisocial development: A dynamic systems approach. *Psychological Review, 113*, 101–131.

Greenberg, D. F. (2016). Criminal careers: Discrete or continuous? *Journal of Developmental and Life-Course Criminology, 2*, 5–44.

Greenwood, P. W. (2006). *Changing lives: Delinquency prevention and crime control.* Chicago, IL: University of Chicago Press.

Griffiths, E., & Chavez, J. M. (2004). Communities, street guns and homicide trajectories in Chicago, 1980–1995: Merging methods for examining homicide trends across space and time. *Criminology, 42*, 941–978.

Grimm, K. J., Ram, N., & Estabrook, R. (2010). Nonlinear structured growth mixture models in M plus and OpenMx. *Multivariate Behavioral Research, 45*, 887–909.

Grisso, T., & Schwartz, R. G. (Eds.). (2000). *Youth on trial: A developmental perspective on juvenile justice.* Chicago, IL: The University of Chicago Press.

Haase, C.M., Heckhausen, J., & Wrosch, C. (2013). Developmental regulation across the life span: Toward a new synthesis. *Developmental Psychology, 49*, 964–972.

Han, S.-K., & Moen, P. (1999). Work and family over time: A life course approach. *The ANNALS of the American Academy of Political and Social Science, 562*, 98–110.

Hanson, R. K., Bourgon, G., Helmus, L., & Hodgson, S. (2009). *A meta-analysis of the effectiveness of treatment for sexual offenders: Risk, need, and responsivity* (Report 2009-1). Ottawa: Project Safety Canada. Retrieved from www.publicsafety.gc.ca

Hart, S. D., Cox, D. N., & Hare, R. D. (1995). *Hare Psychopathy Checklist: Screening Version.* Toronto, Canada: Multi-Health Systems.

Hartmann, D. P., Abbott, C. B., & Pelzel, K. E. (2015). Design, measurement, and analysis in developmental research. In M. H. Bornstein & M. E. Lamb (Eds.), *Developmental science: An advanced textbook* (7th ed., pp. 113–213). New York, NY: Psychology Press.

Haviland, A., Nagin, D. S., & Rosenbaum, P. R. (2007). Combining propensity score matching and group-based trajectory analysis in an observational study. *Psychological Methods, 12,* 247–267.

Haviland, A., Nagin, D. S., Rosenbaum, P. R., & Tremblay, R. E. (2008). Combining group-based trajectory modeling and propensity score matching for causal inferences in nonexperimental longitudinal data. *Developmental Psychology, 44,* 422–436.

Haviland, A. M., Jones, B. L., & Nagin, D. S. (2011). Group-based trajectory modeling extended to account for nonrandom participant attrition. *Sociological Methods & Research, 40,* 367–390.

Haviland, A. M., & Nagin, D. S. (2005). Causal inferences with group based trajectory models. *Psychometrika, 70,* 557–578.

Hayes, A. F. (2013). *Introduction to mediation, moderation, and conditional process analysis: A regression-based approach.* New York, NY: Guilford.

Head, B. W. (2008). Wicked problems in public policy. *Public Policy, 3,* 101–118.

Healy, D. (2013). Changing fate? Agency and the desistance process. *Theoretical Criminology, 17,* 557–574.

Heckhausen, J., Wrosch, C., & Schulz, R. (2010). A motivational theory of life-span development. *Psychological Review, 117,* 32–60.

Hedecker, D. (2004). An introduction to growth modeling. In D. Kaplan (Ed.), *The SAGE handbook of quantitative methodology for the social sciences* (pp. 215–234). Thousand Oaks, CA: Sage.

Helson, R., & Soto, C. J. (2005). Up and down in middle age: Monotonic and non-monotonic changes in roles, status, and personality. *Journal of Personality and Social Psychology, 89,* 194–204.

Helzer, J. E., Kraemer, H. C., & Krueger, R. F. (2006). The feasibility and need for dimensional psychiatric diagnoses. *Psychological Medicine, 36,* 1671–1680.

Herrenkohl, T. I., Maguin, E., Hill, K. G., Hawkins, J. D., Abbott, R. D., & Catalano, R. F. (2000). Developmental risk factors for youth violence. *Journal of Adolescent Health, 26,* 176–186.

Higgins, G. E., Kirchner, E. E., Ricketts, M. L., & Marcum, C. D. (2013). Impulsivity and offending from childhood to young adulthood in the United States: A developmental trajectory analysis. *International Journal of Criminal Justice Sciences, 8,* 182–197.

Hill, C. J., Bloom, H. S., Black, A. R., & Lipsey, M. W. (2008). Empirical benchmarks for interpreting effect sizes in research. *Child Development Perspectives, 2,* 172–177.

Hill, J. M., Blokland, A. A. J., & van der Geest, V. R. (2016). Desisting from crime in emergent adulthood: Adult roles and the maturity gap. *Journal of Research in Crime and Delinquency, 53,* 506–535.

Hipp, J. R., & Bauer, D. J. (2006). Local solutions in the estimation of growth mixture models. *Psychological Methods, 11,* 36–53.

Hirsch, B. J., & DuBois, D. L. (1991). Self-esteem in early adolescence: The identification and prediction of contrasting longitudinal trajectories. *Journal of Youth and Adolescence, 20,* 53–72.

Hirschi, T. (1969). *Causes of delinquency*. Berkeley: University of California Press.

Hochstetler, A., Peters, D. J., & DeLisi, M. (2016). Classifying risk development and predicting parolee recidivism with growth mixture models. *American Journal of Criminal Justice, 41*, 602–620.

Hogan, D. P. (1978). The variable order of events in the life course. *American Sociological Review, 43*, 573–586.

Hoge, R. D. (2001). *The juvenile offender: Theory, research and applications*. Norwell, MA: Kluwer Academic Publishers.

Hoge, R. D., & Andrews, D. A. (1996). *Assessing the youthful offender: Issues and techniques*. New York, NY: Plenum.

Hoge, R. D., & Andrews, D. A., & Leschied, A. W. (2002). *The Youth Level of Service/Case Management Inventory*. Toronto, Canada: Multi-Health Systems.

Hollenstein, T. (2011). Twenty years of dynamic systems approaches to development: Significant contributions, challenges, and future directions. *Child Development Perspectives, 5*, 256–259.

Horney, J. Osgood, D. W., & Marshall, I. H. (1995). Criminal careers in the short-term: Intra-individual variability in crime and its relation to local life circumstances. *American Sociological Review, 60*, 655–673.

Hox, J., & Stoel, R. D. (2005). Multilevel and SEM approaches to growth curve modeling. In B. S. Everitt & D. C. Howell (Eds.), *Encyclopedia of statistics in behavioral science* (Vol. 3, pp. 1296–1305). Chichester, England: Wiley.

Hoyt, S., & Scherer, D. G. (1998). Female juvenile delinquency: Misunderstood by the juvenile justice system, neglected by social science. *Law and Human Behavior, 22*, 81–107.

Hubbard, D. J., & Pratt, T. C. (2002). A meta-analysis of the predictors of delinquency among girls. *Journal of Offender Rehabilitation, 34*, 1–13.

Huh, J., Huang, Z., Liao, Y., Pentz, M., & Chou, C. P. (2013). Transitional life events and trajectories of cigarette and alcohol use during emerging adulthood: Latent class analysis and growth mixture modeling. *Journal of Studies on Alcohol & Drugs, 74*, 727–735.

Huizinga, D., & Elliott, D. S. (1986). Reassessing the reliability and validity of self-report delinquency measures. *Journal of Quantitative Criminology, 2*, 293–327.

Huizinga, D., Wylie Weiher, A., Espiritu, R., & Esbensen, F. (2003). Delinquency and crime: Some highlights from the Denver Youth Survey. In T. P. Thornberry & M. D. Krohn (Eds.), *Taking stock of delinquency: An overview of findings from contemporary longitudinal studies* (pp. 47–91). New York, NY: Kluwer Academic/Plenum.

Hussong, A. M., Curran, P. J., Moffitt, T. E., Caspi, A., & Carrig, M. M. (2004). Substance abuse hinders desistance in young adults' antisocial behavior. *Development and Psychopathology, 16*, 1029–1046.

Jackson, K. M., Sher, K. J., & Schulenberg, J. E. (2005). Conjoint developmental trajectories of young adult alcohol and tobacco use. *Journal of Abnormal Psychology, 114*, 612–626.

Jaffee, S. R., Strait, L. B., & Odgers, C. L. (2012). From correlates to causes: Can quasi-experimental studies and statistical innovations bring us closer to identifying the causes of antisocial behavior? *Psychological Bulletin, 138*, 272–295.

Jennings, W. G. (2011). Sex disaggregated trajectories of status offenders: Does CINS/FINS status prevent male and female youth from becoming labeled delinquent? *American Journal of Criminal Justice, 36*, 177–187.

Jennings, W. G., Maldonado-Molina, M. M., & Komro, K. A. (2010). Sex similarities/differences in trajectories of delinquency among urban Chicago youth: The role of delinquent peers. *American Journal of Criminal Justice, 35*, 56–75.

Jennings, W. G., Maldonado-Molina, M. M., Piquero, A. R., Odgers, C. L., Bird, H., & Canino, G. (2010). Sex differences in trajectories of offending among Puerto Rican youth. *Crime & Delinquency, 56*, 327–357.

Jennings, W. G., & Reingle, J. M. (2012). On the number and shape of developmental/life-course violence, aggression, and delinquency trajectories: A state-of-the-art review. *Journal of Criminal Justice, 40*, 472–489.

Jennings, W. G., Rocque, M., Fox, B. H., Piquero, A. R., & Farrington, D. P. (2016). Can they recover? An assessment of adult adjustment problems among males in the abstainer, recovery, life-course persistent, and adolescence-limited pathways followed up to age 56 in the Cambridge Study in Delinquent Development. *Development and Psychopathology, 28*, 537–549.

Jennings, W. G., Zgoba, K. M., & Tewksbury, R. (2012). A comparative longitudinal analysis of recidivism trajectories and collateral consequences for sex and non-sex offenders released since the implementation of sex offender registration and community notification. *Journal of Crime and Justice, 35*, 356–364.

Jimerson, S., Egeland, B., Sroufe, L. A., & Carlson, B. (2000). A prospective longitudinal study of high school dropouts examining multiple predictors across development. *Journal of School Psychology, 38*, 525–549.

Jo, B., Wang, C.-P., & Ialongo, N. S. (2009). Using latent outcome trajectory classes in causal inference. *Statistics and its Interface, 2*, 403.412.

Johnson, L. M., Simons, R. L., & Conger, R. D. (2004). Criminal justice system involvementand continuity of youth crime: A longitudinal analysis. *Youth & Society, 36*, 3–29.

Johnson, W., Hicks, B. M., McGue, M., & Iacono, W. G. (2007). Most of the girls are alright, but some aren't: Personality trajectory groups from ages 14 to 24 and some associations with outcomes. *Journal of Personality and Social Psychology, 93*, 266–284.

Jolliffe, D., Farrington, D. P., Piquero, A. R., Loeber, R., & Hill, K. G. (2017) Systemic review of the early risk factors for life-course persistent, adolescence-limited, and late-onset offenders in prospective longitudinal studies. *Aggression and Violent Behavior, 33*, 15–23.

Jolliffe, D., Farrington, D. P., Piquero, A. R., MacLeod, J. F., & van de Weijer, S. (2017) Prevalence of life-course persistent, adolescence-limited, and late-onset offenders: A systematic review of prospective longitudinal studies. *Aggression and Violent Behavior, 33*, 4–14.

Jones, B. L., & Nagin, D. S. (2007). Advances in group-based trajectory modeling and an SAS procedure for estimating them. *Sociological Methods & Research, 35,* 542–571.

Jones, B. L., & Nagin, D. S. (2013). A note on a Stata plugin for estimating group-based trajectory models. *Sociological Methods & Research, 42,* 608–613.

Jones, B. L., Nagin, D. S., & Roeder, K. (2001). A SAS procedure based on mixture models for estimating developmental trajectories. *Sociological Methods & Research, 29,* 374–393.

Jones, P. R., Harris, P. W., Fader, J., & Grubstein, L. (2001). Identifying chronic juvenile offenders. *Justice Quarterly, 18,* 479–507.

Kagan, J., & Snidman, N. (2004). *The long shadow of temperament.* Cambridge, MA: Belknap Press.

Kass, R. E., & Raftery, A. E. (1995). Bayes factor. *Journal of the American Statistical Association, 90,* 773–795.

Kazdin, A. E. (1995). *Conduct disorders in childhood and adolescence* (2nd ed.). Thousand Oaks, CA: Sage.

Kazdin, A. E., Kraemer, H. C., Kessler, R. C., Kupfer, D. J., & Offord, D. R. (1997). Contributions of risk-factor research to developmental psychopathology. *Clinical Psychology Review, 17,* 375–406.

Kazdin, A. E., & Nock, M. K. (2003). Delineating mechanisms of change in child and adolescent therapy: Methodological issues and research recommendations. *Journal of Child Psychology and Psychiatry, 44,* 1116–1129.

Kazemian, L. (2007). Desistance from crime: Theoretical, empirical, methodological, and policy considerations. *Journal of Contemporary Criminal Justice, 23,* 5–27.

Kazemian, L. (2012). Pushing back the frontiers of knowledge on desistance from crime. In R. Loeber & B. C. Welsh (Eds.), *The future of criminology* (pp. 134–140). Oxford, England: Oxford University Press.

Kazemian, L. (2015). Desistance from crime and antisocial behavior. In J. Morizot & E. Kazemian (Eds.), *The development of criminal and antisocial behavior: Theory, research, and practical applications* (pp. 295–312). New York, NY: Springer.

Kazemian, L., Farrington, D. P., & Le Blanc, M. (2009). Can we make accurate long-term predictions about patterns of de-escalation in offending behavior? *Journal of Youth and Adolescence, 38,* 384–400.

Kazemian, L., & Travis, J. (2015). Imperative for inclusion of long termers and lifers in research and policy. *Criminology & Public Policy, 14,* 355–395.

Kerr, D. C. R., Capaldi, D. M., Owen, L. D., Wiesner, M., & Pears, K. C. (2011). Changes in at-risk American men's crime and substance use trajectories following fatherhood. *Journal of Marriage and the Family, 73,* 1101–1116.

Kewley, S. (2017). Strength based approaches and protective factors from a criminological perspective. *Aggression and Violent Behavior, 32,* 11–18.

Kirk, D. (2012). Residential change as a turning point in the life course of crime: Desistance or temporary cessation? *Criminology, 50,* 329–358.

Kitzmann, K. M., Gaylord, N. K., Holt, A. R., & Kenny, E. D. (2003). Child witnesses to domestic violence: A meta-analytic review. *Journal of Consulting and Clinical Psychology*, *71*, 339–352.

Knight, R. D. (2008). *Physics for scientists and engineers: A strategic approach* (2nd ed.). Upper Saddle River, NJ: Pearson Addison Wesley.

Koegl, C. J. (2011). *High-risk antisocial children: Predicting future criminal and health outcomes* (Unpublished doctoral dissertation). University of Cambridge, Cambridge, England.

Kohli, N., Harring, J. R., & Hancock, G. R. (2013). Piecewise linear-linear latent growth mixture models with unknown knots. *Educational and Psychological Measurement*, *73*, 935–955.

Kraemer, H. C., Kazdin, A E., Offord, D. R., Kessler, R. C., Jensen, P. S., & Kupfer, D. J. (1997). Coming to terms with the terms of risk. *Archives of General Psychiatry*, *54*, 337–343.

Kraemer, H. C., Stice, E., Kazdin, A. E., Offord, D. R., & Kupfer, D. J. (2001). How do risk factors work together? Mediators, moderators, and independent, overlapping, and proxy risk factors. *The American Journal of Psychiatry*, *158*, 848–856.

Kreager, D. A., Matsueda, A. L., & Erosheva, E. A. (2010). Motherhood and criminal desistance in disadvantaged neighborhoods. *Criminology*, *48*, 221–258.

Kreuter, F., & Muthén, B. (2008a). Analyzing criminal trajectory profiles: Bridging multilevel and group-based approaches using growth mixture modeling. *Journal of Quantitative Criminology*, *24*, 1–31.

Kreuter, F., & Muthén, B. (2008b). Longitudinal modeling of population heterogeneity: Methodological challenges to the analysis of empirically derived criminal trajectory profiles. In G. R. Hancock & K. M. Samuelsen (Eds.), *Advances in latent variable mixture models* (pp. 53–75). Charlotte, NC: Information Age Publishing.

Krohn, M. D., Thornberry, T. P., Rivera, C., & Le Blanc, M. (2001). Later delinquency careers. In R. Loeber & D. P. Farrington (Eds.), *Child delinquents: Development, intervention, and service needs* (pp. 67–93). Thousand Oaks, CA: Sage.

Krohn, M. D., Ward, J. T., Thornberry, T. P., Lizotte, A. J., & Chu, R. (2011). The cascading effects of adolescent gang involvement across the life course. *Criminology*, *49*, 991–1028.

Krueger, R. F., Moffitt, T. E., Caspi, A., Bleske, A., & Silva, P. A. (1998). Assortative mating for antisocial behavior: Developmental and methodological implications. *Behavior Genetics*, *28*, 173–186.

Kruttschnitt, C., Uggen, C., & Shelton, K. (2000). Predictors of desistance among sex offenders: The interaction of formal and informal social controls. *Justice Quarterly*, *17*, 61–87.

Kurlychek, M. C., Bushway, S. D., & Brame, R. (2012). Long-term crime desistance and recidivism patterns-evidence from the Essex County Convicted Felon study. *Criminology*, *50*, 71–103.

LaFree, G., Morris, N. A., & Dugan, L. (2010). Cross-national patterns of terrorism: Comparing trajectories for total, attributed and fatal attacks, 1970–2006. *The British Journal of Criminology*, *50*, 622–649.

Lageson, S., & Uggen, C. (2013). How work affects crime-and crime affects work-over the life course. In C. L. Gibson & M. D. Krohn (Eds.), *Handbook of life-course criminology: Emerging trends and directions for future research* (pp. 201–212). New York, NY: Springer.

Lahey, B. B., & Waldman, I. D. (2003). A developmental propensity model of the origins of conduct problems during childhood and adolescence. In B. B. Lahey, T. E. Moffitt, & A. Caspi (Eds.), *Causes of conduct disorder and juvenile delinquency* (pp. 76–117). New York, NY: Guilford.

Lahey, B. B., & Waldman, I. D. (2005). A developmental model of the propensity to offend during childhood and adolescence. In D. P. Farrington (Ed.), *Integrated developmental and life-course theories of offending* (Advances in Criminological Theory, Vol. 14, pp. 15–50). New Brunswick, NJ: Transaction.

Lambie, I., & Randell, I. (2013). The impact of incarceration on juvenile offenders. *Clinical Psychology Review, 33*, 448–459.

Lanctôt, N. (2015). Development of antisocial behavior in adolescent girls. In J. Morizot & L. Kazemian (Eds.), *The development of criminal and antisocial behavior: Theory, research and practical applications* (pp. 399–411). New York, NY: Springer.

Latessa, E., Cullen, F. T., & Gendreau, P. (2002). Beyond correctional quackery—Professionalism and the possibility of effective treatment. *Federal Probation, 66*, 43–49.

Laub, J. H. (2016). Life course research and the shaping of public policy. In M. J. Shanahan, J. T. Mortimer, & M. Kirkpatrick Johnson (Eds.), *Handbook of the life course* (Vol. 2, pp. 623–637). New York, NY: Springer.

Laub, J. H., Nagin, D. S., & Sampson, R. J. (1998). Trajectories of change in criminal offending: Good marriages and the desistance process. *American Sociological Review, 63*, 225–239.

Laub, J. H., & Sampson, R. J. (1993). Turning points in the life course: Why change matters to the study of crime. *Criminology, 31*, 301–325.

Laub, J. H., & Sampson, R. J. (2001). Understanding desistance from crime. In M. Tonry (Ed.), *Crime and justice* (Vol. 28, pp. 1–69). Chicago, IL: University of Chicago Press.

Laub, J. H., & Sampson, R. J. (2003). *Shared beginnings, divergent lives: Delinquent boys to age 70*. Cambridge, MA: Harvard University Press.

Laub, J. H., Sampson, R. J., & Sweeten, G. A. (2006). Assessing Sampson and Laub's life-course theory of crime. In F. T. Cullen, J. P. Wright, & K. R. Belvins (Eds.), *Taking stock: The status of criminological theory* (pp. 313–33). London, England: Transaction Publishers.

Lauritsen, J. L. (1998). The age-crime debate: Assessing the limits of longitudinal self-report data. *Social Forces, 77*, 127–154.

Laursen, B., Little, T. D., & Card, N. A. (Eds.). (2012). *Handbook of developmental research methods*. New York, NY: Guilford.

LeBel, T. P., Burnett, R., Maruna, S., & Bushway, S. (2008). The 'chicken and egg' of subjective and social factors in desistance from crime. *European Journal of Criminology, 5*, 130–158.

Le Blanc, M. (1993). Late adolescence deceleration of criminal activity and development of self- and social control. *Studies on Crime and Crime Prevention, 2,* 51–68.

Le Blanc, M. (1997). A generic control theory of the criminal phenomenon: The structural and dynamic statements of an integrative multilayered control theory. In T. P. Thornberry (Ed.), *Developmental theories of crime and delinquency* (Advances in Criminological Theory, Vol. 7, pp. 215–285). New Brunswick, NJ: Transaction Publishers.

Le Blanc, M. (2002). Review of clinical assessment strategies and instruments for adolescent offenders. In R. R. Corrado, R. Roesch, S. D. Hart, & J. K. Gierowski (Eds.), *Multi-problem violent youth: A foundation for comparative research on needs, interventions, and outcomes* (pp. 171–190). Amsterdam, The Netherlands: IOS Press.

Le Blanc, M. (2005). An integrated personal control theory of deviant behavior: Answers to contemporary empirical and theoretical developmental criminology issues. In D. P. Farrington (Ed.), *Integrated developmental and life-course theories of offending* (Advances in Criminological Theory, Vol. 14, pp. 125–163). New Brunswick, NJ: Transaction.

Le Blanc, M. (2012). Twenty five years of developmental criminology: What we know, what we need to know. In R. Loeber & B. C. Welsh (Eds.), *The future of criminology* (pp. 124–133). Oxford, England: Oxford University Press.

Le Blanc, M., & Fréchette, M. (1989). *Male criminal activity from childhood through youth: Multilevel and developmental perspectives.* New York, NY: Springer.

Le Blanc, M., & Loeber, R. (1998). Developmental criminology updated. In M. Tonry (Ed.), *Crime and justice: A review of research* (Vol. 23, pp. 115–198). Chicago, IL: University of Chicago Press.

Lee, C., & Berrick, J. D. (2014). Experiences of youth who transition to adulthood out of care: Developing a theoretical framework. *Children and Youth Services Review, 46,* 78–84.

Lee, S., & McLachlan, G. J. (2014). Finite mixtures of multivariate skew *t*-distributions: Some recent and new results. *Statistics and Computing, 24,* 181–202.

Lenzenweger, M. F. (2004). Consideration of the challenges, complications, and pitfalls of taxometric analysis. *Journal of Abnormal Psychology, 113,* 10–23.

Lerner, R. M. (2002). *Concepts and theories of human development* (3rd ed.). Mahwah, NJ: Erlbaum.

Lerner, R. M. (2004). *Liberty: Thriving and civic engagement among America's youth.* Thousand Oaks, CA: Sage.

Lerner, R. M. (2005). *Promoting positive youth development: Theoretical and empirical bases* (White paper prepared for the Workshop on the Science of Adolescent Health and Development, National Research Council/Institute of Medicine). Washington, DC: National Academy of Sciences.

Lerner, R. M., Agans, J. P., DeSouza, L. M., & Hershberg, R. M. (2014). Developmental science in 2025: A predictive review. *Research in Human Development, 11,* 255–272.

Lerner, R. M., Hershberg, R. M., Hilliard, L. J., & Johnson, S. K. (2015). Concepts and theories of human development. In M. H. Bornstein & M. E. Lamb (Eds.),

Developmental science: An advanced textbook (7th ed., pp. 3–41). New York, NY: Psychology Press.

Lerner, R. M., Lerner, J. V., von Eye, A., Bowers, E. P., & Lewin-Bizan, S. (2011). Individual and contextual bases of thriving in adolescence: A view of the issues. *Journal of Adolescence, 34*, 1107–1114.

Lerner, R. M., & Ryff, C. D. (1978). Implementation of the life-span view of human development: The sample case of attachment. In P. B. Baltes (Ed.), *Life-span development and behavior* (Vol. 1, pp. 1–44). New York, NY: Academic Press.

Lerner, R. M., Theokas, C., & Bobek, D. L. (2005). Concepts and theories of human development: Historical and contemporary dimensions. In M. C. Bornstein & M. E. Lamb (Eds.), *Developmental science: An advanced textbook* (5 ed., pp. 3–43). Mahwah, NJ: Erlbaum.

Leschied, A., Chiodo, D., Nowicki, E., & Rodger, S. (2008). Childhood predictors of adult criminality: A meta-analysis drawn from the prospective longitudinal literature. *Canadian Journal of Criminology and Criminal Justice, 50*, 435–467.

Leve, L. D. & Cicchetti, D. (2016). Longitudinal transactional models of development and psychopathology. *Development and Psychopathology, 28*, 621–622.

Lewontin, R. (2000). *The triple helix: Gene, organism, and environment*. Cambridge, MA: Harvard University Press.

Li, L., & Hser, Y.-I. (2011). On inclusion of covariates for class enumeration of growth mixture models. *Multivariate Behavioral Research, 46*, 266–302.

Li, M., & Harring, J. R. (2016). Investigating approaches to estimating covariate effects in growth mixture modeling: A simulation study. *Educational and Psychological Measurement, 77*, 766-791.

Lipman, E. L., Offord, D. R., & Boyle, M. H. (1994). Relation between economic disadvantage and psychosocial morbidity in children. *Canadian Medical Association Journal, 151*, 431–437.

Lipsey, M. W., & Derzon, J. H. (1998). Predictors of serious and violent or serious delinquency in adolescence and early adulthood: A synthesis of longitudinal research. In D. P. Farrington & R. Loeber (Eds.), *Serious & violent juvenile offenders: Risk factors and successful intervention* (pp. 86–105). Thousand Oaks, CA: Sage.

Lipsey, M. W., & Wilson, D. B. (1998). Effective intervention for serious juvenile offenders: A synthesis of research. In D. P. Farrington & R. Loeber (Eds.), *Serious & violent juvenile offenders: Risk factors and successful intervention* (pp. 313-345). Thousand Oaks, CA: Sage.

Little, T. D. (2013). *Longitudinal structural equation modeling*. New York, NY: Guilford.

Livingston, M., Stewart, A., Allard, T., & Ogilvie, J. (2008). Understanding juvenile offending trajectories. *Australian & New Zealand Journal of Criminology, 41*, 345–363.

Lochman, J. E. (2006). Translation of research into interventions. *International Journal of Behavioral Development, 30*, 31–38.

Loeber, R. (1985). Patterns and development of antisocial child behavior. *Annals of Child Development, 2*, 77–116.

Loeber, R. (1990). Development and risk factors of juvenile antisocial behavior and delinquency. *Clinical Psychology Review, 10*, 1–41.

Loeber, R., & Ahonen, L. (2014). What are the policy implications of our knowledge on serious, violent, and chronic offenders. *Criminology & Public Policy, 13*, 117–125.

Loeber, R., Burke, J. D., & Pardini, D. A. (2009). Development and etiology of disruptive and delinquent behavior. *Annual Review of Clinical Psychology, 5*, 291–310.

Loeber, R., Byrd, A. L., & Farrington, D. P. (2015). Why developmental criminology is still coming of age: The influence of biological factors on within-individual change. In J. Morizot & L. Kazemian (Eds.), *The development of criminal and antisocial behavior: Theory, research and practical applications* (pp. 65–73). New York, NY: Springer.

Loeber, R., Farrington, D. P., Stouthamer-Loeber, M., Moffitt, T. E., & Caspi, A. (1998). The development of male offending: Key findings from the first decade of the Pittsburgh Youth Study. *Studies on Crime and Crime Prevention, 7*, 141–172.

Loeber, R., Farrington, D. P., Stouthamer-Loeber, M., Moffitt, T. E., Caspi, A., White, H. R., . . . Beyers, J. M. (2003). The development of male offending: Key findings from fourteen years of the Pittsburgh Youth Study. In T. P. Thornberry & M. D. Krohn (Eds.), *Taking stock of delinquency: An overview of findings from contemporary longitudinal studies* (pp. 93–136). New York, NY: Springer.

Loeber, R., Farrington, D. P., Stouthamer-Loeber, M., & van Kammen, W. B. (1998). *Antisocial behavior and mental health problems: Explanatory factors in childhood and adolescence.* Mahwah, NJ: Erlbaum.

Loeber, R., Farrington, D. P., Stouthamer-Loeber, M., & White, H. R. (Eds.). (2008). *Violence and serious theft: Development and prediction from childhood to adulthood.* New York, NY: Routledge.

Loeber R., Farrington, D. P., & Waschbusch, D. A. (1998). Serious and violent juvenile offenders. In R. Loeber & D. P. Farrington (Eds.), *Serious and violent juvenile offenders: Risk factors and successful interventions* (pp. 13–29). Thousand Oaks, CA: Sage.

Loeber, R., & Hay, D. (1997). Key issues in the development of aggression and violence from childhood to early adulthood. *Annual Review of Psychology, 48*, 371–410.

Loeber, R., Jennings, W. G, Ahonen, L., Piquero, A. R., & Farrington, D. P. (2017). *Female delinquency from childhood to young adulthood: Recent results from the Pittsburgh Girls Study.* New York, NY: Springer.

Loeber, R., & Le Blanc, M. (1990). Toward a developmental criminology. In M. Tonry (Ed.), *Crime and justice: A review of research* (Vol. 12, pp. 375–473). Chicago, IL: University of Chicago Press.

Loeber, R. & Pardini, D. (2008). Neurobiology and the development of violence: Common assumptions and controversies. *Philosophical Transactions of The Royal Society, 363*, 2491–2503.

Loeber, R., Slot, N. W., & Stouthamer-Loeber, M. (2008). A cumulative developmental model of risk and promotive factors. In R. Loeber, N. W. Slot, P. H. van der Laan, & M. Hoeve (Eds.), *Tomorrow's criminals: The development of child delinquency and effective interventions* (pp. 133–164). Burlington, VT: Ashgate.

Loeber, R., & Stouthamer-Loeber, M. (1996). The development of offending. *Criminal Justice and Behavior, 23*, 12–24.

Loeber, R., Wei, E., Stouthamer-Loeber, M., Huizanga, D., & Thornberry, T. P. (1999). Behavioral antecedents to serious and violent offending: Joint analyses from the Denver Youth Survey, Pittsburgh Youth Study and the Rochester Youth Development Study. *Studies on Crime & Crime Prevention, 8*, 245–263.

Loeber, R., Wung, P., Keenan, K., Giroux, B., Stouthamer-Loeber, M., van Kammen, W. B., & Maughan, B. (1993). Developmental pathways in disruptive child behavior. *Development and Psychopathology, 5*, 103–133.

Lombroso, C. (1876). *L'uomo delinquente* [The delinquent man]. Milan, Italy: Hoepli.

Lösel, F., & Bender, D. (2003). Protective factors and resilience. In D. P. Farrington & J. W. Coid (Eds.), *Early prevention of adult antisocial behavior* (pp. 130–204). Cambridge, England: Cambridge University Press.

Lösel, F., & Bender, D. (2006). Risk factors for serious and violent antisocial behaviour in children and youth. In A. Hagell & R. Jeyarajah-Dent (Eds.), *Children who commit acts of serious interpersonal violence: Messages for best practice* (pp. 42–72). London, England: Jessica Kingsley Publishers.

Loughran, T., & Nagin, D. S. (2006). Finite sample effects in group-based trajectory models. *Sociological Methods & Research, 35*, 250–278.

Lowe, K., & Dotterer, A. M. (2013). Parental monitoring, parental warmth, and minority youths' academic outcomes: Exploring the integrative model of parenting. *Journal of Youth and Adolescence, 42*, 1413–1425.

Lubke, G. H., Campbell, I., McArtor, D., Miller, P., Luningham, J., & van den Berg, S. M. (2017). Assessing model selection uncertainty using a bootstrap approach: An update. *Structural Equation Modeling: A Multidisciplinary Journal, 24*, 230–245.

Lussier, P. (2005). The criminal activity of sexual offenders in adulthood: Revisiting the specialization debate. *Sexual Abuse: A Journal of Research and Treatment, 17*, 269–292.

Lussier, P. (2015). Sex offending and developmental criminology: A research agenda for the description, explanation, and prediction of juvenile sex offending. In J. Morizot & L. Kazemian (Eds.), *The development of criminal and antisocial behavior: Theory, research and practical applications* (pp. 413–430). New York, NY: Springer.

Lussier, P., Corrado, R., Healey, J., Tzoumakis, S., & Deslauriers-Varin, N. (2011). The Cracow instrument for multi-problem violent youth: Examining the postdictive validity with a sample of preschoolers. *International Journal of Child, Youth and Family Studies, 2*, 294–329.

Lussier, P., Healey, J., Tzoumakis, S., Deslauriers-Varin, N., & Corrado R. (2010). *Criminal Activity of Adjudicated Youth 36 2010 The CRACOW instrument: A new framework for the assessment of multi-problem violent youth* (Research Report 2011–01). Ottawa, Ontario: National Crime Prevention Centre, Public Safety Canada. Retrieved from www.publicsafety.gc.ca

Lussier, P., McCuish, E., & Corrado, R. R. (2015). The adolescence-adulthood transition and desistance from crime: Examining the underlying structure of desistance. *Journal of Developmental and Life Course Criminology, 1*, 87–117.

Lussier, P., Tzoumakis, S., Cale, J., & Amirault, J. (2010). Criminal trajectories of adult sex offenders and the age effect: Examining the dynamic aspect of offending in adulthood. *International Criminal Justice Review, 20*, 147–168.

Lyngstad, T. H., & Skardhamar, T. (2013). Changes in criminal offending around the time of marriage. *Journal of Research in Crime and Delinquency, 50*, 608–615.

MacCallum, R. C., Zhang, S., Preacher, K. J., & Rucker, D. D. (2002). On the practice of dichotomization of quantitative variables. *Psychological Methods, 7*, 19–40.

MacDonald, J. M., Haviland, A., & Morral, A. R. (2009). Assessing the relationship between violent and nonviolent criminal activity among serious adolescent offenders. *Journal of Research in Crime and Delinquency, 46*, 553–580.

MacLeod, J. F. Grove, P. G., & Farrington, D. P. (2012). *Explaining criminal careers: Implications for justice policy*. Oxford, England: Oxford University Press.

MacMillan, H. L., Fleming, J. E., Trocmé, N., Boyle, M. H., Wong, M., Racine, Y. A., . . . Offord, D. R. (1997). Prevalence of child physical and sexual abuse in the community: Results from the Ontario Health Supplement. *JAMA, 278*, 131–135.

Magnusson, D. (1995). Individual development: A holistic integrated model. In P. Moen, G. H. Elder, & K. Lusher (Eds.), *Linking lives and contexts: Perspectives on the ecology of human development* (pp. 19–60). Washington, DC: APA Books.

Magnusson, D. (1998). The logic and implications of a person-oriented approach. In R. B. Cairns, L. R. Bergman, & J. Kagan (Eds.), *Methods and models for studying the individual* (pp. 33–64). Thousand Oaks, CA: Sage.

Magnusson, D. (1999). Holistic interactionism: A perspective for research on personality development. In L. A. Pervin & O. P. John (Eds.), *Handbook of personality: Theory and research* (2nd ed., pp. 219–247). New York, NY: Guilford Press.

Magnusson, D., & Stattin, H. (2006). The person in context: A holistic-interactionistic approach. In R. M. Lerner (Ed.), *Handbook of Child Psychology, Vol. 1: Theoretical models of human development* (6th ed., pp. 400–464). Hoboken, NJ: Wiley.

Maldonado-Molina, M. M., Piquero, A. R., Jennings, W. G., Bird, H., & Canino, G. (2009). Trajectories of delinquency among Puerto Rican children and adolescents at two sites. *Journal of Research in Crime and Delinquency, 46*, 144–181.

Manning, M., Smith, C., & Homel, R. (2013). Valuing developmental crime prevention. *Criminology & Public Policy, 12*, 305–332.

Manski, C. F. (2007). *Identification for prediction and decision*. Cambridge, MA: Harvard University Press.

Marshall, J. (2006). *Juvenile offending trajectories: A South Australian study*. Adelaide: Office of Crime Statistics and Research, South Australia Department of Justice.

Marshall, P. J. (2013). Coping with complexity: Developmental systems and multilevel analyses in developmental psychopathology. *Development and Psychopathology, 25*, 1311–1324.

Martinez, N. N., Lee, Y. J., Eck, J. E., & O, S. H. (2017). Ravenous wolves revisited: A systematic review of offending concentrations. *Crime Science, 6*, 10.

Maruna, S. (2001). *Making good: How ex-convicts reform and re-build their lives*. Washington, DC: American Psychological Association.

Maruna, S., & Toch, H. (2005). The impact of imprisonment on the desistance process. In J. Travis & C. Visher (Eds.), *Prisoner reentry and crime in America* (pp. 139–178). New York, NY: Cambridge University Press.

Mash, E. J., & Wolfe, D. A. (2019). *Abnormal child psychology* (7th ed.). Boston, MA: Cengage Learning.

Masten, A. S. (2006). Developmental psychopathology: Pathways to the future. *International Journal of Behavioral Development, 30*, 47–54.

Masten, A. S., Burt, K. B., & Coatsworth, J. D. (2006). Competence and psychopathology in development. In D. Cicchetti & D. J. Cohen (Eds.), *Developmental psychopathology: Risk, disorder and adaptation* (2nd ed., Vol. 3, pp. 696–738). Hoboken, NJ: Wiley.

Masten, A., S., & Cicchetti, D. (2010). Developmental cascades. *Development and Psychopathology, 22*, 491–495.

Masten, A. S., & Coatsworth, J. D. (1998). The development of competence in favorable and unfavorable environments: Lessons from research on successful children. *American Psychologist, 53*, 205–220.

Masyn, K. E., Petras, H., & Liu, W. (2014). Growth curve models with categorical outcomes. In G. Bruinsma & D. Weisburd (Eds.), *Encyclopedia of criminology and criminal justice* (pp. 2013–2025). New York, NY: Springer.

Maughan, B. (2005). Developmental trajectory modeling: A view from developmental psychopathology. *The ANNALS of the American Academy of Political and Social Science, 602*, 118–130.

Maxfield, M. G., Weiler, B. L., & Widom, C. S. (2000). Comparing self-reports and official records of arrests. *Journal of Quantitative Criminology, 16*, 87–110.

McAra, L., & McVie, S. (2012). Critical debates in developmental and life-course criminology. In M. Maguire, R. Morgan, & R. Reiner (Eds.), *The Oxford handbook of criminology* (5th ed., pp. 531–560). Oxford, England: Oxford University Press.

McArdle, J. J., & Epstein, D. (1987). Latent growth curves within developmental structural equation models. *Child Development, 58*, 110–133.

McArdle, J. J., & Nesselroade, J. R. (2014). *Longitudinal data analysis using structural equation models*. Washington, DC: American Psychological Association.

McCall, P. L., Land, K. C., & Parker, K. F. (2011). Heterogeneity in the rise and decline of city-level homicide rates, 1976–2005: A latent trajectory analysis. *Social Science Research, 40*, 363–378.

McCollister, K. E., French, M. T., & Fang, H. (2010). The cost of crime to society: New crime-specific estimates for policy and program evaluation. *Drug and Alcohol Dependence, 108*, 98–109.

McCormick, C. M., Kuo, S. I.-C., & Masten, A. S. (2011). Developmental tasks across the life span. In K. L. Fingerman, C. A. Berg, J. Smith, & T. C. Antonucci (Eds.), *Handbook of life-span development* (pp. 117–140). New York, NY: Springer.

McCuish, E. C., Corrado, R. R., Hart, S. D., & DeLisi, M. (2015). The role of symptoms of psychopathy in persistent violence over the criminal career into full adulthood. *Journal of Criminal Justice, 43*, 345–356.

McCuish, E. C., Corrado, R. R., Lussier, P., & Hart, S. D. (2014). Psychopathic traits and offending trajectories from early adolescence to adulthood. *Journal of Criminal Justice, 42,* 66–76.

McGee, T. R., & Farrington, D. P. (2010). Are there any true adult-onset offenders? *The British Journal of Criminology, 50,* 530–549.

McGee, T. R., & Farrington, D. P. (2016). Developmental and life-course theories of crime. In A. R. Piquero (Ed.), *The handbook of criminological theory* (pp. 336–354). Chichester, England: John Wiley & Sons.

McGloin, J. M., Sullivan, C. J., Piquero, A. R., Blokland, A., & Nieuwbeerta, P. (2011). Marriage and offending specialization: Expanding the impact of turning points and the process of desistance. *European Journal of Criminology, 8,* 361–376.

McLachlan, G., & Peel, D. (2000). *Finite mixture models.* New York, NY: Wiley.

McMillan, D., Hastings, R. P., Salter, D. C., & Skuse, D. H. (2008). Developmental risk factor research and sexual offending against children: A review of some methodological issues. *Archives of Sexual Behavior, 37,* 877–890.

Mehta, P. D., & West, S. G. (2000). Putting the individual back into individual growth curves. *Psychological Methods, 5,* 23–43.

Meredith, W., & Tisak, J. (1990). Latent curve analysis. *Psychometrika, 55,* 107–122.

Michel, G. F., Babik, I., Sheu, C.-F., & Campbell, J. M. (2014). Latent classes in the developmental trajectories of infant handedness. *Developmental Psychology, 50,* 349.

Miers, A. C., Blöte, A. W., de Rooij, M., Bokhorst, C. L., & Westenberg, P. M. (2013). Trajectories of social anxiety during adolescence and relations with cognition, social competence, and temperament. *Journal of Abnormal Child Psychology, 41,* 97–110.

Miller, P., Henry, D., & Votruba-Drzal, E. (2016). Strengthening causal inference in developmental research. *Child Development Perspectives, 10,* 275–280.

Miller, S., Malone, P. S., Dodge, K. A., & Conduct Problems Prevention Research Group (2010). Developmental trajectories of boys' and girls' delinquency: Sex differences and links to later adolescent outcomes. *Journal of Abnormal Child Psychology, 38,* 1021–1032.

Moffitt, T. E. (1993). Adolescence-limited and life-course-persistent antisocial behavior: A developmental taxonomy. *Psychological Review, 100,* 674–701.

Moffitt, T. E. (1994). Natural histories of delinquency. In E. G. M. Wietekamp & H.-J. Kerner (Eds.), *Cross-national longitudinal research on human development and criminal behavior* (pp. 3–61). Dordrecht, The Netherlands: Kluwer Academic Publishers.

Moffitt, T. E. (1997). Adolescence-limited and life-course-persistent offending: A complementary pair of developmental theories. In T.P. Thornberry (Ed.), *Advances in Criminological Theory, Vol. 7: Developmental theories of crime and delinquency* (pp. 11–54). New Brunswick, NJ: Transaction Publishers.

Moffitt, T. E. (2005). The new look of behavioral genetics in developmental psychopathology: Gene-environment interplay in antisocial behaviors. *Psychological Bulletin, 131,* 533–554.

Moffitt, T. E. (2006a). Life-course-persistent versus adolescence-limited antisocial behavior. In D. Cicchetti & D. J. Cohen (Eds.), *Developmental psychopathology: Risk, disorder, and adaptation* (2nd ed., Vol. 3, pp. 570–598). Hoboken, NJ: Wiley.

Moffitt, T. E. (2006b). A review of research on the taxonomy of life-course persistent versus adolescence-limited antisocial behavior. In F. T. Cullen, J. P. Wright, & K. R. Blevins (Eds.), *Taking stock: The status of criminological theory* (Vol. 15, pp. 277–311). New Brunswick, NJ: Transaction Publishers.

Moffitt, T. E. (2018). Male antisocial behavior in adolescence and beyond. *Nature Human Behaviour, 2,* 177–186.

Moffitt, T. E., Caspi, A., Dickson, N., Silva, P., & Stanton, W. (1996). Childhood-onset versus adolescent-onset antisocial conduct problems in males: Natural histories from ages 3 to 18 years. *Development and Psychopathology, 8,* 339–424.

Moffitt, T. E., Caspi, A., Harrington, H., & Milne, B. J. (2002). Males on the life-course-persistent and adolescence-limited pathways: Follow-up at age 26 years. *Development and Psychopathology, 14,* 179–207.

Moffitt, T. E., Caspi, A., Rutter, M., & Silva, P. A. (Eds.). (2001). *Sex differences in antisocial behaviour: Conduct disorder, delinquency, and violence in the Dunedin Longitudinal Study.* Cambridge, England: Cambridge University Press.

Molero, Y., Larsson, A., Tengström, A., & Eklund, J. (2015). Are offending trajectories identified in population sample studies relevant for treatment settings? A comparison of long-term offending trajectories in individuals treated for substance abuse in adolescence, to a matched general population sample. *Criminal Behaviour and Mental Health, 25,* 416–428.

Monahan, K. C., & Piquero, A. R. (2009). Investigating the longitudinal relation between offending frequency and offending variety. *Criminal Justice and Behavior, 36,* 653–673.

Monahan, K. C., & Steinberg, L. (2011). Accentuation of individual differences in social competence during the transition to adolescence. *Journal of Research on Adolescence, 21,* 576–585.

Monahan, K. C., Steinberg, L., Cauffman, E., & Mulvey, E. P. (2009). Trajectories of antisocial behavior and psychosocial maturity from adolescence to young adulthood. *Developmental Psychology, 45,* 1654–1668.

Monahan, K. C., Steinberg, L., Cauffman, E., & Mulvey, E. P. (2013). Psychosocial (im)maturity from adolescence to early adulthood: Distinguishing between adolescence-limited and persisting antisocial behavior. *Development and Psychopathology, 25,* 1093–1105.

Monsbakken, C. W., Lyngstad, T. H., & Skardhamar, T. (2013). Crime and the transition to parenthood. *British Journal of Criminology, 53,* 129–148.

Morin, A. J. S., Maïano, C., Nagengast, B., Marsh, H. W., Morizot, J., & Janosz, M. (2011). General growth mixture analysis of adolescents' developmental trajectories of anxiety: The impact of untested invariance assumptions on substantive interpretations. *Structural Equation Modeling: A Multidisciplinary Journal, 18,* 613–648.

Morizot, J. (2015). The contribution of temperament and personality traits to criminal and antisocial behavior development and desistance. In J. Morizot & E. Kazemian (Eds.), *The development of criminal and antisocial behavior: Theory, research, and practical applications* (pp. 137–165). New York, NY: Springer.

Morizot, J., & Le Blanc, M. (2007). Behavioral, self, and social control predictors of desistance from crime: A test of launch and contemporaneous effect models. *Journal of Contemporary Criminal Justice, 23*, 50–71.

Morizot, J. & Kazemian, L. (Eds.). (2015). *The development of criminal and antisocial behavior: Theory, research, and practical applications.* New York, NY: Springer.

Morris, N. A., & Slocum, L. A. (2012). Estimating country-level terrorism trends using group-based trajectory analyses: Latent class growth analysis and general mixture modeling. *Journal of Quantitative Criminology, 28*, 103–139.

Morris, R. G., & Piquero, A. R. (2013). For whom do sanctions deter and label? *Justice Quarterly, 30*, 5, 837–868.

Moule, R. K., Burt, C. H., Stewart, E. A., & Simons, R. L. (2015). Developmental trajectories of individuals' code of the street beliefs through emerging adulthood. *Journal of Research in Crime and Delinquency, 52*, 342–372.

Mrazek, P., & Haggerty, R. (1994). *Reducing risks for mental disorders: Frontiers for preventive intervention research.* Washington, DC: National Academy Press.

Mulaik, S. A. (2009). *Linear causal modeling with structural equations.* Boca Raton, FL: Chapman & Hall/CRC Press.

Mulford, C. F., Blachman-Demner, D. R., Pitzer, L., Schubert, C. A., Piquero, A. R., & Mulvey, E. P. (2018). Victim offender overlap: Dual trajectory examination of victimization and offending among young felony offenders over seven years. *Victims and Offenders: An International Journal of Evidence-Based Research, Policy, and Practice, 13*, 1–27.

Mulvey, E. P. (2014). Using developmental science to reorient our thinking about criminal offending in adolescence. *Journal of Research in Crime and Delinquency, 51*, 467–479.

Mulvey, E. P., Schubert, C. A., Piquero, A. R. (2014). *Pathways to Desistance—Final Technical Report.* Washington, DC: National Institute of Justice.

Mulvey, E. P., Steinberg, L., Fagan, J., Cauffman, E., Piquero, A. R., Chassin, L., . . . Losoya, S. H. (2004). Theory and research on desistance from antisocial activity among serious adolescent offenders. *Youth Violence and Juvenile Justice, 2*, 213–236.

Murphy, D. A., Brecht, M.-L., Huang, D., & Herbeck, D. M. (2012). Trajectories of delinquency from age 14 to 23 in the National Longitudinal Survey of Youth sample. *International Journal of Adolescence and Youth, 17*, 47–62.

Murray, J., Farrington, D. P., & Eisner, M. P. (2009). Drawing conclusions about causes from systematic reviews of risk factors: The Cambridge Quality Checklists. *Journal of Experimental Criminology, 5*, 1–23.

Muthén, B. (2010, September 7). Propensity score matching with SEM in Mplus. [Online user discussion interface comment]. Retrieved from www.statmodel.com.

Muthén, B. (2003). Statistical and substantive checking in growth mixture modeling: Comment on Bauer and Curran (2003). *Psychological Methods, 8,* 369–377.

Muthén, B. (2004). Latent variable analysis: Growth mixture modeling and related techniques for longitudinal data. In D. Kaplan (Ed.), *The SAGE handbook of quantitative methodology for the social sciences* (pp. 345–368). Thousand Oaks, CA: Sage.

Muthén, B., & Asparouhov, T. (2009). Growth mixture modeling: Analysis with non-Gaussian random effects. In G. Fitzmaurice, M. Davidian, G. Verbeke, & G. Molenberghs (Eds.), *Longitudinal data analysis* (pp. 143–165). Boca Raton, FL: Chapman & Hall/CRC Press.

Muthén, B., & Asparouhov, T. (2015). Growth mixture modeling with non-normal distributions. *Statistics in Medicine, 34,* 1041–1058.

Muthén, B., Brown, H. C., Hunter, A. M., Cook, I. A., & Leuchter, A. F. (2011). General approaches to analysis of course: Applying growth mixture modeling to randomized trials of depression medication. In P. E. Shrout (Ed.), *Causality and psychopathology: Finding the determinants of disorders and their cures* (pp. 159–178). New York, NY: Oxford University Press.

Muthén, B., Brown, C. H., Masyn, K., Jo, B., Khoo, S.-T., Yang, C.-C., . . . Liao, J. (2002). General growth mixture modeling for randomized preventive interventions. *Biostatistics, 3,* 459–475.

Muthén, B., & Muthén, L. K. (2000). Integrating person-centered and variable-centered analyses: Growth mixture modeling with latent trajectory classes. *Alcoholism: Clinical and Experimental Research, 24,* 882–891.

Muthén, B., & Shedden, K. (1999). Finite mixture modeling with mixture outcomes using the EM algorithm. *Biometrics, 55,* 463–469.

Muthén L., & Muthén, B. (1998–2012). *Mplus user's guide* (7th ed.). Los Angeles, CA: Muthén & Muthén.

Na, C., Loughran, T. A., & Paternoster, R. (2015). On the importance of treatment effect heterogeneity in experimentally-evaluated criminal justice interventions. *Journal of Quantitative Criminology, 31,* 289–310.

Na, C., & Paternoster, R. (2012). Can self-control change substantially over time? Rethinking the relationship between self- and social control. *Criminology, 50,* 427–462.

Nagin, D. S. (1999). Analyzing developmental trajectories: A semiparametric, group-based approach. *Psychological Methods, 4,* 139–157.

Nagin, D. S. (2004). Response to "Methodological Sensitivities to Latent Class Analysis of Long-Term Criminal Trajectories." *Journal of Quantitative Criminology, 20,* 27–35.

Nagin, D. S. (2005). *Group-based modeling of development.* Cambridge, MA: Harvard University Press.

Nagin, D. S. (2011). Group-based trajectory modeling: An overview. In A. R. Piquero & D. Weisburd (Eds.), *Handbook of quantitative criminology* (pp. 53–67). New York, NY: Springer.

Nagin, D. S. (2016). Group-based trajectory modeling and criminal career research. *Journal of Research in Crime and Delinquency, 53,* 356–371.

Nagin, D. S., Cullen, F., & Jonson, C. L. (2009). Imprisonment and reoffending. In M. Tonry (Ed.), *Crime and justice* (Vol. 38, pp. 115–200). Chicago, IL: University of Chicago Press.

Nagin, D. S., Farrington, D. P., & Moffitt, T. E. (1995). Life-course trajectories of different types of offenders. *Criminology, 33,* 111–139.

Nagin, D. S., Jones, B. L., Lima Passos, V., & Tremblay, R. E. (2018). Group-based multi-trajectory modeling. *Statistical Methods in Medical Research, 27,* 2015–2023.

Nagin, D. S., & Land, K. C. (1993). Age, criminal careers, and population heterogeneity: Specification and estimation of a nonparametric, mixed Poisson model. *Criminology, 31,* 327–362.

Nagin, D. S., & Odgers, C. L. (2010a). Group-based trajectory modeling (nearly) two decades later. *Journal of Quantitative Criminology, 26,* 445–453.

Nagin, D. S., & Odgers, C. L. (2010b). Group-based trajectory modeling in clinical research. *Annual Review of Clinical Psychology, 6,* 109–138.

Nagin, D. S., Pagani, L., Tremblay, R. E., & Vitaro, F. (2003). Life course turning points: The effect of grade retention on physical aggression. *Development and Psychopathology, 15,* 343–361.

Nagin, D. S., & Piquero, A. R. (2010). Using the group-based trajectory model to study crime over the life course. *Journal of Criminal Justice Education, 21,* 105–116.

Nagin, D. S., & Tremblay, R. E. (1999). Trajectories of boys' physical aggression, opposition, and hyperactivity on the path to physically violent and nonviolent juvenile delinquency. *Child Development, 70,* 1181–1196.

Nagin, D. S., & Tremblay, R. E. (2001). Analyzing developmental trajectories of distinct but related behaviors: A group-based method. *Psychological Methods, 6,* 18–34.

Nagin, D. S., & Tremblay, R. E. (2005a). What has been learned from group-based trajectory modeling? Examples from physical aggression and other problem behaviors. *The ANNALS of the American Academy of Political and Social Science, 602,* 82–117.

Nagin, D. S., & Tremblay, R. E. (2005b). Developmental trajectory groups: Fact or a useful statistical fiction? *Criminology, 43,* 873–904.

Nation, M., Crusto, C., Wandersman, A., Kumpfer, K. L., Seybolt, D., Morrissey-Kane, E., & Davino, K. (2003). What works in prevention: Principles of effective prevention programs. *American Psychologist, 58,* 449–456.

National Research Council. (2013). *Reforming juvenile justice: A developmental approach.* Washington, DC: The National Academies Press.

Natsuaki, M. N., Ge, X., & Wenk, E. (2008). Continuity and changes in the developmental trajectories of criminal career: Examining the roles of timing of first arrest and high school graduation. *Journal of Youth and Adolescence, 37,* 431–444.

Neale, M. C., Boker, S. M., Xie, G., & Maes, H. H. (2003). *Mx: Statistical modeling* (6th ed.). Richmond: Department of Psychiatry, Virginia Commonwealth University.

Neill, F. (2006). A desistance paradigm for offender management. *Criminology and Criminal Justice, 6,* 39–62.

Newsom, J. T. (2015). *Longitudinal structural equation modeling: A comprehensive introduction.* New York, NY: Routledge.

Nicol, R., Stretch, D., Whitney, I., Jones, K., Garfield, P., Turner, K., & Stanion, B. (2000). Mental health needs and services for severely troubled and troubling young people including young offenders in an N. H. S. Region. *Journal of Adolescence, 23,* 243–261.

Nielsen, J. D., Rosenthal, J. S., Sun, Y., Day, D. M., Bevc, I., & Duchesne, T. (2014). Group-based criminal trajectory analysis using cross-validation criteria. *Communications in Statistics: Theory and Methods, 43,* 4337–4356.

Nieuwbeerta, P., Nagin, D. S., & Blokland, A. A. J. (2009). Assessing the impact of first-time imprisonment on offenders' subsequent criminal career development: A matched samples comparison. *Journal of Quantitative Criminology, 25,* 227–257.

Nores, M. Belfield, C. R., Barnett, W. S., & Schweinhart, L. (2005). Updating the economic impacts of the High/Scope Perry Preschool Program. *Educational Evaluation and Policy Analysis, 27,* 245–261.

Nylund, K. L., Asparouhov, T., & Muthén, B. (2007). Deciding on the number of classes in latent class analysis and growth mixture modeling: A Monte Carlo simulation study. *Structural Equation Modeling: A Multidisciplinary Journal, 14,* 535–569.

Odgers, C. L., Moffitt, T. E., Broadbent, J. M., Dickson, N., Hancox, R. J., Harrington, H., . . . Caspi, A. (2008). Female and male antisocial trajectories: From childhood origins to adult outcomes. *Development and Psychopathology, 20,* 673–716.

Offord, D. R., Boyle, M. H., Racine, Y. A., Fleming, J. E., Cadman, D. T., Blum, H. M., . . . Woodward, C. A. (1992). Outcome, prognosis, and risk in a longitudinal follow-up study. *Journal of the American Academy of Child & Adolescent Psychiatry, 31,* 916–923.

Offord, D. R., Boyle, M. H., Szatmari, P., Rae-Grant, N. I., Links, P. S., Cadman, D. T., . . . Woodward, C. A. (1987). Ontario Child Health Study: II. Six-month prevalence of disorder and rates of service utilization. *Archives of General Psychiatry, 44,* 832.

Ontario Child Health Study. (2018). Retrieved from http://ontariochildhealthstudy.ca /ochs/about/1983-ochs/

Opsal, T. (2012). "Livin' on the straights": Identity, desistance, and work among women post-incarceration. *Sociological Inquiry, 82,* 378–403.

Osgood, D. W. (2005). Making sense of crime and the life course. *The Annals of the American Academy of Political and Social Science, 602,* 196–211.

Osgood, D. W. (2010). Statistical models of life events and criminal behavior. In A. R. Piquero & D. Weisburd (Eds.), *Handbook of quantitative criminology* (pp. 375–396). New York, NY: Springer.

Osgood, D. W., Foster, E. M., Flanagan, C., & Ruth, G. R. (2005). *On our own without a net: The transition to adulthood for vulnerable populations.* Chicago, IL: University of Chicago Press.

Osgood, D. W., Ruth, G., Eccles, J. S., Jacobs, J. E., & Barber, B. L. (2005). Six paths to adulthood: Fast starters, partners without careers, educated partners, educated singles, working singles and slow starters. In R. A. Setterstein, Jr. F. F. Furstenberg, Jr., & R. C. Rumbaut (Eds.), *On the frontier of adulthood* (pp. 320–355). Chicago, IL: University of Chicago Press.

Osofsky, J. D., & Lieberman, A. F. (2011). A call for integrating a mental health perspective into systems of care for abused and neglected infants and young children. *American Psychologist, 66*, 120–128.

Ouimet, M., & Le Blanc, M. (1996). The role of life experiences in the continuation of the adult criminal career. *Criminal Behavior and Mental Health, 6*, 73–97.

Ouwehand, C., de Ridder, D. T., & Bensing, J. M. (2007). A review of successful aging models: Proposing proactive coping as an important additional strategy. *Clinical Psychology Review, 27*, 873–884.

Overton, W. F. (2015). Process and relational developmental systems. In W. F. Overton & P. C. M. Molenaar (Eds.), *Handbook of child psychology and developmental science: Theory and method* (7th ed., Vol. 1, pp. 9–62). New York, NY: Wiley.

Pardini, D. (2016). Empirically based strategies for preventing juvenile delinquency. *Child and Adolescent Psychiatric Clinics of North America, 25*, 257–268.

Parker, K. F., Stansfield, R., & McCall, P. L. (2016). Temporal changes in racial violence, 1980 to 2006: A latent trajectory approach. *Journal of Criminal Justice, 47*, 1–11.

Pastor, D. A., & Gagné, P. (2013). Mean and covariance structure mixture models. In G. R. Hancock & R. O. Mueller (Eds.), *Structural equation modeling: A second course* (2nd ed., pp. 343–393). Charlotte, NC: Information Age Publishing.

Paternoster, R. (2017). Happenings, acts, and actions: Articulating the meaning and implications of human agency for criminology. *Journal of Developmental and Life-Course Criminology, 3*, 350–372.

Paternoster, R., Bachman, R., Bushway, S., Kerrison, E., & O'Connell, D. (2015). Human agency and explanations of criminal desistance: Arguments for a rational choice theory. *Journal of Developmental Life Course Criminology, 1*, 209–235.

Paternoster, R., Bachman, R., Kerrison, E., O'Connell, D., & Smith, L. (2016). Desistance from crime and identity: An empirical test with survival time. *Criminal Justice and Behavior, 43*, 1204–1224.

Paternoster, R., & Bushway, S. (2009). Desistance and the 'feared self:' Toward an identity theory of criminal desistance. *Journal of Criminal Law and Criminology, 99*, 1103–1156.

Patrick, C. J., Zempolich, K. A., & Levenston, G. K. (1997). Emotionality and violent behavior in psychopaths: A biosocial analysis. In A. Raine, P. A. Brennan, D. P. Farrington, & S. A. Mednick (Eds.), *Biosocial bases of violence* (pp. 145–161). New York, NY: Plenum.

Patterson, G. R. (1986). Performance models for antisocial boys. *American Psychologist, 41*, 432–444.

Patterson, G. R. (1993). Orderly change in a stable world: The antisocial trait as Chimera. *Journal of Consulting and Clinical Psychology, 61*, 911–919.

Patterson, G. R. (1996). Some characteristics of a developmental theory for early-onset delinquency. In M. F. Lenzenweger & J. J. Haugaard (Eds.), *Frontiers of developmental psychopathology* (pp. 81–124). New York, NY: Oxford University Press.

Patterson, G. R., Capaldi, D., & Bank, L. (1991). An early starter model for predicting delinquency. In D. J. Pepler & K. H. Rubin (Eds.), *The development and treatment of childhood aggression* (pp. 139–168). Hillsdale, NJ: Erlbaum.

Patterson, G. R., DeBaryshe, B., D., & Ramsey, E. (1989). A developmental perspective on antisocial behavior. *American Psychologist, 44*, 329–335.

Patterson, G. R., Reid, J. B., & Dishion, T. J. (1992). *A social interactional approach: Antisocial boys* (Vol. 4). Eugene, OR: Castalia.

Patterson, G. R., & Yoerger, K. (1993). Developmental models for delinquent behavior. In S. Hodgins (Ed.), *Mental disorder and crime* (pp. 140–172). Thousand Oaks, CA: Sage.

Patterson, G. R., & Yoerger, K. (1997). A developmental model for late-onset delinquency. In D. W. Osgood (Ed.), *Motivation and delinquency: Vol. 44 of the Nebraska Symposium on Motivation* (pp. 119–177). Lincoln: University of Nebraska Press.

Patterson, G. R., & Yoerger, K. (1999). Intraindividual growth in covert antisocial behavior: A necessary precursor to chronic juvenile and adult arrests? *Criminal Behavior and Mental Health, 9*, 24–38.

Patterson, G. R., & Yoerger, K. (2002). A developmental model for early- and late-onset delinquency. In J. B. Reid, G. R. Patterson, & J. Snyder (Eds.), *Antisocial behavior in children and adolescents: A developmental analysis and model for intervention* (pp. 147–172). Washington, DC: American Psychological Association.

Paul, G. I. (1967). Strategy of outcome research in psychotherapy. *Journal of Consulting Psychology, 31*, 109–118.

Payne, J. L., & Piquero, A. R. (2018). The concordance of self-reported and officially recorded criminal onset: Results from a sample of Australian prisoners. *Crime & Delinquency, 64*, 448–471.

Pepler, D., Jiang, D., Craig, W., & Connolly, J. (2008). Developmental trajectories of bullying and associated factors. *Child Development, 79*, 325–338.

Petersen, A. C., & Leffert, N. (1995). What is special about adolescence? In M. Rutter (Ed.), *Psychosocial disturbances in young people: Challenges for prevention* (pp. 3–36). Cambridge, England: Cambridge University Press.

Petersilia, J. (1980). Criminal career research: A review of recent evidence. In M. Tonry (Ed.), *Crime and justice: A review of research* (Vol. 2, pp. 321–379). Chicago, IL: University of Chicago Press.

Petras, H., & Masyn, K. (2010). General growth mixture analysis with antecedents and consequences of change. In A. R. Piquero & D. Weisburd (Eds.), *Handbook of quantitative criminology* (pp. 69–100). New York, NY: Springer.

Peugh, J., & Fan, X. (2012). How well does growth mixture modeling identify heterogeneous growth trajectories? A simulation study examining GMM's performance characteristics. *Structural Equation Modeling: A Multidisciplinary Journal, 19*, 204–226.

Pickles, A., & Angold, A. (2003). Natural categories or fundamental dimensions: On carving nature at the joints and the rearticulation of psychopathology. *Development and Psychopathology, 15*, 529–551.

Pickles, A., & Hill, J. (2006). Developmental pathways. In D. Cicchetti & D. J. Cohen (Eds.), *Developmental psychopathology: Theory and method* (2nd ed., Vol. 1, pp. 211–243). Hoboken, NJ: Wiley.

Piquero, A., & Mazerolle, P. J. (2001). Introduction. In A. Piquero & P. J. Mazerolle (Eds.), *Life-course criminology: Contemporary and classic readings* (pp. viii–xx). Belmont, CA: Wadsworth/Thompson Learning.

Piquero, A. R. (2000). Assessing the relationships between gender, chronicity, seriousness, and offense skewness in criminal offending. *Journal of Criminal Justice, 28,* 103–115.

Piquero, A. R. (2004a). *What have we learned about the natural history of criminal offending from longitudinal studies?* Paper presented at the National Institute of Justice, Washington, DC.

Piquero, A. R. (2004b). Somewhere between persistence and desistance: The intermittency of criminal careers. In S. Maruna & R. Immarigeon (Eds.), *After crime and punishment: Pathways to offender reintegration* (pp. 102–125). Cullompton, England: Willan.

Piquero, A. R. (2008). Taking stock of developmental trajectories of criminal activity over the life course. In A. M. Liberman (Ed.), *The long view of crime: A synthesis of longitudinal research* (pp. 23–78), New York, NY: Springer.

Piquero, A. R., Blumstein, A., Brame, R., Haapanen, R., Mulvey, E. P., & Nagin, D. S. (2001). Assessing the impact of exposure time and incapacitation on longitudinal trajectories of criminal offending. *Journal of Adolescent Research, 16,* 54–74.

Piquero, A. R., Brame, R., Mazerolle, P., & Haapanen, R. (2002). Crime in emerging adulthood. *Criminology, 40,* 137–170.

Piquero, A. R., & Brezina, T. (2001). Testing Moffitt's account of adolescence-limited delinquency. *Criminology, 39,* 353–370.

Piquero, A. R., & Buka, S. L. (2002). Linking juvenile and adult patterns of criminal activity in the Providence cohort of the National Collaborative Perinatal Project. *Journal of Criminal Justice, 30,* 259–272.

Piquero, A. R., Daigle, L. E., Gibson, C., Piquero, N. L., & Tibbetts, S. G. (2007). Are life-course-persistent offenders at risk for adverse health outcomes? *Journal of Research in Crime and Delinquency, 44,* 185–207.

Piquero, A. R., Farrington, D. P, & Blumstein, A. (2003). The criminal career paradigm: Background and recent developments. In M. Tonry (Ed.), *Crime and justice: A review of research* (Vol. 30, pp. 359–506). Chicago, IL: University of Chicago Press.

Piquero, A. R., Farrington, D. P., & Blumstein, A. (2007). *Key issues in criminal career research: New analyses from the Cambridge Study of Delinquent Development.* Cambridge, England: Cambridge University Press.

Piquero, A. R., Farrington, D. P., Fontaine, N. M., Vincent, G., Coid, J., & Ullrich, S. (2012). Childhood risk, offending trajectories, and psychopathy at age 48 years in the Cambridge Study in Delinquent Development. *Psychology, Public Policy, and Law, 18,* 577–598.

Piquero, A. R., Farrington, D. P., Nagin, D. S., & Moffitt, T. E. (2010). Trajectories of offending and their relation to life failure in late middle age: Findings from the Cambridge Study in Delinquent Development. *Journal of Research in Crime and Delinquency, 47*, 151–173.

Piquero, A. R., Farrington, D. P., Shepherd, J. P., & Auty, K. (2014). Offending and early death in the Cambridge Study in Delinquent Development. *Justice Quarterly, 31*, 445–472.

Piquero, A. R., Farrington, D. P., Welsh, B. C., Tremblay, R., & Jennings, W. G. (2009). Effects of early family/parent training programs on antisocial behavior and delinquency. *Journal of Experimental Criminology, 5*, 83–120.

Piquero, A. R., Gonzalez, J. M. R., & Jennings, W. G. (2015). Developmental trajectories and antisocial behavior over the life-course. In J. Morizot & E. Kazemian (Eds.), *The development of criminal and antisocial behavior: Theory, research and practical applications* (pp. 75–88). New York, NY: Springer.

Piquero, A. R., Jennings, W. G., & Barnes, J. C. (2012). Violence in criminal careers: A review of the literature from a developmental life-course perspective. *Aggression and Violent Behavior, 17*, 171–179.

Piquero, A. R., Jennings, W. G., Diamond, B., Farrington, D. P., Tremblay, R. E., Welsh, B. C., & Gonzalez, J. M. R. (2016). A meta-analysis update on the effects of early family/parent training programs on antisocial behavior and delinquency. *Journal of Experimental Criminology, 12*, 229–248.

Piquero, A. R., Jennings, W. G., & Farrington, D. P. (2013). The monetary costs of crime to middle adulthood: Findings from the Cambridge Study in Delinquent Development. *Journal of Research in Crime and Delinquency, 50*, 53–74.

Piquero, A. R., Jennings, W. G., Farrington, D. P., Diamond, B., & Gonzalez, J. M. R. (2016). A meta-analysis update on the effectiveness of early self-control and improvement programs to improve self-control and reduce delinquency. *Journal of Experimental Criminology, 12*, 249–264.

Piquero, A. R., Monahan, K. C., Glasheen, C., Schubert, C. A., & Mulvey, E. P. (2012). Does time matter? Comparing trajectory concordance and covariate association using time-based and age-based assessments. *Crime & Delinquency, 59*, 738–763.

Piquero, A. R., Paternoster, R., Mazerolle, P., Brame, R., & Dean, C. W. (1999). Onset age and offense specialization. *Journal of Research in Crime and Delinquency, 36*, 275–299.

Piquero, A. R., Shepherd, I., Shepherd, J. P., & Farrington, D. P. (2011). Impact of offending trajectories on health: disability, hospitalization, and death in middle-aged men in the Cambridge Study in Delinquent Development. *Criminal Behavior and Mental Health, 21*, 189–201.

Piquero, A. R., Schubert, C. A., & Brame, R. (2014). Comparing official and self-report records of offending across gender and race/ethnicity in a longitudinal study of serious youthful offenders. *Journal of Research in Crime and Delinquency, 51*, 526–556.

Piquero, A. R., Sullivan, C. J., & Farrington, D. P. (2010). Assessing differences between short-term, high-rate offenders and long-term, low-rate offenders. *Criminal Justice and Behavior, 37*, 1309–1329.

Piquero, A. R., Theobald, D., & Farrington, D. P. (2014). The overlap between offending trajectories, criminal violence, and intimate partner violence. *International Journal of Offender Therapy and Comparative Criminology, 58,* 286–302.

Piquero, A. R., & Weisburd, D. (Eds.). (2010). *Handbook of quantitative criminology.* New York, NY: Springer.

Piquero, N. L., & Piquero, A. R. (2006). Democracy and intellectual property: Examining trajectories of software piracy. *The ANNALS of the American Academy of Political and Social Science, 605,* 104–127.

Piquero, N. L., Piquero, A. R., & Farrington, D. P. (2010). Criminal offender trajectories and (white-collar) occupational prestige. *American Journal of Criminal Justice, 35,* 134–143.

Preacher, K. J., & Merkle, E. C. (2012). The problem of model selection uncertainty in structural equation modeling. *Psychological Methods, 17,* 1–14.

Preacher, K. J., Wichman, A. L., MacCallum, R. C., & Briggs, N. E. (2008). *Latent growth curve modeling.* Thousand Oaks, CA: Sage.

Prendergast, M., Huang, D., Evans, E., & Hser, Y.-I. (2010). Are there gender differences in arrest trajectories among adult drug abuse treatment participants? *Journal of Drug Issues, 40,* 7–26.

Prior, D., Farrow, K., Hughes, N., Kelly, G., Manders. G., White, S., & Wilkinson, B. (2011). *Maturity, young adults and criminal justice: A literature review.* Birmingham, England: Institute of Applied Social studies, School of Social Policy, University of Birmingham. Retrieved from www.t2a.org.uk

Public Safety Canada. (2016). *Tyler's troubled life: The study of one young man's path towards a life of crime* (Research Division, Catalogue No. PS18–33/2016E-PDF). Ontario: Author. Retrieved from www.publicsafety.gc.ca

Raftery, A. E. (1995). Bayesian model selection in social research. *Sociological Methodology, 25,* 111–163.

Ram, N., & Grimm, K. J. (2007). Using simple and complex growth models to articulate developmental change: Matching theory to method. *International Journal of Behavioral Development, 31,* 303–316.

Ram, N., & Grimm, K. J. (2009). Methods and measures: Growth mixture modeling: A method for identifying differences in longitudinal change among unobserved groups. *International Journal of Behavioral Development, 33,* 565–576.

Ramaswamy, V., Desarbo, W. S., Reibstein, D. J., & Robinson, W. T. (1993). An empirical pooling approach for estimating marketing mix elasticities with PIMS data. *Marketing Science, 12,* 103–124.

Raudenbush, S. W. (2001). Comparing personal trajectories and drawing causal inferences from longitudinal data. *Annual Review of Psychology, 52,* 501–525.

Raudenbush, S. W. (2005). How do we study "what happens next"? *The ANNALS of the American Academy of Political and Social Science, 602,* 131–144.

Raudenbush, S. W., & Bryk, A. S. (2002). *Hierarchical linear models: Applications and data analysis methods* (2nd ed.). Thousand Oaks, CA: Sage.

R Development Core Team (2009). *R: A language and environment for statistical computing*. Vienna, AT: R Foundation for Statistical Computing. Retrieved from www.R-project.org

Reid, J. B., Patterson, G. R., & Snyder, J. (Eds.). (2002). *Antisocial behavior in children and adolescents: A developmental analysis and model for intervention*. Washington, DC: American Psychological Association.

Reijntjes, A., Vermande, M., Goossens, F. A., Olthof, T., van de Schoot, R., Aleva, L., & van der Meulen, M. (2013). Developmental trajectories of bullying and social dominance in youth. *Child Abuse & Neglect, 37*, 224–234.

Rein, M., & Winship, C. (2000). The danger of strong causal reasoning in social policy. *Society, 36*, 38–46.

Reingle, J. M., Jennings, W. G., & Maldonado-Molina, M. M. (2011). The mediated effect of contextual risk factors on trajectories of violence: Results from a nationally representative, longitudinal sample of Hispanic adolescents. *American Journal of Criminal Justice, 36*, 327–343.

Reingle, J. M., Jennings, W. J., & Maldonado-Molina, M. M. (2012). Risk and protective factors for trajectories of violent delinquency among a nationally representative sample of early adolescents. *Youth Violence and Juvenile Justice, 3*, 260–276.

Reppucci, N. D., Fried, C. S., & Schmidt, M. G. (2002). Youth violence: Risk and protective factors. In R. R. Corrado, R. Roesch, S. D. Hart, & J. K. Gierowski (Eds.), *Multi-problem violent youth: A foundation for comparative research on needs, interventions and outcomes* (pp. 3–22). Amsterdam, The Netherlands: IOS Press.

Rhodes, W. (2013). Machine learning approaches as a tool for effective offender risk prediction. *Criminology & Public Policy, 12*, 507–510.

Rindskopf, D. (2003). Mixture or homogeneous? Comment on Bauer and Curran (2003). *Psychological Methods, 8*, 364–368.

Rittel, H. W., & Webber, M. M. (1973). Dilemmas in a general theory of planning. *Policy Sciences, 4*, 155–169.

Roberts, B. W., Walton, K. E., & Viechtbauer, W. (2006). Patterns of mean-level change in personality traits across the life course: A meta-analysis of longitudinal studies. *Psychological Bulletin, 132*, 1–25.

Robins, L. N. (1966). *Deviant children grown up: A sociological and psychiatric study of sociopathic personality*. Baltimore, MD: Williams & Wilkins.

Robins, L. N., & Price, R. K. (1991). Adult disorders predicted by childhood conduct problems: Results from the NIMH Epidemiologic Catchment Area Project. *Psychiatry, 54*, 116–132.

Rocque, M. (2014). The lost concept: The (re)emerging link between maturation and desistance from crime. *Criminology & Criminal Justice, 15*, 340–360.

Rocque, M. (2017). *Desistance from crime: New advances in theory and research*. New York, NY: Palgrave Macmillan.

Roebuck, J. B. (1967). *Criminal typology*. Springfield, IL: Charles C Thomas.

Roeder, K., Lynch, K. G., & Nagin, D. S. (1999). Modeling uncertainty in latent class membership: A case study in criminology. *Journal of the American Statistical Association, 94*, 766–776.

Roisman, G. I., Aguilar, B., & Egeland, B. (2004). Antisocial behavior in the transition to adulthood: The independent and interactive roles of developmental history and emerging developmental tasks. *Development and Psychopathology, 16*, 857–871.

Ronel, N., & Elisha, E. (2011). A different perspective: Introducing positive criminology. *International Journal of Offender Therapy and Comparative Criminology, 55*, 305–325.

Ronel, N., & Elisha, E. (2014). Positive criminology in practice. *International Journal of Offender Therapy and Comparative Criminology, 58*, 1389–1407.

Ronis, S. T., & Borduin, C. M. (2013). Antisocial behavior trajectories of adolescents and emerging adults with histories of sexual aggression. *Psychology of Violence, 3*, 367–380.

Roth, J. L., & Brooks-Gunn, J. (2003). What is a youth development program: Identification of defining principles. In F. Jacobs, D. Wertlieb, & R. M. Lerner (Eds.), *Handbook of applied developmental science: Promoting positive child, adolescent, and family development though research, policies, and programs* (Vol. 2, pp. 197–223). Thousand Oaks, CA: Sage.

Rothermund, K., & Brandtstädter, J. (2003). Coping with deficits and losses in later life: From compensatory action to accommodation. *Psychology and Aging, 18*, 896–905.

Rubin, D. B. (2008). For objective causal inference, design trumps analysis. *The Annals of Applied Statistics, 2*, 808–840.

Rühs, F., Greve, W., & Kappes, C. (2017). Coping with criminal victimization and fear of crime: The protective role of accommodative self-regulation. *Legal and Criminological Psychology, 22*, 359–377.

Rutter, M., Giller, H., & Hagell, A. (1998). *Antisocial behavior by young people.* Cambridge, England: Cambridge University Press.

Rutter, M., Pickles, A., Murray, R., & Eaves, L. (2001). Testing hypotheses on specific environmental causal effects on behavior. *Psychological Bulletin, 127*, 291–324.

Rutter, M., & Sroufe, L. A. (2000). Developmental psychopathology: Concepts and challenges. *Development and Psychopathology, 12*, 265–296.

Ryan, J. P., Hernandez, P. M., & Herz, D. (2007). Developmental trajectories of offending for male adolescents leaving foster care. *Social Work Research, 31*, 83–93.

Ryan, J. P., & Testa, M. F. (2005). Child maltreatment and juvenile delinquency: Investigating the role of placement and placement instability. *Children and Youth Services Review, 27*, 227–249.

Ryan, J. P., Testa, M. F., & Zhai, F. (2008). African American males in foster care and the risk of delinquency: The value of social bonds and permanence. *Child Welfare, 87*, 115–140.

Ryff, C. D. (1989). Happiness is everything, or is it? Explorations on the meaning of psychological well-being. *Journal of Personality and Social Psychology, 57*, 1069–1081.

Salihovic, S., Özdemir, M., & Kerr, M. (2014). Trajectories of adolescent psychopathic traits. *Journal of Psychopathology and Behavioral Assessment, 36,* 47–59.

Salihovic, S., & Stattin, H. (2017). Psychopathic traits and delinquency trajectories in adolescence. *Journal of Psychopathology and Behavioral Assessment, 39,* 15–24.

Sample, L. L., & Bray, T. M. (2006). Are sex offenders different? An examination of rearrest patterns. *Criminal Justice Policy Review, 17,* 83–102.

Sampson, R. J. (2001). Foreword. In A. R. Piquero & P. J. Mazerolle (Eds.), *Life-course criminology: Contemporary and classic readings* (p. v–vii). Belmont, CA: Wadsworth/Thompson Learning.

Sampson, R. J., & Laub, J. H. (1990). Crime and deviance over the life course: The salience of adult social bonds. *American Sociological Review, 55,* 609–627.

Sampson, R. J., & Laub, J. H. (1993). *Crime in the making: Pathways and turning points through life.* Cambridge, MA: Harvard University Press.

Sampson, R. J., & Laub, J. H. (1997). A life-course theory of cumulative disadvantage and the stability of delinquency. In T. P. Thornberry (Ed.), *Advances in criminological theory: Developmental theories of crime and delinquency* (Vol. 7, p. 133–161). New Brunswick, NJ: Transaction Publishers.

Sampson, R. J., & Laub, J. H. (2003). Life-course desisters? Trajectories of crime among delinquent boys followed to age 70. *Criminology, 41,* 555–592.

Sampson, R. J., & Laub, J. H. (2005a). A life-course view of the development of crime. *The ANNALS of the American Academy of Political and Social Science, 602,* 12–45.

Sampson, R. J., & Laub, J. H. (2005b). Seductions of method: Rejoinder to Nagin and Tremblay's "Developmental Trajectory Groups: Fact or Fiction?" *Criminology, 43,* 905–913.

Sampson, R. J., & Laub, J. H. (2005c). A general age-graded theory of crime: Lessons learned and the future of life-course criminology. In D. P. Farrington (Ed.), *Integrated developmental and life-course theories of offending* (Advances in Criminological Theory, Vol. 14, pp. 165–181). New Brunswick, NJ: Transaction.

Sampson, R. J., & Laub, J. H. (2009). A life-course theory and long-term project on trajectories of crime. *Monatsschrift fuer Kriminologie und Strafrechtsreform, 92,* 226–239.

Sampson, R. J., & Laub, J. H. (2016). Turning points and the future of life-course criminology: Reflections on the 1986 Criminal Careers report. *Journal of Research in Crime and Delinquency, 53,* 321–335.

Sampson, R. J., Laub, J. H., & Eggleston, E. P. (2004). On the robustness and validity of groups: Response to Daniel Nagin. *Journal of Quantitative Criminology, 20,* 37–42.

Sampson, R. J., Laub, J. H., & Wimer, C. (2006). Does marriage reduce crime? A counterfactual approach to within-individual causal effects. *Criminology, 44,* 465–508.

Sampson, R. J., Winship, C., & Knight, C. (2013). Translating causal claims: Principles and strategies for policy-relevant criminology. *Criminology & Public Policy, 12,* 587–616.

Sanders, M. R. (1999). Triple P-Positive Parenting Program: Towards an empirically validated multilevel parenting and family support strategy for the prevention of behavior and emotional problems in children. *Clinical Child and Family Psychology Review, 2,* 71–90.

Savolainen, J. (2009). Work, family, and criminal desistance: Adult social bonds in a Nordic welfare state. *British Journal of Criminology, 49,* 285–304.

Sawyer, A. M., Borduin, C. M., & Dopp, A. R. (2015). Long-term effects of prevention and treatment on youth antisocial behavior: A meta-analysis. *Clinical Psychology Review, 42,* 130–144.

Schwarz, G. (1978). Estimating the dimension of a model. *The Annals of Statistics, 6,* 461–464.

Schmid, K. L., & Lopez, S. J. (2011). Positive pathways to adulthood: The role of hope in adolescents' constructions of their futures. *Advances in Child Development and Behavior, 41,* 69–88.

Schmid, K. L., Phelps, E., & Lerner, R. M. (2011). Constructing positive futures: Modeling the relationship between adolescents' hopeful future expectations and intentional self-regulation in predicting positive youth development. *Journal of Adolescence, 34,* 1127–1135.

Schmidt, F., Campbell, M. A., Houlding, C. (2011). Comparative analyses of the YLS/CMI, SAVRY, and PCL: YV in adolescent offenders: A 10-year follow-up into adulthood. *Youth Violence and Juvenile Justice, 9,* 23–42.

Schulenberg, J. E., Bryant, A. L., & O'Malley, P. M. (2004). Taking hold of some kind of life: How developmental tasks relate to trajectories of well-being during the transition to adulthood. *Development and Psychopathology, 16,* 1119–1140.

Schulenberg, J. E., Sameroff, A. J., & Cicchetti, D. (2004). The transition to adulthood as a critical juncture in the course of psychopathology and mental health. *Development and Psychopathology, 16,* 799–806.

Schwartz, J. A. (2016). Biosocial prevention science: Synthesis of two interrelated perspectives. *Criminology & Public Policy, 15,* 677–681.

Schweinhart, L. (2007). Crime prevention by the High/Scope Perry Preschool Program. *Victims and Offenders, 2,* 141–160.

Sclove, S. L. (1987). Application of model-selection criteria to some problems in multivariate analysis. *Psychometrika, 52,* 333–343.

Selman, R. L., & Adalbjarnardottir, S. (2000). A developmental method to analyze the personal meaning adolescents make of risk and relationship: The case of "drinking." *Applied Developmental Science, 4,* 47–65.

Shadish, W. R. (2013). Propensity score analysis: Promise, reality, and irrational exuberance. *Journal of Experimental Criminology, 9,* 129–144.

Shadish, W. R., Cook, T. D., & Campbell, D. T. (2002). *Experimental and quasi-experimental designs for generalized causal inference* (2nd ed.). Boston, MA: Houghton Mifflin.

Shadish, W. R., & Sullivan, K. J. (2012). Theories of causation in psychological science. In H. Cooper (Ed.), *APA Handbook of Research Methods in Psychology: Vol. 1. Foundations, planning, measures, and psychometrics* (pp. 23–52). Washington, DC: American Psychological Association.

Shanahan, M. J., Sulloway, F. J., & Hofer, S. M. (2000). Change and constancy in devel-opmental contexts. *International Journal of Behavioral Development, 24,* 421–427.

Shannon, L. W. (1982). *Assessing the relationship of adult criminal careers to juvenile ca-reers: A summary.* Washington, DC: Office of the Juvenile Justice and Delinquency Prevention, US Department of Justice. Retrieved from http://files.eric.ed.gov

Shaw, D. S., Hyde, L. W., & Brennan, L. M. (2012). Early predictors of boys' antisocial trajectories. *Development and Psychopathology, 24,* 871–888.

Shaw, P., Kabani, N. J., Lerch, J. P., Eckstrand, K., Lenroot, R., Gogtay, N., . . . Wise, S. P. (2008). Neurodevelopmental trajectories of the human cerebral cortex. *Journal of Neuroscience, 28,* 3586–3594.

Sherman, L. W. (1995). Hot spots of crime and criminal careers of places. In R. V. Clarke (Ed.), *Crime and place: Crime prevention studies* (Vol. 4, pp. 35–52). Monsey, NY: Willow Tree Press.

Shirk, S., Talmi, A., & Olds, D. (2000). A developmental psychopathology perspective on child and adolescent treatment policy. *Development and Psychopathology, 12,* 835–855.

Shiyko, M. P., Ram, N., & Grimm, K. J. (2012). An overview of growth mixture model-ing: A simple nonlinear application in OpenMx. In R. H. Hoyle (Ed.), *Handbook of structural equation modeling* (pp. 532–546). New York, NY: Guilford.

Shonkoff, J. P., & Bales, S. N. (2011). Science does not speak for itself: Translating child development research for the public and its policymakers. *Child Development, 82,* 17–32.

Shover, N. (1996). *Great pretenders: Pursuits and careers of persistent thieves.* Boulder, CO: Westview Press.

Silverthorn, P., & Frick, P. J. (1999). Developmental pathways to antisocial behavior: The delayed-onset pathway in girls. *Development and Psychopathology, 11,* 101–126.

Simons, R. L., Johnson, C., Conger, R. D., & Elder, G. (1998). A test of latent trait versus life-course perspectives on the stability of adolescent antisocial behavior. *Criminol-ogy, 36,* 217–243.

Simons, R. L., Wu, C.-I., Conger, R. D., & Lorenz, F. O. (1994). Two routes to delin-quency: Differences between early and late starters in the impact of parenting and deviant peers. *Criminology, 32,* 247–276.

Singer, J. D., & Willett, J. B. (2003). *Applied longitudinal data analysis: Modeling change and event occurrence.* New York, NY: Oxford University Press.

Sivertsson, F., & Carlsson, C. (2014). Continuity, change, and contradictions risk and agency in criminal careers to age 59. *Criminal Justice and Behavior, 42,* 382–411.

Skardhamar, T. (2009). Reconsidering the theory on adolescent-limited and life-course persistent anti-social behavior. *The British Journal of Criminology, 49,* 863–878.

Skardhamar, T. (2010). Distinguishing facts and artifacts in group-based modeling. *Criminology, 48,* 295–320.

Skardhamar, T., Monsbakken, C. W., & Lyngstad, T. H. (2014). Crime and the transi-tion to marriage: The role of the spouse's criminal involvement. *British Journal of Criminology, 54,* 411–427.

Skardhamar, T., & Savolainen, J. (2014). Changes in criminal offending around the time of job entry: A study of employment and desistance. *Criminology, 52,* 263–291.

Skardhamar, T., Savolainen, J., Aase, K. N., & Lyngstad, T. H. (2015). Does marriage reduce crime? *Crime & Justice, 44,* 385–446.

Skeem, J. L., Scott, E., & Mulvey, E. P. (2014). Justice policy reform for high-risk juveniles: Using science to achieve large-scale crime reduction. *Annual Review of Clinical Psychology, 10,* 709–739.

Spaeth, M., Weichold, K., Silbereisen, R. K., & Wiesner, M. (2010). Examining the differential effectiveness of a life skills program (IPSY) on alcohol use trajectories in early adolescence. *Journal of Consulting and Clinical Psychology, 78,* 334–348.

Sroufe, L. A. (1979). The coherence of individual development: Early care, attachment, and subsequent developmental issues. *American Psychologist, 34,* 834–841.

Sroufe, L. A. (1997). Psychopathology as an outcome of development. *Development and Psychopathology, 9,* 251–268.

Sroufe, L. A. (2009). The concept of development in developmental psychopathology. *Child Development Perspectives, 3,* 178–183.

Sroufe, L. A. (2013). The promise of developmental psychopathology: Past and present. *Development and Psychopathology, 25,* 1215–1224.

Sroufe, L. A., & Rutter, M. (1984). The domain of developmental psychopathology. *Child Development, 55,* 17–29.

Stander, J., Farrington, D. P., Hill, G., & Altham, P. M. E. (1989). Markov chain analysis and specialization in criminal careers. *British Journal of Criminology, 29,* 317–335.

Stattin, H., & Magnusson, D. (1991). Stability and change in criminal behavior up to age 30. *British Journal of Criminology, 31,* 327–346.

Steffensmeier, D., & Allan, E. (1996). Gender and crime: Toward a gendered theory of female offending. *Annual Review of Sociology, 22,* 459–487.

Steinberg, L. (2008). A social neuroscience perspective on adolescent risk-taking. *Developmental Review, 28,* 78–106.

Steinberg, L. (2010a). A dual systems model of adolescent risk-taking. *Developmental Psychobiology, 52,* 216–224.

Steinberg, L. (2010b). A behavioral scientist looks at the science of adolescent brain development *Brain and Cognition, 72,* 160–164.

Steinberg, L., Albert, D., Cauffman, E., Banich, M., Graham, S., & Woolard, J. (2008). Age differences in sensation seeking and impulsivity as indexed by behavior and self-report: Evidence for a dual systems model. *Developmental Psychology, 44,* 1764–1778.

Steinberg, L., & Cauffman, E. (1996). Maturity of judgment in adolescence: Psychosocial factors in adolescent decision making. *Law and Human Behavior, 20,* 249–272.

Steinberg, L., Chung, H. L., & Little, M. (2004). Reentry of young offenders from the justice system: A developmental perspective. *Youth Violence and Juvenile Justice, 2,* 21–38.

Sterba, S. K. (2014). Fitting nonlinear latent growth curve models with individually varying time points. *Structural Equation Modeling: A Multidisciplinary Journal, 21,* 630–647.

Sterba, S. K., Baldasaro, R. E., & Bauer, D. J. (2012). Factors affecting the adequacy and
preferability of semiparametric groups-based approximations of continuous growth
trajectories. *Multivariate Behavioral Research, 47,* 590–634.

Sterba, S. K., & Bauer, D. J. (2010). Matching method with theory in person-oriented
developmental psychopathology research. *Development and Psychopathology, 22,*
239–254.

Stewart, A. J. (1982). The course of individual adaptation to life changes. *Journal of
Personality and Social Psychology, 42,* 1100–1113.

Stoll, M. A., & Bushway, S. D. (2008). The effect of criminal background checks on hir-
ing ex-offenders. *Criminology and Public Policy, 7,* 371–404.

Stone, M. (1974). Cross-validatory choice and assessment of statistical predictions.
Journal of the Royal Statistical Society. Series B (Methodological), 36, 111–147.

Stoolmiller, M. (1995). Using latent growth curve models to study developmental
processes. In J. M. Gottman (Ed.), *The analysis of change* (pp. 103–138). Mahwah,
NJ: Erlbaum.

Stouthamer-Loeber, M. (2012). The next generation of longitudinal studies. In
R. Loeber & B. C. Welsh (Eds.), *The future of criminology* (pp. 94–100). New York,
NY: Oxford University Press.

Stouthamer-Loeber, M., Loeber, R., Wei, E., Farrington, D. P., & Wikström, P. O. H.
(2002). Risk and promotive effects in the explanation of persistent serious delinquency in boys. *Journal of Consulting and Clinical Psychology, 70,* 111–123.

Stouthamer-Loeber, M. & van Kammen, W. B. (1995). *Data collection and management:
A practical guide.* Thousand Oaks, CA: Sage.

Stright, A. D., Gallagher, K. C., & Kelley, K. (2008). Infant temperament moderates
relations between maternal parenting in early childhood and children's adjustment
in first grade. *Child Development, 79,* 186–200.

Sullivan, C. J. (2013). Change in offending across the life course. In F. T. Cullen, &
P. Wilcox (Eds.), *The Oxford handbook of criminological theory* (pp. 205–225). Oxford, England: Oxford University Press.

Sullivan, C. J., & Piquero, A. R. (Eds.). (2016a). Criminal careers and Career Criminals
Report, 30th anniversary [Special Issue]. *Journal of Research in Crime and Delinquency, 53*(3).

Sullivan, C. J., & Piquero, A. R. (2016b). The criminal career concept: Past, present and
future. *Journal of Research in Crime and Delinquency, 53,* 420–442.

Szatmari, P., Boyle, M. H., & Offord, D. R. (1993). Familial aggregation of emotional
and behavioral problems of childhood in the general population. *American Journal
of Psychiatry, 150,* 1398–1403.

Tackett, J. L. (2010). Toward an externalizing spectrum in DSM-V: Incorporating
developmental concerns. *Child Development Perspectives, 4,* 161–167.

Tahamont, S., Yan, S., Bushway, S. D., & Liu, J. (2015). Pathways to prison in New York
State. *Criminology & Public Policy, 14,* 431–453.

Tanner-Smith, E. E., Wilson, S. J., & Lipsey, M. W. (2013). Risk factors and crime. In F. T. Cullen & P. Wilcox (Eds.), *The Oxford handbook of criminological theory* (pp. 89–114). Oxford, England: Oxford University Press.

Tarling, R., & Morris, K. (2010). Reporting crime to the police. *The British Journal of Criminology, 50,* 474–490.

Tewksbury, R., & Jennings, W. G. (2010). Assessing the impact of sex offender registration and community notification on sex-offending trajectories. *Criminal Justice and Behavior, 37,* 570–582.

Tewksbury, R., Jennings, W. G., & Zgoba, K. M. (2012). A longitudinal examination of sex offender recidivism prior to and following the implementation of SORN. *Behavioral Sciences & the Law, 30,* 308–328.

Theobald, D., & Farrington, D. P. (2009). Effects of getting married on offending: Results from a prospective longitudinal survey of males. *European Journal of Criminology, 6,* 496–516.

Theobald, D., & Farrington, D. P. (2014). Onset of offending. In G. Bruinsma & D. Weisburd (Eds.), *Encyclopedia of criminology and criminal justice* (pp. 3332–3342). New York, NY: Springer.

Thornberry, T. P. (1987). Toward an interactional theory of delinquency. *Criminology, 25,* 863–891.

Thornberry, T. P. (Ed.). (1997). *Developmental theories of crime and delinquency* (Advances in Criminological Theory, Vol. 7). New Brunswick, NJ: Transaction Publishers.

Thornberry, T. P. (2009). The apple doesn't fall far from the tree (or does it?): Intergenerational patterns of antisocial behavior. *Criminology, 47,* 297–325.

Thornberry, T. P., Ireland, T. O., & Smith, C. A. (2001). The importance of timing: The varying impact of childhood and adolescent maltreatment on multiple problem outcomes. *Development and Psychopathology, 13,* 957–979.

Thornberry, T. P., & Krohn, M. D. (2001). The development of delinquency: An interactional perspective. In S. O. White (Ed.), *Handbook of youth and justice* (pp. 289–305). New York, NY: Plenum.

Thornberry, T. P., & Krohn, M. D. (Eds.). (2003a). *Taking stock of delinquency: An overview of findings from contemporary longitudinal studies.* New York, NY: Kluwer Academic Publishers.

Thornberry, T. P., & Krohn, M. D. (2003b). Comparison of self-report and official data for measuring crime. In J. V. Pepper & C. V. Petrie (Eds.), *Measurement problems in criminal justice research: Workshop summary* (pp. 43–94). Washington, DC: National Academies Press. Retrieved from www.nap.edu

Thornberry, T. P., & Krohn, M. D. (2005). Applying interactional theory to the explanation of continuity and change in antisocial behavior. In D. P. Farrington (Ed.), *Integrated developmental and life-course theories of offending* (Advances in Criminological Theory, Vol. 14, pp. 183–209). New Brunswick, NJ: Transaction.

Thornberry, T. P., Lizotte, A. J., Krohn, M. D., Smith, C. A., & Porter, P. K. (2003). Causes and consequences of delinquency: Findings from the Rochester Youth

Development Study. In T. P. Thornberry & M. D. Krohn (Eds.), *Taking stock of delinquency: An overview of findings from contemporary longitudinal studies* (pp. 11–46). New York, NY: Kluwer Academic Publishers.

Titterington, D. M., Smith, A. F. M., & Makov, U. E. (1985). *Statistical analysis of finite mixture distributions.* New York, NY: Wiley.

Tofighi, D., & Enders, C. K. (2008). Identifying the correct number of classes in growth mixture models. In G. R. Hancock & K. M. Samuelsen (Eds.), *Advances in latent variable mixture models* (pp. 317–341). Charlotte, NC: Information Age Publishing.

Tolan, P. H., & Gorman-Smith, D. (2002). What violence prevention research can tell us about developmental psychopathology. *Development and Psychopathology, 14,* 713–729.

Tolan, P. H., Gorman-Smith, D., & Loeber, R. (2000). Developmental timing of onsets of disruptive behaviors and later delinquency of inner-city youth. *Journal of Child and Family Studies, 9,* 203–220.

Tolvanen, A. (2007). *Latent growth mixture modeling: A simulation study* (Unpublished doctoral dissertation). Department of Mathematics, University of Jyväskylä, Finland.

Tomasik, M. J., & Silbereisen, R. K. (2012). Beneficial effects of disengagement from futile struggles with occupational planning: A contextualist-motivational approach. *Developmental Psychology, 48,* 1785–1796.

Tracy, P. E., Wolfgang, M. E., & Figlio, R. M. (1990). *Delinquency careers in two birth cohorts.* New York, NY: Plenum.

Tremblay, R. E. (2012). Development of antisocial behavior during childhood. In C. L. Gibson & M. D. Krohn (Eds.), *Handbook of life-course criminology: Emerging trends and directions for future research* (pp. 3–19). New York, NY: Springer.

Tremblay, R. E. (2015). Antisocial behavior before the age-crime curve: Can developmental criminology continue to ignore developmental origins? In J. Morizot & E. Kazemian (Eds.), *The development of criminal and antisocial behavior: Theory, research and practical applications* (pp. 39–49). New York, NY: Springer.

Tremblay, R. E., & Craig, W. M. (1995). Developmental crime prevention. *Crime and Justice, 19,* 151–236.

Tripodi, S. J., Kim, J. S., & Bender, K. (2010). Is employment associated with reduced recidivism? The complex relationship between employment and crime. *International Journal of Offender Therapy and Comparative Criminology, 54,* 706–720.

Tzoumakis, S., Lussier, P., Le Blanc, M., & Davies, G. (2013). Onset, offending trajectories, and crime specialization in violence. *Youth Violence and Juvenile Justice, 11,* 143–164.

UCLA Fielding School of Public Health. (n.d.). John Snow and the Broad Street pump. Retrieved from http://www.ph.ucla.edu/epi/snow/snowcricketarticle.html

Uggen, C. (2000). Work as a turning point in the life course of criminals: a duration model of age, employment, and recidivism. *American Sociological Review, 65,* 529–546.

Uggen, C., & Piliavin, I. (1998). Asymmetrical causation and criminal desistance. *Journal of Criminal Law and Criminology, 88,* 1399–1422.

van de Schoot, R., Sijbrandij, M., Winter, S. D., Depaoli, S., & Vermunt, J.K. (2017). The GRoLTS-Checklist: Guidelines for reporting on latent trajectory studies. *Structural Equation Modeling, 24*, 451–467.

van der Geest, V. R., Bijleveld, C. C. J. H., & Blokland, A. A. J. (2011). The effects of employment on longitudinal trajectories of offending: A follow-up of high-risk youth from 18 to 32 years of age. *Criminology, 49*, 1195–1234.

van der Geest, V., Blokland, A. A. J., & Bijleveld, C. (2009). Delinquent development in a sample of high-risk youth: Shape, content, and predictors of delinquent trajectories from age 12 to 32. *Journal of Research in Crime and Delinquency, 46*, 111–143.

Vandevelde, S., Vander Laenen, F., Van Damme, L., Vanderplasschen, W., Audenaert, K., Broekaert, E., & Vander Beken, T. (2017). Dilemmas in applying strengths-based approaches in working with offenders with mental illness: A critical multidisciplinary review. *Aggression and Violent Behavior, 32*, 71–79.

van Domburgh, L., Loeber, R., Bezemer, D., Stallings, R., & Stouthamer-Loeber, M. (2009). Childhood predictors of desistance and level of persistence in offending in early onset offenders. *Journal of Abnormal Child Psychology, 37*, 967–980.

van Domburgh, L., Vermeiren, R., Blokland, A. A. J., & Doreleijers, Th. A. H. (2009). Delinquent development in Dutch childhood arrestees: Developmental trajectories, risk factors, and co-morbidity with adverse outcomes during adolescence. *Journal of Abnormal Child Psychology, 37*, 93–105.

van Dulmen, M. H. M., Goncy, E. A., Vest, A., & Flannery, D. J. (2009). Group-based trajectory modeling of externalizing behavior problems from childhood through adulthood: Exploring discrepancies in the empirical findings. In J. Savage (Ed.), *The development of persistent criminality* (pp. 288–314). New York, NY: Oxford University Press.

van Schellen, M., Poortman, A.-R., & Nieuwbeerta, P. (2012). Partners in crime? Criminal offending, marriage formation, and partner selection. *Journal of Research in Crime and Delinquency, 49*, 545–571.

Vaughn, M. G., DeLisi, M., Gunter, T., Fu, Q., Beaver, K. M., Perron, B. E., & Howard, M. O. (2011). The severe 5%: A latent class analysis of the externalizing behavior spectrum in the United States. *Journal of Criminal Justice, 39*, 75–80.

Verbruggen, J., van der Geest, V. R., & Blokland, A. A. J. (2016). Adult life adjustment of vulnerable youths. The relationship between criminal history, employment history, and adult life outcomes. *Journal of Developmental and Life-Course Criminology, 2*, 466–493.

Vermunt, J. K. (2010). Latent class modeling with covariates: Two improved three-step approaches. *Political Analysis, 18*, 450–469.

Vermunt, J. K., & Magidson, J. (2005). *Technical guide for Latent GOLD 4.0: Basic and advanced*. Belmont, MA: Statistical Innovations Inc.

Viding, E., Larsson, H., & Jones, A. P. (2008). Quantitative genetic studies of antisocial behavior. *Philosophical Transactions of The Royal Society, 363*, 2519–2527.

Vrieze, S. I. (2012). Model selection and psychological theory: A discussion of the differences between the Akaike information criterion (AIC) and the Bayesian information criterion (BIC). *Psychological Methods, 17*, 228–243.

Walters, G. D. (2012). Developmental trajectories of delinquent behavior: One pattern or several? *Criminal Justice and Behavior, 39*, 1192–1203.

Walters, G. D. (2015). The latent structure of criminal persistence: A taxometric analysis of offending behavior from late adolescence to early adulthood in adjudicated male delinquents. *American Journal of Criminal Justice, 40*, 542–559.

Wang, C.-P., Brown, C. H., & Bandeen-Roche, K. (2005). Residual diagnostics for growth mixture models: Examining the impact of a preventive intervention on multiple trajectories of aggressive behavior. *Journal of the American Statistical Association, 100*, 1054–1076.

Ward, A. K., Day, D. M., Bevc, I., Sun, Y., Rosenthal, J. S., & Duchesne, T. (2010). Criminal trajectories and risk factors in a Canadian sample of offenders. *Criminal Justice and Behavior, 37*, 1278–1300.

Ward, T., Mann, R. E., & Gannon, T. A. (2007). The Good Lives Model of offender rehabilitation: Clinical implications. *Aggression and Violent Behavior, 12*, 87–107

Warr, M. (1998). Life-course transitions and desistance from crime. *Criminology, 36*, 183–216.

Warren, J. R., Luo, L., Halpern-Manners, A., Raymo, J. M., & Palloni, A. (2015). Do different methods for modeling age-graded trajectories yield consistent and valid results? *American Journal of Sociology, 120*, 1809–1856.

Weakliem, D. L., & Wright, B. R. E. (2009). Robustness of group-based models for longitudinal count data. *Sociological Methods & Research, 38*, 147–170.

Weatherburn, D. (2010). *The effect of prison on adult reoffending* (Crime and Justice Bulletin No. 143). Sydney, Australia: NSW Bureau of Crime, Statistics, and Research.

Webster, C. D., Augimeri, L. K., & Koegl, C. J. (2002). The Under 12 Outreach Project for antisocial boys: A research based clinical program. In R. R. Corrado, R. Roesch, S. D. Hart, & J. K. Gierowski (Eds.), *Multi-problem violent youth: A foundation for comparative research on needs, interventions, and outcomes* (pp. 201–218). Amsterdam, The Netherlands: IOS Press.

Webster, C. D., Douglas, K. S., Eaves, D., & Hart, S. D. (1997). *The HCR-20: Assessing risk for violence (Version 2)*. Burnaby, Canada: Simon Fraser University.

Weisburd, D., Bushway, S., Lum, C., & Yang, S.-M. (2004). Trajectories of crime at places: A longitudinal study of street segments in the city of Seattle. *Criminology, 42*, 283–322.

Welsh, B. C., Braga, A. A., & Bruinsma, G. J. N. (2013. *Experimental criminology: Prospects for advancing science and public policy*. Cambridge, England: Cambridge University Press.

Welsh, B. C., & Farrington, D. P. (2012). Science, politics, and crime prevention: Toward a new crime policy. *Journal of Criminal Justice, 40*, 128–133.

Welsh, B. C., Farrington, D. P., & Gowar, B. (2015). Benefit-cost analysis of crime prevention programs. In M. Tonry (Ed.), *Crime and justice* (Vol. 44, pp. 447–516). Chicago, IL: University of Chicago Press.

Welsh, M. C., Pennington, B. F., & Groisser, D. B. (1991). A normative-developmental study of executive function: A window on the prefrontal function in children. *Developmental Neuropsychology, 7*, 131–149.

Wexler, D. B. (2014). *New wine in new bottles: The need to sketch a therapeutic jurisprudence 'code' of proposed criminal processes and practices* (Therapeutic Jurisprudence, Paper 7). Retrieved from www.civiljustice.info

Wheeler, A. P., Worden, R. E., & McLean, S. J. (2016). Replicating group-based trajectory models of crime at micro-places in Albany, NY. *Journal of Quantitative Criminology, 32*, 589–612.

White, H. R., Bates, M. E., & Buyske, S. (2001). Adolescence-limited versus persistent delinquency: Extending Moffitt's hypothesis into adulthood. *Journal of Abnormal Psychology, 110*, 600–609.

Whitten, T., McGee, T. R., Homel, R., Farrington, D. P., & Ttofi M. (2017). Disentangling operationalizations of persistent offending. *Journal of Criminal Justice, 52*, 22–33.

Wiesner, M., & Capaldi, D. M. (2003). Relations of childhood and adolescent factors to offending trajectories of young men. *Journal of Research in Crime and Delinquency, 40*, 231–262.

Wiesner, M., Capaldi, D. M., & Kim, H. K. (2007). Arrest trajectories across a 17-year span for young men: Relation to dual taxonomies and self-reported offense trajectories. *Criminology, 45*, 835–863.

Wiesner, M., Capaldi, D. M., & Kim, H. K. (2010). Arrests, recent life circumstances, and recurrent job loss for at-risk young men: An event-history analysis. *Journal of Vocational Behavior, 76*, 344–354.

Wiesner, M., Capaldi, D. M., & Kim, H. K. (2011). Early adult outcomes of male arrest trajectories: Propensity versus causation effects. *Western Criminology Review, 12*, 75–89.

Wiesner, M., Capaldi, D. M., & Kim, H. K. (2012). General versus specific predictors of male arrest trajectories: A test of the Moffitt and Patterson theories. *Journal of Youth and Adolescence, 41*, 217–228.

Wiesner, M., Capaldi, D. M., & Patterson, G. R. (2003). Development of antisocial behavior and crime across the life-span from a social interactional perspective: The coercion model. In R. L. Akers & G. F. Jensen (Eds.), *Social learning theory and the explanation of crime: A guide for the new century* (Vol. 11, pp. 317–338). New Brunswick, NJ: Transaction Publishers.

Wiesner, M., & Kim, H. K. (2006). Co-occurring delinquency and depressive symptoms of adolescent boys and girls: a dual trajectory modeling approach. *Developmental Psychology, 42*, 1220–1235.

Wiesner, M., Kim, H. K., & Capaldi, D. M. (2005). Developmental trajectories of offending: Validation and prediction to young adult alcohol use, drug use, and depressive symptoms. *Development and Psychopathology, 17*, 251–270.

Wiesner, M., Silbereisen, R. K., & Weichold, K. (2008). Effects of deviant peer association on adolescent alcohol consumption: A growth mixture modeling analysis. *Journal of Youth and Adolescence, 37*, 537–551.

Wiesner, M., & Windle, M. (2004). Assessing covariates of adolescent delinquency trajectories: A latent growth mixture modeling approach. *Journal of Youth and Adolescence, 33*, 431–442.

Wiesner, M., & Windle, M. (2006). Young adult substance use and depression as a consequence of delinquency: Trajectories during middle adolescence. *Journal of Research on Adolescence, 16*, 239–264.

Wikström, P.-O. H. (2005). The social origins of pathways in crime: Towards a developmental ecological action theory of crime involvement and its changes. In D. P. Farrington (Ed.), *Integrated developmental and life-course theories of offending* (Advances in Criminological Theory, Vol. 14, pp. 211–245). New Brunswick, NJ: Transaction.

Willett, J. B., & Sayer, A. G. (1994). Using covariance structure analysis to detect correlates and predictors of individual change over time. *Psychological Bulletin, 116*, 363–381.

Williams, K. R., Guerra, N. G., & Elliot, D. S. (1997). *Human development and violent prevention: A focus on youth.* Boulder, CO: The Center for the Study and Prevention of Violence, Institute of Behavioral Science.

Wimer, C., Sampson, R. J., & Laub, J. H. (2008). Estimating time-varying causes and outcomes, with application to incarceration and crime. In P. Cohen (Ed.), *Applied data analytic techniques for turning points research* (pp. 37–59). New York, NY: Routledge.

Windle, M., Mun, E. Y., & Windle, R. C. (2005). Adolescent-to-young adulthood heavy drinking trajectories and their prospective predictors. *Journal of Studies on Alcohol, 66*, 313–322.

Witkiewitz, K., & Masyn, K. E. (2008). Drinking trajectories following an initial lapse. *Psychology of Addictive Behaviors, 22*, 157–167.

Wohlwill, J. F. (1973). *The study of behavioral development* (The Child Psychology Series). New York, NY: Academic Press.

Wolfgang, M. E., Figlio, R. M., & Sellin, J. T. (1972). *Delinquency in a birth cohort.* Chicago, IL: University of Chicago Press.

Wright, J. P., & Cullen, F. T. (2004). Employment, peers, and life-course transitions. *Justice Quarterly, 21*, 183–205.

Wrosch, C., Scheier, M.F., Carver, C.S., & Schulz, R. (2003). The importance of goal disengagement in adaptive self-regulation: When giving up is beneficial. *Self and Identity, 2*, 1–20.

Yessine, A. K., & Bonta, J. (2009). The offending trajectories of youthful Aboriginal offenders. *Canadian Journal of Criminology and Criminal Justice, 51*, 435–472.

Yonai, S., Levine, S. Z., & Glicksohn, J. (2013). A national population based examination of the association between age-versatility trajectories and recidivism rates. *Journal of Criminal Justice, 41*, 467–476.

Zara, G., & Farrington, D. P. (2009). Childhood and adolescent predictors of late onset criminal careers. *Journal of Youth and Adolescence, 38,* 287–300.

Zara, G., & Farrington, D. P. (2016). Chronic offenders and the syndrome of antisociality: Offending is a minor feature. *Irish Probation Journal, 13,* 40–64.

Zimmerman, G. M., & Messner, S. F. (2012) Person-in-context. In R. Loeber & B. C. Walsh (Eds.), *The future of criminology* (pp. 70–76). Oxford, England: Oxford University Press.

Zimmerman, S. M., Phelps, E., & Lerner, R.M. (2007). Intentional self-regulation in early adolescence: Assessing the structure of selection, optimization, and compensation processes. *International Journal of Developmental Science, 1,* 272–299.

Zimmerman, S. M., Phelps, E., & Lerner, R. M. (2008). Positive and negative developmental trajectories in U.S. adolescents: Where the Positive Youth Development perspective meets the deficit model. *Research in Human Development, 5,* 153–165.

Zopluoglu, C., Harring, J. R., & Kohli, N. (2014). FitPMM: An R routine to fit finite mixture of piecewise mixed-effect models with unknown random knots. *Applied Psychological Measurement, 38,* 583–584.

Zucker, R. A., Fitzgerald, H. E., & Moses, H. D. (1995). Emergence of alcohol problems and the several alcoholisms: A developmental perspective on etiologic theory and life course trajectory. In D. Cicchetti & D. J. Cohen (Eds.), *Developmental psychopathology: Risk, disorder, and adaptation* (Vol. 2, pp. 677–711). Oxford, England: Wiley.

INDEX

acceleration, of offending, 42

accommodative coping, 144

Achenbach System of Empirically Based Assessment, 262, 263

action theory-guided research, 142–43; dual-process assimilative and accommodative coping in, 144

action theory of human development, of Brandtstädter, 136, 141, 142–44

activation, of offending, 42

adaptation, 48; Baltes on, 265; hierarchical concept of, 11; life-span psychology on, 49–50, 55, 241, 252

adaptational failure, 11, 50, 171, 265

adaptive functioning, 3, 16, 233, 246, 248, 270; SOC theory and, 49–50, 55, 241, 242

adolescence, 47–48; developmental tasks of, 10; deviant peer groups and, 31, 44, 173; as late starters, 3, 44; offending in, 42; SOC processes and development in, 53; Steinberg on risk-taking in, 218

adolescence limited (AL) trajectory, of antisocial behavior, 54, 180–83, 247, 276; Assink meta-analysis on predictors of, 255–56; late starters and, 44, 129–30; maturity gap of, 22, 130, 131; normal development until age 15 of, 22; normative brain maturity gap and, 131

advanced causal analysis, in GMM and SGBTM, 98–99

adverse health, later life outcomes of, 228

"Age, Criminal Careers, and Population Heterogeneity—Specification and Estimation of a Nonparametric, Mixed Poisson Model" (Nagin and Land), 37

age-crime curve, 146, 246; criminal career paradigm and, 39, 70; heterogeneity of, 150; Nagin and Land on, 189; on recidivism, 232

age-graded: changes in social bonds, 127–28; developmental processes, 13, 29; environmental discontinuities, 211; levels of functioning, 13; psychosocial maturity, 13; transitions, 45

age-graded theory of informal social control, of Sampson and Laub, 125, 135–36

age of onset: antisocial behavior and, 134–35, 257–58; policy and practice implication for, 257–58; subgroup, of offenders, 19, 257–58

aggravation, of offending, 42

AL. See adolescence limited trajectory

Allard, T., 166

Anderson, Elijah, 160

antecedents or covariates dependency, 114–16

antisocial behavior, 1, 2, 3, 47–48; age of onset and, 134–35, 257–58; behavioral trajectory of, 133; causal loops across life course for, 133–34; Day on early onset of, 194; of female offenders, 152–53; interactional theory and, 133–34; late starters and, 44, 129–30, 134; meta-analysis of early family/ parenting programs for, 251; multiple pathways research of, 24; Robins on, 18; transitions and nonnormative stressors increase from, 48. See also adolescence limited trajectory; dual taxonomy model

Laub, John, 63, 117, 149, 204, 219; age-graded theory of informal social control, 125, 135–36; on developmental perspective, 124–25, 127; on employment and desistance from crime, 214; on marriage and offending, 233, 235; on stakes in conformity, 237

Laursen, B., 75

LCGA. *See* latent class growth analysis

LCGCM. *See* latent class growth curve model

LCP. *See* life-course persistent trajectory

Le Blanc, Marc, 37, 41, 214; developmental and life-course model of, 129; on developmental trajectories, 43; on offending frequency declines, 208; on offending in adolescence, 42

Lerner, Richard: relational developmental systems metamodel, 137–41, *139–40*; on SOC theory and ISR, 53

Level of Service/Case Management Inventory, 159

Level of Service Inventory-Ontario Revision, 159

levels of functioning, age-graded, 13

life-course approaches: defined, 127–28; on personality traits, 217; variability and exogenous influences emphasis, 128

life-course persistent (LCP) trajectory, of antisocial behavior, 180–83, 247, 276; Assink meta-analysis on predictors of, 255–56; childhood conduct problem behavior of, 22; crime variability of, 130; criminal activity through adulthood of, 129–30; cumulative and contemporary consequences for, 130–31; early starters and, 44, 129–30; propensity factors for, 130–31

life-course sociology, of Elder, 15, 37, 46, 48, 62, 127, 133, 135, 141; life-span psychology differences from, 49; on trajectories, 45; on transitions, 45, 47

life-course trajectories: in arrests, 46–47; in birth of child, 46

life span: criminal behavior across, 8; developmental needs across, 3; within-person development across, 13, 273

life-span psychology, of Baltes, 37, 128, 141; on adaptation and adaptive functioning, 49–50, 55, 241, 242; on development from birth to death, 48–49; as family of perspectives, 48; gains and losses in, 52; life-course sociology differences from, 49; on long-term patterns of change, 49; objectives of, 49

Little, T. D., 75

Loeber, Rolf, 37, 40, 41, 257, 276; on criminal behavior, 16–17; developmental and life-course model of, 129; on developmental trajectories, 43; on dual taxonomy theory, 255–56; multiple pathways model of, 24–26, *25*, 71; on offending in adolescence, 42; on versatile offenders, 26

longitudinal growth patterns, for offending, 146; for female offenders, 152, 154

longitudinal research, 126–27, 170–71; for assessments of individual change, 8–9; causal variables and, 171; criminal career paradigm use of, 39; developmental perspective and, 14; Laursen, Little and Card on, 75; McArdle and Nesselroade on, 75; of Ontario Child Health Study, on developmental risk factors, 40–41; prospective longitudinal designs, 171; on temporal sequence of life events, 14; Toronto study, 63–64; on within-person analysis of behavior, 14

loss-based selection, 51, 240, 243

low-level-chronic group, 23

low rate offenders, 3, 149, 175, 177, 186; long-term, 72, 73; monetary costs of, *165*, *166*, *167*; psychopathy and, 183

Lussier, P., 157; on psychopathy, 183–84

Patterson, Gerald: coercion model of, 125, 131–33; developmental theory of antisocial behavior of, 30–31, *31*; early-/ late-starter model of, 195; theory of criminality of, 43–44
peers, 214; delinquent group of, 191–92; deviant groups of, 31, 44, 173, 191–92; relations formation, 10; risk factors of, 61
persistent label, for criminal trajectory, 149
personality characteristics, criminal typologies of, 21
person-centered analysis, of behavior, 8, 9–10, 175–76
Petras, H., 101
Philadelphia Birth Cohort Study, 19, 20, 155
phrenology theory, of Gall, 21
piecewise GMM, with unknown random knots, 98
Piquero, A. R., 119, 121, 147, 148, 149, 178; on classify/analyze approach, 176; on criminal career, 264–65; cumulative risk index of, 259; on desistance from delinquency, 55; on developmental risk factors, 189; on dual taxonomy theory, 255–56; on early intervention and prevention programs, 251; on female offenders, 154; on health outcomes, 228; on incarceration, 238; on life failure at age 48, 230; on monetary costs, 163–64, 166; on problem behaviors, 229; on psychopathy, 185
Pittsburgh Youth Study, 17, 24–26, 40, 257
plasticity, 48, 57, 137, 200
policy and practice implication: for age of onset, 257–58; application of developmental tasks to criminal justice system, 266–68; broad perspective of, 247; within criminal justice system, 263–70; criminal trajectory research, 252–54; cumulative risk, 256–57; on developmental tasks, 265–66; early invention and prevention, 249–52;

from monetary costs, 163, 166; narrow perspective of, 245–47; outside criminal justice system, 248–63; risk assessment instruments, 258–63; on sense of agency, 268–70; trajectory group membership prediction, 254–56; trajectory research and, 246; Tyler case study and, 248–50, 264
population trajectories, unknown continuous distribution of, 104–9, *106*
Positive Youth Development (PYD), 53–55, 269–70
Preacher, K. J., 110
predictors and correlates, of trajectory groups, 203; causes, correlates and risk factors, 170–71; Day on, 192–93; dose effect and, 189–90, 256–57; literature on, 194–95, *196–200*, 200–202; longitudinal research, 170–71; risk factor research and variables, 172–74; role of theory for, 171; root causes and, 169–70; trajectory groups membership correlates, 179–88; trajectory groups membership predictors, 188–94; Ward study on, 193–94
prevention programs, 3, 15; Greenwood on, 246. *See also* early intervention and prevention programs
prison populations, 72
probabilistic developmental pathways, 48
probabilistic risk factors, 18, 29
process concept, risk factor as, 30, 183
process models: Cicchetti on, 29; developmental psychopathology and, 30; Kazdin on risk factor as process concept, 30, 183; Krohn on gang involvement and street crime, 33; on parental and adolescent alcohol and drug use pathways, 32; Patterson developmental theory of antisocial behavior, 30–31, *31*; for understanding criminal behavior, 28–33. *See also* developmental processes

variability: in LCP trajectory, of antisocial behavior, 130; life-course approaches emphasis on, 128; among offender population, 18; onset, 119; trajectory, in GMM approach within classes, 83–84
variable-centered analysis, of behavior, 175–76
variables: causal, 171; contributing to high rate offenders, 201; in criminal trajectories, 7; discrete, 190–91; future research on biological, 276; for high rate offenders, 201; instrumental variable approaches, 245–46; risk factor identification and, 172–73; in risk factor research, 172–74
versatile offenders, 26
versatility, of offending, 70–71; of sex offenders, 157
violent offenses,: in criminal trajectory, 71; neurobiological characteristics and, 276

Waldman, I. D., 129
Ward, A. K., 193–94
Welsh, B. C., 248
White, H. R., 181, 183
Wiesner, M., 97, 119, 223, 229, 231; on discrete variables of risk factors, 190–91
Wikström, P.-O. H., 129, 257
Williams, Kirk, 266
Willoughby, M. T., 63
Winship, C., 253–54
within-person: development, across life span, 13, 273; differences, in offending, 126; models, 76, 77, 78, 78, 79
within-person analysis, of behavior, 8, 9–10; in developmental and life-course theories, 126; longitudinal data on, 14
Wohlwill, J. F., 70
Wolfgang, M. E., 19, 20, 155, 175, 176

Youth Inclusion Program, 250
Youth Level of Service/Case Management Inventory, 260

ABOUT THE AUTHORS

David M. Day is Professor in the Department of Psychology at Ryerson University in Toronto. He is a registered psychologist who received his PhD in 1990 in applied social psychology from the University of Windsor. His research interests are in the areas of developmental criminology, risky behavior among young people, and access to justice for crossover youth.

Margit Wiesner is Associate Professor in the Department of Psychological, Health, and Learning Sciences at the University of Houston in Houston, Texas. She received her PhD in developmental psychology in 1999 from the Friedrich Schiller University of Jena, Germany. Her research interests include longitudinal modeling of trajectories of offending and substance use, youth violence exposure, and measurement invariance of mental health screening instruments.